The Transfer Pricing Problem

The Transfer Pricing Problem

A Theory for Practice

Robert G. Eccles
Harvard University Graduate School of
Business Administration

Lexington Books
D.C. Heath and Company/Lexington, Massachusetts/Toronto

Library of Congress Cataloging in Publication Data
Eccles, Robert G.
The transfer pricing problem.

Bibliogrphy: p.
Includes index.
1. Transfer pricing. I. Title.
HF5416.5.E27 1985 338.5'2 85-4572
ISBN 0-66909029-8 (alk. paper)

Published simultaneously in Canada
Printed in the United States of America on acid-free paper
International Standard Book Number: 0-669-09029-8
Library of Congress Catalog Card Number: 84-48024

To My Parents, Robert and Georgia,
Who Taught Me How to Learn

Contents

List of Figures xi

List of Tables xiii

Preface and Acknowledgments xv

1. The Problem with a Solution 1

    The Nature of the Problem 1

    Research Design 5

    Summary of Findings 7

    Overview of This Book 11

2. Theory and Practice 15

    The Origin of Transfer Prices 15

    Early Theory 18

    Economic Theory 21

    Mathematical Programming 25

    Accounting Theory 27

    Management Theory 35

    Data from Practice 40

    Toward a New Theory 49

3. The Case of Alfarabi Chemicals, Inc. 51

    Company Background and Strategy 51

    Transfer Pricing Policies 56

Changes in Transfer Pricing Policies 57

Transfer Pricing Processes 62

Economic Decisions 66

Performance Measurement, Evaluation, and Reward 68

The Effects of Volume and Business Performance 70

Discussion 71

4. A Theory for Practice 77

How Strategy Determines Transfer Pricing Policy 79

Mandated Full Cost 82

Mandated Market-Based 91

Exchange Autonomy 97

Dual Pricing 101

Some Empirical Support 106

The Role of Administrative Process 113

5. Exchange Autonomy: Pricing in a Market Context 117

Transfer Pricing as External Pricing 119

Disincentives to Trade Internally 124

Incentives Through the Management Hierarchy 132

Incentives Through Market Mechanisms 137

Incentives Through Dual Pricing 139

Dual Pricing as a Limited and Temporary Solution 144

Managing Disincentives 147

6. Mandated Full Cost: Measuring the Cost of Production 149

Measuring Standard and Actual Costs 149

The Need for Strategic Clarity 151

Problems in Allocating Variances 162

Managing Costs and Variances 172

7. **Mandated Market-Based: Searching for the Just Price 175**

External Market-Based Pricing 178

Cost Plus Markup Pricing 184

Managing the Ambiguity of Price 190

Competitive Problems Resulting from Market-Based Transfers 195

The Dual Pricing Solution 200

A Remaining Question 203

8. **Managing Conflict for Information and Control 205**

The Conflict Dynamics of Interdependence 206

How Top Management Can Use Conflict 213

Evaluating the Benefits of Conflict 222

Implications for Dual Pricing 225

9. **Pressures for Endless Change 227**

The Product/Process Life Cycle 228

The Introduction of Transfer Pricing 238

Reorganizing Exchange Relationships 248

Uniformity for Administrative Simplicity and Fairness 256

The Inherent Value of Change 266

10. **The Manager's Analytical Plane 269**

Strategy and Its Implementation 269

Four Pure Organizational Types 273

The MAP and Transfer Pricing 279

Other Uses of the MAP 288

Next Steps 293

Appendix A: The Methodology of Practice-Based Theory 295

Appendix B: A Revision of Rumelt's Typology of Corporate Strategy 309

Notes 315

Bibliography 325

Index 333

About the Author 343

List of Figures

1–1. The Causes and Effects of Transfer Pricing 7

1–2. The Relationship between Strategy and Transfer Pricing Policy 9

2–1. Economic Theory's Definition of the Transfer Pricing Problem 24

2–2. Accounting Theory's Definition of the Transfer Pricing Problem 34

2–3. Management Theory's Definition of the Transfer Pricing Problem 39

3–1. Alfarabi Chemicals, Inc., Organization Chart (1981) 55

4–1. The Relationship between Strategy and Transfer Pricing Policy 80

4–2. A Framework for Describing Responsibility Centers: Mandated Full Cost Transfers 86

4–3. A Framework for Describing Responsibility Centers: Mandated Market-Based Transfers 92

4–4. A Framework for Describing Responsibility Centers: Exchange Autonomy Transfers 98

4–5. A Framework for Describing Responsibility Centers: Dual Pricing Transfers 102

4–6. A Theory of Transfer Pricing 115

9–1. Characteristics of the Phases of the Product/Process Life Cycle 229

9–2. Transfer Pricing Policy Preferences in the Product/Process Life Cycle 236

9–3. A Continuum of Exchange Relationships for Transfer Pricing 249

9–4. Pressures for Diversity and Uniformity 258

9–5. The Task Force's Evaluation of Four Transfer Pricing Methods 264

9–6. The Cicero Systems Transfer Pricing Policy 265

10–1. A Model of Strategy Implementation 270

10–2. The Manager's Analytical Plane (MAP) 271

10–3. Four Pure Organizational Types in the MAP 274

10–4. Transfer Pricing Policies in the MAP 279

10–5. Locations of Companies in the MAP 281

10–6. Dual Pricing in the MAP 284

10–7. Changes in Locations in the MAP 286

A–1. Letter to Obtain Research Sites for Pilot Phase Study of Vertical Integration 299

A–2. Letter to Obtain Research Sites for Transfer Pricing Project 300

List of Tables

1–1. Extent of Internal Transfers 3

1–2. Summary of Data Collection Effort 6

2–1. Solomons' Recommendations on Transfer Pricing 29

2–2. Transfer Pricing Methods Used in Practice 41

2–3. Evaluation of Transfer Pricing 46

2–4. Comparison of the Four Theories 48

3–1. Intergroup Task Interdependencies 53

3–2. Major Intergroup Transfers at Alfarabi Chemicals, Inc. (1980) 58

3–3. Major Intra–Commodity Group Transfers at Alfarabi Chemicals, Inc. (1980) 60

3–4. Major Intra–Chemicals Group Transfers at Alfarabi Chemicals, Inc. (1980) 60

4–1. Transfer Pricing Policies Used in Thirteen Companies 78

4–2. Extent of Transfers, by Strategic Type 109

4–3. Transfer Pricing Method, by Strategic Type 110

4–4. Profit Center Managers' Authority to Choose between Internal and External Vendors, by Strategic Type 114

5–1. The Effects of Dual Pricing on a Consolidated Income Statement 145

10–1. Implementation Modes of the Four Pure Organizational Types 275

10–2. Transfer Pricing Policy, by Strategic Type 280

A–1. Summary of Data Collection Effort 302

B–1. Strategic Classification Scheme Used by Vancil 311

B–2. Reclassification of Vancil's Eleven Strategic Types 313

Preface and Acknowledgments

I became interested in the transfer pricing problem five years ago. In my initial research, I was struck by the divergence between academic theory and managerial practice. As a result of this divergence, many managers today are struggling with what often proves to be a very complex and irritating problem. The purpose of this book is to provide some help to these managers and also to contribute to academic theory in the disciplines that are relevant to the transfer pricing problem—business policy, control, economics, organizational behavior, and sociology.

This was a difficult book to write for several reasons. First, many disciplines involve concepts that are useful for understanding the transfer pricing problem. Thus, I had to become familiar with various disciplines, their different vocabularies, and their often conflicting assumptions. Combining these disciplines in a useful way proved to be a challenging task.

Even more challenging was the process of data collection and analysis. As anyone knows who has studied a complex management problem using field-based research methods, organizing complex and often contradictory data to derive conclusions that are useful both in theory and in practice is an arduous task, fraught with inefficiencies, detours, and dead ends. It is also an exciting task, made enjoyable for me by the many conversations I had with the managers who participated in this study and the colleagues with whom I discussed this intriguing question.

The central conclusion of this study is that transfer pricing policies are an integral aspect of strategy implementation and that effective management of these policies requires careful attention to administrative process. The first four chapters of this book elaborate this finding by showing how strategy determines transfer pricing policy and by identifying the elements of administrative process that are especially crucial. The next five chapters examine in depth the management challenges of the most common transfer pricing policies. These chapters include descriptions of both successful and unsuccessful experiences at a number of companies. The final chapter presents a general framework for strategy implementation that is designed to help managers analyze their own company's transfer pricing practices. This framework also has other applications, some of which are mentioned.

I began this research project soon after joining the faculty of the Harvard Business School. I took a position there because the school's mission of doing research that contributes to both theory and practice and of training general managers was compatible with my own epistemological preferences and career objectives. It has proved to be the kind of stimulating, supportive, and ambiguous environment that nurtures the type of project I undertook. I would like to thank Dean John McArthur for fostering and sustaining this environment and for his support on this project, including ways in which I probably remain unaware.

Ray Corey, director of the Division of Research, has been of great help to me since the inception of my research on this problem. He has always struck the right balance between encouragement and criticism, both substantively and in terms of the research and writing process itself. Joan Terrell and Judy Uhl, also of the Division of Research, have been extremely helpful to me as editors and critics.

The person who is most familiar with this project and who saw me through all of its ups and downs is Harrison White, whom I first met when I was a graduate student in the Department of Sociology at Harvard University. As a mentor, his intellectual influence on me has been great, but equally important have been his roles of colleague and friend. Since words alone cannot express the debt I owe him, my thanks must be expressed in terms of the joys of intellectual discovery and teaching we have shared and continue to share together.

Paul Lawrence, in the Organizational Behavior/Human Resource Management area at the school, has also been a continuing source of support and encouragement since the beginning of this project, especially since I selected a subject that traditionally had been defined as an accounting problem. Richard Vancil, in the Control area, offered some of the earliest and most penetrating criticism of my work. I admire his intellectual honesty, and I have benefited greatly from his insights. Robert Hayes, in the Production and Operations Management area, also played a crucial early role in this project; it was in a conversation with him that I decided to focus on the transfer pricing problem. I also want to thank Howard Stevenson, in the General Management area, for many useful suggestions on the many drafts he so willingly read.

Many others have contributed to this project. In particular, I would like to thank the many managers who were so generous with their time and so open in their discussions with me about what can be a very sensitive problem. Since they must remain anonymous to preserve the company disguises, I hope their participation was at least interesting to them and, in some cases, even useful in providing some insight into a problem in which we share a strong mutual interest. I would also like to thank Daniel Keegan and Kirthi Govindarajan of Price Waterhouse for making data available to me from their own study of transfer pricing and for performing additional analyses of these data so that I could include some of their important findings in this book. Bruce Katz, my editor at Lexington Books, assisted me in a number of ways through his understanding of the dilemmas involved in writing for both managers and academics.

The difficulty of writing this book was reflected in the number of drafts it went through. At each stage, I received many useful comments from a large number of colleagues; the number was large because of the broad range of expertise that is relevant to this problem. At the Harvard Business School, various drafts were read by individuals in four areas. In the Organizational Behavior/Human Resource Management area, my administrative home, I benefited from comments by By Barnes, Michael Beer, Daniel Isenberg, John Kotter, Jay Lorsch, Paul Lawrence, Janice McCormick, Leonard Schlesinger, and Richard Walton. Within the Control area, where the most research has been done on this problem, I benefited from conversations with Robert Anthony, James Cash, Robert Kaplan, Warren McFarlan, Richard Vancil, and Michael Vitale. In the Business Policy group of the General Management area, Kenneth Andrews, Norman Berg, Joseph Bower, Richard Hamermesh, Michael Porter, and Howard Stevenson helped broaden my appreciation of the strategic aspects of the problem. Robert Hayes and Robert Stobaugh in the Production and Operations Management area helped me through their industry knowledge of and experience with this particular problem and more general aspects of vertical integration. Barbara Jackson, formerly of the Harvard Business School and currently at Index Systems, made a number of helpful suggestions and offered some important insights on product pricing practices. Chris Argyris, at the Harvard School of Education, was especially helpful to me in discussions about how to write up clinical research. Finally, Paul Hirsch, of the University of Chicago, gave me a very useful critique both as a sociologist and as a professor of business administration.

The production of this book involved a number of people. Valerie Kerr, Lynn de Barros, and Pam Lovell assisted me at various stages of the preparation of the manuscript. They also served as intelligent readers who had no prior familiarity with this problem and, as such, could critique the clarity and logic of the presentation. Rose Giacobbe and members of the word processing staff at the Harvard Business School patiently typed my many drafts, often under severe time pressures.

Anne Laurin Eccles made this already enjoyable project even more so through her constant emotional support and critical insights on presentation and style. I also want to thank her for her willingness to endure innumerable discussions of the subject. As a novelist, her writing habits are very different from mine, which she accepted with good humor and understanding.

It is customary for the author to accept full responsibility for the final product, including errors and omissions, while absolving of any blame those who were helpful to him or her. This I easily and willingly do. As an author knows better than even the strongest critic, however, a book can always be improved and, in this sense, is never finished. Therefore, I especially look forward to the additional insights into the fascinating transfer pricing problem that will come from those who read and use this book.

The Transfer Pricing Problem

In every department of human affairs, Practice long precedes Science: systematic enquiry into the modes of action of the powers of nature is the tardy product of a long course of efforts to use those powers for practical ends.

John Stuart Mill
Principles of Political Economy (1884)

1
The Problem with a Solution

The transfer pricing problem is a difficult and frustrating one. Although there has been substantial interest in this problem among academics, many managers regard it as unsolved or unsolvable. The current state of knowledge has been well summarized by Richard Vancil (1978), a leading authority on management control systems. Vancil had hoped to further our understanding of transfer pricing in his general study of decentralization but fell short of this objective:

> My third disappointment in this study is that I have been unable to say anything definitive—or even mildly useful—on the subject of transfer prices. . . . The issue remains a perennial puzzle for academicians, while practitioners continue to cope. I wish the best of good fortune to the next researcher to tackle this problem. (p. 142)

This book is based on the coping efforts of the many managers who have struggled with this vexing problem. Their experience clearly demonstrates (1) that transfer pricing policies must be based on strategy, (2) that careful attention to administrative process is essential to successful implementation of these policies, and (3) that no single policy is an ultimate solution for every situation once and for all. The beginning of wisdom for those involved with and interested in transfer pricing lies in recognizing that it is a problem that must be constantly managed in order to adapt transfer pricing practices to changing circumstances. This book thus presents a theory of transfer pricing for managers and academics who wish to understand the causes and effects of transfer pricing practices.

The Nature of the Problem

A common response to the administrative complexity presented by firms that have diversified into a number of industries or that have identified a number of product/market segments within a single industry is to subdivide the company into profit centers under the direction of general managers, including group general managers, division general managers, and even product managers. (The terms *profit center manager* and *general manager* will be used interchangeably.) Since each general manager is given "bottom line" responsibility for one or more businesses and most of the resources necessary for achieving profit objectives, the decision-making burden on the chief executive officer (CEO) and other corporate-level managers is reduced, and they can concentrate on longer-term strategic issues. However, since these lower-level general managers never have all of the necessary resources, they depend on corporate line and staff functions, other profit centers, and outside suppliers for goods and services not provided within the profit center.

The interdependence created when profit centers buy from and sell to each other—or have the potential to do so—necessitates a transfer price, since profit center managers are held responsible for both revenues and costs. Transfer pricing is at the heart of inter–profit center relationships, and it must be effectively managed to prevent the advantages of a multiple profit center form of organization from being overwhelmed by the problems of inter–profit center relationships. The more top management must get involved in these relationships, the less the advantages of decentralization are obtained.

The multiple profit center organizational form has become extremely popular among large, diversified firms. In a survey conducted nearly twenty years ago, Mauriel and Anthony (1966) found that 82 percent of the 2,658 firms in a sample of the 3,525 largest U.S. corporations were organized into multiple profit centers. More recently, Reece and Cool (1978) found that 95.8 percent of 620 responding companies from a survey of the *Fortune* 1,000 had this form. This figure closely matches the 94.6 percent of respondents to Vancil's (1978) survey that reported two or more profit centers. Of the multiple profit center companies in the Reece and Cool survey, 94 percent had been organized as such for at least six years and 38 percent for twenty-five years or more. Thus, among large manufacturing firms, nearly all have the potential for transfer pricing.

In fact, data from several surveys suggest that the proportion is about 85 percent. Mautz (1968) reported that 341 of the 404 companies in his survey (84 percent) had internal transfers. Vancil (1978) found that 249 of the 291 companies in his sample (85 percent) had internal transfers, and 121 of Tang's (1979) American companies (91 percent) used transfer prices. Thus, it can be estimated that about 80 percent of the *Fortune* 1,000 companies are confronted by the transfer pricing problem. Although this percentage is lower for smaller firms—because they tend to be less diverse and because their size makes it difficult to retain economies of scale in a multiple profit center form—transfer pricing is by no means an unknown problem among them.

The importance of transfer pricing, measured in terms of amount of goods traded internally, varies across firms from 1 percent of total sales or total cost of goods sold to over 40 percent. Although all three of the aforementioned surveys

Table 1–1
Extent of Internal Transfers

Percentage of Transfers of Goods[a]	*Number of Respondents*	*Percentage of All Respondents*	*Percentage of Respondents With Transfers*
0	42	15.1	—
1–3	55	19.7	23.2
4–7	60	21.5	25.3
8–15	58	20.8	24.5
15 +	64	22.9	27.0
Total	279	100.0	100.0
Minimum		0.0	1.0
Median		5.0	8.0
Mean		10.8	12.7
Maximum		65.0	65.0
Standard Deviation		12.8	13.0

Source: Data from Vancil (1978), p. 176, exhibit B–1.

[a]Intracompany cost of sales elimination to total external cost of sales or intracompany cost of goods sold to total cost of goods sold.

reported data on extent of internal transfers, because of the way the data were reported and the lack of strict comparability between categories across studies, it is impossible to arrive at a precise measure of an average figure. However, a reasonable estimate of the extent of internal transfers is the 10 percent computed by Vancil.

Vancil's data, which are fairly representative of all three surveys and are the most complete, are shown in table 1–1. These data show that the majority of firms with internal transfers have amounts equal to or less than 15 percent. Vancil found a statistically significant relationship between firm size and extent of internal transfers, with larger firms having a greater percentage of internal transfers. Mautz (1968) found a similar pattern, although he did not compute any statistics of significant difference. Vancil stated that "the reasons behind this relationship are not exactly clear" (p.171). Although I, too, do not have a ready explanation for this relationship, I agree with Vancil that "one suspects an intervening variable is involved, and diversification is a likely candidate" (p.171).

If there is an intervening relationship between diversification strategy and extent of internal transfers, it must be somewhat complex, since Vancil found a statistically significant negative relationship between diversification strategy and extent of internal transfers but a positive (though not significant) relationship between firm size and diversification strategy. Not unexpectedly, 85 percent of the firms with a corporate strategy of "unrelated businesses" had less than 10 percent internal transfers, while only 62 percent of the firms with corporate strategies identified as "single business," "dominant business," or "related businesses" had less than 10 percent. Also, although about 30 percent of the single business and dominant business firms had internal transfers over 15 percent, the percentage was only 23 percent for related businesses firms and 13 percent for unrelated businesses firms.

These findings do not support a simple positive relationship between firm size and extent of internal transfers through diversification strategy, since the more diversified firms tend to be larger but have smaller amounts of internal transfers. Perhaps the relationship is not linear, and firms of intermediate diversification are both largest and have the greatest amount of internal transfers. The relationship between corporate strategy and extent of internal transfers is discussed in greater depth in chapter 4.

Finally, Vancil (1978) found positive and statistically significant relationships between extent of internal transfers and (1) profit as a percentage of sales, (2) return on investment, and (3) earnings per share (EPS) growth rate. These findings suggest that amount of internal transfers is related to financial performance. Possible explanations of this relationship include economies of scale from concentrating capacity in one division and competitive advantages from the development of products that are based on proprietary technology and are only sold internally. Again, however, there is the possibility, noted by Vancil, of one or more intervening variables. For example, Vancil found negative, though statistically insignificant, relationships between the three measures of financial performance and diversification strategy. It is possible that highly diversified firms have lower performance for a number of reasons other than the lack of internal transfers. In any case, it is clear that internal transfers do not negatively affect company performance, which suggests that managers have found ways to manage internal transfers effectively.

One indication of the complexity of these internal transfers is the number of times a good is transferred between profit centers before it is sold externally. In a recent Price Waterhouse (1984) survey of 74 of the *Fortune* 150, one-third of the respondents reported four or more as the maximum number of sequential transfers; one firm reported six. For the typical number of transfers, however, 56 percent had one and another 32 percent reported two. Somewhat amazingly, two firms reported four as the typical number.[1]

A central aspect of managing these internal transfers is balancing them with external transfers. Goods sold internally can also be sold externally, and those purchased internally can also be bought from external suppliers. The Price Waterhouse (1984) survey found that 60 percent of the firms always sold internally transfer-priced items externally and 40 percent did so sometimes.

External purchases were less common than external sales. Only 20 percent of the firms responded yes to the question: "Do the 'buyers' of goods which are produced internally also obtain them from outside sources?" Another 58 percent responded "sometimes," and the remaining 22 percent responded that they fulfilled all needs internally when these goods were made in other profit centers.

About half of the firms had profit centers that purchased goods externally and resold them internally.

A variety of reasons were cited for external sourcing. The most common ones were better quality, better availability, better price, better service, internal capacity constraints, and the desire to maintain a second source.[2] It is clear from these data that transfer pricing cannot be studied in isolation from the external relationships that profit centers have with outside suppliers and customers.

Research Design

One of the reasons transfer pricing has remained a puzzle for academics for so long is the dearth of research on how it is actually done in companies. A few questionnaire surveys have been conducted that rely on data provided by financial executives (National Industrial Conference Board, 1967; Mautz, 1968; Vancil, 1978; Tang, 1979; Price Waterhouse, 1984). There have also been some limited field studies, also based primarily on interviews with financial executives (National Association of Accountants, 1956; Solomons, 1965; Larson, 1974; Benke and Edwards, 1980). Although some individual cases have been written, no study based on in-depth clinical research—involving collection of extensive data on the company and its transfer pricing practices from the perspective of both general and functional managers—has ever been conducted.

The purpose of my research was to determine, through such a clinical study, how transfer pricing is managed in practice. By studying a number of companies in several industries, I hoped to be able to understand why particular policies were chosen and how these policies were implemented. This focus on practice was intended to yield prescriptions that would be relevant to practice and, at the same time, would be scientifically rigorous in the sense that they generated empirically disconfirmable hypotheses.

I began the pilot phase of this project in the spring of 1980. (Appendix A discusses research methodology in more depth.) Between May and August 1980, I conducted interviews with fifty-three managers in four companies, two in the chemicals industry and two in the electronics industry. Subsequently, I obtained access to nine more companies, some in the chemicals and electronics industries and several in the heavy machinery and machinery components industries. Table 1–2 lists the companies, using disguised names, and the number of persons interviewed, according to function. All of the companies studied in this research were promised anonymity, and all data presented in this book have been approved by them for release. In all cases, individuals' names have been disguised; in some cases, individual products have also been disguised. When quantitative information has been disguised, all ratios have been preserved.

The size range of these companies in terms of 1980 sales, was between $475 million and over $6 billion. The number of persons interviewed in each company

Table 1–2
Summary of Data Collection Effort

		Number of Interviews					
Company Name (Disguised)	*Data Collection Period*	*General Managers*	*Financial Managers*	*Other Managers*[a]	*Total*	*Number of Visits*	*Total Days on Site*
Alfarabi Chemicals, Inc.	May–June 1981	5	5	4	14	2	4
Aquinas Chemicals Co., Inc.[b]	June–August 1980	3	1	5	9	2	3
Bacon & Bentham, Inc.[b]	June–August 1980	3	4	3	10	2	4
Blackstone Machinery Co., Inc.	May 1981	1	4	3	8	1	2
Cicero Systems, Inc.	June 1981	0	4	0	4	1	1
Dewey & Burke, Inc.	September 1981	3	3	1	7	1	1
Grotius Equipment Co., Inc.	July 1981	1	1	0	2	1	1
Hobbes Instrument Co., Inc.	May 1981	3	7	3	13	1	3
Hume Fabrication Co., Inc.	April–June 1981	9	8	1	18	3	5
Locke Chemical Co., Inc.	April–November 1981	5	10	2	17	3	5
Milton, Inc.[b]	May–August 1980	5	4	4	13	4	4
Paine Chemical Co., Inc.[b]	June–August 1980	14	3	4	21	4	10
Rousseau Chemical Corporation	November 1981	2	3	3	8	1	1
Total	May 1980–November 1981	54	57	33	144	26	44

[a]Primarily in manufacturing, marketing and planning.
[b]Pilot phase.

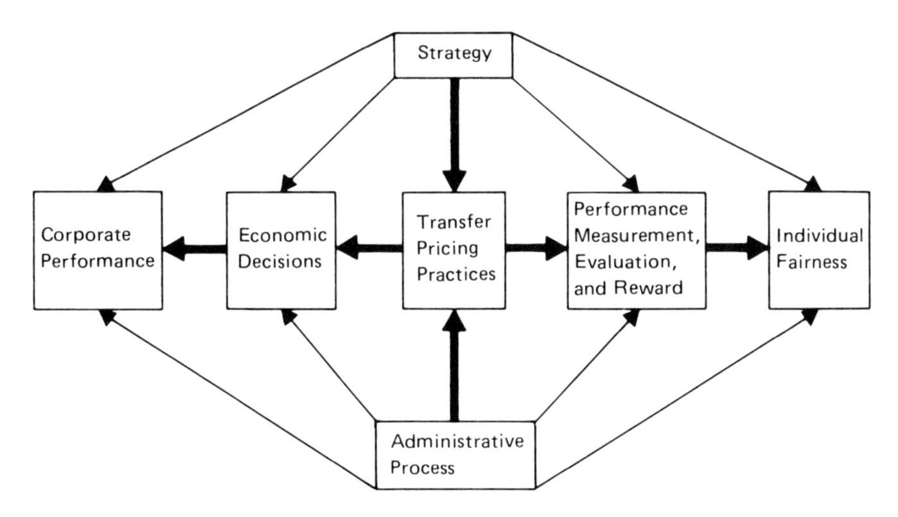

Figure 1–1. The Causes and Effects of Transfer Pricing

varied between 2 and 21, with a mean of 11. A total of 144 managers were interviewed during 44 days in the field. I made between one and four trips to each company, and the number of days spent at each company ranged from one to ten.

The largely unstructured interviews lasted from a half-hour to four hours, averaging about one hour. During these interviews, I obtained backgound data on the company, including its history, current strategy and organizational design, transfer pricing policies, especially important or interesting transfer pricing situations, and current high-priority management issues. When documents were cited during the interviews, such as internal studies of transfer pricing or memoranda on specific transfer pricing situations, I obtained copies whenever possible. Through these interviews and documents, I obtained a wealth of data from each company, which I used to develop a practical theory of transfer pricing.

Summary of Findings

The important relationships between transfer pricing practices and other variables are shown in figure 1–1. At the center of the diagram are transfer pricing practices—the phenomenon to be explained both descriptively (what is done) and prescriptively (what should be done). The prescriptive findings are obtained by separating the described practices into situations in which transfer pricing was managed effectively and situations in which it was not.

Figure 1–1 shows that there are two principal determinants of transfer pricing practices: strategy and administrative process. Transfer pricing practices affect economic decisions, which in turn affect corporate performance. Transfer pricing practices also affect performance measurement, evaluation, and reward, which in turn affect perceptions of fairness by individual managers. (Figure 1–1 also shows that strategy and administrative process each directly affect economic decisions; corporate performance; performance measurement, evaluation, and reward; and individual fairness.) The fundamental difficulty in managing transfer pricing involves establishing practices that will lead to decisions that enhance corporate performance, while at the same time measuring, evaluating, and rewarding performance in light of these practices in a way that managers perceive as fair.

Strategy

Both corporate strategy and unit strategies—such as strategies for groups, divisions, or even individual products—affect transfer pricing practices. Every company in my study had a general transfer pricing policy determined by its corporate strategy. For example, some companies had a corporate policy on intergroup transfers, but intragroup policies were left to the discretion of the group general manager. Typically, a variety of practices were used, according to variations in group, division, or product strategies. Further evidence of the importance of strategy was that as strategies changed, so, too, did transfer pricing practices.

I have identified three basic policies and a fourth hybrid policy that account for all of the transfer pricing situations described by managers in this research project: exchange autonomy, mandated full cost transfers, mandated market-based transfers, and dual pricing. The relationship between strategy and transfer pricing policy depends on two key aspects of strategy (see figure 1–2). The first aspect is whether or not there is a strategy of vertical integration for managing the interdependence between profit centers. When there is not, a policy of exchange autonomy is used. Inter–profit center transactions occur only when they are agreed upon by managers in both the buying and selling roles.

When there is a strategy of vertical integration, internal transactions are mandated. If the selling profit center is viewed as a distinct business for external sales only and as a manufacturing unit for internal sales to other profit centers—similar to manufacturing units within a profit center—these transfers are at full cost. If the selling profit center is viewed as a distinct business for both internal and external sales, transfers are market-based so that they include a profit or loss to the seller. These transfer prices may be based on external market prices, on markups on cost designed to approximate market prices, or on both. Slight variations occur in transfer pricing policies for vertical integration when only internal purchases or internal sales are mandated, but these asymmetries were relatively uncommon in my study.

The hybrid policy, dual pricing, is so named because it involves two prices—

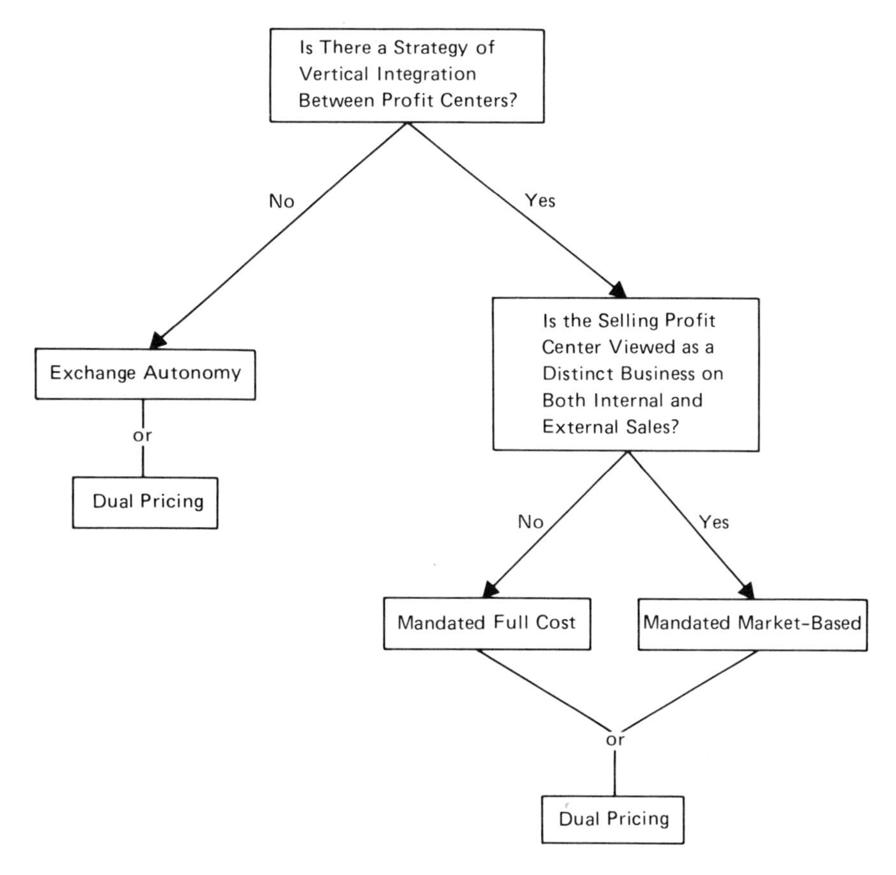

Figure 1–2. The Relationship between Strategy and Transfer Pricing Policy

full cost (or, very rarely, variable cost) to the buying profit center and a market-based price to the selling profit center. Dual pricing is used both when internal transactions are mandated and when they are not. When they are mandated, this hybrid policy is designed to compensate the management of the buying profit center for the lack of authority to select outside vendors. When internal transactions are not mandated, it is designed to provide an incentive to buying profit centers to source internally.

The relationship between strategy and transfer pricing policy is so intimate that it is nearly a tautology. Without a policy of mandated transactions, it is difficult, if not impossible, to implement a strategy of vertical integration. Conversely, mandated internal transactions are tantamount to a declaration of a vertical integration strategy. Similarly, when mandated transactions are transferred at full cost, it is understood that all profits (or losses) on the external sale of the final good are contained in the unit receiving the transferred good, just as would be the case if this unit manufactured the intermediate good for itself. (Usually, full cost is less than market price, but this is not always the case, so there may be losses as well as profits.) But when the selling unit transfers the intermediate good at a price similar to external transactions, it is held responsible for all profits and losses, just as if its entire output were sold externally. In this sense, it is identical to profit centers defined in terms of distinct businesses that have no interdependencies with businesses in other profit centers.

The relationship between strategy and transfer pricing policy is the basis for the first general prescriptive statement. A company's transfer pricing policy should match its strategy, as shown in figure 1–2. If it does not, the policy it does use will be less effective for implementing its strategy than the appropriate policy would be. Although this seems rather obvious, there were examples in my study in which the transfer pricing policy was inconsistent with corporate or unit strategies. These examples are discussed in chapters 5 through 9.

Administrative Process

The second principal determinant of a company's transfer pricing practices is the administrative process used for implementing its transfer pricing policy. Whereas strategy determines what a company does, administrative process determines how it does it. Five major administrative process components are especially relevant to transfer pricing: (1) how the transfer price is set (from programmed to unprogrammed decision making), (2) the individuals involved (different levels of general managers, financial managers, and other managers), (3) what information is used (on costs, other external transactions, and other internal transactions), (4) when transfer prices are set (how frequently and under what conditions they are changed), and (5) how conflict is managed (what conflict resolution mechanisms are used and who is involved).

Although there is some relationship between policy and the nature of the administrative process used to implement it, a great deal of variation is possible, which makes it difficult to make general prescriptive statements. Administrative process is also affected by other aspects of the company's strategy, by the management style of the managers involved, by company culture, by technological and market characteristics of the transferred product and the products that incorporate it, and by general business conditions. Chapters 5 through 9 discuss in more detail the factors that affect the administrative process of transfer pricing, both descriptively and prescriptively.

Criteria for Evaluating Transfer Pricing Practices

There are two principal criteria for evaluating the effectiveness of a company's transfer pricing practices. The first criterion is whether these practices lead to economic decisions that positively affect corporate performance, including capital investment decisions, output level decisions for both the intermediate and the final good, and product pricing decisions for the external sales of both the intermediate and the final good. As figure 1–1 shows, corporate performance is affected by strategy and administrative process both directly and through their effect on transfer pricing practices.

Although transfer pricing can affect corporate performance, my study suggests that managing this relationship is less difficult than managing the relationship between transfer pricing practices and performance measurement, evaluation, and reward. The second criterion for evaluating transfer pricing practices—and the one that is the most difficult to satisfy—is whether managers feel that they are being fairly rewarded for the contribution they are making to the company. If they do not, there may be short- and long-term negative effects on corporate performance. Administrative process plays an important role in creating the perception of fairness through its effects on transfer pricing practices, on how performance is measured, evaluated, and rewarded, and on other variables that affect an individual's perception of how he or she is being treated.

A tension can exist between these two criteria of effectiveness, since transfer pricing practices that lead to the best economic decisions for corporate performance may not result in perceptions of fairness regarding how performance is measured, evaluated, and rewarded—and vice versa. In such cases, the solution to the transfer pricing problem lies not in changing transfer pricing practices but in changing other factors that influence economic decisions or how performance is measured, evaluated, and rewarded, or both. A major objective of this book is to enable managers to determine whether changes are necessary in transfer pricing practices or in other variables that affect the effectiveness of transfer pricing. These prescriptions for practice will also be formulated as hypotheses that can be put to empirical test.

Overview of This Book

This book is written for both managers and academics who are interested in the transfer pricing problem, and it is intended to be relevant for both practice and theory. The book is organized to satisfy the objectives of both audiences.

Chapter 2, "Theory and Practice," reviews the major theoretical contributions to the transfer pricing problem by academics and shows that these theories are of limited utility for understanding or improving current practice. The gap between theory and practice is demonstrated by the presentation of survey data from some of the previously cited studies. This chapter will be the most difficult one for those whose interests are primarily practical; those who have had experience with transfer pricing probably already know that current theory is of little help. However, for those readers who have strong theoretical interests and little practical experience, this chapter will be crucial in demonstrating the need for a new theory.

Chapter 3, "The Case of Alfarabi Chemicals, Inc.," examines in detail the transfer pricing practices of one company. The primary interest of this chapter for managers is to help them see similarities and differences in the experiences of their companies and Alfarabi as a way of motivating a theory to explain these similarities and differences. For academics, the purpose of this chapter is to give an example of the full administrative complexity faced by managers who deal with transfer pricing and to identify the variables that must be incorporated in the formal theory. From a more practical standpoint, this case also emphasizes the inadequacy of existing theory.

The most crucial chapter of the book is chapter 4, "A Theory for Practice," since it presents the theoretical framework that serves as the basis for what follows. Both managers and academics can evaluate the validity of this framework. Managers will base this evaluation on how much it helps them understand their experiences with transfer pricing and on the guidance it gives them for managing it more effectively. Academics will base their evaluation on how consistent this theory is with data presented in the book and other data that might be collected. Toward this end, a limited statistical test of the relationship between strategy and transfer pricing policy is provided, using Vancil's (1978) data base.

Chapters 5 through 7 ("Exchange Autonomy: Pricing in a Market Context," "Mandated Full Cost: Measuring the Cost of Production," and "Mandated Market-Based: Searching for the Just Price") explore each of the three basic policies in depth, using extensive clinical data from my study. The hybrid policy of dual pricing is discussed in chapters 5, 7, and 8. The value to managers of these chapters is to help them learn how to better manage transfer pricing according to the experiences of other companies. The generalizations about and recommendations for using each of the three basic policies and the fourth hybrid policy elaborate the theory presented in chapter 4 and can be framed as hypotheses that are testable through independently collected data.

Chapter 8, "Managing Conflict for Information and Control," deals with the emotionally charged issue of how to manage the conflict that frequently surrounds transfer pricing, especially when transactions are mandated. Again, extensive use is made of clinical data, and the suggestions for improving practice are testable propositions.

Whereas chapters 5 through 8 focus on managing an established transfer pricing policy, chapter 9, "Pressures for Endless Change," explores the variables leading to changes in transfer pricing policies and the problems that arise in implementing these changes. It is hoped that by this point, all readers—both managers and academics—will be persuaded of the intimate relationship between theory and practice. If so, the chapter should be equally valuable to both audiences.

In chapter 10, "The Manager's Analytical Plane," I step back from the very detailed examination of transfer pricing that characterizes the rest of the book to present a framework for strategy implementation. I then use this framework to establish a more general context for pulling together the data presented throughout the book—a context that should also be useful for thinking about problems other than transfer pricing. Finally, since the utility of the framework for managers depends on its validity, I also indicate possible directions for further theoretical development through empirical efforts by both managers and academics.

2
Theory and Practice

A large gap exists between the various theories of transfer pricing and its practice. This gap is evident in three ways. First, the highly regarded policies of marginal cost and mathematical programming are rarely used in practice, although economic theory suggests that these are the most appropriate policies for many transfer pricing situations. The second piece of evidence is that although full cost transfers are quite popular in practice, they are considered to be highly inadequate by economists and academic accountants. Thus, there is a divergence between what companies should do, according to economic and accounting theory, and what they actually do. This divergence occurs because the theories ignore the role of strategy. The third piece of evidence is the relative lack of theoretical attention to administrative processes for implementing transfer pricing policies—an area of central concern to practitioners.

Since most of the theoretical work on transfer pricing has been done by economists and academic accountants, who have defined the problem in a very narrow way—that is, profit maximization—their theories are limited both scientifically and practically. The work done by academics who have taken a broader perspective to examine how transfer pricing is managed recognizes some important issues that are ignored by those who focus on the role of transfer prices in resource allocation for profit maximization. Unfortunately—and ironically—these theorists pay little attention to the role of transfer prices in resource allocation.

The reason for the gap between theory and practice is obvious. Most of the work to date has been conducted by people who are committed to a particular discipline. They have been more concerned with fitting the problem to their already existing theories than with developing multidisciplinary theories that address the problem. As a result, this problem is regarded by many as intractable.[1]

The Origin of Transfer Prices

The concept of a transfer price can be traced at least as far back as 1883. Harry Sidgwick (1901), in *The Principles of Political Economy,* recognized the possibility that producers can consume some of their output in his discussion of the theory of exchange value of material products. This possibility complicated his assumption that products were produced to be sold. But since "in the existing organization of industry, the extent to which any producer supplies his own consumption is trifling in most industries," he suggested that internal consumption be treated "by the fiction of supposing the producer to sell to himself at the market-rate" the share of the product consumed internally (p. 181). He noted, however, that producers also filled the role of consumers when internal consumption was high and that "their gains in the latter character will partially counterbalance any losses through cheapness that may befall them in the former character" (p. 181).

At the time Sidgwick was writing, most firms manufactured only one product or a narrow line of products. During the late nineteenth and early twentieth centuries, the "modern multi-unit business enterprise replaced small traditional enterprises when administrative coordination permitted greater productivity, lower costs, and higher profits than coordination by market mechanisms" (Chandler, 1977, p. 6). As distribution firms integrated backward into manufacturing and as manufacturing firms integrated forward into distribution, they adopted centralized functional structures (Chandler, 1962). There was only one profit center—the entire firm—organized into such departments as engineering, manufacturing, and marketing/sales. Firms also diversified into new products and markets. Sometimes diversification and vertical integration came about simultaneously when a firm entered new product markets that were potential suppliers or customers for existing businesses. So long as a centralized functional structure was retained, there could be no transfer prices in the purest technical sense of values set on transactions between profit centers. The problem was simply one of cost accounting to determine the costs of products sold externally.

Chandler (1962) has shown how vertical integration and diversification ultimately led to the breakdown of these centralized functional structures into a decentralized structure based upon divisional profit centers reporting to a corporate office. The profit centers had responsibility for operating the businesses on a day-to-day basis, while the corporate office was responsible for long-range strategic planning and interdivisional coordination. The new strategy ("the basic long-term goals and objectives of an enterprise") based on vertical integration and diversification required a new structure ("the design of the organization through which the enterprise is administered").[2] The increased complexity of vertical integration and diversification overwhelmed top management's ability to combine the entrepreneurial activities of strategy formulation and the operating responsibilities of implementation. Implementation was assigned to product-based division general managers whose profit centers contained most of the functions necessary for an independent business, such as research and development (R&D), engineering, manufacturing, marketing, and finance. To varying degrees, the corporate office supplied staff support for both operating functions and such administrative functions as legal counsel, public relations, finance, purchasing, and personnel.

Among the many management challenges of administering the new structure was the problem of interdivisional transfers. The seeds of this problem had been sown before the decentralized multidivisional structure was invented; as a result of vertical integration, a substantial portion of the total output of products sold externally was also transferred internally. With the changes in company and industry structure described by Chandler, Sidgwick's observation about the low significance of internal transfers was no longer true.

The sub-subcommittee at Du Pont that recommended a multidivisional structure in its report submitted March 16, 1920, had interviewed executives in other companies as part of a study it undertook to solve the administrative problems that had developed at Du Pont with its diversification strategy.[3] The committee "found that those firms which produced both semifinished and finished goods transferred the bulk goods to the finishing division 'either at a fixed profit or at market prices'" (Chandler, 1962, p. 94). The term *division* as used here refers to a manufacturing department, not the multifunctional division that soon evolved, but the committee's finding demonstrates that questions arose about the valuation of transferred goods as soon as both external and internal transactions were involved. For goods involved only in internal transactions, the valuation problem would be to measure the cost, but when the same goods were also sold in external transactions, market price was an obvious alternative valuation. This was a pressing problem at Du Pont because large quantities of raw materials were supplied internally. When Du Pont finally implemented its multidivisional structure in 1921, the decision was made to use current market prices for interdivisional transfers to facilitate evaluation of the divisions in terms of return on investment (ROI), as defined by Donaldson Brown's (1927) now-famous formula.[4]

Although executives of General Motors initially decided not to integrate vertically backward to the extent that Ford did, when the company adopted a multidivisional structure between 1921 and 1925, they faced the same problem Du Pont executives had had to cope with. The decision was made to transfer goods internally at current market prices—the same prices outside customers paid—although the practice had been to let divisions negotiate these prices between themselves. This negotiated approach was no doubt a result of General Motors having been built upon the acquisitions of formerly independent automobile and automobile supply companies. Donaldson Brown, who had left his position as treasurer at Du Pont to go to General Motors, was instrumental in developing this policy. He commented: "The question of pricing product from one division to another is of great importance" (Brown, 1927, p. 8). Here, again, he was concerned with being able to measure the divisions' return on investment. He was especially concerned with the possibility that parts and accessories divisions might conceal inefficiencies if they negotiated prices higher than current market prices.

Brown also examined the problem of the lack of external sales for obtaining market prices and the problem of divisions sourcing externally. "Where there are no substantial sales outside," he stated, "such as would establish a competitive basis, the buying division determines the competitive picture—at times partial requirements are actually purchased from outside sources so as to perfect the competitive situation" (p. 8). In this case, supplying divisions are more properly conceived of as quasi profit centers.[5] Divisions that sourced externally had to state their reasons in detailed reports to the Executive Committee of General Motors (Chandler, 1962, p. 144). This suggests that buying divisions at General Motors had some autonomy to source externally—and may have done so when outside prices were more attractive—whereas at Du Pont, internal transactions were probably required if capacity existed. The issue of how much autonomy managers have to choose between internal and external transactions is a central aspect of the transfer pricing problem.

Early Theory

The transfer pricing problem first appeared in the business and accounting literature soon after large industrial companies began to adopt the decentralized multidivisional structure. *The Proceedings of the Sixth International Cost Conference* of the National Association of Cost Accountants, held in 1925, included a discussion on "Competing with your Customers"—the last question addressed at the conference. This discussion applied to the situation preceding "transfer pricing proper," such as existed at Du Pont before the 1921 reorganization. C.H. Scovell, chairman of the session, framed the issue:

> We have two lines of argument in this question. The management may say "You take this product on the same basis we sell competitors, and you make some money on it if you can." The other line of reasoning is that the business stands as Division A and Division B, and there is no reason why Division B should pay Division A anything more than cost for what it takes over from Division A. Now which should prevail? (NACA, 1925, p. 194)

Among the variety of opinions expressed at the session were arguments that the cost method of transfer pricing protects the business of the transferred good from entry by competitors, that it reduces taxes on inventories, and that it reduces dividends on potentially unrealized profits by producing an income statement that eliminates intracompany profits. Arguments in favor of market price transfers were that "it is only fair to the manager" (p. 195) of the supplying division to get a profit on the transfers, especially if his performance is evaluated in terms of profitability; that it forces the finishing division to be competitive, since its competitors often pay market price for raw materials; and that "you have got to treat your competitors fairly by putting them on the same basis with yourself" (p. 197). One participant observed that it depends on whether the divisions are viewed as separate entities and measured on the basis of profits.

Camman (1929), a partner at Peat, Marwick, Mitchell and Company,[6] admitted that "the further one enters into the subject, the more perplexing become the considerations" (p. 37). He contrasted the advantages of cost and market price transfers, and although he did not offer a final solution, he clearly favored cost. The advantages of using market price were in judging managers, evaluating decisions to make or buy, and measuring ROI, but they were offset by five problems: (1) bickering, (2) difficulties in determining market price, (3) inadequate incentives for the selling division when market prices did not provide sufficient profits (even if the buying division could make high profits on the final product), (4) the viewing of intracompany profits by division managers as less significant than profits earned on external transactions, and (5) the buying division's lack of knowledge of the cost of the transferred good.

Camman chaired the session "Inter-department and Inter-branch Transfers of Products—At Cost or Market Price?" at the Eleventh International Cost Conference of the National Association of Cost Accountants. In his introductory comments, he remarked:

> A topic of growing importance that is being considered and discussed more and more frequently today concerns the problem of how to transfer products between departments or between plants. The problem arises from the expansion of business enterprises through mergers and consolidations. The questions relating to it are of very practical interest. (NACA, 1930, p. 205)

In this session, arguments were made for both cost and market price. One of the participants in the session had prepared a survey of forty-one companies, ranging from large to small in different industries, and reported that 70 percent used cost in all instances and the rest used it in some. Those favoring cost noted that it passed the savings of vertical integration on to the external consumer;[7] that it was a positive incentive to the sales organization, since it stimulated more competitive pricing; that the plant transferring the product was in a position to supply the buying plant with low-cost materials; that the accounting was simpler; and that "while it is interesting to know profits by branches, the vital thing is to know the combined profit of all branches" (p. 211). A number of problems with the cost approach were also noted, and solutions were offered for some of them. These problems included an insufficient markup on the final good; difficulties in making comparisons with outside competitors' plants when all the product was sold externally; the use of actual costs, which resulted in inevitable variations in the transfer price according to source plant and other factors beyond the control of the buying departments; and situations in which market price was less than cost.

Standard costs were suggested as one solution to the problems of actual costs. As a way of solving the performance evaluation problem, internal and external transactions could be separated in measuring plant performance. Two suggestions were offered to deal with the problem of standard costs exceeding market price. One was to charge the buying department market price and to charge the negative variance between market price and standard cost to the selling department. The other suggestion was to allow the buying department to source externally. The issue of which department would be responsible for variances caused some heated discussion.

Market prices were suggested as preferable in helping management arrive at make-or-buy decisions. They could also more effectively prevent the advantages of vertical integration from being passed on to the consumer, and they could ensure that excessive costs did not limit or reduce the sales volume of the final product or keep the buying department ignorant of the costs of the intermediate good. Problems that were identified included the possibility of pricing the final product too high (which could be resolved by pricing committees that were informed about costs of the intermediate good) and difficulties in calculating the profitability of the total product flow (which could be resolved by performing special calculations using cost).

Although the problem was elaborated and better understood than it had been five years earlier, no consensus was reached. V.W. Collins, treasurer of the Rome Wire Company, called internal transfers "one of those indefinite subjects on which no one seems to be able to reach a satisfactory conclusion" (NACA, 1930, p. 209). After presenting four different points of view that he had collected from managers in his company and that were contradictory in many ways, he concluded: "I feel it much better to leave the questions unanswered insofar as I am concerned as I am frank to admit that each one of these gentlemen's point of view is exactly the same as mine in every respect, strange as it may seem to you, both for and against, and I remain as I am, confident that the majority of you are still to be convinced as to the proper procedure" (p. 216).

Professor J.B. Heckert of Ohio State University opened his presentation with the observation that "this question impresses me as one entirely of policy and expediency. I know of no theoretical reason why we should select any certain method of transferring our products along from department to department, or from branch to branch, so long as we are within the same corporate organization" (p. 218). B.A. Brady, comptroller and assistant treasurer of International Inks, Inc., echoed this view when he summarized his own presentation:

> In conclusion, it seems fairly obvious that operating rather than accounting executives should decide this question and that it is the accountant's duty to provide records that will overcome accounting objections to transfers at market should that course be deemed necessary. It seems fairly obvious also that no rule can be applied universally and that the circumstances in each case will dictate the policy which the operating management will be forced to adopt. (pp. 208–209)

From the time the transfer pricing problem first appeared, it was framed in terms of cost versus a market price that gave profits or losses on the transferred good to the selling division. There was also some concern about choosing between internal and external transactions, although this received less attention at two cost accounting conferences. Although a variety of opinions existed about which policy (cost or market price) was best, there was strong support for the view that a determination of which was best depended on a company's objectives. Although no explicit guidelines were suggested for determining the circumstances in which each policy was most appropriate, the managers were very aware of the advantages and disadvantages of each.

By 1930, if not before, it was possible to codify the experiences of practitioners into a rigorous and formal theory, but this was not done. Instead, this problem appears to have been largely ignored by academics for more than thirty years after it first appeared in practice. When academics finally turned their attention to the problem, they focused on certain variables while ignoring some other crucial ones.

Economic Theory

In economic theory, the role of prices is to allocate resources in the market. Similarly, the role of transfer prices is to allocate resources within the firm, under the assumption that managers are motivated to maximize the profits of their division because at least some of their rewards are tied to divisional financial performance. The objective is to find the price that will lead both the selling and buying divisions to choose output levels that maximize the total profits of the firm. Autonomy is preserved in setting output levels but not in establishing transfer prices. Arrow (1959) argued more generally that some form of price system could be used to facilitate management of the decentralized firm. Through a "supple and understanding" application of the concept of a price system, more individual latitude could be given to individual departments.

The first formal treatment of the transfer pricing problem based on economic theory was made by Hirshleifer (1956), who approached it as a problem in marginal analysis. In doing so, he implicitly assumed that the selling division was not operating at full capacity. Noting that some authors had advocated market prices (Cook, 1955) or negotiated competitive prices (Dean, 1955), he showed that market price was correct only when the transferred or intermediate good was traded in a perfectly competitive market; here, the price was determined by "the market." In other cases, the solution that optimized corporate profits was marginal cost; here the price had to be calculated. In neither case was the price negotiated by the divisions involved.

In practice, a small percentage of transferred goods are traded in perfectly competitive markets. But the use of marginal cost faces two major difficulties: marginal cost is difficult to calculate from information collected by cost accounting systems, and no provision is made for fixed costs, overhead, and profit for the selling division. This is not true, of course, when marginal costs increase with volume. Although this is a standard assumption in economic theory, it frequently does not hold in practice. As a result, the selling division can argue that it does not produce a fair measure of the division's contribution to the company. This argument, often made about full cost transfers, is even more applicable to marginal cost or to its closest real-world equivalent, variable cost. One of the biggest disparities between theory and practice is that economists regard fixed costs as "sunk costs," whereas businessmen expect to be reimbursed for them.

Hirshleifer's (1956) marginal cost solution applies only when two conditions hold. The first is that the operating costs of each division are independent of those of the other (the assumption of *technological independence*). When there is a high degree of vertical integration, this assumption does not apply. Since many transfer pricing situations involve such vertically integrated profit centers, the failure of economic theory to yield a solution limits its influence on practice. In this situation, a technical solution requires mathematical programming.

Hirshleifer's second assumption was *demand independence*, whereby an external sale by either division has no effect on the demand of the other. Although demand independence is not as complex as technological dependence, "the analysis is rather complex . . . the solution falls between market price and marginal cost" (p. 183). The solution here requires a method of successive approximations. As Arrow (1959) stated: "We must abandon the impossible ideal of actually achieving a maximum profit at any time" and settle for "a procedure which will always lead to an improvement, at least if conditions remain unchanged" (p. 13).

When market price is the appropriate solution, both divisions can be given the autonomy to trade inside or outside, because the assumptions leading to this solution anticipate that firm profits will be maximized in either case. If the selling division sells all of an intermediate good externally, the buying division will source its requirements externally. In practice, this is most likely to occur when the amount of interdivisional trading is minimal. Thus, the solution of market price with divisional trading autonomy applies to what in practice is a trivial case, although it is a policy that is easy to implement. Hirshleifer gave no attention to the actual implementation of the marginal cost or more complex solutions (when either or both assumptions do not hold) in terms of the administrative processes that would be needed.

For all other solutions, the divisions are required to trade with each other. In imperfectly competitive markets, since the transfer price is less than market price, it is likely that the buying division would source internally. This is by no means certain, however, since the decision depends on the difference between these prices and on variations in quality, service, and delivery. The selling division may find that outside opportunities are more attractive and that it can increase its profits by trading externally (albeit at the expense of total company profits) when it is operating at full capacity. In this case, mathematical programming is required to obtain transfer prices that provide the appropriate incentives for the volume of internal transactions.

Hirshleifer (1956) concluded his analysis with the qualification that transfer prices applied only to short-term decisions, assuming no change in existing capacity: "When nonmarginal decisions like abandoning a subsidiary are under consideration, a calculation of the incremental revenues and costs of the operation as a whole to the firm should be undertaken" (p. 184).

Gould (1964) built upon the work of Hirshleifer and Arrow to examine the important practical case of determining the transfer price when net prices that the buyer and seller could get on the outside were different. Cook (1955) cited transportation costs, selling expenses, credit terms, and bad debt expenses as factors that would lead to differences in buying and selling price. Indeed, these reduced transaction costs have been cited as one of the fundamental reasons for vertical integration (Coase, 1937; Williamson, 1975).

Gould (1964) used the method of successive approximations suggested by Arrow (1959) for this problem. In this procedure, corporate headquarters announces an arbitrary (and presumably reasonable) transfer price for the intermediate good. Each division calculates the output level that would maximize its profit, given this transfer price, and reports to corporate headquarters the quantity of this good that it will produce (as the selling division) or consume (as the buying division). If supply exceeds demand, the transfer price is lowered; if demand exceeds supply, it is raised. This procedure is repeated until supply and demand converge. With this procedure, corporate headquarters ultimately sets the transfer price, thus interfering with the pricing autonomy of the selling division.

A number of severe problems plague this procedure. First, it requires a great deal of knowledge on the part of both divisions to determine maximum profitability levels. Second, as Gould (1964) himself pointed out, division managers are often measured and rewarded on the basis of divisional profits, which are affected by transfer prices. Since division managers must supply information for determining the transfer price, "each divisional manager has the incentive and the opportunity to rig the procedure so that a transfer price is determined which is more favorable to his division than the one which would maximize the firm's overall profits" (p. 66). Even without these incentives for gaming, this procedure would be impractical if there were a large number of iterations before the output levels converged. The procedure would have to be incorporated in a company's budgeting process and would take so much time and energy that the number of iterations would have to be limited. The method of successive approximations ignores these administrative costs in establishing the transfer price, although in theory they would have to be subtracted from the gains in firm profitability over suboptimal transfer prices. Thus, like Hirshleifer's solution, it is adminstratively impractical.

Arrow (1964a) identified uncertainty as an important limitation in using a

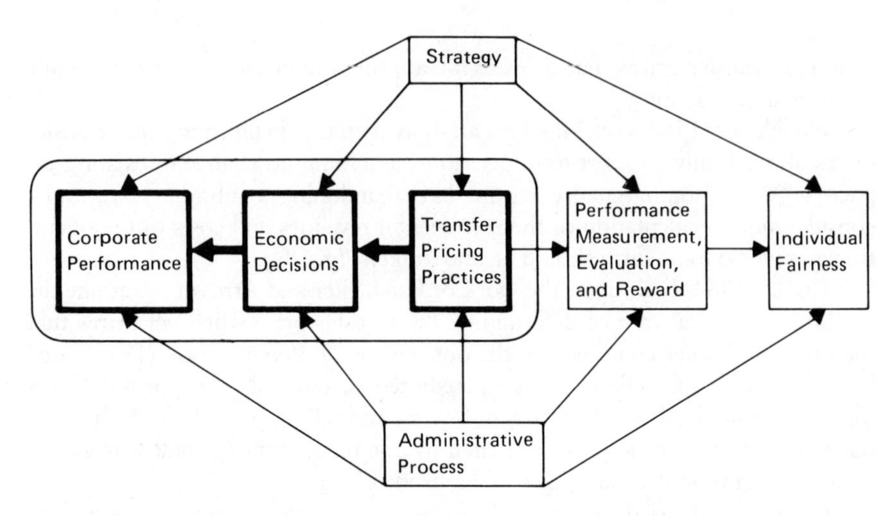

Figure 2–1. Economic Theory's Definition of the Transfer Pricing Problem

price system to control an organization—that is, to ensure that members act in the interest of corporate objectives. Kanodia (1979) extended Hirshleifer's analysis, which assumed certainty about the environment, to the case of uncertain environments. But the transfer price systems he developed, which could be modified to include both price and technological uncertainty, were not incentive-compatible in the presence of risk. This is the identical problem of Gould's solution, whereby division general managers "would have an incentive to misrepresent their demand and supply functions in order to secure a more favorable transfer price, and thus would induce a suboptimal solution" (Gould, 1964, p. 77). But again, even if these problems were resolved, the complexity of the solution would make it impractical to apply in an actual organization.

Abdel-khalik and Lusk (1974) criticized the marginal cost approach on a number of grounds, including its assumptions of (1) temporal stability, such as in cost relationships, (2) technological independence and (3) linear production functions. They also criticized it for its susceptibility to gaming by division general managers, for permitting inefficiencies in the selling division to be passed on to the buying division, for providing no cost-benefit analysis for a marginal cost-pricing system, and for being applicable to two divisions only.

Figure 2–1 illustrates the definition of the transfer pricing problem according to economic theory. It ignores strategy, since it does not address the question of what businesses a company chooses to be in or how it chooses to compete in these businesses. Instead, it focuses on profit maximization under the unstated assumption that the other factors are given. Also, although it focuses on economic decisions, it does so primarily in terms of output levels. It ignores the effect of transfer prices on product pricing for external transactions and on capital investment decisions, and it ignores the administrative processes necessary for implementing the recommended policies of marginal cost or successive approximations. Finally, it largely fails to address the implications of these policies for performance measurement, evaluation, and reward in terms of perceptions of individual fairness. This is a critical omission, since these policies restrict the autonomy of managers to set transfer prices themselves and since the transfer prices given by corporate headquarters do not reflect the profits and losses that would be earned on market price transfers.

Mathematical Programming

Mathematical programming procedures introduce a pricing mechanism to determine how resources should be allocated in situations with more than one buying division and with constraints on capacity. The same assumptions about the motivation and incentives of managers used in economic theory are used in mathematical programming techniques. In generalizing on the economic approach, these techniques replace marginal cost with opportunity cost as the basic concept for determining transfer prices. However, the application of mathematical programming has the same problems as the method of successive approximations described earlier: it ultimately centralizes the determination of transfer prices, it permits gaming, and it would be difficult to apply in practice. It would also be difficult to establish the equations representing the divisions' profitability, since assumptions would have to be made about costs and revenues. Finally, it applies only to short-term operating decisions, not to strategic decisions such as whether or not to enter or leave a market.

The first breakthrough in the use of mathematical programming for problems of substantial complexity was Baumol and Fabian's (1964) application of the Dantzig and Wolfe (1960) decomposition theorem. This approach employs a generalized interpretation of shadow prices from linear programming duality theory.[8] A major advantage of this approach is that it resolves problems of external economies and diseconomies. In this procedure, central management need not know anything about the internal technological arrangements of the divisions. The basic procedure can be described in five steps:

1. Corporate headquarters sends prices to divisions.
2. Divisions submit plans to corporate headquarters based on these prices.
3. Headquarters uses these plans and the mathematical model to determine new prices by looking at the net benefits and costs of the plans of the divisions on each other.
4. Repeat steps 2 and 3 until the prices do not change.
5. Corporate headquarters tells the divisions what weights to employ—that is, what combination of their proposals the company wants them to produce.

Hass (1968) offered a more general approach, using a decomposition algorithm for quadratic programming. He cited four prevalent phenomena that dictate the need for planning in the decentralized firm: (1) demand dependence (for example, competing goods), (2) variable cost dependence (for example, quantity discounts), (3) corporate resource limitations (for example, working capital), and (4) corporate policy (for example, restricting output of a product in a particular market for fear of antitrust action). Hass noted some important limitations in the linear programming approach: it cannot deal with oligopolistic industries (which he claimed most industries are), and it cannot take account of demand or supply dependence. His algorithm contains the same steps proposed by Baumol and Fabian, but it uses a different mathematical model. Externalities are taken into account, and divisions pay opportunity costs for scarce resources. Also, as in Baumol and Fabian's linear programming approach, the best solution for the firm may require that one or more divisions produce less than they could. This would be perceived as suboptimal from a divisional perspective.

Verlage (1975) reviewed the many mathematical programming methods that have been developed for using transfer prices to allocate resources in the decentralized firm, including linear programming, separable convex programming, general convex programming, separable nonconvex programming, mixed programming, and geometric programming. He pointed out that solutions in practice would be optimal only by accident and, for purposes of profit maximization, should be rejected from a theoretical point of view. However, he also recognized the limitations of mathematical programming. Even assuming that the practical problems could be overcome, which is highly unlikely, the irony remains that these mathematical approaches to the transfer pricing problem would substantially reduce divisional decision-making autonomy:

> When shadow prices are used as transfer prices, decentralization has a fairly narrow meaning. Decentralization here is not delegation of authority to lower levels of the hierarchy, combined with a centralized control system, but means centralized guidance (by a central staff department) of input and output decisions to be taken by lower levels in the hierarchy via transfer prices. (Verlage, 1975, p. 41)

Assuming that gaming did not occur, these transfer prices would maximize profits only so long as the conditions of the world remained the same as when the mathematical model was specified. As conditions changed, the procedure would have to be repeated. Although the use of mathematical programming bases resource allocation decisions on a pricing mechanism, it is centrally administered and thus quite unlike the market pricing mechanisms of economic theory, which preserve the firm's autonomy to make output-level decisions. Since transfer prices in mathematical programming are based on information collected at the top of the hierarchy, they are prices in name only. For this reason, Godfrey

(1971) concluded that the allocation of scarce resources should be treated as a short-run planning problem in which the corporate headquarters collects information and makes allocation and pricing decisions in one step.

Kaplan (1982) noted three problems with mathematical programming approaches to transfer pricing. First, linear approaches yield multiple optimal solutions, only one of which is globally optimal. Second, a great deal of information must be supplied to and analyzed by corporate staff, which gives division managers the opportunity to manipulate this information to their advantage. Third, the division managers have a strong incentive to do so, since shadow prices impute all profits to the scarcest resource, thereby penalizing divisions that have adequate or surplus capacity. "This induces a strange set of incentives, encouraging each division to limit capacity so that any profits will be imputed to use of its resources" (Kaplan, 1982, p. 496).

The shortcomings of mathematical programming prevent it from being a solution to the transfer pricing problem, even if it is narrowly defined in terms of profit maximization. Figure 2–1 also illustrates the approach to transfer pricing according to mathematical programming theory. Although mathematical programming requires a less restrictive set of assumptions than the marginal cost analysis of economic theory, it ignores strategy, administrative process, and individual fairness through performance measurement, evaluation, and reward, and focuses only on the economic decision of divisional output levels. Although development of this theory may be mathematically interesting, it offers little promise to managers who are confronted with the transfer pricing problem.

Accounting Theory

Both practicing and academic accountants have written extensively on the transfer pricing problem. Like the economists and the mathematical programmers, their objective is to find a way of determining the transfer price that will result in decisions at the divisional level that are optimal for the firm as a whole, using the same assumptions about motivation and incentives. Accounting theorists assume that transfer prices affect such resource allocation decisions as the amount of intermediate product the selling division is willing to transfer, the amount the buying division will source internally, output levels of both divisions, make-or-buy decisions, capital budgeting decisions, decisions on whether or not to drop products, and pricing of the final goods (although this is often assumed as set by the market). But they are equally concerned with the effects of transfer prices on performance measurement and evaluation. As a result, they are especially aware that transfer prices that lead to profit maximization for the firm as a whole interfere with the objective of measuring divisions as independent profit centers. This creates the potential problem that "much of the motivational advantage of a profit center will be lost" (Benke and Edwards, 1980, p. 24).

The debate in accounting theory centers on whether market price or standard variable cost (an approximation of marginal cost) should be used. The former is best for evaluating divisional performance, and the latter is best for maximizing profits. Another important aspect of the debate is whether or not divisions should be free to choose between internal and external transactions. Less attention has been given to this issue than to the type of transfer price.

Solomons (1965) was the first to attempt to adapt the conclusions from economic theory (Hirshleifer, 1956) to practice. Although he recognized the tension between transfer prices for resource allocation and transfer prices for performance evaluation, his analysis focused on the former; in practice, the latter is of greater concern.

> What we are seeking is more than merely a method of fixing transfer prices. We need a procedure for ensuring that transactions between divisions are of a kind and volume which will maximize corporate profits. The transfer prices are not the only element in this procedure, but they are probably the most important element. (Solomons, 1965, p. 198)

Solomons identified five situations, based on the nature of external markets and the extent of internal transfers, and specified the transfer pricing method most appropriate for each situation. Table 2–1 summarizes his conclusions and my assessments of the practical importance of the situation and the administrative complexity of the transfer pricing policy. The table shows that for Solomons' recommendations, the greater the practical importance of the situation, the greater the administrative complexity of the recommended transfer pricing policy.

In the situation of perfectly competitive external markets for the intermediate good, Solomons recommended the use of market price, preserving the autonomy of divisions to choose their suppliers and customers. This solution is identical to having no transfer pricing policy about either price or source. In perfectly competitive markets, divisions would engage in transactions as if they were independent economic entities, and corporate profits would be maximized whether exchanges were internal or external. Although this theoretical solution is easy to implement in practice, it only applies to situations in which transfer pricing is of minor importance.

In the other situations, Solomons implicitly assumed, as have most writers since him, that the buying division is required to source internally. In some cases, the selling division is required to supply as much as is desired by the buying division, assuming that sufficient capacity exists; in other cases, the selling division can choose between internal and external customers.

The second situation involves no competitive outside markets, but the transfers are not important or potentially important. Solomons advocated negotiation, since this preserves divisional decision-making autonomy. He claimed that

Table 2–1
Solomons' Recommendations on Transfer Pricing

Situation	*Transfer Pricing Policy*	*Practical Importance of the Situation*	*Administrative Complexity of the Transfer Pricing Policy*
1. There is a competitive outside market, and the buying division has free access to its use.	Outside price	Low	Low
2. No competitive outside market exists, but the transfers are not important or potentially important.	Negotiation, typically based on a standard full cost plus a "fair ROC markup"	Low	Low
3. Transfers are significant or potentially significant, no outside market exists, and the product is not a predominant part of the supplying division's business.	Two-part transfer price based on (1) a charge per unit that equates the marginal cost of the producer with the marginal revenue ultimately received by the buying division (this covers the variable and perhaps some of the fixed costs of the selling division) and (2) an annual lump sum payment to cover fixed costs and profit, which is fixed by negotiation once per year on the basis of the expected volume of transfers	Medium	High
4. No competitive outside market exists, transfers are a predominant part of the supplying division's business, and it can meet all probable requirements.	Standard variable cost plus period charges for fixed costs, and treating the supplying division as a service center	High	High
5. No competitive outside market exists, transfers are in significant amounts, and the supplying division does not have the capacity to meet all requirements.	Programming methods	Very high	Very high

Source: Solomons (1965), pp. 198–205.

this policy usually resulted in a price approximating standard full costs plus a "fair" profit. There are strong economic theoretical grounds for objecting to the use of full cost transfers, since they turn one division's fixed costs into another division's variable costs; this can lead to suboptimal profits for the firm as a whole, because the division selling the final product will forgo outside sales that might be unprofitable to it but profitable for the corporation as a whole. Solomons regarded this as only a minor practical problem when the amount of transferred product was small. In this situation, too, transfer pricing is a relatively unimportant management concern, which is not the case for the other three situations.

In the third situation, when the amount of transferred product is substantial but is not a major part of the selling division's total output, Solomons recommended the use of a two-part transfer price. The first part is the marginal cost per unit, to provide the appropriate incentive to the buying division to source the optimal amount of the intermediate good. This assumes that the price of the final good is given by the market or, possibly, that it is priced at some markup over marginal cost. The second part of the transfer price is a lump sum payment to cover fixed costs, including a margin for profit, so that the division selling the intermediate good can continue to measure financial performance accurately. Presumably, this would also increase the motivation of the selling division to cooperate with internal customers. Solomons assumed that in this situation, the buying division would use only the information on marginal cost in setting output levels.

In the fourth situation, when the transferred product is a major part of the internal supplier's output but capacity is adequate to meet all requirements, Solomons recommended treating the supplying division as a service or cost center, with standard variable cost as the transfer price. Fixed costs, including cost of capital, are to be charged on a period basis to prevent the suboptimization problem described earlier. In the fifth situation, when capacity is not sufficient to meet all requirements, Solomons concluded that mathematical programming methods were necessary. "In these circumstances, transfer prices cease to be important in arriving at short-run decisions about the volume and allocation of transfers" (p. 204).

Ronen and McKinney (1970) also offered an adaptation of Hirshleifer's (1956) analysis that was designed to ensure "corporate as well as divisional profit maximization" and that would "preserve the operating autonomy of the divisional manager" (Ronen and McKinney, 1970, p. 101). Instead of using discrete situations, they recommended that corporate staff establish supply (by the selling division) and demand (by the buying division) schedules for determining the optimum transfer price. If necessary, corporate headquarters pays the selling division a subsidy or assesses a tax so that it receives credit for the total profits earned by the corporation on the sales of the final good. This results in a double counting of profits, since the buying division also shows these profits. Ronen and

McKinney did not address the administrative concerns of how this double counting would affect perceptions of performance measures or how it would be eliminated in the preparation of consolidated financial statements.

Benke and Edwards (1980) took an approach similar to that of Solomons by identifying particular situations, but they qualified the objective of profit maximization. They were willing to sacrifice this for the objective of performance measurement, so long as the transfer price resulted in profit maximization in most instances. The "general transfer pricing rule" they established for all situations was that "the transfer price equals the standard variable cost plus the lost contribution margin" (p. 77). Depending on the situation, they recommended prevailing market price, adjusted market price, phantom market price, or standard variable cost. Like Solomons, Benke and Edwards recommended against treating fixed costs as variable costs to prevent suboptimization. However, for the sake of simplicity, they suggested variable costs instead of marginal costs, and they did not recommend any use of mathematical programming.

In addition to the highly theoretical and somewhat technical work of the foregoing academic accountants, a number of articles, addressed primarily to practitioners, have been published since the early 1950s in such journals as the *Harvard Business Review* and *Management Accounting*. Virtually every method—including market price, adjusted market price, some type of cost-based method, dual price (market price to the selling division and cost to the buying division), and negotiation—has had its proponents. Many writers have observed that the correct method depends on management's objectives.[9] The current accounting view on the transfer pricing problem that is of practical relevance is reflected in two recent textbooks, Anthony and Dearden (1980) and Kaplan (1982).

Anthony and Dearden emphasized two objectives for a transfer price system:

1. It should motivate the division manager to make sound decisions, and it should communicate information that provides a reliable basis for such decisions. This will happen when actions that division managers take to improve the reported profit of their divisions also improve the profit of the company as a whole.
2. A distress price, that is, a temporarily low price offered by an outside vendor, should ordinarily be disregarded in arriving at the transfer price for products made internally. (p. 235)

They also explicitly recognized that determining a source and establishing the transfer price could be two separate decisions.

Anthony and Dearden advocated the use of market prices when they exist, since they force the selling division to review make-or-buy decisions constantly and to produce only products on which it can earn sufficient profits. When both divisions have autonomy to trade internally or externally, "the sourcing and pricing decisions are resolved simultaneously" (p. 236), and price determines source. Since this method does not necessarily optimize company profits, certain restrictions should be established, including (1) internal sourcing when prices are equal, (2) disregarding temporarily low prices from an outside vendor, and (3) involvement of corporate headquarters, at the request of either division, to review sourcing changes. These restrictions interfere with the autonomy of the trading divisions.

In many instances, outside sourcing is restricted—for example, for goods that are only produced internally or for products with a high volume of internal transfers. In some cases, it is possible to get roughly comparable outside market prices to which adjustments should be made for reduced transaction costs on internal transfers. In these circumstances, transfer prices should be negotiated by the division general managers who have the relevant information, and involvement of headquarters should be minimal.

Anthony and Dearden recommended cost-based methods only when neither market prices nor rough estimates are available. Under this method, the transfer price is the sum of standard full costs and a margin for profit. The profit margin is either based on the average profit margin of external sales when they exist or adjusted for the type of equipment on which the product is made, or it is estimated on some other basis, such as typical industry margins when external sales do not exist. Like many others who have examined full cost transfers, Anthony and Dearden recognized that this method does not provide an incentive for the division producing the final good to optimize corporate profits, since it may produce at a level that optimizes its profits but is too low for optimizing corporate profits.[10] They suggested three solutions to this problem, the first of which is to use standard variable costs as unit transfer prices plus a fixed monthly charge for fixed costs—based on the percentage of capacity reserved for the internal customer—that includes a profit margin. This solution is very similar to recommendations made by Solomons and by Benke and Edwards. The second solution is to transfer at standard variable cost and split the contribution earned—the selling price minus the variable manufacturing and marketing costs—between the two divisions. Their third solution is to use two sets of prices; that is, the selling division receives an outside sales price less a discount based on marketing costs, but the buying division pays standard variable cost. The difference is charged to a headquarters account when consolidated statements are prepared.

Kaplan (1982) identified the conflict between economic decisions and performance measurement and evaluation as "the essence of the transfer-pricing conundrum" (p. 483). He also identified the further conflict of short-term versus long-term considerations. Like Anthony and Dearden, he advocated market prices when the intermediate good is traded in a highly competitive market, with an adjustment for reduced transaction costs. This price forces the division producing the intermediate good—and the division making the final product—to be competitive. Kaplan cautioned against accepting exceptionally low outside prices, since such short-term optimization could have long-term disadvantages. He also recognized the importance of upward market price adjustment for internally traded goods of higher quality.

To illustrate the complexities of the transfer pricing problem when perfectly competitive markets do not exist, Kaplan considered the case of a product that is only available internally. His analysis of this situation followed that of Solomons, and he reached the same conclusion: marginal cost. Kaplan used the concept of "opportunity cost" to unify market price and marginal cost. Despite its advantages for resource allocation, he noted some serious problems, including (1) a lack of profit to the supplying division, which interferes with performance measurement; (2) complexities that arise when marginal cost varies over the range of output; (3) inapplicability of this rule when the supplying division is at full capacity; and (4) incentives for the selling division general manager to misrepresent the cost function of the intermediate good.

Kaplan proposed using the two-part transfer price of variable unit costs and a fixed fee, charged on a period basis, when the transfer represents a small part of the supplying division's total output. (Otherwise, the supplying division should be defined as a standard cost center.) But problems also arise with this method if the selling division is operating at full capacity; if demand for the final good contracts (although variable costs for units taken go down, the fixed fee is still charged, forcing the buying division to absorb market uncertainty); and because it gives the manager of the selling division an incentive to misrepresent the division's cost structure.

Full cost was the one method for which Kaplan could find no justification besides simplicity. He believed that this method does not contribute to measuring and evaluating divisional performance; that it provides the wrong incentives for the selling division, which can add markups to generate profits; and that it neither rewards efficiency nor penalizes inefficiency. He also argued that when the division selling the final good prices it as a markup on total cost, it may become uncompetitive in the marketplace. The seriousness of this problem increases as more and more items are identified as being part of full cost—such as divisional general and administrative (G&A) expenses, working capital charges, and a margin for profit.

Given the limitations of cost-based methods, Kaplan expressed enthusiasm for negotiated market-based prices when perfectly competitive markets do not exist. Use of this method would depend on the following conditions: (1) some form of outside market for the intermediate good, to avoid a bilateral monopoly situation that favors "the strength and skill of each negotiator" (p. 492); (2) sharing of all information among the negotiators, so that the transfer price will be close to the opportunity cost of both divisions; (3) freedom to buy or sell outside, which provides the necessary discipline for the bargaining process; (4) willingness of external suppliers or purchasers to submit legitimate bids to the company, which are difficult to obtain unless some external transactions actually take

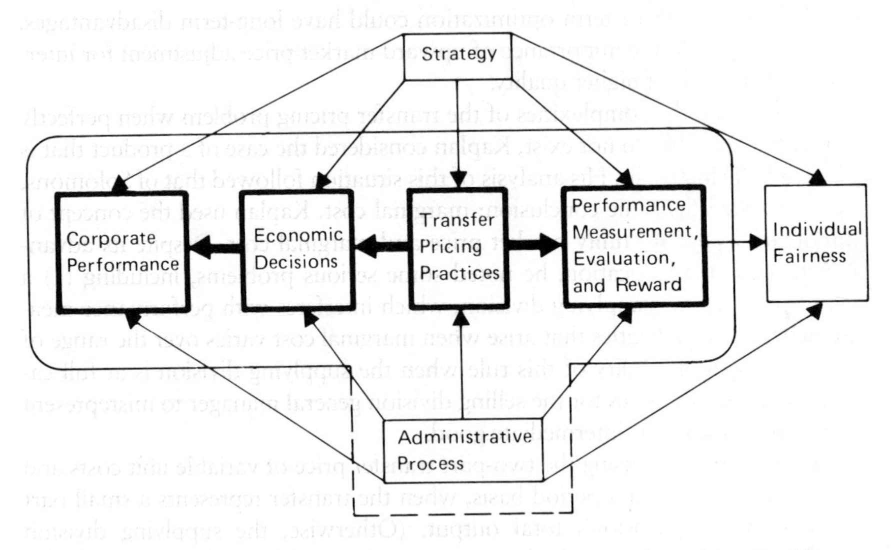

Figure 2–2. Accounting Theory's Definition of the Transfer Pricing Problem

place; and (5) the support and occasional involvement of top management—for example, for resolving disputes or preventing obvious cases of suboptimization. Unless top management involvement is limited, however, it will undermine the negotiating process and the benefits of decentralization.

Like all other methods, negotiation has its drawbacks. As Kaplan (1982) noted:

> 1. It is time consuming for the managers involved.
> 2. It leads to conflict between divisions.
> 3. It makes the measurement of divisional profitability sensitive to the negotiating skills of managers.
> 4. It requires the time of top management to oversee the negotiating process and to mediate disputes.
> 5. It may lead to a suboptimal (too low) level of output if the negotiated price is above the opportunity cost of supplying the transferred goods. (p. 493)

Kaplan's claim that these aspects of negotiation are drawbacks is not unreasonable, but he did not pursue his arguments in depth. Also, it reflects another narrow view, ignoring the importance of developing negotiating skills in general managers and permitting those who can negotiate effectively to benefit from it.

Figure 2–2 summarizes the definition of the transfer pricing problem in accounting theory. Like economic theory and mathematical programming, accounting theory focuses on how transfer prices affect economic decisions and thus one aspect of corporate performance. It also is concerned with such economic decisions as product pricing of goods sold externally, an aspect largely ignored by the other two theories. But accounting theory also pays more attention to the role of transfer prices in measuring and evaluating divisional performance, even if this implies some sacrifice of profit maximization. In doing so, it recognizes that policies that optimize short-term profits may not be optimal over the longer term. However, strategy plays no role in the accounting theory of transfer pricing. There is also little recognition of the criterion of individual fairness, although it is somewhat implicit in the treatment of performance measurement and evaluation. Finally, administrative processes are considered to only a limited extent. Kaplan (1982) summarized the contribution of accounting theory, mathematical programming, and economic theory to the transfer pricing problem:

> Accounting and economic researchers now realize that under conditions that make decentralization worthwhile—that is, an uncertain environment with private information possessed by local managers—we do not know a great deal about optimal transfer-pricing policies. Research, though, is actively in progress, and future editions of this text may have more to say on this subject. (p. 497)

Management Theory

A limited amount of work has been done on the relationship between transfer pricing practices and administrative processes—primarily by academics in the fields of business policy and organizational behavior. The term *management theory* is used to refer to this somewhat eclectic collection, since its proponents share a broader perspective on the problems of management than is the case for economic theory, mathematical programming, or accounting theory. Management theorists even include a few academic accountants who have a broader interest in administration than is covered by their field. Assumptions about the motivation of managers and the incentives established for them vary and are not always made explicit. In general, however, they replace the strict profit maximizer with a profit "satisficer" and do not tie rewards as strictly to divisional financial performance. For example, more subjective qualitative criteria and total corporate performance may influence such rewards as bonuses and salary increases.

Thompson (1967) regarded transfer pricing as "an attempt to substitute arbitrarily for the missing market mechanism" to get each division "to behave as if it were independent with respect to the others." He noted that "the fact that such accounting and statistical schemes are socially invented and validated means that they are more vulnerable to attack than are empirical referents, and leads to some important consequences for the behavior of individuals and groups within organizations" (p. 95).

Cyert and March (1963) provided some insights into what these consequences might be. Rejecting economists' schemes designed to achieve an efficient allocation of resources, as well as transfer pricing methods used in practice that are aimed at making "a 'fair' division among the subunits," they viewed an organization as a coalition of participants in which conflict is only partially resolved and "the concepts of 'efficiency' and 'fairness' have limited utility" (pp. 275–276). They postulated that organizational participants would view the rules for establishing transfer prices as largely arbitrary and as something to be negotiated to improve the measured performance of the unit. Cyert and March also suggested that "subunits that have been successful will be less active in seeking new transfer rules than will units that have been unsuccessful" (p. 276). Cyert and March viewed transfer prices as part of a long-run bargaining process in which division managers are attempting to solve divisional problems, especially when little can be done about transactions with the external environment, rather than as problem-solving solutions for economic decisions. They concluded:

> In general, we should find that transfer payments are made on the basis of a few simple rules that (1) have some crude face validity and (2) have shown some historic viability. We should find that they are the focus of conflict among subunits in the same way as other allocative devices. (p. 276)

Bower and Doz (1979) provided a business policy perspective in their article on the role of the chief executive officer in formulating company strategy. They used the illustration of a transfer pricing problem in the "Dennison Manufacturing Company" case and claimed that since any number of transfer prices could be justified, the important question became *how* the CEO went about resolving a transfer pricing dispute between two key division general managers:

> Who "won?" Who "lost?" and "Why?" are the questions of interest. The organization members' *perception* of patterns of decision making to answer questions like this will determine the strategy of rapid growth. (p. 152)

They emphasized the social and political processes involved in strategy formulation and saw transfer pricing as one particular way of communicating corporate strategy.

The behavioral model of Cyert and March is one of four organizational perspectives used by two accounting theorists, Swieringa and Waterhouse (1982), to examine the transfer pricing problem. They used this model, the garbage can model (Cohen and March, 1974; Cohen, March, and Olsen, 1972), the organizing model (Weick, 1969, 1979), and the markets and hierarchies model (Williamson, 1975, 1979) to present different interpretations of the classic "Birch Paper Company" case, borrowing Allison's (1971) approach of using each model as a conceptual lens to interpret the events in the case. Swieringa and Waterhouse (1982) noted: "Each model leads to different definitions of the problem, to different diagnostic questions, and to different answers to the questions" (p. 150).

The four lenses presented very different perspectives from the traditional one of rational choice in pursuit of profit-maximizing objectives.

Swieringa and Waterhouse concluded that the behavioral model depicted the situation in the case as an "episode in an ongoing, long-term bargaining process between the division managers" (p. 153). They found that the garbage can model analyzed the situation as a choice opportunity that "provides an occasion for executing standard operating procedures, for defining what the organization is all about, for distributing glory or blame for what has happened in the organization, for expressing and discovering self-interest, for having a good time and so forth" (p. 154). They noted that Weick's organizing model, which emphasized the retrospective meaning given to events, viewed the selection of a transfer pricing rule "as a means for legitimating past action" (p. 155). Finally, they concluded that the markets and hierarchies model, which described when market transactions based on contracts would be replaced by transactions within a hierarchical authority structure,

> . . . suggests that the decision about whether to purchase the order outside or inside the hierarchy should involve a consideration of whether the contract terms are likely to require revision. If contract revision is expected, outside contracting will become less attractive. (p. 157)

Swieringa and Waterhouse contrasted these four perspectives in terms of goals versus determinants, adaptability versus stability, simplicity versus complexity, and process versus outputs. They concluded that each model summarized a different conception of determinants and that these conceptions were complementary. Thus, it was possible to combine all four models to understand the problem. As a *process* through which structure and control evolve, transfer pricing can contribute to organizational learning and adaptation, but as a *rule* it can contribute to stability. The appropriate balance between adaptability and stability depends on the environmental pressures on the organization. They further suggested that when learning and adaptability are important, "transfer pricing rules should incorporate specific last date of use routines" (p. 161). All four models present a more complex view of the transfer pricing problem than the rational choice view of economic and accounting theory. In contrast to the simple profit-maximizing perspective, which ignores the organizational context of the problem, these four models demonstrate that "the choice and process of choice cannot be conveniently abstracted from the complications of the context" (p. 162).

Their widest departure from the traditional view was in concluding, as Bower and Doz did, that "the process of devising pricing rules, procedures, and prices may be as important in achieving some degree of organizational control as the rules, procedures, and prices themselves" (pp. 159–160). Whereas the profit-maximizing perspective completely ignores the problem of process (except as it is implicit in determining the transfer price which achieves this rule), Swieringa and

Waterhouse suggested that the processes—for determining what type of policy to use and for using this policy to price transfers in a particular situation—are far more important than the transfer price itself. In doing so, they recognized the role of transfer pricing in establishing a "shared set of beliefs which in turn may form the basis for structuring and controlling" (p. 160).

Swieringa and Waterhouse's analysis is interesting and makes some useful points—such as the crucial role of processes—but it does not directly grapple with some of the practical problems of managing transfer pricing. Other accounting theorists have addressed the concrete implications of behavioral or administrative process issues, although fifty years after transfer pricing came into existence, Fantl (1974) noted that accountants were only beginning to investigate the behavioral effects of the different policies.[11] These investigations sometimes pointed out the shortcomings of economic theory and mathematical programming, as Anthony (1965) did in criticizing the approaches of Arrow and Hirshleifer for treating "the problem as one of economics rather than social psychology" (p. 89). He emphasized the importance of the exercise of subjective judgment by division managers.

Those who have studied the behavioral effects have emphasized the importance of fairness and managing conflict. Shillinglaw (1977), for example, identified the problem of fairness as one of the three criteria for the design of a transfer pricing system:

> *The transfer pricing system should be designed so that the division managers will regard the transfer prices as fair.* Fairness is a subjective quality, and what one manager regards as fair may seem totally unfair to another. This second principle, therefore, is a statement of a goal, not an absolute quantity. (p. 851)

He regarded this criterion, along with making profit-maximizing economic decisions, as more important than evaluating divisional profitability.[12]

Dean (1955), Dearden (1960a), and Watson and Baumler (1975) all examined the problem of managing conflict. Dean believed that the parties should be able to resolve disputes among themselves, without a mediator.[13] Dearden disagreed. He thought that adjudication procedures for handling disputes would always be necessary, and he suggested that top management, special committees, and members of the central staff could all play a role. Dearden regarded "chronic quarreling" as an especially nagging problem associated with transfer pricing, and he believed that the people involved should be replaced if necessary: "Although disputes are the result of many causes, it may be well to review the personnel involved in areas where the number of price disputes is inordinately large" (p. 124).[14] He concluded that "there is no royal road to interdivisional pricing" (p. 125).

Watson and Baumler (1975) examined transfer pricing in terms of Lawrence and Lorsch's (1967) theory of differentiation and integration and the ordered set of integrating devices identified by Galbraith (1973).[15] They decided that transfer

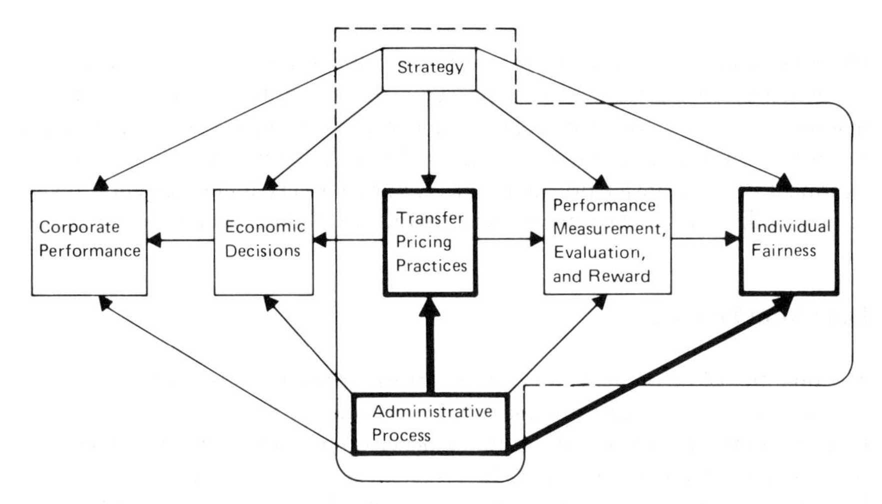

Figure 2–3. Management Theory's Definition of the Transfer Pricing Problem

pricing contributed to both differentiation and integration. They thought that it enhanced differentiation because it pinpointed the responsibility of profit centers, and they believed that proper determination of transfer prices would facilitate integration of the divisions' efforts.

From this perspective, a programmed transfer pricing system based on some formula for determining cost- or market-based prices represents the simplest integrating device of rules and is appropriate only in the simplest integrating situations. Watson and Baumler (1975) thus noted that mathematical programming methods "concentrate on the behaviorally simple integration problems. The environments are stable and the interdependencies are of the simplest kinds" (p. 470). They also criticized these approaches because they sacrificed decentralized responsibility for profit maximization. However, they argued, when the behavioral aspects are taken into account, negotiation has much to recommend it, despite theoretical objections to its ability to maximize profits.

Watson and Baumler drew this conclusion by regarding transfer pricing as a problem in conflict resolution. They argued that transfer pricing is often only part of a multidimensional conflict. Since Lawrence and Lorsch found that negotiation ("confrontation" in their terminology) was the preferred conflict resolution mechanism, Watson and Baumler (1975) concluded that this finding could be directly applied to the transfer pricing problem. Noting the lack of empirical research in this area, they suggested as a hypothesis for further exploration "that accounting data are completely irrelevant or unimportant in the more difficult integrating situations" (p. 472).

Figure 2–3 summarizes the management theory perspective of the transfer pricing problem. The primary focus is on individual fairness and administrative process, and managing conflict is the central concern in administrative process.

Other elements of process—such as what information is used, who is involved, and when transfer prices are set—receive much less attention. Similarly, little attention is given to performance measurement, evaluation, and reward, although this is how fairness is ensured. Strategy is also included in management theory's treatment of the transfer pricing problem, but to a very limited extent. Finally, economic decisions and corporate performance are almost completely ignored.

Data from Practice

The quantity of theoretical literature on transfer pricing is vast compared to the quantity of literature reporting the results of studies of the transfer pricing practices of actual companies. Most of the evidence on practice comes from questionnaire surveys. These surveys, and the results of the few field studies which have been done, are reviewed in this section. They clearly demonstrate a gap between theory and practice, as would be expected from our review of the four theories. Managers eventually must cope with all aspects of a problem, and they do not have the luxury of using a particular theory that ignores some key variables or that cannot be implemented in their particular situations.

There are obvious limitations in using survey data. The principal ones in the surveys discussed here are (1) reporting of data by categories in a way that is inconsistent with how policies are viewed in practice, (2) a confusion between policies and administrative processes, (3) a lack of data on processes, and (4) a lack of data on variables related to transfer pricing practices, such as sourcing policies. I will rely on insights gained from my own clinical study to aid in the interpretation of these data.[16]

In the surveys by Mautz (1968), Vancil (1978), and Tang (1979), transfer pricing policies (usually referred to as *methods*) were classified into two broad categories: cost-based methods and market-based methods. Cost-based methods include variable and full cost (both actual and standard) and full cost plus an additional markup. This markup can be established in a number of ways, such as a fixed percentage of full cost or a percentage calculated to yield a predetermined return on sales or return on investment. Market-based methods include market prices in actual transactions, market prices less some discount, list prices (perhaps with a discount), bid prices from external suppliers or purchasers (perhaps with a discount), and negotiation.

One finding of these surveys that is consistent with an implication of theory, though in a very general way, is that many companies use more than one policy. The theories reviewed in the preceding sections maintained that transfer pricing policy is determined by situation and that if a company has multiple situations, it should have multiple policies. Mautz found that 51.3 percent of the companies in his survey used more than one policy, and Tang found that 44.4 percent did. (Vancil's survey did not ask this question.) Three or more policies were used by

Table 2–2
Transfer Pricing Methods Used in Practice

Methods	*Number of Companies*	*Percentage*
Cost-Based Methods		
Standard variable cost	7	2.9
Actual variable cost	4	1.7
Standard full cost	30	12.5
Actual full cost	31	13.0
Full cost plus profit markup based on corporate return on sales	7	2.9
Full cost plus profit markup based on corporate return on investment	7	2.9
Full cost plus some other defined profit	26	10.9
Subtotal of cost-based methods	112	46.8
Market-Based Methods[a]		
Competitor's price	28	11.7
Company's list price	41	17.2
Most recent bid price received	5	2.1
Negotiation	53	22.2
Subtotal of market-based methods	127	53.2
Total	239	100.0

Source: Data from Vancil (1978), p. 180, exhibit B–9.
[a]Because of the wording in the questionnaire, competitor's price, company's list price, and most recent bid price received may or may not include a discount.

27.9 percent of the companies in Mautz's survey and by 21.8 percent in Tang's survey.

Vancil surveyed the largest number of companies, and his findings, which are consistent with those of the other two surveys, are reported in table 2–2. His data show that cost-based and market-based methods are about equally popular.[17]

Several key conclusions can be drawn from these data. First, policies that are highly recommended in economic theory, mathematical programming, and accounting theory are almost completely absent in practice. Although many situations in practice would require marginal cost, standard variable cost, or mathematical programming, these methods are rarely used. Tang listed mathematical programming in his survey but found absolutely no use of this method. Nor was any use made of marginal cost. Standard variable cost was reported by 2.9 percent of Vancil's firms and was the dominant method used by 1.5 percent of Tang's firms.[18] Actual variable cost was used by 1.7 percent of Vancil's firms and 0.0 percent of Tang's firms. I interpret the absence of mathematical programming and marginal cost to be due to their administrative impracticality, and I concur with Vancil's (1978) analysis of why variable cost receives such limited use: "From a business perspective, this is not surprising because the profit center managers of supplying divisions would have little incentive to produce if their output were to be transferred on the basis of variable costs" (p. 173).

A similar problem exists with full cost transfers that do not include a margin for profit, yet 25.5 percent of Vancil's firms used actual or standard full cost transfers. Tang reported 25.9 percent and Mautz 19.8 percent. Especially interesting are the findings of the Price Waterhouse (1984) survey of 74 of the *Fortune* 150, which reported that 31 percent of these firms used full cost transfers that did not include a margin for profit. Of these, only 27 percent had considered implementing a policy that would add a markup, either directly on cost or through the use of market-based prices. The popularity of this method, especially among these very large and probably financially sophisticated firms, defies explanation according to economic theory, mathematical programming, or management theory. Kaplan (1982) was frustrated by this finding reported by Vancil, as well as by the extent to which cost plus profit markup methods were used:

> It is discouraging to find that one-fourth of the companies use a full-cost scheme and an additional one-sixth use full cost plus markup. Thus 42 percent of companies use a scheme for which we have no theoretical justification other than simplicity and objectivity. . . . The survey raises the disturbing question as to why 42 percent of companies use a full-cost based transfer-pricing rule. (p. 500)

The popularity of full cost transfers (without a markup) is something any empirically based theory of transfer pricing must explain.

Kaplan's inclusion of full cost plus markup transfers in the foregoing quotation is a common misconception. From my study, I know that managers use this method to establish what they think the "market price" should be of products that are not sold externally. Thus, such transfers should more properly be included in market-based methods. The Price Waterhouse (1984) data show that 44 percent of companies with transfers that included a markup (market price or cost plus) calculated markups on cost. About 70 percent of that 44 percent also used market prices. Eight of the seventy-four companies used cost plus calculations without any use of market price or negotiation.

Kaplan (1982) was much more pleased with Vancil's findings on the use of market price and negotiated transfer prices: "In light of our previous analysis it is encouraging to see that 53 percent of companies use a market-price or negotiated-market-price scheme" (p. 499). In many situations, however, this method can lead to suboptimal decisions if the buying divisions make output-level decisions based only on this information.

Data from the Price Waterhouse (1984) survey show that in only one-third of the companies with profit markups on transfers was the selling division's cost kept secret from the buying division. (However, it was purposely made available in only 27 percent of the cases.) These data show that buying divisions often have the information—full cost—that enables them to make decisions that maximize corporate profits, albeit at the expense of their own division's profits. Managers use information on full cost in a way similar to accounting theorists' recommendations about the use of information on standard cost. This disparity points to yet another nagging gap between theory and practice. Whereas economic theory, mathematical programming, and accounting theory treat fixed costs as "sunk costs," managers expect to be reimbursed for them on both external and internal sales.

Another problem with these surveys is the treatment of negotiation as a market-based method (22.2 percent in Vancil's survey, 18.1 percent in Tang's, and 23.6 percent in Mautz's). It is more accurate to think of negotiation as describing the administrative process of determining the transfer price. In this sense, a negotiated transfer price can be contrasted with one that is established by a rule or calculation (for example, outside market price less 10 percent or standard full cost plus 25 percent). This follows the general distinction March and Simon (1958) made between programmed and unprogrammed decisions.

This distinction between policy (or method) and process was made explicit by Shilinglaw (1977), who contrasted the transfer pricing basis (cost or market) and the transfer pricing mechanism (negotiation or dictation). Negotiation can be used with all policies (actual or standard variable cost, actual or standard full cost, full cost plus profit markup, and various market-based prices). The Price Waterhouse (1984) survey recognized the distinction between process and policy by asking firms that transferred at a profit markup (whether cost or market-based) if some type of negotiation was *also* involved. Seventy-two percent of these firms said yes. It is interesting that 62.8 percent of the firms that used market prices to determine transfer prices also used negotiation, whereas 79.2 percent of those that used cost plus factors also used negotiation.

It is not certain how respondents interpreted negotiation as a transfer pricing method (or basis). It is most likely that they assumed that it referred to situations in which both divisions have autonomy to choose either internal or external transactions, top management is not involved in the transfers or is involved only rarely, and the negotiated transfer price determines whether or not the exchange is internal or external. This is how Kaplan defined this method; he emphasized the importance to managers of having the freedom to select external transactions over internal ones. Negotiation is the form of market-based transfer pricing that most closely approximates the pricing of external transactions.

It is impossible to verify this interpretation, since the three surveys that treated negotiation as a transfer pricing policy did not collect data on sourcing policies. The nature of interdivisional negotiations is greatly affected by whether either or both divisions have the option to trade externally if negotiations do not produce a satisfactory transfer price. The Price Waterhouse (1984) survey found that, of those firms transferring at a markup, 55.6 percent of those that also used negotiation and 75 percent of those that did not also use negotiation at least sometimes permitted divisions to buy externally when internal sources existed.

When transfer prices are market-based and do not involve negotiations, they are typically based on prices of transactions to external customers. It is not uncommon for transfer prices to be somewhat lower than external prices; for example, they may be based on prices for the largest-volume customers or they may include a discount to reflect lower costs on internal transactions because of lower selling expenses, no receivables expenses, and no bad debt expenses. This was true in at least some cases for 80 percent of the companies in the Price Waterhouse survey.

Besides confounding transfer pricing policy with the administrative process of determining the transfer price and presenting some limited data on what information is used, these surveys have little to say about administrative processes. Only the Price Waterhouse survey collected information on who sets transfer prices, when these prices are set, and how conflict is managed.[19] The survey found substantial variation in who sets transfer prices, including managers from the profit center level to corporate headquarters and general managers, financial managers and other managers, individually or jointly.

In many cases, transfer prices were changed annually, although there were also many cases of changes on a quarterly basis or as needed. The factors that determined this timing, in order of importance, were (1) changes in market conditions of the transferred good, (2) changes in the price of a raw material used to make the transferred good, (3) revaluations of standard costs, (4) labor or other major contract negotiations, (5) development of the operating plan, and (6) fiscal year end. It was fairly unusual for transfer prices to be changed because of changes in volume—for example, being increased if actual volume of the buying division turned out to be less than was projected when the transfer prices were set. Similarly, most companies did not charge the buying division for the difference between planned and actual quantities. Those firms that did use these "take or pay" provisions frequently employed them in external contracts as well. In general, though, most companies did not write contracts for internal transactions. (Only 28 percent of the firms in the Price Waterhouse survey did so.)

The only question about managing conflict asked in the Price Waterhouse survey was whether there were mechanisms that enabled either the buyer or the seller to appeal decisions on transfer prices. A great deal of variety was found in how these disputes were handled. In some cases, no mechanisms existed; for example, one company simply claimed that these disputes were "not allowed." When mechanisms did exist, they might involve division general managers, group general managers, the chief executive officer, the corporate controller, the corporate purchasing manager, the chief financial officer, or even a transfer pricing committee.

Conflict may be a result of dissatisfaction with the company's transfer pricing policy. Larson (1974) conducted a field study in eight firms, based on in-depth interviews with nine division controllers or assistant controllers and eight top-level managers. He found that division management did not "like the present system, but, as yet, have not been successful in changing it" (p. 29). One reason for their dissatisfaction was the high level of conflict. Thus, conflict can only lead to dissatisfaction. Larson's conclusion about how to manage this aspect of the transfer pricing problem was a pessimistic one:

> The overall conclusion that emerges here is that the problem of conflict resolution that surrounds transfer pricing and decentralization is of such a complex nature that it is very doubtful that any present method of transfer pricing would be successful. (p. 32)

In another field study, Benke and Edwards (1980) also found conflict to be a major problem, although to some extent this may have been a result of how they selected firms. They interviewed corporate controllers and/or members of their staffs in nineteen companies that had at least 5 percent internal transfers, had recently changed their methods, and had expressed some concern about transfer pricing. They found that conflict resolution often involved high levels of the organization and that the greater the dollar value of the transaction, the higher the level to which disputes went to be resolved. In some instances, conflict resolution involved the company president. Only "minor problems or problems emanating from low down in the organizational structure tended to be resolved by the controller or his staff" (p. 25).

Benke and Edwards also found that controllers played a relatively limited role in transfer pricing; in most cases, they felt they were advisors rather than policymakers. Benke and Edwards argued that controllers and their staffs are seen as experts because transfer pricing is a "technical function," but inasmuch as it affects performance, "important decisions are not made by the controller, but by key operating executives" (p. 10). They somewhat disapprovingly described the consequences of the central role played by general managers:

> As a result, the technique used frequently reflected some compromise between interested parties, which almost invariably led to a transfer pricing technique that varied from those described in textbooks. The variation was designed to solve a particular problem, reflect a certain circumstance, or conform to a certain objective. (p. 10)

This attitude of implying that practice is wrong if it does not conform to theory—rather than recognizing that there must be significant problems with a theory that is rarely used in practice—enabled them to develop a set of recommendations through their "general rule" that completely ignored the data they collected.

Lambert (1979) conducted a questionnaire survey about conflict in transfer

Table 2–3
Evaluation of Transfer Pricing

	Mechanical Aspects	*Conceptual and Motivational Basis*
Very satisfied	46%	57%
Somewhat satisfied	46%	35%
Somewhat dissatisfied	6%	8%
Very dissatisfied	2%	0%

Source: Data from Price Waterhouse (1984).

pricing through a random selection of 200 of the *Fortune* 500, of which 84 responded and 61 responses could be used. He found statistically significant relationships between degree of conflict and whether or not the buying division was able to buy outside ($p = .10$ for higher conflict without this option) and when it affected the buying division's profits ($p = .05$). For all four independent variables combined (the other two were method of transfer pricing and how transfer pricing affected the corporation's profits), the relationship with conflict was significant at the .02 level. Lambert found that the degree of conflict was about equal for market price and full cost methods and greater for negotiation. He reported that the corporate controllers who responded to his survey "seemed to perceive interdivisional conflict arising from transfer pricing as dysfunctional" (p. 73).

Although the findings of Larson, Benke and Edwards, and Lambert suggest that conflict is fairly common and is perceived as problematic, the Price Waterhouse (1984) survey found that companies that transferred at a markup were generally satisfied with their policies.[20] Respondents were asked to evaluate executive management's perception of the mechanical aspects of their transfer pricing system as well as the conceptual and motivational basis. The responses are summarized in table 2–3. Respondents also indicated that financial mangement held similar views.

It is difficult to reconcile these findings with those on conflict for two reasons. First, the data on conflict primarily reflect the views of financial managers at the division and corporate levels and, to a lesser extent, division general managers, while the data on satisfaction primarily reflect the views of corporate-level general and financial managers. Second, none of these studies examined conflict and satisfaction with transfer pricing policies in terms of a theory of transfer pricing that explains current practice. Such a theory could offer insight into whether increased conflict leads to decreased satisfaction with transfer pricing policies and whether this results in an ineffective policy.

Although the Price Waterhouse study did not attempt to develop an explicit theory for explaining its findings, it did report data on the objectives of companies that had established transfer pricing policies based on a markup. It asked respondents to rank-order five objectives from most important (1) to least important (5). First in importance was performance evaluation (1.95). Although it was not always easy to establish transfer prices, it was believed that this was important for measuring the results of profit centers. Managerial motivation was the second most important reason (2.21), since transfer prices provide "a 'profit making' orientation throughout the company" (Price Waterhouse, 1984, section J).

Objectives related to economic decisions were ranked third and fourth. The third objective (pricing-driven = 2.44) was to ensure that the products sold externally by the buying division carried a sufficient markup while, at the same time, they enabled the selling division to earn the profits it would as a "stand-alone business." The fourth objective (market-driven = 2.94) was to maintain internal competitiveness by ensuring that internal transfers were "in balance with outside market forces."

The least important objective (convenience = 3.97) was not really an objective at all. In this case, transfer pricing was used between "nonvertically integrated entities" that traded at small volumes simply because it was more convenient to treat these transactions as if they were similar to external ones.

Of all the empirical studies cited here, Vancil (1978) made the most complete attempt to understand why companies used the transfer pricing policies they did.[21] He analyzed the relationship between transfer pricing method and the seven variables he correlated with extent of internal transfers (diversification strategy, sales revenue, profit margins, EPS growth rate, return on investment, typical profit center sales, and number of profit centers), but he found no statistically significant correlations except for sales revenue; that is, larger companies were more likely to use negotiation and other market-based methods. The Price Waterhouse (1984) survey did not support this finding, since nearly one-third of the very large companies in its survey used full cost transfers. Mautz (1968), however, obtained a finding similar to Vancil, especially for negotiation, which was used by 15.5 percent of the companies with sales revenues of less than $100 million, compared to 26.7 percent of companies with $100 million or more.

Vancil (1978) was unable to offer an explanation for this and was generally discouraged by his inability to find any explanations for why companies used the methods they did:

> From the above discussion, it is clear that though transfer prices are very important, we have not been successful in our attempt to explain why a particular manufacturing firm makes use of a particular method for transfer pricing. An answer to this question would be quite useful to practitioners involved in transfer pricing issues, and hence this topic offers much potential for further research. (p. 176)

His failure to find a relationship between diversification strategy and transfer pricing policy is of special interest, given the emphasis placed on strategy in chapter 1 and in the review of theories in this chapter. Chapter 4 explains why Vancil

Table 2–4
Comparison of the Four Theories

	Economic Theory	*Mathematical Programming*	*Accounting Theory*	*Management Theory*
Principal criterion	Profit maximization	Profit maximization	Profit maximization	Individual fairness
Assumptions	Highly restrictive	Restrictive	Somewhat restrictive	Not restrictive
Completeness	Ignores many variables	Ignores many variables	Ignores some key variables	Ignores some key variables
Empirical support	Almost none	Almost none	Some	Some
Usefulness to managers	None	None	Limited	Limited

got this result and shows that, using a revised typology of strategic types, transfer pricing policy is highly correlated with corporate strategy. It is also interesting to note that Vancil found no correlation between transfer pricing policy and measures of financial performance. In particular, companies that used full cost and full cost plus markup policies, which concerned Kaplan, did not appear to be suffering as a result.

Toward a New Theory

In light of all the advances in management theory, accounting theory, and even economic theory and mathematical programming that have made their way into practice over the past fifty years, it is curious that the transfer pricing problem has remained so vexing. Some managers and academics have described it as intractable. Compared to such advances as multidivisional and matrix structures, techniques of financial analysis for capital budgeting decisions, portfolio-planning approaches to formulating corporate strategy, and the application of computer systems to many different aspects of business, transfer pricing would appear to be a relatively small nut. However, it has proved very difficult to crack.

This chapter has shown that the reason for this difficulty is the failure of any of the theories to adequately address the phenomenon in all its complexity. Instead, these theories have focused on only some of the key variables—and often under restrictive assumptions that preclude the situations in practice that present the greatest challenge to management. Table 2–4 summarizes these theories in terms of their principal criterion of explanation (which is the basis for prescriptive statements), assumptions, completeness, empirical support, and usefulness to managers.

A theory that is supported by empirical data and thus useful to managers must be complete in its inclusion of key variables and must not be based on assumptions that rule out the more complicated and managerially challenging situations. It must also address the two criteria of corporate performance—beyond short-term profit maximization—and individual fairness. Since such a theory must incorporate the complex variables of strategy and administrative process, it must be developed according to extensive clinical data from practice. As Vancil (1978) noted: "Deep, intensive clinical studies are not only the best way to obtain such understanding, they are the only way" (p. 142).

The case of Alfarabi Chemicals in the next chapter illustrates how one company managed transfer pricing. By reviewing one company's transfer pricing practices, we can see what variables are important and what problems can arise, thereby motivating the general theory presented in chapter 4. This case will also be used to generate some specific hypotheses that can be derived from this theory. The hypotheses are explored in greater detail in chapters 5 through 9.

3
The Case of Alfarabi Chemicals, Inc.

The senior executives at Alfarabi Chemicals, Inc., were very satisfied with the company's transfer pricing practices. Stuart Tishman, chairman and chief executive officer, explained why he believed transfer pricing was managed effectively at his company:

> I think we have less hassle because I wouldn't tolerate it. The president wouldn't have any patience with it either. People fairly well understand that the financial vice president can call it. It's been a couple of years since I heard of any problems. Two and a half years ago I saw a memo complaining about it. That person was advised very quickly that this was a poor move to make. It wasn't acceptable. It is not too useful to spend a lot of time on this.

Andrew Littel, the financial vice-president and chief financial officer, said he was the final arbiter on transfer pricing and agreed with his CEO. "From where I sit," he said, "I don't see any problems with transfer prices." He added, "There is probably no right way or wrong way to set transfer prices. It has a lot to do with the philosophy of the executive office and senior management." Bruce Cedar, vice-president and controller, pointed out that although he and Littel were the final arbiters, "we try to encourage the managers involved to work it out amongst themselves."

Company Background and Strategy

Alfarabi Chemicals was founded as a commodity chemical company that used raw materials to produce a few basic chemicals that it sold outside and that it also transformed into products for agricultural markets. Both its commodity chemical and agricultural chemical products were highly capital-intensive. Since most of its products were commodities, the company competed on the basis of price augmented by service. Vertical integration was an important part of its strategy to keep costs as low as possible.

The company's principal products were Commodity A, Commodity B, B-Upgrade (Commodity B with further processing), and end-use products sold to farmers that used all three (A, B, and B-Upgrade). Throughout the 1950s, the company had been organized into three divisions—one for Commodity A, one for Commodity B, and one for B-Upgrade and end-use products—each with its own manufacturing and sales functions. Internal transfers were made on a full cost basis, even though each division was a profit center. Because of this organization, multiple salesmen called on the same accounts. In the early 1960s, to avoid the problems created by this arrangement, the three divisions were consolidated into the Commodity Division, the precursor of the Commodity Group.

By the late 1960s, commodity chemicals businesses anticipated slow growth and were perceived to lack glamor. Throughout the decade, Alfarabi's financial performance was poor, and the company began a diversification strategy into specialty chemicals and other businesses to make the company more attractive in the stock market. For most of these businesses as well, the company competed on the basis of price and service.

In the late 1960s, when Stuart Tishman was chief financial officer, he had initiated a major upgrade in the company's accounting system to give as much emphasis to balance sheet measures as to income measures. Since that time, return on invested capital (ROIC) had become a key measure of performance. Capital included property, plant and equipment, goodwill, and net working capital. The ROIC for all products was measured at least once a year, which resulted in careful management of inventories and receivables. Littel considered the company to have very sophisticated measures of financial performance.

By the mid-1970s, two acquisitions, Ammonia Corporation and Chelsea Chemicals, along with others, contributed to three major changes. First, the group structure was instituted, with acquisitions as the basis of the Chemicals Group and the Metals Group. The Agricultural Group was formed in 1978 by separating out from the Commodity Group the end products of the three commodities—A, B, and B-Upgrade. A second change was that "transfer pricing really became an issue," according to the controller, with new interdependencies across groups as well as within them.

Hypothesis 1: The importance of transfer pricing increases when a company makes acquisitions that buy from and/or sell to other parts of the company or have the potential to do so.

Hypothesis 2: The importance of transfer pricing increases when a company subdivides a single profit center into two or more profit centers.

Hypothesis 3: The importance of transfer pricing decreases when a company combines two or more profit centers into a single profit center.

Table 3–1
Intergroup Task Interdependencies

Investment	*Production*	*Marketing*
Agricultural	Commodity	Agricultural
Commodity	Commodity	Agricultural
Chemicals	Agricultural	Chemicals
Chemicals	Commodity	Chemicals
Chemicals	Agricultural	Chemicals

Table 3–1 illustrates the interdependencies of the group with investment responsibility, the group with production responsibility, and the group with marketing responsibility. For example, the first line of the table shows that the Commodity Group had production responsibility for some products marketed by the Agricultural Group, which also owned the plants in the sense that it was responsible for the return on investment of these plants. Although the Agricultural Group had been established as a separate group, the two groups still had plants located next to each other, and some plants could still be used to make products for both groups. This task interdependence, stemming from past business and manufacturing strategies, required substantial coordination between the Commodity Group and the Agricultural Group. Other interdependencies existed for similar reasons or because related businesses from acquisitions were reorganized into separate groups.

A third change in the 1970s was that the company adopted a more formal management style and issued a policy manual for the first time. The manual was short and simple, in keeping with the company's tradition of informality.

Between 1971 and 1980, revenues increased more than threefold to nearly $2 billion, while earnings increased tenfold and ROIC increased fourfold. By 1980, however, earnings in the Chemicals Group and the Metals Group were very low. By 1981, the company had been unsuccessful in integrating its acquisitions, many of which were in the Chemicals Group, and had failed to change its image as a commodity and agricultural products company. The highly capital-intensive nature of the company's major businesses was causing top management to consider whether this was where resources should be concentrated.

Even with diversification, Alfarabi had remained a highly centralized company in which a few people made most of the key decisions, as Tishman, the CEO, acknowledged. "Alfarabi is highly centralized," he said. "Very few people make it work, but we have 65 people in the long-term income plan. They share and share alike in terms of how well the corporation does."

Hypothesis 4: The greater the concentration of authority at the top of the organization, the more likely that disputes over transfer pricing will be definitively resolved here.

Except for Mal Fisher, corporate executive vice-president and president of the Agricultural Group, all group general managers reported to the president, Mike Clarkson, whom many people in the company thought was the most likely successor to Tishman. Clarkson and Fisher both reported to Tishman, as shown in the organization chart in figure 3–1.

The strategy of the Commodity Group was well understood; and it was said to have been established by Tishman ten years ago. Some of its plants could be used to manufacture either commodity or agricultural products, which required trade-off decisions. It was heavily interdependent with the Agricultural Group, to which it supplied a large volume of B-Upgrade as well as some Commodity A, about one-fifth of which was simply resold in Agricultural's markets without further processing.

Dan Wyckoff was a corporate senior vice-president and president of the Commodity Group. The group was organized on a functional basis, the two principal functions being marketing and operations. Henry Jackson, a corporate vice-president and executive vice-president of the Commodity Group, was in charge of operations. A product management function coordinated marketing and operations through activities such as scheduling and making allocations, but it was not a profit center. This group also had a Retail Division, which sold Commodity A, Commodity B, and B-Upgrade to the retail market. It was a separate profit center within the larger profit center of the Commodity Group (see figure 3–1).

The Agricultural Group had been created in 1978 and Mal Fisher was made president. Fisher was scheduled to retire within a year, at which time he would be replaced by Earl Richards (see figure 3–1). Richards had spent fifteen years in the Commodity Group and four years as president of the Metals Group.

Alfarabi managers gave several reasons for separating the agricultural businesses into a separate group. One was that Fisher was a highly respected executive who planned to retire in a few years. As Tishman said: "We pulled it out for people reasons. I had a capable senior manager approaching retirement and I didn't want to subordinate him on paper." Another reason given was that products in the Agricultural Group had a higher growth rate. The separate group was consistent with the company's desire to emphasize its diversification efforts to outside investors by profiling different businesses. Some hoped this would improve the company's stock multiple, but this had not happened. Tishman thought that the group might be recombined with the Commodity Group at some future date. (Many of the Agricultural Group's competitors were still part of a larger group.) However, he also contemplated the possibility of recombining the Ani-

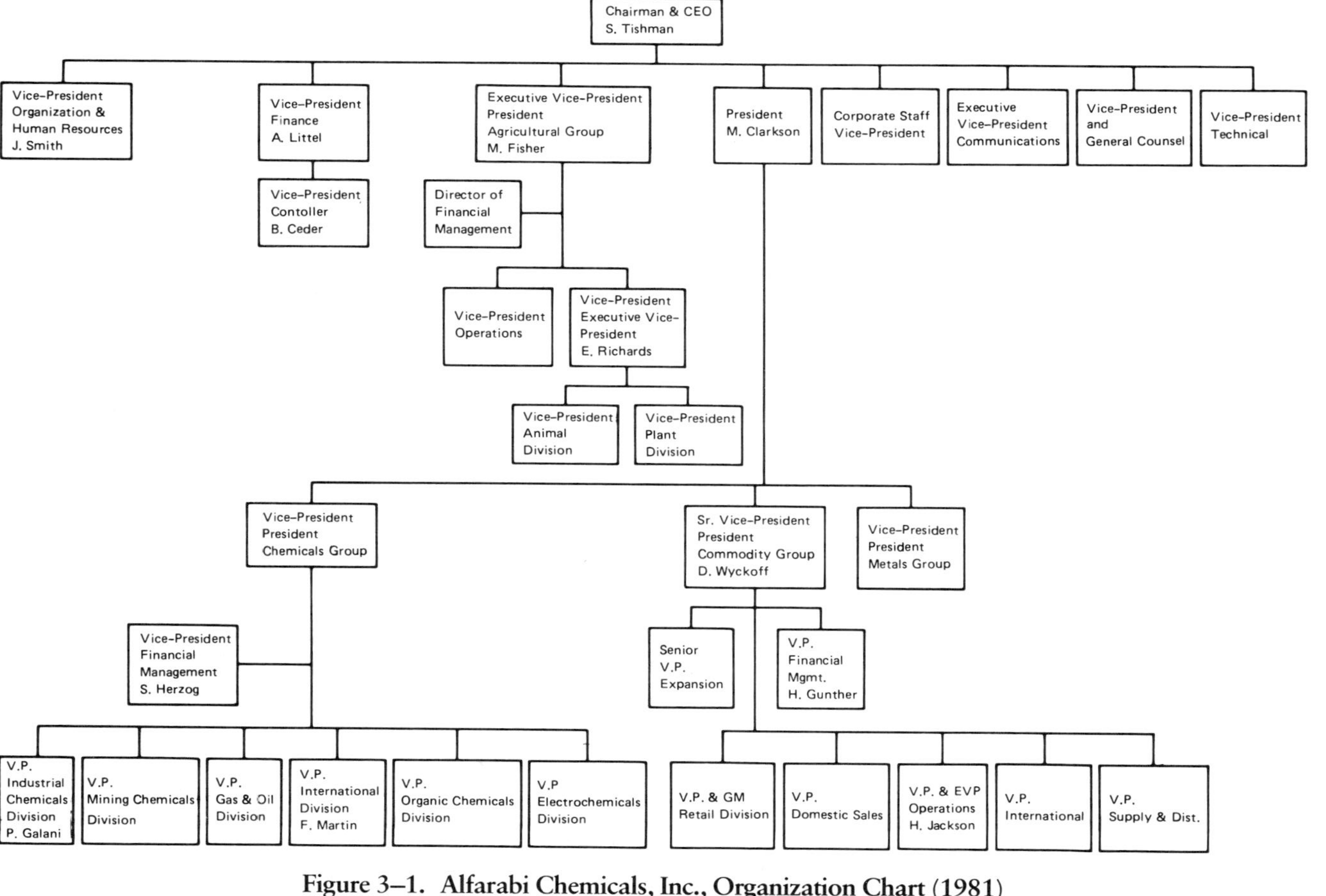

Figure 3–1. Alfarabi Chemicals, Inc., Organization Chart (1981)

mal Division, the primary user of Commodity's products, into the Commodity Group and leaving the Plant Division separate.

The Chemicals Group consisted of six divisions: Organic Chemicals, Industrial Chemicals, Electrochemicals, Mining Chemicals, Gas and Oil, and International (see figure 3–1)—what one manager described as all the "cats and dogs businesses." The Chemicals Group, formed in 1976, had been based primarily on the acquisitions of Ammonia Corporation and Chelsea Chemicals.

Managers at Alfarabi spoke of Tishman, the CEO, with great respect both for his abilities and for the kind of person he was. He was seen as the driving force behind the company and as the man who set the basic tone. Managers gave him credit for the "lack of politicking" in the company ever since he had become president and had fired several prima donna managers.

Several managers referred to Tishman's intuitive ability to make investment decisions. Littel expressed this view:

> Our CEO is a very unique individual. We laugh and say he is chief everything. His background is in finance. For years we had no top financial officer. It was really done by Tishman as CEO and chairman.

In addition to being brilliant financially, Tishman was also good at conceptualizing strategy. He was impatient with bureaucracy and did not hesitate to jump several levels to obtain information. In his firm, quiet manner he could do this without antagonizing intervening managers. About himself, Tishman stated:

> People are conscious of my financial background. I expect good control. I expect numbers to be accurate. I expect high moral standards on the part of people and I get them.

Transfer Pricing Policies

Company policy for transfer pricing applied only to intergroup transfers. The four groups (Agricultural, Chemicals, Commodity, and Metals) were required to buy from and sell to each other on a market price basis, with a discount to reflect the lower selling costs, lack of receivables, and other cost reductions on internal transfers. Group executives established the transfer pricing policy for transfers within their group, and these varied by group. The only constraint on intragroup transfer pricing policies was that return on investment for each product could be measured. As the chief financial officer said: "Within groups I don't care what they do as long as the ROI can be measured."

The Commodity Group used mandated full cost transfers. For the most part, the Chemicals Group used mandated market-based transfers. Tishman remarked: "Within the Chemicals Group I don't pay too much attention to how things are transferred." Both mandated full cost and mandated market-based transfer prices were used for intradivisional transfers with the Chemicals Group.

> **Hypothesis 5:** Internal transfers will be mandated when a company has a strategy of vertical integration.

Tables 3–2, 3–3, and 3–4 report the major intergroup, major intra-Commodity Group, and major intra-Chemicals Group transfers at Alfarabi Chemicals. Transfer prices could be different for the same product sold to different buyers. Factors that influenced the transfer price included volume, whether the product was simply resold by the buying division, volatility of external prices of the transferred good, external demand for the transferred good, and external demand for the products manufactured by the buying divisions. Variations were reflected in how market price was defined and in the size of any discount taken from this price. Wyckoff, president of the Commodity Group, explained why the policy for intergroup transfers required some flexibility:

> We basically try to follow market price or our best calculation so we have a reasonably good feel for what each division does. At the same time, once in a while a situation comes up where we depart from this and give a group that is not doing too well a break on a product in order to help their motivation. It's not an exact science. We play it by ear.

> **Hypothesis 6:** Basic transfer pricing policies are adjusted according to the circumstances of particular transactions.

Within the Commodity Group, transfers between operations and marketing were made on a standard full cost basis. Managers used the term *transfer price* when they discussed these transfers.[1] Marketing was held responsible for price variances, and manufacturing was responsible for cost and volume variances, even when volume was the result of marketing's over- or underprojections. Top management understood these businesses so well that it knew how to interpret these performance measures. The same transfer prices were used for transfers to the Retail Division.[2]

Changes in Transfer Pricing Policies

The transfer pricing policies used at Alfarabi Chemicals had not been constant over time. Changes had occurred in the cases of products sold to the Retail Division, natural gas, and methanol. In some cases, these changes had followed reorganizations and changes in strategy.

Until about twenty years ago, transfers to the Retail Division had been done

Table 3–2
Major Intergroup Transfers at Alfarabi Chemicals, Inc. (1980)

Seller	*Product*	*Buyer*	*Transfer Price*
Commodity Group	Commodity A	Agricultural Group	Average domestic sales price for the year from external sales less a 10% commission less $5.00/unit of volume if low-grade product; resold externally through Agricultural's distribution channels
Commodity Group	Commodity A	Chemicals Group—Electrochemicals Division	Domestic seasonal list price less the same discount from actual market price given to a major national account (currently 5%)
Commodity Group	Commodity A	Chemicals Group—Industrial Chemicals Division	Sold as both a raw material and for resale at list price less 5%, which was considered by the buyer to be market-competitive; used as both a raw material and resold externally
Commodity Group	Commodity B	Agricultural Group—Animal Division	Highest overseas market price less 20%
Commodity Group	B-Upgrade, brown form	Agricultural Group—Animal Division	Market price to largest outside customer less 20% less an additional discount for taking product in less finished form than that sold externally

Commodity Group	Ammonia	Agricultural Group—Animal Division	Average spot price FOB U.S. Gulf, which was adjusted quarterly
Commodity Group	Ammonia	Chemicals Group—Industrial Chemicals, Mining Chemicals, and Organic Chemicals Divisions	Average spot price FOB U.S. Gulf, which was adjusted quarterly
Chemicals Group—Industrial Chemicals Division	Methanol	Agricultural Group—Animal Division	Lowest price sold to any external customer (currently list price less 10%) plus an additional 7% discount since no freight expenses; renegotiated if market price decreased
Chemicals Group—Mining Chemicals Division	Explosive caps	Commodity Group	Purchased from external supplier and resold internally at outside purchase price (currently list price less 20%) plus a small handling fee
Chemicals Group—Gas and Oil Division	Natural gas	Commodity Group	Very complex pricing due to federal regulations, but essentially opportunity cost—defined as highest price that could be obtained from external customer on a long-term contract

Table 3–3
Major Intra–Commodity Group Transfers at Alfarabi Chemicals, Inc. (1980)

Seller	*Product*	*Buyer*	*Transfer Price*
Operations	Commodity A	Marketing	Standard full cost adjusted for grade; lower grades costed at lower cost than difference in production cost, and higher grades costed at higher cost to encourage use of lower grades
Operations	Commodity A	Retail Division	Same as above
Operations	Commodity B	Marketing	Same as above
Operations	Commodity B	Retail Division	Same as above
Operations	B-Upgrade	Marketing	Standard full cost
Operations	B-Upgrade	Retail Division	Standard full cost

Table 3–4
Major Intra–Chemicals Group Transfers at Alfarabi Chemicals, Inc. (1980)

Seller	*Product*	*Buyer*	*Transfer Price*
Organic Chemicals	Chemical A	Mining Chemicals	List price less 5%, resold externally (price to outside distributors, list less 7%)
Organic Chemicals	Chemical B	Industrial Chemicals	List price

according to a mandated market-based policy. Tishman explained why the transfer pricing method had been changed:

> I was here when we went from market price to cost for transfers to the Retail Division. They had a special value to us, such as being a training ground for developing general managers, since for a long time that was the only job in the company except for the president's which involved multiple functions.
>
> They couldn't go outside for raw materials and they took off-grade and out-of-season product. To pretend that they should develop a return based on market prices was a stupid exercise which made them look bad on paper for no purpose. There was a time when Retail would have shown a loss with market transfers.

Henry Jackson, executive vice-president for operations, had been in charge of the Retail Division when this change was made. He recalled a great deal of disagreement about the transfer prices to this division—for example, about determining the discount from market price for off-grade product that was not sold externally. In some instances, Retail had sourced product externally when it could, even when spare capacity existed internally. The change from market-based to cost-based transfer prices had occurred when Retail, which had formerly reported directly to the president, was placed in the Commodity Group. The Commodity Group's general manager implemented the change with the full concurrence of the executive office.

> **Hypothesis 7:** Changes in organizational structure can result in changes in the transfer pricing policy for particular products.

When Alfarabi acquired the Ammonia Corporation, it obtained properties producing natural gas, which is a key raw material for making ammonia. The ammonia facilities had been the original purpose of the acquisition, since at that time ammonia was not easily available and it was a key material for B-Upgrade. Originally, both ammonia and natural gas were a part of the Chemicals Group, and natural gas was transferred on a mandated full cost basis.

Ammonia prices started to fall in the late 1970s, and it was decided that to evaluate Alfarabi's backward integration into ammonia, natural gas had to be valued on a market basis to best measure ammonia's cost of production. Initially, this was done simply for purposes of analysis, but soon internal transfers were also made on the basis of market price. The ammonia business was transferred to the Commodity Group when a new ammonia plant was built, although natural gas remained in the Chemicals Group. At about the same time, an aggressive manager had been hired to run the Gas and Oil Division in the Chemicals Group. Escalating energy prices and the decontrol of natural gas made this an attractive business in its own right, while ammonia was looking much less attractive.

Steve Herzog, vice-president for finance and administration in the Chemicals Group, described the shift in strategy for natural gas:

> When gas was first acquired in 1975 my impression was that many thought the gas was acquired to supply Commodity for manufacturing ammonia. Since then we have tended to look at Gas and Oil as its own business. It is completely self-financing. It takes its earnings and plows them back into exploration. By adjusting the amount of money spent on exploration it can control its level of earnings. Our strategy is to build reserves through explorations and acquisitions. With the decontrol of natural gas there will be a nice leverage on the value of the inventory, i.e., the gas in the ground.

> **Hypothesis 8:** Changes in strategy can result in changes in the transfer pricing policy for a product.

Of less importance than these changes was the shift in the policy of transfers of methanol from the Industrial Chemicals Division to the Animal Division in the Agricultural Group from mandated full cost to mandated market-based. The

Animal Division was Industrial Chemicals' largest customer and took about one-third of its methanol sales. Pat Galani, division general manager, explained why he had made the change:

> I decided to sell at market. I was paying market price for products, so why shouldn't they? I'm pretty nice to these guys but they don't believe it.

Galani doubted that the Animal Division could buy methanol more cheaply in the external market.

In all three of these cases, changes in transfer pricing policy had affected the comparability of performance measures with historical results. Tishman (the CEO) regarded this as an important disincentive to changing transfer pricing policies:

> When you make a change, it is hard to compare with past numbers. Last year we tried to make a capital charge to everyone. It was a fiasco. We had two sets of numbers: before and after the change. You need a very good reason to make a change. The language has to be the same before and after.

> **Hypothesis 9:** Difficulty in comparing present and past measures of performance is a disincentive to changing transfer pricing policies.

Transfer Pricing Processes

Transfer prices for intergroup transfers were established on an annual basis during budget preparation and usually were not changed during the year. Typically, these prices were agreed upon by group-level executives, although there were exceptions. Herman Gunther, vice-president for financial management in the Commodity Group, described one example:

> The transfer of Commodity A to Electrochemicals was settled at a lower level of management and negotiated a bit more than is the case with some other products. Our domestic marketing guy established a 5 percent discount with the division manager of Electrochemicals.

Table 3–2 gives more information on when intergroup transfer prices were set. For some products (such as ammonia), they were set quarterly; for others, transfer prices were adjusted as external prices changed. Within the Chemicals Groups, transfer prices were set at both the group and the divisional level.

Establishing transfer prices was sometimes a source of controversy, such as when adjustments were not made to reflect changed market conditions. The Commodity Group had once purchased ammonia from the Chemicals Group when Mal Fisher, currently president of the Agricultural Group, was president of Chemicals, and he had experienced problems then in establishing the transfer price:

> For one or two years the price of ammonia dropped a lot and the Commodity Group was feeling justifiably ripped off. Their price had been set at the beginning of the year, which was higher than the market at the end of the year. There is a question of what is the market price. It is often difficult to arrive at and set a figure. When I was selling ammonia, we made adjustments to more closely reflect market price.

However, he also felt that there were advantages in not being too quick to change transfer prices in response to changes in market prices:

> There are some benefits to the corporation in not giving ground too easily on lowering transfer prices. This can be an incentive to the downstream division to work at keeping prices up.

Hypothesis 10: Conflict will exist when transfer prices are not adjusted for changes that occur in the cost or market prices used to determine them.

Another problem, also involving Fisher but this time in the role of buyer, had occurred in 1980, when transfer prices on B-Upgrade were changed. Littel, the chief financial officer, recalled this issue:

> Last year the transfer price for B-Upgrade was too low so Commodity raised prices. Fisher was not pleased. I talked to him and tried to persuade him. Although it would have cost him 5–10K in bonus, he was more concerned in terms of pride than money.
>
> Tishman was very concerned about this. He came into my office eight to ten times in the space of two to three weeks to discuss it. But he supported me and told me I was the final arbiter. Tishman was a little annoyed with Fisher and concerned that I do the right thing.

Wyckoff, president of the Commodity Group, noted the difficulties these adjustments could make, even when the transfer prices were very favorable:

> We recognize that they are a big customer, totally reliable, and we don't have to wait for our money. We give them a better price than our two biggest outside customers who buy about the same amount. If in a year our judgment turns out to be wrong, we adjust the price retroactively. We did this last month and gave them a $1.8 million reduction. Once before we upped it and they screamed. It cuts both ways.

> **Hypothesis 11:** Conflict will exist when adjustments in transfer prices negatively affect performance measures and financial rewards.

A more general controversy arose over the transfer pricing policy applied to B-Upgrade. Managers in both the buying and the selling groups were unhappy, but for different reasons. The original policy, established when the Agricultural Group was created in 1978, was market price less 10 percent. According to Gunther, the vice-president for finance in the Commodity Group, "there was some arm twisting from the corporation" to increase the discount to 20 percent. He, for one, felt that this discount was too high. The difference in discounts represented an extra 2.5 to 3 percent in ROIC for the Agricultural Group. One justification for the discount was that the Agricultural Group, complaining about a decline in profits, argued that some competitors received their raw materials from internal suppliers at full cost. Some managers felt that the higher discount was based more on Fisher's seniority and relationship with Tishman than on economic considerations.

Although the Agricultural Group did benefit from the increased discount, Fisher, who had good working relationships with managers in the Commodity Group for many years, was unhappy with the current transfer pricing method. Two of his concerns were how the decision to use this policy had been made and what its effects would be on the performance measurement of his group:

> This was a decision made in the executive office. I was not involved in this decision although I would have liked to have been. I've suggested substantial changes but haven't sold them yet. What I want is for part of the capital of Plant B-Upgrade to be placed on the books of the Agricultural Group, prorated based on the percent of output we take, and move the product at cost. We should be held accountable for making a profit on an enlarged asset basis. As a major user of B-Upgrade, it seems to me a sharing of assets would be appropriate. It would more accurately reflect the contribution the Agricultural Group makes to the corporation. We should show a larger contribution, although our ROI might go down. Right now a lot of the dollars of profit we make are taken by the Commodity Group.

> **Hypothesis 12:** The process by which a transfer pricing policy is designed affects the perceived fairness of this policy by those who implement it.

Fisher explained that although he thought the wrong policy was being used, the current one was being fairly applied:

> On B-Upgrade the price is fair enough. They make a market price adjustment if market price turns out to be more or less than budgeted. It is not a thing that

> engenders personal animosity. It is just a sloppy way of doing business. Tishman has not seen fit to change the policy so far. I would be pushing harder if I were not retiring in eleven months.

In support of his argument, Fisher pointed out that he was completely satisfied with the market price less 10 percent transfer price for Commodity A: "I don't have a strong argument here for assigning part of the capital to us since we take a smaller percent (2 percent) of their total output." The Agricultural Group purchased 19 percent of the output of B-Upgrade.

Support for this variation on a mandated full cost policy for B-Upgrade transfers varied throughout the corporation. Fisher had advocated cost and investment transfer prices when he was head of Chemicals. Fred Martin, vice-president of the International Division, explained why Fisher had not been able to persuade his division general managers to use this method:

> We chose market price because we didn't want to have to make allocations of capital to other divisions for measuring ROI. Making allocations is a pain in the ass. It just creates jobs for accountants. There are already too many accountants in the world now.

Tishman's comment on Fisher's proposal was simply that transfers based on "cost and assets involved a lot of bookkeeping," but Wyckoff was agreeable to this approach:

> I don't have any particular objection to their getting costs and assets. It's a question of what is the most accurate way to get a look at how a business is performing. I don't care how you count the beans, but don't divide the responsibility for running those plants.

Other managers had various reactions. Richards, executive vice-president of the Agricultural Group, thought that cost transfers of B-Upgrade should only be used if investment allocations were also made:

> If the transfers were to be done on a cost basis I would want a share of the investment so I could get a true measure of the division as a stand-alone business.

Henry Jackson, executive vice-president for operations in the Commodity Group, actually preferred a cost approach, since he felt it would eliminate much of the dissension:

> I'd prefer to move internally to other groups at cost. We spend too much time on this without making any progress. We can make calculations on a pro forma basis using market price. It would be cleaner and simpler.

Hypothesis 13: Mandated transfers in a vertical integration strategy will be market-based when buying and selling profit centers are viewed as distinct businesses.

Hypothesis 14: Mandated transfers in a vertical integration strategy will be at full cost when the assets in the selling profit center used for internal sales are viewed as part of the business of the buying profit center.

Although there were disagreements over choices of transfer pricing policies and implementation of these policies, overt conflict between groups rarely exceeded a moderate level. This was largely because of a lack of tolerance for conflict, given the company's culture and the management style of its CEO. One reason given by several managers for the lack of conflict was the atmosphere of informal gentility created by the southern backgrounds of a number of high-level managers. Littel, the chief financial officer, noted: "We're a company with less conflict than most companies. This is not all good or all bad. It is good in our circumstances." Tishman said emphatically: "On conflict I have a simple rule—you fire both of them and that ends that." He explicitly included transfer pricing as an issue in which he regarded conflict as inappropriate:

> I have a financial background. I know the futility of hassling. We don't tolerate it. I don't hear much complaining. What we have works pretty well.

The low level of conflict was most apparent within the Commodity Group and the Agricultural Group. The culture of the Chemicals Group, however, fostered higher levels of conflict. Jim Smith, corporate vice-president for organization and human resources, compared the Commodity and Chemicals groups:

> Commodity is one big happy family. Chemicals is not. It is full of a lot of young, hard-charging guys who are a little more selfish and more focused on their own profit centers. They are a reflection of the head of the Chemicals Group, although he spent some time in Commodity.

Hypothesis 15: The degree of conflict over transfer pricing is affected by company culture and subcultures of units within the company.

Hypothesis 16: The degree of conflict over transfer pricing is affected by the management style of the individuals involved.

Economic Decisions

Managers at Alfarabi expressed very little concern about the influence of transfer prices on output levels, product pricing, capital investment, and plant closings, although some possible negative effects of specific transfer pricing policies were noted by several managers.

Two problems with market price transfers that Richards identified were that if profits were low in the receiving division, morale would be low, and that the division might forgo outside business at prices that would not ensure a profit, even if this business would be profitable for the company as a whole. No current examples of this problem were cited.

Richards noted that a full cost policy avoided these problems, but he did not feel that it was an intrinsically superior policy:

> The question is whether or not one division should earn profit at the expense of another. The cost transfer works great in Commodity today. The decision was made so long ago that the present wholesale people have never known any differently.

But this policy had its own shortcomings. Jackson pointed out that "there might be some negative impact since some profits would show up in the other groups." He also recalled some concern that had been expressed when the full cost policy for transfers to the Retail Division had first been implemented:

> There was some muttering that our division would cut price now that we had cheaper raw materials. They said that we were used to small margins and we wouldn't get the full markup possible. The complaints almost disappeared by the end of the year.

Littel had also heard this argument, but he discounted its validity:

> One argument against cost is that margins are dissipated without appropriate controls. I heard this when I was at the Retail Division. I have enough confidence in the quality of management to keep this from happening.

One reason for this concern about whether the Retail Division would receive the highest possible markup on its products was that some competitors that were not vertically integrated paid the going market price for their raw materials.

> **Hypothesis 17:** Transfer prices will result in suboptimal decisions on output levels and product pricing by the buying profit center only when they are the only information used to make these decisions.

Wyckoff admitted the possibility of transfer prices leading to incorrect non-incremental decisions (capital investment and plant closing), but he doubted that this had actually occurred. He cited the example of the transfer prices of the natural gas used to make ammonia, which he felt were too high:

> It never gets bad enough to affect our decision on whether to run a plant or not. Where you get into trouble is when they charge so much that we can't sell ammonia; so we shut the plant down, and they turn out not to be able to sell the gas outside.

One reason transfer prices did not affect nonincremental decisions was that top management was able to evaluate a business using both full cost and market-based transfers. These reviews of return on invested capital (ROIC) were conducted on a quarterly basis. For example, to compute the ROIC of products transferred within the Commodity Group, a market-based transfer price of average domestic price less 15 percent was used. Tishman described his role in reviewing these numbers:

> Once a year we make an adjustment to market price and produce an ROI book so I can look at it both ways. This enables me to make some comparisons I might want to make to a free-standing business. When I convert to market and develop the ROI book, the purpose is to make decisions on whether or not to keep a business.

> **Hypothesis 18:** Transfer prices will result in suboptimal decisions on capital investment and plant closings only when they are the only information used to make these decisions.

Performance Measurement, Evaluation, and Reward

More concern was expressed about the effect of transfer prices on performance measurement, evaluation, and reward than about their effect on economic decisions. Two examples already cited were Fisher's preference for full cost transfers on B-Upgrade and the effect of the increased transfer price of B-Upgrade the previous year. For the most part, however, managers believed that transfer prices did not inhibit fairness in performance measurement, evaluation, and reward. This was largely because of how these were done.

Tishman was cautious about basing performance evaluation and bonuses solely on financial measures:

> It depends on what the numbers are used for. You shouldn't use them to beat people over the head. Compensation plans have a lot to do with how numbers are perceived. I've heard of CEOs who use numbers to hide behind when giving a bonus.

Individual managers were evaluated both by objective, quantitative factors and by subjective, qualitative factors, since, as Cedar (the controller) said, "You can't formalize all of this. A lot ends up as subjective interpretation." He connected employees' respect for Tishman with their willingness to accept subjective performance evaluation:

> A lot of people being willing to accept subjective judgments is attributable to Tishman. Tishman is a very informal guy. He calls plant managers directly but at the same time respects the organization chart. He wanders around a lot. He is just a remarkable person. He has amazing retention. He avidly reads, consumes, and retains information on the company you wouldn't think someone in his position would remember. He is very much interested in individuals as individuals and is very committed to the welfare of employees.

Hypothesis 19: The exercise of subjective judgment in measuring and evaluating performance can reduce conflict over transfer prices.

To the extent that financial criteria were used to measure and evaluate performance, managers believed that if it was done properly, whether transfers were at full cost or market-based should be a matter of indifference. Richards, executive vice-president of the Agricultural Group, explained why this should be true in discussing the relative advantages and disadvantages of these two policies:

> It is a moot point in a way. The point is what is expected of you and how well you do what is expected of you. If upper management is happy with how you are achieving expectations, there should be no problem. We all work against a profit plan. In large part your success or failure depends on how you compare to that plan.

Hypothesis 20: Evaluation of measures of financial performance in terms of budgeted objectives can reduce conflict over transfer pricing policies.

The company had designed a system for determining annual and long-term bonuses for group executives that emphasized total corporate performance. Twenty-five percent of their annual bonus was based on group results and 75 percent was based on corporate results. Division managers' bonuses were based entirely on group results. Tishman believed that these financial incentives reduced conflict over transfer prices:

> Bonuses are paid like a World Series pool. We've removed the bonus incentive hassle related to transfer pricing. It makes no difference to the long-run bonus plan, either.

Hypothesis 21: Financial incentives that are based on the combined results of two or more profit centers can reduce conflict over transfer prices.

The Effects of Volume and Business Performance

The extent to which managers were concerned about transfer prices varied according to the volume of transfers, as a percentage of total sales or total costs, and the group's or division's business performance. In 1981, the Commodity Group—the largest group at Alfarabi—accounted for 50 to 55 percent of the company's sales, 50 to 60 percent of its investment, and 75 to 80 percent of its profits. Some managers thought this was why Wyckoff was relatively unconcerned about transfer prices. Jackson contrasted Wyckoff's attitude with that of managers in other groups:

> Wyckoff is pretty relaxed about these things. Some of the other groups are more tense, such as Chemicals. They're having more trouble with their profit plan. They also have a different management, which has different careers and philosophies.

The Chemicals Group had an ROIC of 5 to 7 percent, compared to the 14 percent ROIC of the Commodity Group.

The Agricultural Group had the highest ROIC of any group at Alfarabi, in the range of 16 to 20 percent. Richards, the group's executive vice-president, admitted that this was a major reason why he accepted the current transfer price of B-Upgrade at market price less 20 percent and was not arguing for a full cost policy:

> I'm satisfied because the margins we can generate are good. Our group has the highest ROIC in Alfarabi. If this were not the case, I'd be yelling. If our return was less, I'd complain more. After all, Plant B-Upgrade is not Commodity's asset, it's Alfarabi's.

Hypothesis 22: The lower the level of business performance, the higher the level of conflict over transfer prices and/or transfer pricing policy.

Although the performance of the Commodity Group was good in general, the performance of its ammonia production had suffered over the past few years. Since natural gas represented 80 percent of the cost of producing ammonia, the transfer prices of natural gas had become a major issue as gas prices had increased while ammonia prices had decreased. Because no discount was given for reduced working capital, sales, or administrative expenses, many managers in the Commodity Group believed that the price for natural gas was too high. Gunther, finance vice-president of the group, admitted that "we're sensitive because ammonia has been a bad market until recently." The situation was exacerbated by the fact that market prices of natural gas were set by federal regulations and were higher than the prices paid by many ammonia competitors who had long-term contracts for cheap gas. Gunther also acknowledged that this was of greater concern to the managers reponsible for manufacturing and marketing ammonia than it was to Wyckoff:

> Wyckoff doesn't worry too much. The plant guys get upset, as do the marketing guys who have to sell the ammonia. You'd feel a lot better if they could show an actual sale for this volume. It is a loosely defined opportunity price. This is the policy and it won't change. It has some pretty high-level support.

Furthermore, Wyckoff expected disagreement to wind down, since demand for ammonia was increasing and competitors' long-term natural gas contracts were about to expire. Both factors would contribute to higher ammonia prices and profits.

While the Commodity Group purchased natural gas from the Gas and Oil Division in the Chemicals Group, the Organic Chemicals Division in that group purchased ammonia from Commodity, creating what Wyckoff described as "a sort of equilibrium situation." Speaking of Organic Chemicals' purchases of 2 percent of the Commodity Group's ammonia output, Gunther said: "There are more arguments on the pricing of this 2 percent than on anything else." He attributed this to the division's poor financial results.

Others who purchased ammonia also believed the price was too high. They were less concerned, however, because their performance was better and they purchased a smaller amount, both absolutely and relatively in terms of their total costs. The Agricultural Group, for example, purchased only about 0.3 percent of the total ammonia output. Richards commented:

> We pay market price for ammonia—maybe more. These prices are set and not argued and you go ahead as long as it doesn't make you or break you. We don't take much ammonia of theirs. You don't wear yourself out much talking about the small things.

Several years ago, the general manager of the Industrial Chemicals Division had been dissatisfied with the transfer price of ammonia and had made some outside purchases. Top management had then instructed him to buy inside, and since ammonia was an "insignificant part" of his products' costs, he found it easy to acquiesce.

> **Hypothesis 23:** The greater the volume of internal transfers the higher the level of conflict.

Discussion

Was transfer pricing managed effectively at Alfarabi Chemicals? For the most part, senior management—including the CEO, the CFO, and the president of the largest and most important group—thought that it was. They expressed little, if any, concern that the company's transfer pricing practices were leading to suboptimal economic decisions. Also, although they were aware that problems could and did arise over perceptions of fairness, they believed these problems were not significant given the company's performance measurement, evaluation, and reward practices. As a result, there was little patience with conflict over transfer prices, which was consistent with the company's distaste for conflict in general. This attitude inhibited the expression of dissatisfaction over transfer prices, which was more prevalent lower in the organization, particularly among profit center managers who purchased high volumes or whose businesses were suffering poor performance. The general attitude of senior management, exemplified by Tishman, was that transfer pricing was a subject that did not deserve a lot of time and energy.

The case of Alfarabi Chemicals is a significant challenge to the theories reviewed in chapter 2. In a number of cases, the company's transfer pricing policies deviated substantially from what would be recommended by economic theory, accounting theory, or mathematical programming. An example would be the transfer of B-Upgrade from the Commodity Group to the Agricultural Group. The high level of interdependence between these two groups on this product (recall that Agricultural purchased 19 percent of Commodity's total output of this product) would require a mathematical programming technique, particularly when demand exceeded supply. Instead, a policy of market price less 20 percent was used. Some managers believed that this decision had been reached somewhat arbitrarily and that it was not based solely on economic considerations. Yet there were no complaints that this policy was the cause of suboptimal economic decisions.

In general, managers at Alfarabi were aware of the potential problems of both mandated full cost and mandated market-based policies. (They did not even consider the possibility of permitting outside purchase of goods produced internally, except in the rarest of instances.) However, they did not believe that transfer prices had resulted in any incorrect product-pricing, output-level, capital-investment, or plant-closing decisions. Although economists or accounting theorists might argue that they were making bad decisions and were simply unaware of them, the company's strong performance, especially in the Commodity and Agricultural groups, contradicts this assertion. A better explanation is simply that managers had access to enough other information to prevent them from making obviously incorrect decisions based on information from transfer prices. Furthermore, Alfarabi was described as a "highly centralized" company in which a few managers made all the key decisions. This suggests that transfer prices were not used as a way of decentralizing decision-making responsibility, which is how they are used in the theories that focus on economic issues.

However, if transfer prices play a relatively small role in economic decision making, what is their purpose? At Alfarabi Chemicals, they were used to measure the performance of profit centers. Strong evidence of the importance of this approach was that adjustments could be made retroactively, as occurred with B-Upgrade, if resulting market prices turned out to be greater or less than was anticipated when the transfer prices were set during the budgeting process. (This is another strong contradiction to economic theory, accounting theory, and mathematical programming, since these theories assume that information is used to make decisions; when retroactive adjustments are made, the information is generated after the decisions have been made.)

Given the role of transfer prices in the performance measurement of profit centers, the principal concern of managers was whether these prices resulted in accurate measures of profit center profitability. One manager remarked that a problem with full cost transfers was that "some profits would show up in other groups." However, another manager pointed out that this was a "moot point" so long as the evaluation of performance measures was in terms of budgeted objectives that reflected the type of transfer pricing policy being used. From this perspective, conflict over transfer prices should occur only when they deviate from budget, whether they are full cost or market-based.

The necessity to get involved in the intricacies of establishing which profit center should be held responsible for deviations in actual results from projected results—measured in financial terms in order to evaluate and reward performance—is mitigated by the use of nonfinancial measures of performance and the exercise of subjective judgment. This was the case at Alfarabi Chemicals, where Tishman was able to make an assessment of a manager's contribution to the company on the basis of a great deal more information than simply profit center financial results. He was able to do this because he had access to very detailed information beyond financial results and because he was held in very high regard by the managers at the company. The use of subjective and other information in performance measurement and evaluation of individual managers reduced the role of transfer prices in this activity.

The effect of transfer prices on rewards was also limited because annual and long-term bonuses were based on the results of the next-level profit center. Thus, division general managers were rewarded on the basis of group results, and group general managers were rewarded primarily on the basis of corporate results. So long as transfer prices did not affect group results from the perspective of a division general manager or corporate results from the perspective of a group general manager, financial rewards were not affected by these prices. At Alfarabi, it was unlikely that transfer prices hurt corporate or group results, given their minimal role in economic decision making.

This analysis suggests that transfer prices did not play a dominant role at Alfarabi Chemicals in the performance measurement of profit centers or in the performance measurement, evaluation, and reward of individual managers. With the possible exception of B-Upgrade, managers accepted the transfer pricing policies used for the various transferred products and had learned to manage with these policies, although disputes did arise over the implementation of the policies. Over time, these managers had developed a view of the company's businesses and expectations of performance based on these policies. For example, they were accustomed to evaluating the Retail Division in terms of full cost transfers. One reason Tishman cited for keeping the same policies was that it made it possible to compare present and historical results.

Even though transfer prices did not play a dominant role in either economic decision making or performance measurement, evaluation, and reward, some conflict still existed. It was most likely to occur when transfers were of large volume or when one or the other profit centers or both were suffering poor performance. In these cases, transfer prices would have a material effect on performance measurement. Given the qualifications that have already been observed about the role of transfer prices at Alfarabi Chemicals, a possible explanation for this effect lies in the fact that individuals either have an absolute sense of what represents good performance or compare their performance to other profit centers in the company. Even when they are achieving their budgeted objectives and receiving the expected financial rewards, they may be dissatisfied if their reported profitability is lower than this absolute standard or that of other profit centers in the company.

Financial results can be very much a matter of status; therefore, managers may be dissatisfied with transfer prices if these prices lower their status. Perceptions of fairness can be affected as much by these absolute standards and relative comparisons as by the rewards for achieving objectives. Thus, transfer prices may be actually used as a form of reward to ensure measures that preserve the status of profit center managers. Evidence of this is the fact that transfers to the Retail Division were changed from market-based to full cost to improve the managers' profitability, to prevent them from "feeling bad," and to improve their "motivation." The president of the Agricultural Group argued that full cost transfers on B-Upgrade would "more accurately reflect the contribution the Agricultural Group makes to the corporation." In other words, his group would show a greater percentage of total corporate profits. And the CFO believed that the adjusted transfer price to the group had affected its president more "in terms of pride" than in terms of his reduced bonus. Given this individual's salary and the fact that he was about to retire, this could have very well been true.

The effect of status concerns on perceptions of fairness resulted in some dissension over transfer pricing policies or over the application of particular policies. But conflict over transfer prices was rarely expressed openly to senior management, given the CEO's aversion to conflict, which was mirrored in the company culture. Evidence from this case suggests that satisfaction with transfer pricing practices was directly related to the level in the organization of the profit center managers who were involved with the transfers. Senior management was most satisfied, followed by group management, with division management least satisfied.

An important question is whether the suppression of this conflict was in the best interest of the company. Should the lack of conflict be regarded as an indicator of an effective transfer pricing policy? Two closely related questions are (1) how administrative processes affect the level of conflict and (2) what the relationship is between transfer pricing policy and level of conflict. At Alfarabi Chemicals, the ability to reduce conflict by exercising the option to purchase externally did not exist, since all transfers were mandated. This raises a fourth question: When should buying profit centers be given the option to source externally goods that are available internally?

The answers to these questions require a theory of transfer pricing that addresses the practical concerns of managers, which have been illustrated in the case of Alfarabi Chemicals. However, it cannot be assumed that the transfer pricing practices of this company furnish a model that all other companies can use. The next chapter presents a theory that is intended to help managers determine whether transfer pricing is being managed effectively in their company.

4
A Theory for Practice

Transfer pricing concerns both general managers of profit centers engaged in internal transactions and their bosses.[1] Their challenge is to establish appropriate transfer pricing policies to govern these transactions. On what basis should these policies be established?

In my field study of thirteen companies, I identified three basic policies and one hybrid policy in use: (1) mandated full cost transfers, (2) mandated market-based transfers, (3) exchange autonomy, and (4) dual pricing. Table 4–1 shows the use of these policies in the companies I studied. Survey data indicate that the first three policies alone account for over 95 percent of the policies used in practice.[2] If an explanation can be found for why companies use these policies, the foundation for a theory of transfer pricing that has practical utility will have been established.

The first three policies can be described in terms of two questions, the first of which is whether or not internal transactions are mandated. If the answer is that they are mandated, the second question is how these transactions are valued. There are two principal choices, full cost and market price—the first and second policies, respectively. The other obvious alternative, variable cost, is rarely chosen because it seriously interferes with the performance measurement of the trading profit centers.[3]

If the answer to the first question is that transactions are not mandated, then profit center managers can choose between internal and external exchanges, which is the third policy. Here, the transfer price, which must be acceptable to both parties for the transaction to take place, can range between cost and market price. Typically, market price is greater than cost, but this is not always true.

The fourth, and rarely observed, hybrid policy of dual pricing can be used with either mandated or nonmandated transactions. In both cases, two transfer prices are used—full cost to the buying profit center and market price to the selling profit center. This policy is established when both options in the second question are selected, no matter what the answer is to the first question.

Table 4–1
Transfer Pricing Policies Used in Thirteen Companies

Company	*Industry*	*Exchange Autonomy*	*Mandated Full Cost*	*Mandated Market-Based*	*Dual Pricing*
Alfarabi Chemicals, Inc.	Chemicals		X	X	
Aquinas Chemicals Co., Inc.	Chemicals		X	X	
Bacon & Bentham, Inc.	Electronics and machinery	X		X	X
Blackstone Machinery Co., Inc.	Heavy machinery		X		
Cicero Systems, Inc.	Electronics		X	X	
Dewey & Burke, Inc.	Electronics		X	X	
Grotius Equipment Co., Inc.	Machinery components		X	X	
Hobbes Instrument Co., Inc.	Electronics	X	X	X	X
Hume Fabrication Co., Inc.	Heavy machinery and machinery components	X	X	X	
Locke Chemical Co., Inc.	Chemicals		X	X	
Milton, Inc.	Electronics	X	X	X	X
Paine Chemical Co., Inc.	Chemicals		X	X	
Rousseau Chemical Corporation	Chemicals		X	X	

How Strategy Determines Transfer Pricing Policy

What determines the answers to the two transfer pricing questions? For the companies in my study, the answers were based on two elements of strategy.[4] The first was whether or not the company (or group or division) was pursuing a strategy of vertical integration. Porter (1980) defined vertical integration as "the combination of technologically distinct production, distribution, selling, and/or other economic processes within the confines of a single firm" (p. 300). Vertical integration can be employed for a variety of reasons, including the achievement of economies, tapping into technology, assuring supply and/or demand, offsetting bargaining power and input cost distortions, and enhanced ability to differentiate one's product. Mandated internal transactions are required in implementing a strategy of vertical integration. Thus, those companies in my study that had established such a strategy between profit centers also had a policy of mandated internal transactions. Those without such a strategy had a policy of exchange autonomy.

The second element was how the company (or group or division) had defined the businesses in which it competed, where *business* means the product(s) or service(s) for which there is an identifiable set of customers and competitors. When the resources in the selling profit center devoted to internal sales were considered as much a part of the business of the buying profit center as its own manufacturing facilities, transfers were at full cost. When the selling profit center was defined as a distinct business in its own right for both internal and external sales, transfers were at market price. Dual pricing was used when the company was pursuing several objectives simultaneously (as discussed in more detail later). Figure 4–1 diagrams the relationship between these elements of strategy and transfer pricing policy.

This book does not address the two strategic questions of whether or not a company should vertically integrate or when a selling profit center should be defined as a distinct business for both internal and external sales. These are matters of strategy formulation. Our concern here is with transfer pricing as a matter of strategy implementation.[5] However, as is often noted, strategy formulation and strategy implementation are intimately related.[6] This is certainly true of the relationship between strategy and transfer pricing, since particular transfer pricing policies imply particular strategies. Significant problems can arise when an inappropriate policy is being used for a given strategy. Although the relationship between strategy and transfer pricing policy would seem so obvious as to be nearly a tautology, examples will be discussed later in this book of situations in which management failed to match strategy and transfer pricing policy. Since transfer pricing is such a crucial aspect of strategy implementation, this failure creates ambiguities about strategy as well as problems with transfer pricing.

Transfer pricing policy is one way in which a general manager establishes the *authority* of the general managers who report to him or her. Here, authority will

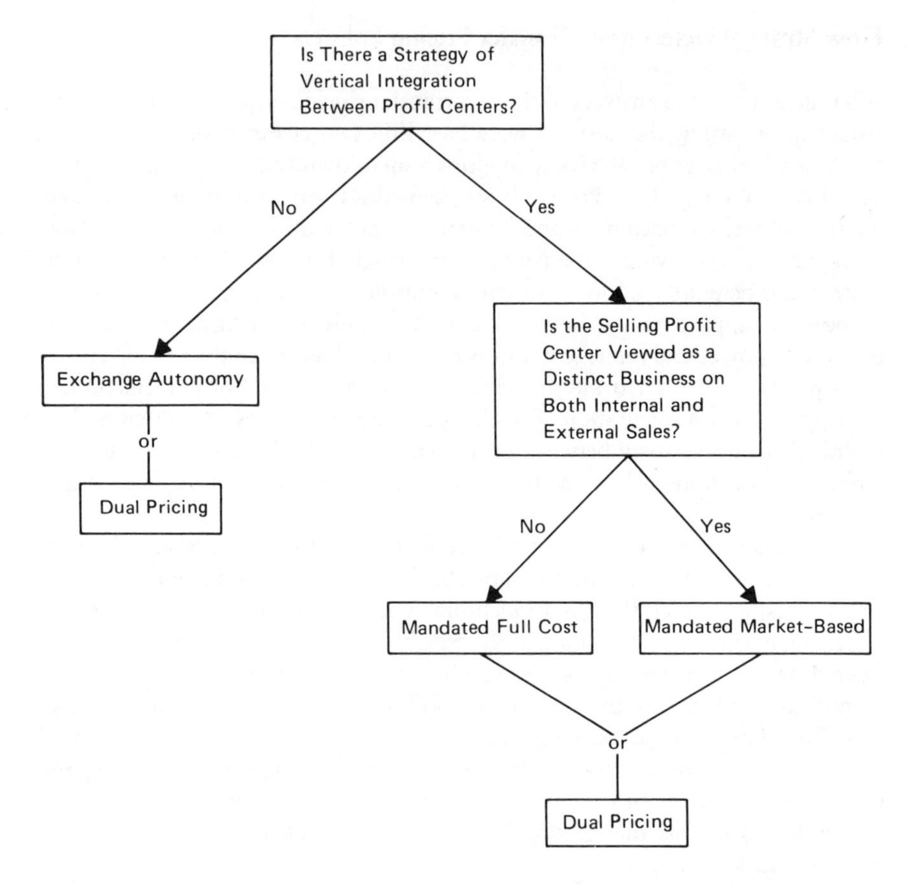

Figure 4–1. The Relationship between Strategy and Transfer Pricing Policy

be defined in terms of decision rights: a manager has authority when he or she has the right to make or influence a particular decision.[7] Often, these decisions involve the allocation of resources. An important authority issue is whether profit center managers can choose between internal and external transactions. When they cannot, as is the case in a strategy of vertical integration, their authority is reduced.

Transfer pricing policy is also one way in which a general manager establishes the *responsibility* of the general managers who report to him or her. Here, responsibility will be defined in terms of the criteria by which a manager's performance is measured, including both quantitative and qualitative criteria measured over both the short and the long term.[8] Although there is usually a fair degree of uniformity in the criteria used to evaluate general managers, variation does exist within companies in terms of specific criteria and the relative weights attached to each criterion according to the manager being evaluated. One of the most important criteria for general managers is profitability, which can be measured in a number of ways, depending on the costs that are charged to the profit center—that is, the costs for which the manager is held responsible.[9] When a mandated full cost policy is used, the general manager of the selling profit center is not held responsible for the profits or losses on the intermediate good.

Of course, transfer pricing policy is only one element in establishing the authority and responsibility of general managers. Strategy also determines the total authority managers have over different economic decisions and their responsibility for the performance of their profit centers, which is a result of these decisions. Economic decisions can be made with respect to both external resources and other internal resources, such as those in corporate line or staff units that are not treated as profit centers. A problem closely related to transfer pricing is cost allocation to profit centers. How much authority should profit center managers have to choose among using corporate resources, using external sources, or establishing the resources within the profit center—and in the first case, how should these costs be charged?[10]

There are two major criteria for evaluating whether the distribution of authority and responsibility is effective for implementing strategy: corporate performance and individual fairness. Have general managers been given the appropriate level of responsibility and sufficient authority over resources to carry out this responsibility in a way that contributes to corporate performance and that is perceived by them as fair? An often-voiced complaint by managers is that their responsibility exceeds their authority—that they are held responsible for outcomes that they cannot control because they do not have the authority over the resources that determine the outcomes. Vancil has shown that responsibility frequently does exceed authority.[11] Although this does not necessarily mean that corporate performance will suffer (in fact, it may be improved, since multiple perspectives on the use of resources must be resolved when these structural interdependencies exist), it does create the possibility that managers will believe that their contributions to the company are not being fairly evaluated and rewarded. The rewards include salary increases, bonuses, promotions, and other nonpecuniary and more symbolic rewards.

The problem of fairness is a central one in managing transfer pricing, since transfer pricing policies affect both the authority and the responsibility of managers. If managers believe that the transfer pricing policy results in performance measures that misrepresent their contributions to the company, or that it interferes with their ability to achieve the objectives they are responsible for, then they will believe that the policy is unfair. Obviously, managers will believe that a transfer pricing policy is unfair when it results in lower rewards than they think they should receive, given their evaluation of their performance—either absolutely, relative to objectives, relative to the performance of others in the company, or relative to the rewards of outside competitors. This is most likely to be the case when rewards are based strictly on financial performance measures evaluated in terms of budgeted objectives. Vancil (1978) found that only 42 percent of the managers in his survey thought that profit alone was a fair measure of their performance. However, he also found that only 30 percent of the managers in his survey reported that their bonuses were determined solely by financial performance.

Although fairness is a central concern of all members of an organization, achieving it can be very difficult indeed. This is because individuals use many criteria for determining whether or not they think the rewards they have received are commensurate with the contributions they have made. Variations exist in relative emphasis on the short and the long term, on the present versus the past, on comparisons with similar and dissimilar others, on internal standards, and on the company's compensation and promotion policies and practices. Because of the importance of comparisons with similar others, achieving fairness for one individual may create a perception of unfairness on the part of another—for example, when one manager defines fairness in terms of being paid more than a counterpart who defines fairness in terms of being paid the same as the first manager. Fairness for all at each point in time is so elusive as to be impossible to achieve. Nevertheless, it is not something that can be ignored.

The use of nonfinancial and subjective criteria in evaluating and rewarding performance can mitigate fairness concerns over transfer prices by recognizing that financial measures alone are imperfect measures of performance. Transfer pricing policies must be considered in the more general context of how much authority the managers have been given, the outcomes for which they are held responsible, and how their performance is evaluated and rewarded. However, since the use of these criteria does not completely eliminate the role of financial measures, it is likely that some tension will persist. Even if individuals believe their managers recognize and reward their contributions fairly, despite reported financial results, this does not mean that others in the organization are able to do so—which affects a manager's status—or that a new boss will be able to do so—which can affect a manager's career prospects.

Thus, each of the three basic transfer pricing policies and the fourth hybrid policy can be characterized in terms of (1) the strategy for which it is appropriate, (2) its effects on the authority and responsibility of profit center managers, (3) potential problems in economic decision making, and (4) potential problems in perceptions of fairness. The remainder of this chapter will discuss these four issues and will also present some empirical support for the contention that strategy determines transfer pricing policy.

Mandated Full Cost

Mandated full cost transfers are used to implement a strategy of backward vertical integration for the purpose of reducing the cost of the intermediate good.[12]

This often results in a large volume of internal transfers, which presents the opportunity for decisions by profit center managers that are optimal for them but suboptimal for the corporation. Mandated transactions partially eliminate this problem. Reducing costs by saving the profit margin paid to an outside supplier or by eliminating other costs, such as freight or transaction costs, is especially important when the final good is sold in a price-competitive market. When this backward vertical integration is contained within a single profit center, the transfer pricing problem does not exist; the profit center manufactures the good for itself, thereby obtaining the desired economies.

However, there are a number of reasons why this intermediate good may be placed in a separate profit center. Two of the most important reasons are (1) that it is manufactured by a technology that another profit center has more expertise in managing or (2) that not all of the intermediate good is used internally and another profit center has more expertise in marketing and selling the leftover product—a problem of balance. Both of these conditions are strong possibilities (Hayes, 1977).

To implement this strategy, mandated full cost transfers are required. The selling profit center must be denied the temptation to forgo internal sales at full cost for external sales that include a profit margin. Also, these transfers are at full cost because the purpose of having manufacturing capacity for the intermediate good is to furnish a low-cost supply to the buying profit center, rather than to enter a new business defined by the intermediate good. If transfers were at market price, the original intention of the strategy would be defeated. Of course, whether the purpose of backward integration is to provide a low-cost supply of the intermediate good in support of the business defined by the final good or to entering a new business is largely a matter of definition. This becomes especially complex when a large proportion of the intermediate good is sold both internally and externally. Therefore, management must be clear about its strategic purpose.

A policy of mandated full cost transfers restricts the authority of the selling profit center, because it must give priority to internal demand at the expense of external opportunities. It also restricts the authority of the buying profit center, since it prevents that profit center from sourcing externally, which it will be tempted to do when market conditions are such that market price is less than full cost or when it is willing to pay more for a better-quality product. At the same time, the responsibility of the selling profit center for the profits on the intermediate good is reduced in proportion to the amount sold internally, and the buying profit center is held responsible for the total profits earned on the final good.

Under this policy, since transfers are mandated, transfer prices do not determine the sourcing decision of the buying profit center, nor do they determine whether or not the selling profit center trades internally. Conceivably, the transfer prices can affect the output-level decisions of the buying profit center—and, indirectly, the output-level decisions by the selling profit center—since full cost transfers enable it to take outside business that would not be profitable at market-based transfer prices. The extent to which this occurs depends on (1) how much authority the buying profit center has in determining output levels (they may be established by higher-level management), (2) what its profit objectives are (these objectives can always be such that the profit center is not penalized for accepting low-margin business), (3) the extent to which the buying profit center faces an upward-sloping cost function (although this is the assumption of economic theory, in practice these curves are typically flat beyond a certain volume), and (4) the extent to which profit margins decrease as volume increases (again, this assumption of economic theory does not always hold in practice). In my study, I did not find any strong evidence that full cost transfer prices were considered to be a positive incentive for increasing volume by the buying profit center.

I also did not find full cost transfer prices to have a significant effect on capital investment decisions. Such nonincremental decisions were made on the basis of special studies using such techniques for calculating financial return as discounted cash flow and return on investment, which considered the economic impact of the decision on both profit centers. Furthermore, Bower (1970) has shown that these decisions are far more complex than is assumed in even the most sophisticated financial techniques. He indicated that strategic considerations, organizational context, and the individuals involved all affected whether or not proposals were accepted.

The managers in my study expressed more concern about the potential of full cost transfer prices to lead to poor pricing decisions on the final good. Their concern was that if product pricing was done by a simple percentage markup added to total cost, the company would not earn the same absolute profits as it would if market price transfers were used, where the same percentage on a larger cost basis would result in larger profits. This was not a concern at Alfarabi Chemicals or at some other companies in my study that used full cost transfer prices. Whether or not this problem arises in using this policy is a complex question that depends on the industry structures of the intermediate and final goods, the extent to which competitors are vertically integrated and what their transfer pricing practices are, and the manner in which product prices are established. For example, when prices on the final good are given by the market (as they often are for commodities), the issue becomes one of output levels, not product pricing.

This policy creates two separate roles for the selling profit center. It is a manufacturing cost center in terms of its internal relationships with other profit centers, and it is a profit center in terms of its external sales. Evaluation of its performance is very complex, since the level of internal demand can affect the profits earned on external sales. Similarly, the level of external sales can affect the full cost transfer price to the buying profit center, which affects its reported profits. The details of the effects of this and other interdependencies on the performance measurement of the two profit centers are discussed in chapter 6. For now, it is sufficient to note that the restriction in authority from this policy can result in variables that affect performance measures for which managers are held responsible but do not have the authority to control. As a result, problems will emerge if performance evaluation and rewards are based solely on measures of individual profit center performance. Instead, the contributions of each profit center to the outcomes of the other must also be assessed, using subjective judgment when necessary.

The existence of profit centers that transfer on a full cost basis raises an important consideration for accounting theory. The typical accounting definition of a profit center is similar to that of Vancil (1978), who defined profit centers as "units, such as a product division, where the manager is responsible for the best combination of costs and revenues. His objective is to maximize the bottom line, the profit that results from his decisions" (p. 77). When full cost transfers are used, the "revenues" on these internal transfers are equal to their costs, and thus no profit is earned.

Kaplan (1982) has suggested that defining a profit center simply as a unit in an organization for which profit is measured is too general, and he has argued that the key criterion should be decision-making authority:

> For our purposes, then, a *profit center* is a unit for which the manager has the authority to make decisions on sources of supply and sources of markets. In general, a profit center will be selling a majority of its output to outside customers and is free to choose sources of supply for a majority of its materials, goods, and services. With this definition, it is unlikely that manufacturing or marketing divisions will be profit centers, even though some firms may evaluate these units using a profit figure. (p. 477)

By his definition, the restriction in authority to determine with whom one will trade is a further restriction on the profit center role of both profit centers. It can also hinder the efforts of managers in these units to earn profits—for example, when external customers are reluctant to place large, long-term orders with the selling profit center for fear of having lower priority than internal customers, or when the buying profit center cannot take advantage of attractive external opportunities.

This analysis suggests that in studying transfer pricing—as well as other problems of strategy implementation—it is overly simplistic to think strictly in terms of either cost centers or profit centers, classifying organizational units as one or the other.[13] Instead, a range of possibilities exist, defined by the authority and responsibility of the general manager. When mandated full cost transfers are used, the authority of both profit centers is restricted, as is the responsibility of the selling profit center for profits on the transferred intermediate good. Figure 4–2 presents a framework for locating cost and profit centers, which will be referred to generally as *responsibility centers*.[14] As the figure shows, a manager of a selling profit center under a mandated full cost policy has more authority and responsibility than the manager of a manufacturing unit. The greater authority comes from control over resources used in the external sales, and the greater re-

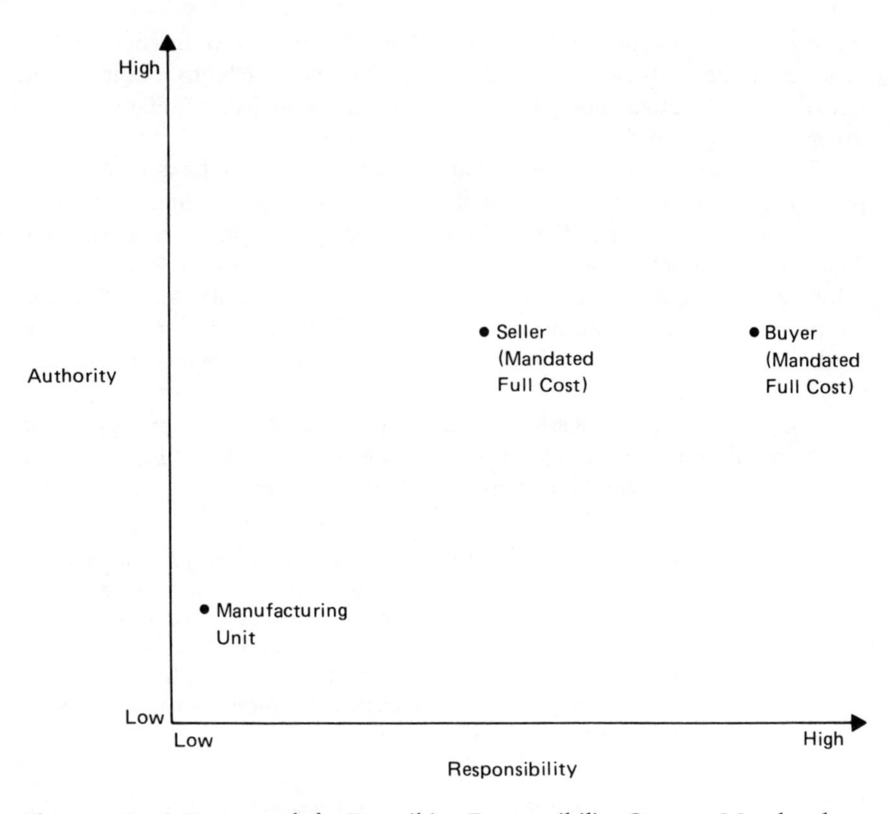

Figure 4–2. A Framework for Describing Responsibility Centers: Mandated Full Cost Transfers

sponsibility comes from being held accountable for the profits on these sales. The manager of the buying profit center has equal authority but greater responsibility, since he or she is accountable for the profits on the internally transferred good as well as for the final good.

Rousseau Chemical Corporation: An Emphasis on Corporate Optimization

Receiving no profits on internally traded goods transferred at full cost can be a major source of concern if profitability (on an absolute or comparative basis) is the primary means of measuring, evaluating, and rewarding the selling division's performance. If managers accept their cost center role, they will be much less concerned when divisional performance targets reflect lower profit expectations as a result of full cost transfers. The use of full cost transfer prices also requires that middle-level general managers focus on their contribution to the total company, not simply on their own performance measures. This is likely to occur only when top management evaluates their contribution to the total company by taking into account the interdependencies that affect performance measures based on the accounting system.

Rousseau Chemical Corporation was a good example of a company that used full cost transfer prices and whose managers were concerned with their contribution to the total company, rather than merely the financial outcomes of their divisions. This successful, multibillion-dollar, highly vertically integrated chemical company produced basic chemicals, basic plastics, and specialties. It had stressed basics until recently, when it switched its emphasis to specialties. The company, one of the major U.S. chemical companies, was located on the East Coast. Speaking about the corporate strategy, Mike Adams, group administrative vice-president, explained: "Until fairly recently, the strategy was not articulated, but we knew what it was. It had remained basically unchanged for many years until the recent change was made."

Of the raw materials and intermediates it produced for internal use, the company furnished nearly 100 percent of its total requirements, although some thought was being given to greater external sourcing. These vertically integrated production processes contained two, three, and sometimes four steps. At each step, it usually sold some of the product in the external market. Thus, the prices set on products for external transactions could have been used to determine market prices for internal transfers.

Organizational Structure

The extremely high degree of interdependence and the complexity of the company's product line were reflected in its three-dimensional matrix structure, based on functions, products, and geographical areas. The matrix resulted from performance problems in the early 1960s caused by some difficulties in coordinating manufacturing, marketing, and R&D. At the same time, the company expanded its overseas activities.

To improve cross-functional coordination, the position of product manager and the concept of a product team were introduced into the company. Each product manager served as chairman of a product team and had profit and loss responsibility for a product or group of products. By the late 1960s, an area structure had been created and the company had installed its three-dimensional matrix.[15]

In 1980, there were nearly fifty product managers, each of whom reported to one of sixteen business department general manages. Functional representatives on the product teams were appointed by the functional head, and these team members had a functional boss in the business department and a product manager boss.

Each business department had a marketing director, an R&D director, and one to five product managers. Marketing directors and R&D directors also reported to group vice-presidents of each respective function. Rousseau Chemical's complex structure led one manager to say that the company was "run by committees and task forces." In its matrix structure, the company had decided to superimpose the product manager and product team on top of its functional structure to retain the advantages of the latter while obtaining necessary interfunctional coordination for separate products. The advantages of the functional structure included its adaptability and economies of scale. Ken Bove, a group vice-president (to whom business department managers reported), thought that the company had not created a structure of autonomous divisions because "if we take a logical grouping of products to set up a division, we find optimizing manufacturing to be an almost impossible task." Another structural variation that had been considered but rejected was to group the basic raw materials into one large cost center. The objection to this was that many of the raw materials produced for internal use yielded coproducts that were primarily sold outside the company. The cost center would have had to sell these coproducts and become partially a profit center, or the coproducts would have had to be transferred internally to other divisions for resale.

Of the sixteen business departments, three-fourths were primarily profit centers that sold most of their product externally. The remaining ones were primarily cost centers that transferred most of their product internally to the downstream departments, but these departments also had external sales. No difference in prestige was attached to being a general manager of either type of department.

Standard Cost System

The foundation of the company's management control system was a standard cost system that had been installed in the early 1950s. This system had been implemented by the chief financial officer. The company's accounting policy and procedures manual stated:

> Standard costs form the nucleus of Rousseau's cost system. They are used not only to value products moving into and out of inventory, but also to distribute utility costs and certain internal services (maintenance, engineering, laboratory) which can be measured by hours or some other unit. By identifying variances, standard costs permit exception reporting.

Standard manufacturing costs were based on a compromise between actual capacity (full capacity less an allowance for maintenance and changeovers) and capacity needed to fulfill demand projections. They were set annually by the production control and accounting departments, with some higher-level management participation. A principal advantage managers identified for using the standard cost system to measure performance was that it established continuity for comparing a plant's current-year performance with its historical performance. In this way, management could evaluate whether it was becoming more or less efficient.

Performance Measurement, Evaluation, and Reward

Return on sales (ROS) was the key measure of business performance. Managers believed that return on investment (ROI) would be preferable to ROS but cited several reasons for using the latter. First, the company already had good systems for reporting ROS on a product-by-product basis. Second, ROI measures would have been difficult to calculate. The high degree of vertical integration would have required allocations to subdivide investments in the plants among their various multiple products. This would have been especially difficult to do in the case of coproducts.

Business performance was evaluated primarily by comparing actual results to commitments. Little attention was paid to internal comparisons of business performance or to comparing the performance of a business with outside competitors. The company as a whole, however, did compare its net income and sales to a composite of twelve other chemical companies. For more than ten years it had compared very favorably with this composite, and it was considered by competitors and security analysts to be a very well-managed company.

The lack of ROI measures on current performance seemed to be no hindrance to decision making on capital investments. Discounted cash flow (DCF) and ROI calculations were both used in project evaluations, but Adams stated:

> We don't have a hurdle rate that we pursue. Instead, we ask "Does it make strategic sense?" Purely economic studies are suspect anyway since they are sensitive to price and volume. We look at the strategic position of a business more than the numbers. This has worked for us.

In evaluating the "strategic position of a business," the company used a form of portfolio planning that considered the size and growth rate of the market, its market share, how product performance compared to that of competitors, and cost position relative to that of competitors. Alfred Meston, a group manufacturing vice-president, echoed Adams's sentiments: "We don't let business managers tell us where to build a plant. You can't do everything on economic theoretical arguments." The high degree of vertical integration dictated that capital investment decisions be evaluated in terms of their impact on both the upstream and the downstream businesses. It was also necessary to examine their impact on coproducts. For example, although additional capacity was needed for one raw material, its production process yielded a coproduct that was sold in a very competitive market. This reduced the attractiveness of adding capacity.

Performance evaluation and reward of product managers also reflected the high degree of interdependence among the profit centers in the company, since they were measured on more than strictly financial outcomes. Adams distinguished between measurement and evaluation of these profit center managers:

> They are measured on profit before taxes, but we evaluate them more on the quality of their effort. It is a largely subjective judgment and includes a poll of their colleagues.

This method of evaluation did not focus only on financial outcomes, such as profitability, that emphasized individual profit center performance. By evaluating the "quality of their effort" and by taking "a poll of their colleagues," higher-level managers encouraged profit center managers to cooperate with each other. The final evaluation was "largely subjective," but Meston, the group manufacturing vice-president, believed that "we do a really good job of evaluating our people. We spend a hell of a lot of time on it."

Performance was rated according to one of five categories. These performance ratings determined the size of a manager's merit pay increases and his or her career prospects. A bonus system was tied to a manager's performance rating and corporate profits. Every year, the Compensation Committee of the Board of Directors established a target figure for earnings per share; if it was achieved, a bonus pool was established. Middle managers could receive up to 10 percent of their base salary in the annual bonus, and this percentage increased as a manager's level in the hierarchy went up.

The Emphasis on Corporate Optimization

The method of performance evaluation and the manner in which bonuses were allocated provided strong incentives for profit center managers to cooperate for the benefit of the total company. Ken Bove ran his profit center with this point of view:

> Our objective is Rousseau corporate profits. I can make a decision which costs Rousseau U.S. money, but if it makes Rousseau money I'll be okay. It's an inherent philosophical and intellectual thing. We react to overall optimization.

He contrasted the way Rousseau was managed with the way more diversified and less vertically integrated companies were managed:

> Our attitude is that we are not a conglomerate. We do better when we try to operate as a single unit, as a coordinated system. The corporate organization coordinates the global strategy for all products. This is a very difficult way to operate, but that's our mentality.

The ability and willingness of managers to focus on total corporate performance, not simply on their profit center, was facilitated by a number of characteristics of the company. There was a high degree of social relationships between middle and top management; as a result, "we work and play together," which "mitigates the effects of hierarchy." A loose, informal organization enabled people from various levels and functions to associate directly with each other and get the information necessary for decisions that would optimize corporate performance. One consequence of the many close personal and professional ties among managers was a network of relationships that was relatively free of conflict. And while the lack of conflict was perceived as contributing in a positive way to the company's performance, Adams acknowledged that "we really haven't faced up to the question of entrepreneurship."

The familiarity that all managers had with the company's technologies and businesses also facilitated overall corporate optimization. Almost all new professional employees were recruited directly from college and promoted from within. Rousseau recruited most of its chemical engineers and chemists (75 percent of all new hires had degrees in technical fields) from a few large schools that had strong reputations and where the company had facilities; they "grew up in the company, learning its ways." Managers hired into middle-level general management jobs from outside might emphasize their businesses' results at the expense of the total company if they had not "come up through the system." Joel Kanter, a group marketing vice-president, summarized Rousseau's character:

> Twenty-five years ago I told people we operate this company like it is the family drugstore. Everybody understands how things are done. The total enterprise is what really matters. There is a kind of informality that comes from growing up in the system. Today we are almost still like a corner drugstore.

Mandated Market Based

Mandated market-based transfers are used to implement all other types of vertical integration strategies, including backward integration for purposes of ensuring a source of supply, obtaining access to technology, or entering a higher-return business.[16] As with the backward integration strategy for producing low-cost intermediate goods, this often results in large volumes of internal transfers and requires that transactions be mandated to prevent decisions that optimize profit center results at the expense of corporate results. In all of these cases, the intermediate good is still considered to be a distinct business for both internal and external sales, so transfers should be at a market price similar to that of external transactions. Under all types of forward vertical integration—for purposes such as ensuring the volume of the intermediate good, obtaining access to technology, reduced marketing costs, or entering a higher-return business—since the strategy is to improve the business of the intermediate good, it is also necessary to use market-based transfer prices.[17] Under this policy, the transfer price does not determine whether transactions will be internal or external.

Once a company has vertically integrated either forward or backward, the type of vertical integration strategy it is pursuing is largely a matter of definition, and this can change from the original intention. One indication of a change in a strategy is a change in transfer pricing policy—for example, when full cost transfers for implementing a low-cost strategy of backward integration are changed to market price transfers for implementing a forward integration strategy for obtaining access to technology by more aggressively pursuing external sales of the intermediate good.

An interesting example of how vertical integration strategies can change occurred at Alfarabi Chemicals. Originally, the company's natural gas properties were regarded as a source of low-cost raw material for making ammonia, and the natural gas was transferred at cost. However, when the company defined natural gas as a business in its own right, with a broader strategic mandate, it shifted to market price transfer prices, which were higher than some of the company's ammonia competitors were paying.

When market-based transfer prices are used, the selling profit center has greater responsibility for financial outcomes that when full cost transfers are used, since it is measured on the basis of profit for all sales, both internal and external. At the same time, however, it has no greater authority, since it is still required to sell internally, just as the buying profit center is required to purchase internally. Figure 4–3 locates profit centers under this transfer pricing policy in the framework of responsibility centers in relation to manufacturing unit cost centers and profit centers under a mandated full cost policy.

The significant difference between mandated full cost and mandated mar-

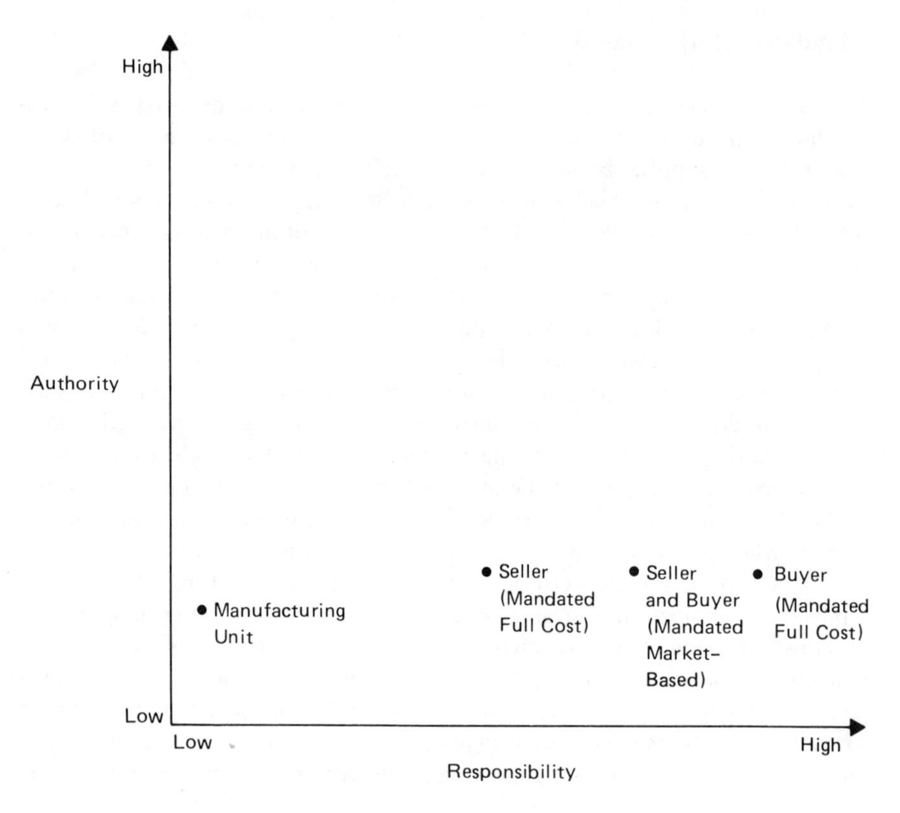

Figure 4–3. A Framework for Describing Responsibility Centers: Mandated Market-Based Transfers

ket-based policies is that in the latter, profits on the intermediate good are reported in the selling profit center, which makes it more directly comparable with the buying profit center than it is when the selling profit center has both cost and profit center roles. The two profit centers share financial responsibility for the use of the resource. This results in a greater emphasis on the profitability of the two businesses than exists in the case of mandated full cost transfers, when the emphasis is on the profitability of the buying profit center. Some managers who used the policy of mandated market-based transfers cited as one of its advantages the greater "entrepreneurial spirit" that it generated, since both profit centers were measured as if they were independent businesses.

However, because of the interdependence created by mandated transactions, each profit center can be affected by actions of the other that affect financial outcomes over which it has no control. (This issue is discussed in more detail in chapter 7.) As with mandated full cost transfers, problems will arise if performance evaluation and reward are based solely on financial measures of the individual profit centers. Their contributions to each other's outcomes must also be assessed, which often requires the exercise of subjective judgment.

As with mandated full cost transfers, capital investment decisions are rarely affected by a mandated market-based policy. A bit more concern was expressed by managers about the disincentive a market-based policy could create for the buying profit center to accept low-margin external business on the final good, although this was mentioned in only a few cases. Whether or not this occurs depends how much authority the profit center manager has in accepting or rejecting external business and on how profit objectives are established.

The greatest concern about mandated market-based transfers expressed by managers in this study was that these transfers would result in uncompetitive pricing of the final good if the selling profit center attempted to obtain the same gross margin percentages as it could get by marking up full cost. In doing so, it could lose market share. Whether or not this occurs is a complex question and depends on the same factors that must be considered in assessing the consequences of full cost transfers on the pricing of the final good.

Hobbes Instrument Company: An Emphasis on Entrepreneurship

Rousseau Chemical Corporation can be contrasted with Hobbes Instrument Company, another successful company. Rousseau emphasized total corporate results and used mandated full cost transfers in support of a vertical integration strategy for supplying low-cost raw materials. Hobbes also made extensive use of a strategy of vertical integration, but typically for other reaons, such as supplying proprietary technology to buying profit centers to obtain competitive advantages on the final good. As a result, it placed greater emphasis on measuring profit centers as distinct businesses and thus used a policy of mandated market-based transfers for transfers within the Electronics Group. (Transfers between this group and the Semiconductor Group were typically done through exchange autonomy.) The origin of this transfer pricing policy dated back to the middle 1960s, when product matrix management had been installed on top of an organization that then comprised two major profit centers—distribution and operations.

The Prevalance of Internal Competition and Conflict

Relationships between profit center managers were much more competitive at Hobbes than they were at Rousseau. The exercise of subjective judgment in evaluating and rewarding performance and the use of negotiation to resolve conflicts helped keep the entrepreneurial emphasis from resulting in decisions that optimized profit center performance at the expense of total corporate performance.

Al Webster, director of financial analysis in the Electronics Group, explained why the product manager role was introduced:

> The current president of the company was the head of the Electronics Group at one time. He and the current vice-chairman created the product

manager concept at Hobbes in the mid-1960s in order to increase entrepreneurial focus.

He thought the use of market-based transfer prices was consistent with this entrepreneurial focus, which held product managers responsible for specific businesses. Webster continued:

> All of the rest comes from this. With the entrepreneurial approach you need transfer pricing. But you also want to look at a total Hobbes point of view. The president pushed for both consolidated statements and transfer pricing negotiations. The latter is one of our conflict management tools.

In general, there was a high level of conflict in the group, and it was considered to be useful. As one manager remarked: "The Electronics Group has a lot of conflict, and this is considered healthy. We have a sarcastic atmosphere." The conflict derived from a high degree of interdependence combined with an emphasis on profit measurement all the way down to the product manager level. This measurement required substantial cost allocations between product managers, in addition to transfer pricing.

Organization of the Electronics Group

The Electronics Group was organized into four divisions: Distribution, International, Components, and Systems. Each division was subdivided into units, also called divisions, which were, in turn, subdivided into departments. Each department in the Components and Systems divisions contained five to ten product managers—125 in all. The president of the company believed in the small business concept; once the sales of a product group exceeded $50 million, the group was split between two product managers. Distribution and International were subdivided into market segments. Profit and loss (P&L) statements were reported on both a market and a product basis.

Cost Allocations

Substantial allocations were required to generate the P&L statements for product groups. (A product group was a collection of products under a product manager.) The single largest item charged to a product manager's budget was distribution costs. Since sales and service personnel were organized on a market basis, a product manager received cost allocations representing the proportion of his or her quota to the total quota for the market. Allocations were based on orders rather than shipments. Distribution costs, which could amount to 20 to 40 percent of sales, could be increased or decreased depending on the level of orders placed by product groups that shared distribution capacity. In effect, actual full cost transfers were used to allocate distribution costs.

Even though P&L statements were calculated on a market basis for Distribution and were aggregated to produce an overall statement, Distribution was not considered to be as much of a profit center as the Components and Systems divisions were. As one manager explained:

> The general manager of Distribution doesn't rise and fall on his P&L statement. His performance is evaluated more on quotas. P&L does not get a heavy weighting. Other things which are important are morale, quality of people, market share, customer service, and receivables.

Another interdependence existed as a result of sharing of plant facilities by product managers. As with distribution costs, actual full cost allocations were made across the products manufactured in a plant. (When a product manager bought a product from another product manager, he or she paid a market-based price, even if the product was manufactured in the same plant that the buying manager used.) Manufacturing costs involved the same problem—the volume of one product group affecting the costs of another for a given volume. John Coulter, vice-president and director of business management for the Electronics Group, admitted that this created problems:

> At the plant the product managers get allocated costs. When actuals occur, they pay for what actually happened. If someone doesn't take what he said he would, others may pay more. This is one of our largest conceptual problems to the P&Ls. We have difficulty attributing causes of variance on allocations—who or what it is due to.
>
> This is so complicated that it's mind-boggling, and it affects the effectiveness of P&L measures. We're thinking of doing another approach, to keep it simple. But even these are very complicated. Most product managers say "My P&L is up for grabs. Finance can change it at will."

The emphasis on viewing each product group as a distinct business, indicated by market-based transfer prices and by allocating all distribution and manufacturing costs, was reinforced by allocating interest expense and assigning capital on a departmental basis. These charges and asset assignments had been in place for several years, since the company first emphasized return on net assets (RONA) as a key performance measure. So far, the company had been unable to make these interest charges and asset allocations at the product manager level, because it was even more complicated than allocating distribution and manufacturing costs.

Conflict Management

The competitiveness of external markets created pressures to offer substantial pricing discounts. Distribution had the authority to take these discounts, which further restricted the authority of product managers. This made the effects of cost allocations and transfer prices all the more apparent in P&L statements. Top management recognized that product managers might consider performance measures so arbitrary as to be meaningless. Thus, since the product managers were held responsible for all costs, they were provided the opportunity to affect the performance measures. This was the foundation for the management of conflict at this company. Coulter explained how this process contributed to overall group performance:

> The product manager has clout. He can go to the factory and distribution people and point out errors and problems. Product managers can disagree amongst themselves and get heard in court. We have a lot of inde-

> pendence and an upward wheeler-dealer environment. Anybody can be heard.
>
> It's a complicated system, but it helps ensure that the total business comes out properly. The conflict in the Electronics Group is very well contained on an emotional level, but there is a healthy discontent.

Webster elaborated on how this process worked:

> Right now, product managers are held responsible for every item of cost. They kick about it. But the president won't accept them saying they're not responsible. In conflict management they can always come and argue. If they say they don't want R&D charges, that's fine, but they had better not ask for R&D in the future.

When asked why product managers accepted this management approach, he replied: "If someone doesn't like it, we can always find someone else to take his job."

One consequence of this conflict was that it produced a great deal of information for managers at various levels in the different departments and divisions and thus contributed to making decisions that optimized group performance. It also made higher-level management aware of any obvious optimization in one profit center at the expense of others. The emphasis on information sharing made it possible for product managers to calculate their proportional contribution to division results, which reinforced competition and conflict. This was more significant than comparison with total group results, given the large number of small product groups.

Performance Measurement, Evaluation, and Reward

Although a great deal of emphasis was placed on calculating P&L at all general management levels and RONA at the department level and above, this was not the sole basis for evaluating and rewarding performance. An incentive bonus system weighted short-term financial goals as 30 percent of the bonus and long-term goals as 70 percent. The long-term goals included quality of strategy and personnel and new product development. Evaluating a manager's performance on these objectives required the subjective judgment of higher-level management.

Corporate Transfer Pricing Policy

Corporate headquarters had very little involvement in the Electronics Group's transfer pricing and cost allocation policies. One manager explained: "There is no corporate policy on transfer pricing. There are many different situations and you need a degree of flexibility." Transfer prices were derived on the basis of both market price and cost plus markup. For the most part, these transfers were not seen as creating competitive problems in the pricing of final products. Although some lower-level managers advocated changes in transfer pricing policies, there was little support for such change in higher-level management. The current approach was considered consistent with the group's strategy, and any change would result in a different definition of this strategy. Coulter explained why he did not expect any major changes in the group's transfer pricing practices:

We've had very little change in transfer pricing. The standard practices of transfers among domestic divisions are very similar to what we've done the past ten to fifteen years. One of the reasons there has been little change is that we haven't structurally changed our organization.

We use transfer pricing as a fundamental document in measuring operations. If we change transfer prices, we change profitability and how they see themselves.

Exchange Autonomy

Exchange autonomy is used when there is no strategy of vertical integration to link the business stategies of the two profit centers. Each profit center is regarded as a distinct business with a strategy that is independent of the other profit center's strategy. Because transactions are not mandated, the transfer price determines whether the buying profit center chooses internal sources over external ones and whether the internal sources are willing to sell internally. Since the lack of a vertical integration strategy is often due to the fact that significant benefits from mandated internal transactions do not exist, internal transfers are typically smaller in volume than in cases where a vertical integration strategy does exist. When the potential for internal transfers is small, the consequences of a profit center optimizing its own results at the expense of corporate results—for example, sourcing externally when spare capacity exists internally—are also small. The cause–effect relationship is reciprocal, of course, since the lack of such a strategy can inhibit the development of these internal transfers.

Under this policy, profit center managers have a significant element of authority that is missing in the other two policies, since they are not required to trade internally. Therefore, their authority is more equal to their financial responsibility, as shown in figure 4–4. This makes it possible to base performance evaluation and reward more strictly on financial outcomes, without taking into consideration the effects of their actions on other profit centers. Profit center managers who are high in both authority and responsibility are very similar to entrepreneurs in independent firms.

A greater emphasis on financial outcomes of individual profit centers typically exists when a company is in many unrelated businesses. The number and diversity of businesses explain both the lack of opportunities for internal transfers and the necessity to place a greater emphasis on financial outcomes in measuring, evaluating, and rewarding performance, since higher-level managers cannot be as familiar with the details of many diverse businesses as they can be with a smaller number of more related businesses.

The lack of mandated interdependence eliminates consideration of the effect of transfer prices on capital investment decisions, output levels, and pricing of the final good. Since profit center managers have a high level of responsibility for

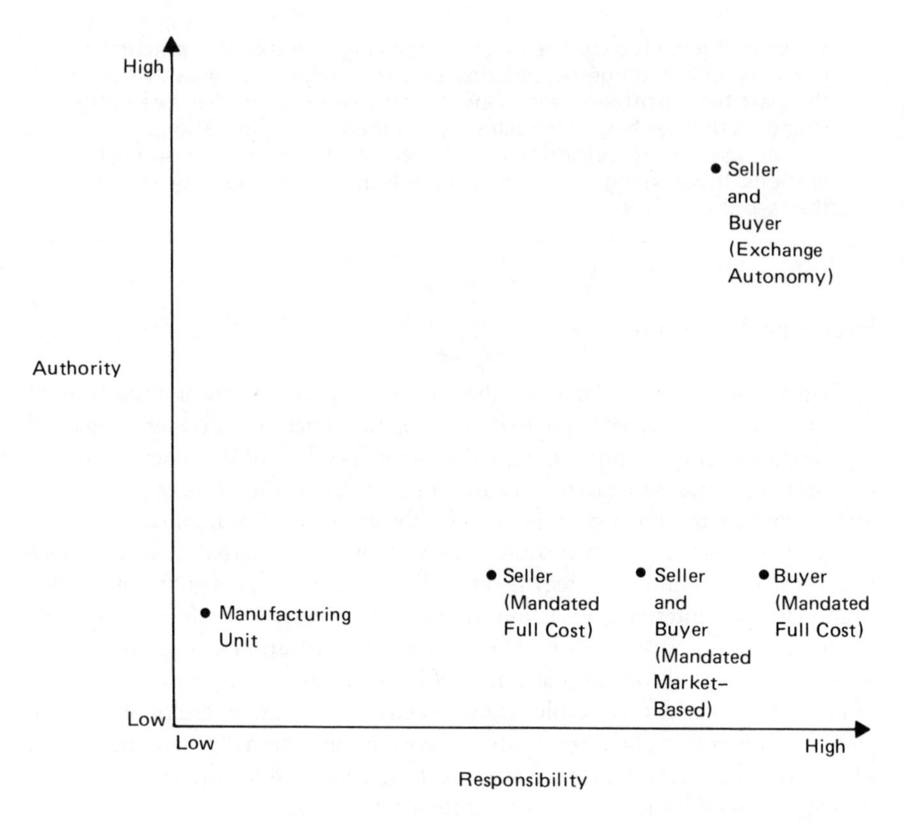

Figure 4–4. A Framework for Describing Responsibility Centers: Exchange Autonomy Transfers

the financial outcomes of these decisions, and since they have the authority to trade externally, it is up to them to select the exchange relationships that enable them to achieve their financial objectives. Consistent with their high levels of authority and responsibility, these managers typically have more authority over capital investment decisions, output levels, and product pricing than do those who are required to trade internally.

Although the prices profit center managers pay to suppliers and receive from customers obviously affect profit center results, they do so in the context of the profit center's relationships with other firms in the market—and it is the profit center manager's job to manage these relationships effectively. Under a policy of exchange autonomy, intrafirm transactions take place as if they were market transactions, since they are determined by the market mechanism of price for resource allocation, rather than by the organizational mechanism of authority for resource allocation. No special consideration for intrafirm transactions needs to be given in evaluating and measuring performance under exchange autonomy, since profit center managers are free to engage in such transactions or not with the same degree of choice they have in selecting external relationships.

Bacon & Bentham, Inc.: An Emphasis on Divisional Autonomy

Bacon & Bentham was a company that used a policy of exchange autonomy on internal transfers. It was a diversified company that participated in a variety of electronics and machinery businesses. In contrast to both Rousseau and Hobbes, very little interdependence existed between profit center managers in most cases. As a result of a diversified corporate strategy and the lack of interdependence, division general managers had substantial autonomy. Like Hobbes, the company emphasized entrepreneurship in the profit centers, but at Bacon & Bentham the profit center managers more closely approximated the entrepreneurs of independent firms than was the case at Hobbes. Financial outcomes were the most important criterion in measuring and evaluating performance, and rewards were almost totally based on the results of individual profit centers.

Strategy and Structure

The company was built largely on acquisitions. In 1980, it was organized into twenty-four divisions contained in six groups. Each division had between $50 million and $100 million in sales. Division general managers were described by one manager as "kings in their little fiefdoms." They were considered to be entrepreneurial and concerned about their employees. Group general managers were perceived as having relatively little authority over the division general managers. Just as the division general managers were concerned about too much involvement by group executives, so were the group general managers concerned about too much corporate involvement in their affairs.

Keith Reis, vice-president of special programs, described the company:

> What is Bacon & Bentham? It is not a combination of companies which are horizontally or vertically integrated where there is a flow of product between divisions. We have organized divisions to have different products serving different market niches. Each product has 10 to 40 percent of the market share in its niche. This is typical of capital goods companies. Each division has four to six product lines, so they are all pretty small in sales. All divisions are in capital goods in electronics or machinery and equipment, with the exception of the Semiconductor Group.

The company's strategy in all divisions was to be a specialist. Although it never made one-of-a-kind products, it was willing to enter a market to make two or more, but it dropped out of the market once the product became a commodity item. The company preferred to compete in markets where there were only two or three competitors. These markets tended to be between $50 million and $100 million, with a few as large as $500 million. Great attention was given to defining these markets very carefully.

Given the specialized nature of the company's products and the need to be constantly developing new ones as markets evolved into commodities, a strong emphasis was placed on giving division general managers substantial responsibility and the authority to fulfill it. Each division was functionally self-contained, with its own sales, manufacturing, engineering, and financial personnel. The role of the corporate staff was to offer expertise and assistance to divisional personnel but to refrain from interfering with divisional operations. One manager who had worked at several other companies described Bacon & Bentham as "the most decentralized company I've ever seen."

Mark Overhold, vice-president and corporate controller, elaborated on this:

> At Bacon & Bentham we have attempted to become as decentralized as we safely can. We delegate as far down as possible while retaining control. The CEO has full control and delegates authority to officers and line management through the use of policy bulletins. We have an internal audit staff to audit compliance with policy. Once per quarter we listen to what the internal auditors have done.

There were fifty-three policy statements and eight internal auditors. Audits were arranged in advance with the division general managers, since "we do not conduct ourselves as policemen or spies." The plan for an audit was reviewed with the division general manager, as was a draft of the audit. Overhold believed that the use of audits enabled top management to delegate authority while retaining control: "We don't tell them what to do. If they don't comply with policy, they get caught in the audit."

Performance Measurement, Evaluation, and Reward

Division general managers were measured on sales, profits, and return on equity. Evaluation of these measures was based on budgeted objectives established in the annual plan and on performance of the top one-third of their competitors. These objectives, intended to be "achievable but tough," were evaluated on a quarterly, annual, and five-year basis. Divisional plans included the volume of interdivisional sales, but little effort was made to coordinate plans across divisions, since they did not affect each other very much. The company's philosophy was that if one division sold more than 10 percent of its output to another division, it was questionable whether it should be a separate division.

A large portion of the division general manager's salary—up to 25 to 40 percent—was based on incentive compensation. If division general managers missed their plans two years in a row, they were given a staff job or placed on special assignment. The reward system was designed to closely approximate the risks and rewards of the independent entrepreneur.

Internal Transfers

The substantial authority granted division general managers included the right to choose vendors and customers. There was no formal policy mandating internal purchases, although one manager claimed that the company had adopted the attitude of "ceterus paribus—if it makes sense to use a Bacon and Bentham product, a division should do it." Overhold explained the current sourcing policy as follows:

"We've told division general managers we'd appreciate it very much if they would use our own products, including on internal applications." However, he emphasized that internal transactions were not a requirement. Overhold believed that the policy they had adopted was appropriate for their situation, but he did not think it was best in all cases:

> Everybody has their own method, which depends on their management philosophy. If we interfere with the management of profit incentives, we have to reimburse them. Once we interfere with their day-to-day operations, they can complain to us.

Reis confirmed the importance of not having a transfer pricing policy that would interfere with divisional autonomy: "We don't mandate Bacon & Bentham products because we don't want to give division general managers any excuses for why they can't make money."

One consequence of this policy was that internal transfers were lower than they could have been. For example, the company sourced only $1 million of its $20 million in semiconductor purchases from itself; one manager estimated that the amount could double. However, increasing the level of internal transfers would have required that the two divisions work together so that the buying division could design products that would use products of the selling division, and vice versa. Four years ago, there had been some discussion about making internal sourcing an explicit policy. The most that had happened was informal pressure and encouragement by the CEO, but this conflicted with his strong belief in decentralized responsibility.

The vice-president of technology in the Semiconductor Group pointed out this dilemma:

> The CEO's bent is toward decentralization and nonintegration. Then on Sunday afternoons he worries about the lack of integration. He has come to the conclusion that in key areas, such as integrated circuits, we have to get more cross-contamination. Other divisions are to use more of our stuff. But we've got too much business. If left to our own devices, we'd say screw it to the other divisions.

Dual Pricing

Dual pricing, which involves two transfer prices—full cost to the buying profit center and market price to the selling profit center—can be used both when a strategy of vertical integration exists and when it does not. This policy requires the elimination of the double-counted profit at a higher level in the organization.[18] It is used when a strategy of vertical integration exists as a means of eliminating the problems in economic decision making that can result from both mandated full cost and mandated market-based policies. It is designed to eliminate the problem in full cost transfers of treating the selling profit center as both a cost center and as a profit center, which top management may find difficult to

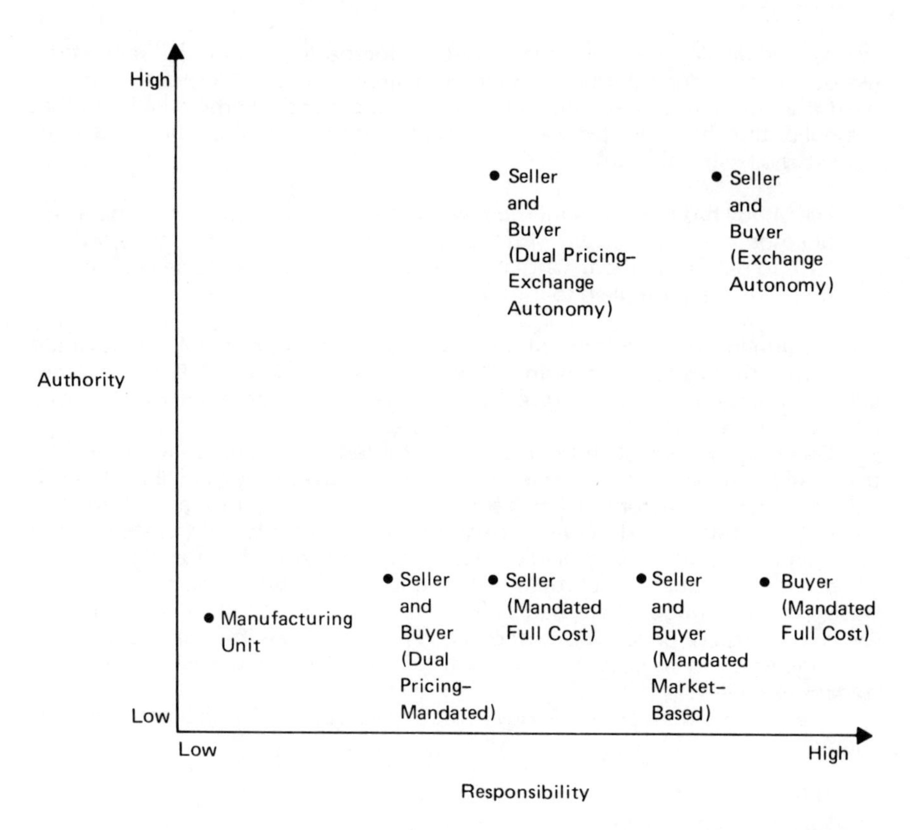

Figure 4–5. A Framework for Describing Responsibility Centers: Dual Pricing Transfers

do. By transferring at a market price to the selling profit center, this policy eliminates objections its managers may have to receiving only full cost. At the same time, since the buying profit center pays only full cost, possible disincentives to setting output levels or product prices that optimize corporate results at the expense of profit center results do not exist.

Under a strategy of vertical integration, dual pricing is an attempt to "have one's cake and eat it, too." It does not change the authority of profit center managers in any way, but it does lessen their responsibility, as indicated in figure 4–5. Unlike the case with mandated full cost transfers, the buying profit center is not held responsible for the total profits earned on the intermediate good, which are incorporated into the final good. And unlike the case with mandated market-based transfers, the selling profit center is not held responsible for the total profitability of the intermediate good on both internal and external sales. This dilution in responsibility is accompanied by a simultaneous statement of two mutually exclusive strategies. The intermediate good is regarded as a business in its own right from the perspective of the selling profit center while, at the same time, it is considered a manufacturing cost center on internal transfers from the perspective of the buying profit center.

Dual pricing can also be used when exchange autonomy exists as a means of increasing the incentive for buying profit centers to source internally without restricting their authority by mandating internal transactions. This is another form of "having one's cake and eating it, too," since dual pricing used in this fashion is an attempt to obtain the advantages of a vertical integration strategy without the disadvantages that arise from mandating transactions. The result here is also a dilution of responsibility (see figure 4–5) and an ambiguous message on strategy—in this case, whether or not a strategy of vertical integration exists.

Although this policy—which offers something to everyone—at first glance seems to be an excellent way to resolve the problems inherent in the three basic policies, it is rarely found in practice. It has its own problems—especially the double counting of profits and the ambiguity about strategy it creates—which make it an inherently unstable policy. A more detailed explanation of why this is the case is presented in chapter 5.

Hume Fabrication Company: A Dual Pricing Proposal

Managers at Hume Fabrication Company, a manufacturer of heavy machinery and machinery components, were generally dissatisfied with how transfer pricing was being managed. Their company policy was a combination of two basic policies: mandated market-based and exchange autonomy. Buying profit centers were able to source externally, but if they elected to buy from internal sources, the selling profit centers were required to supply them. Besides creating ambiguity about strategy, this mixed policy resulted in problems inherent in both of the basic policies. At times—especially for certain products—the company also used full cost transfers in which only the selling profit center was required to trade internally. Mitchell Bernard, corporate controller, developed a proposal for using dual pricing, since he felt that it would solve many of the problems the company had experienced with transfer pricing for many years.

Hume Fabrication's transfer pricing policy had evolved from full cost excluding general and administrative (G&A) expenses to the inclusion of G&A costs in the late 1960s and then to market price less a discount in the mid-1970s, which was the present policy. It had been implemented when the company reorganized into a multidivisional structure with divisions collected into groups. Pressures to change to a market price policy had been felt for a number of years, and the new structure facilitated it. The same asymmetry was retained. Bernard explained the rationale for market price less a discount:

> The normal procedure is best price less a discount to reflect that there are no selling or collection expenses. The objective is to have the same gross margin for the selling division whether the sale is inside or outside.

He also noted a major complaint that this policy hurt the ability of the buying divisions to price their final products competitively:

> Some of us feel this is a double profit for Hume. Some think that a margin on top of a margin ends up making products too expensive.

Others believed that when a final good was competitively priced, the end-product division showed a low return on assets (ROA), even though the ROA for the company as a whole was quite good.

Preferences for External Sources

Although the policy was designed to encourage buying divisions to source internally, Julian Haynes, vice-president and treasurer, noted that buying divisions often used external sources when internal ones were available. One manager commented: "I've gone to customers' operations and looked at our machines with other people's parts. This is dumb." Another confirmed this and noted that, if anything, internal sources were given last rather than first consideration:

> I've been disturbed that divisions don't use products available from this company. They even go out of their way not to. When I joined Hume ten years ago, a division manager said, "I wouldn't use *any* products from this company." Some of the reasoning was not totally emotional. There were difficulties with deliveries. Nobody cared about internal accounts.

He did not think this problem could be solved through transfer prices alone:

> Cooperation on transfers emanates from the top. This can't be done with pricing or service. The CEO has to say we want to use Hume products whenever possible. He has to order it to be done. If he makes that mandate, the subject does not have that prominence.

Other managers believed that this would create its own set of problems. One manager said it would be impossible to determine what was a "good deal" on internal exchanges:

> If inside buyers can only buy inside, the ballgame is already 80 to 90 percent lost. You've taken away the freedom to negotiate and get the best deal. This is the beginning of the end. It establishes an unfair negotiating position. One party can say, "Take it or leave it." Structurally, psychologically, and politically, if I must buy product from sister divisions, I already have two strikes against me. If I can't prove to myself I've gotten a good deal, the negotiations are no good.

He also said it would be difficult to get outside prices when suppliers knew they were simply being used to supply bids for determining transfer prices: "The outside market is not interested in dealing with you. They may give you an outside price that's too high just to get rid of you."

The Foundry Division

The negative consequences of a market-based policy with sourcing autonomy for buying divisions were greatest for the company's Foundry Division. Problems in using the foundry capacity were exacerbated by the fact that the division's role had changed over the years. During some periods, it had been allowed to sell externally and transfer internally on a market basis. In other periods, it had been restricted to internal sales only on a full cost basis.

When market-based pricing was used, the Foundry Division sought to obtain a profit on internal transactions. This created problems because of the structure of the industry in which it competed. Many outside foundries tended to be specialists, whereas the Foundry Division manufactured a broad product line. Specialists were able to manufacture a narrow line of products more efficiently than the Foundry Division could, which gave them a competitive advantage in pricing the product. If the Foundry Division attempted to get the same profit margins, which it often did, buying divisions preferred to source externally.

Buying divisions also preferred external sources in times of low demand. Many external foundries were closely held businesses that attempted to retain their work force through good times and bad. Because of this and because of their lower overhead costs as a percentage of total costs, they priced very competitively in times of low demand to keep their plants operating. Customers who continued to buy from them in slow periods were rewarded in periods when demand was high by not having their orders rejected or given low priority—a practice foundries were notorious for following.

Thus, buying divisions had a strong incentive, for both price and longer-term relationship reasons, to maintain their purchases from external sources at precisely the time when the Foundry Division was having the most difficulty obtaining business. But if the buying divisions turned inside when demand was high to avoid the long lead times with external suppliers, the Foundry Division, which also had strong external demand and long lead times before it could fill orders, would have to give these external customers lower priority. There was no reward in this, however, since the buying divisions increased their external purchases when conditions changed back to low demand. In a recent year, this divisional optimization at the expense of corporate optimization was reflected in the foundry's operating at 8,700 tons per year on a total capacity of 25,000 tons per year.

Problems also arose with full cost transfers. In some situations, these were not always less than market price. Managers in the Foundry Division had been reluctant to accept the role of manufacturing unit for internal buying divisions. One concern was that their performance would not be properly evaluated. Another was based on the claim by a group general manager that he would not be able to hire a Foundry Division general manager unless it was a profit center, and the high turnover of this position in the industry made this an important consideration. There had also been complaints at one time about determining full cost transfer prices when the price was based on dollars per pound. Purchasers of long production runs believed that they were subsidizing purchasers of short runs. A better costing system was developed that would have eliminated this problem for full cost transfer prices, but by then the company had shifted to market-based transfer prices.

A Proposal for Dual Pricing

In early 1980, Bernard proposed a dual pricing policy to top management, which would not have required mandated internal transactions. He saw it as a way to resolve the continuing conflict and ambiguity over the mission of the Foundry Division and to correct transfer pricing problems throughout the company. For example, he felt that it would solve the problem of the company pricing itself out of the market "because we require the buying division to earn an acceptable return on intracompany items on which Hume had already generated such a return (by the selling division). In other words, the compounding effect of generating gross margin upon gross margin can price us out of the market." Bernard's proposal identified the advantages of this approach to the selling division, to the buying division, and to the company as a whole.

For both buying and selling divisions, he believed that dual pricing would reduce the amount of time spent on transfer pricing negotiations and would lead to increased intracompany trading as a corporate benefit. Full cost transfers would also reduce the inventory values of the buying divisions and increase their ROS measures and would mean that the profit margins they reported would reflect "the total gross margin earned by Hume on sales to outsiders."

Bernard identified four potential problems. First, divisions selling the final product might not add a sufficient markup in pricing the final product: "In other words, a 20 percent ROA division purchasing from a 40 percent ROA division may establish prices based on a 20 percent return." Second, buying divisions that made large internal purchases would have trouble estimating these costs when they prepared their budgets. Third, his proposal would not enable one buying division that bought from another to report the full gross margin of these two-step transfers. Fourth, "based on past experience, there are strong objections in communicating gross margins realized by selling divisions." He was concerned that if buying divisions knew the gross margin, they would attempt to negotiate further the market-based portion of the transfer price.

The problems in this proposal were considered to outweigh its advantages, and it was rejected by top management. Bernard believed he had not adequately prepared managers to accept it:

> I tried to introduce a new concept. I was the only one for it. I got a lot of opposition. It was not accepted. I didn't prepare and present it properly.

Some Empirical Support

Thus far, this chapter has presented a theoretical explanation of why companies use the transfer pricing policies they do. The theory is based on the assertion that strategy determines transfer pricing policy. It was developed by first finding that all the practices I observed in my study could be classified as one of three basic policies and a fourth hybrid policy and then recognizing that the reasons given for the use of these policies were similar in each category and that these reasons were strategic in nature. Examples have been presented to show the circumstances in which each policy was used or, in the case of dual pricing, proposed. However, these examples are by no means a test of the theory based on management practice that is asserted here.

To assess the validity of this theory, it is necessary to use data that have been collected independently of the data used to develop it.[19] Although, ideally, these data would have been collected specifically to test this theory, I have not attempted to do this. (Here is an opportunity for another researcher.) Some data do exist, however, that can provide a limited test of the theory presented here. These data were collected by Vancil (1978) in his more general study of decentralization in American manufacturing firms.

Some important limitations must be recognized in using these data. First, the response categories Vancil used do not match the three basic policies and fourth hybrid policy described here. He did not include dual pricing, and he did include a category called "negotiation," which requires some interpretation since it confounds policy and process. He also did not ask specifically whether internal transfers were mandated or not, although he did ask in another questionnaire about the authority of profit center managers to make sourcing decisions.[20]

Another problem is that his questionnarie was ambiguous regarding the level of profit center transfers, and he only provided for one response. As the case of Alfarabi Chemicals shows, companies can use several different policies, and these can vary by organizational level. Since respondents were asked "how you most commonly set transfer prices," it is unclear whether the question referred to intergroup transfers, interdivisional transfers, intradivisional transfers, or some combination of the three. Despite these limitations, the results are very strong, which warrants regarding them as a partial verification of this theory and certainly as a test that does not disconfirm it.

These findings are especially important because Vancil himself did not find any relationship between transfer pricing policy and diversification strategy. My results are based on a revised strategic typology that has more general implications for strategy implementation beyond transfer pricing, as discussed in chapter 10. Vancil used a classification scheme developed by Rumelt, which combined a "specialization ratio" (the proportion of a firm's revenues derived from its largest single business) and a "related ratio" (the proportion of a firm's revenues derived from its largest single group of related businesses).[21] This scheme fails to distinguish between the vertical integration strategy in which the supplying division is a manufacturing unit for the buying division and the one in which both units are viewed as distinct businesses. Examples of both of these strategies are found in the strategic types he labeled "single business," "dominant business," and "related businesses."

In the first situation, "single business vertical integration," full cost transfer prices are used. In the second situation, "distinct businesses vertical integration," transfer prices that include a profit (market price and cost plus profit markup) are used. Both of these can be distinguished from the third situation—with no explicit vertical integration strategy—"unrelated businesses," in which negotiation and market price are used for establishing transfer prices and for choosing between internal and external suppliers.

The firms in Vancil's survey were categorized according to these three strategic types. (See appendix B for a detailed discussion of the procedure for classification.) Table 4–2 shows the extent of transfers by strategic type for all firms and for only those firms with internal transfers. These results conform to expectations for each type and are statistically significant. Over 40 percent of the single business vertical integration firms do not have internal transfers between profit centers.[22] This is because the interdependencies in these firms are contained within single profit centers. Units that supply raw materials are considered to be cost centers on internal transfers.

In contrast, very few of the distinct businesses vertical integration firms do not have transfers. Substantial interdependencies exist with a strategy of vertical integration, as reflected in over 30 percent of these firms having 16 percent or more internal transfers, while the emphasis on treating units as distinct businesses results in most of these firms having transfers between profit centers. Only 5.5 percent of these firms do not have internal transfers between profit centers.

When the two vertical integration strategies are compared for only those firms that have transfers between profit centers (that is, supplying divisions are profit centers because they have both internal and external sales), the results are very similar. About 15 percent of firms in both types have 3 percent or less internal transfers, and approximately 30 percent have 16 percent or more. Explicit vertical integration strategies result in similar distributions of extent of inter–profit center transfers. It is reasonable to assume that many firms of these two types have corporate policies that mandate internal transactions.

Firms in the unrelated businesses strategic type have much lower extents of internal transfers than those in the other two types. The 18 percent with no transfers are cases in which profit centers are in such different businesses that no possible exchange relationships exist. For firms of this type that do have internal transfers, 40 percent have 3 percent or less, and only 15.6 percent have 16 percent or more. The lack of an explicit vertical integration strategy between profit centers in these firms results in lower internal transfers. It is reasonable to assume that in many of these firms, most internal transactions are mutually agreed upon by the managers involved and are not mandated by corporate policy.

This threefold typology gives a statistically significant distribution of transfer pricing policies (see table 4–3) that is consistent with the theory presented here. The policies are ranked along a rough continuum ranging from pure organizational mechanisms of resource allocation to pure market mechanisms of resource allocation. At one extreme are full cost transfers, assumed to be mandated, which are similar to transfers from the manufacturing function to the sales function within an organizational hierarchy. At the other extreme are combination policies, which are not really ranked since it is impossible to interpret this category, and variable cost.

Table 4–2
Extent of Transfers, by Strategic Type

Extent	*Single Business Vertical Integration*		*Distinct Businesses Vertical Integration*		*Unrelated Businesses*		*Total*	
All Firms[a]								
No transfers	43.5%	(30)	5.5%	(7)	18.0%	(17)	18.6%	(54)
1–3%	8.7%	(6)	14.1%	(18)	33.0%	(31)	18.9%	(55)
4–7%	18.8%	(13)	23.4%	(30)	18.1%	(17)	20.6%	(60)
8–15%	13.0%	(9)	25.0%	(32)	18.1%	(17)	19.9%	(58)
>16%	15.9%	(11)	32.0%	(41)	12.8%	(12)	22.0%	(64)
Total	100.0%	(69)	100.0%	(128)	100.0%	(94)	100.0%	(291)
Firms with Internal Transfers[b]								
1–3%	15.4%	(6)	14.9%	(18)	40.2%	(31)	23.2%	(55)
4–7%	33.3%	(13)	24.8%	(30)	22.1%	(17)	25.3%	(60)
8–15%	23.1%	(9)	26.4%	(32)	22.1%	(17)	24.5%	(58)
>16%	28.2%	(11)	33.9%	(41)	15.6%	(12)	27.0%	(64)
Total	100.0%	(39)	100.0%	(121)	100.0%	(77)	100.0%	(237)

Note: Extent of transfers = internal transfers as a percentage of total cost of goods sold or as a percentage of total sales, depending on how the transfers are valued.

[a]Chi-square = 65.162; sig = .000; df = 8.

[b]Chi-square = 21.882; sig = .001; df = 6.

Table 4–3
Transfer Pricing Method, by Strategic Type

Method	*Single Business Vertical Integration*		*Distinct Businesses Vertical Integration*		*Unrelated Businesses*		*Total*	
Full cost	48.8%	(20)	23.0%	(29)	15.0%	(12)	24.7%	(61)
Cost plus profit	14.6%	(6)	15.9%	(20)	17.5%	(14)	16.2%	(40)
Market price	22.0%	(9)	35.7%	(45)	25.0%	(20)	30.0%	(74)
Negotiation	12.2%	(5)	16.7%	(21)	33.8%	(27)	21.5%	(53)
Variable cost	0.0%	(0)	5.6%	(7)	5.0%	(4)	4.5%	(11)
Combination	2.4%	(1)	3.2%	(4)	3.8%	(3)	3.2%	(8)
Total	100.0%	(41)	100.0%	(126)	100.0%	(80)	100.0%	(247)

Chi-square = 26.892; sig = .003; df = 10.
Note: Of the 291 firms in Vancil's (1978) survey, 247 answered this question.

The ordering of variable cost requires some explanation, since most implicit rankings of transfer pricing policies typically put it before full cost.[23] I have placed it otherwise, however, because I found a few examples in which it was used on international transfers when it was purely incremental volume to the selling profit center, which had already satisfied external sales and had spare capacity available. In such cases, variable cost plays a very similar role to marginal cost, which, according to economic theory, is supposed to be equal to market price when perfectly competitive conditions exist. Thus, it is very much a market resource allocation mechanism.

Cost plus profit markup transfers are usually mandated and combine the full cost organizational resource allocation mechanism with some profit added to approximate external exchanges. Market price transfers may or may not be mandated, as is the case with negotiation. Negotiated transfer prices are most similar to a market resource allocation mechanism when both parties can forgo the transaction if a favorable price cannot be agreed upon. I have placed negotiation after market price based on the fact that in my field study and subsequent discussions with managers, I found that negotiation typically includes exchange autonomy. Market price often occurs with mandated transactions when external prices are easy to determine.

The fact that Vancil's unidimensional strategic typology did not produce a statistically significant result shows the importance of treating vertical integration as a decision independent of the definition of distinct businesses. Full cost is the most popular policy for firms in the single business vertical integration category, accounting for nearly 50 percent. Market price is the next most popular policy, followed by cost plus profit and negotiation. None of the firms in this category used variable cost. This is an important finding given its popularity in theory, especially for situations of vertical integration. Variable cost was used by only 5 percent of the firms in the unrelated businesses category and by 5.6 percent in the distinct businesses vertical integration category. This is consistent with the aforementioned interpretation of variable cost, since these types of firms have more "marketlike" relationships between their profit centers.

The popularity of various transfer pricing policies is very different in the unrelated businesses category than it is in the single business vertical integration category. In the former, negotiation is the most popular policy, accounting for one-third of all cases, followed by market price in one-quarter. Although it is not possible to ascertain whether profit centers in these companies have trading autonomy—the critical characteristic of the transfer pricing policy for firms in this category—the large use of negotiation and market price, combined with the small use of full cost (15 percent) suggests that this is the case. Exchange autonomy is most likely to be associated with the negotiation policy, as discussed earlier. The infrequency of its use in single business vertical integration firms (12 percent) is consistent with this argument.

For firms in the distinct businesses vertical integration category, market price is the most popular policy (36 percent) followed by full cost (23 percent), negotiation (17 percent), and cost plus profit markup (16 percent). These firms are similar to single business vertical integration firms in the extent of internal transfers when they exist, and they are similar to unrelated businesses firms in their emphasis on including a profit on internal transfers. Three-quarters of the unrelated businesses firms include a profit on internal transfers (cost plus profit markup, market price, and negotiation), which is consistent with the emphasis in these firms on measuring each profit center as a distinct business. Similarly, nearly 70 percent of the distinct businesses vertical integration firms include a profit on internal transfers. However, whereas negotiation is the most popular policy in the unrelated businesses firms, restrictions on trading autonomy make it much less popular in the distinct businesses vertical integration firms, where market prices for external transactions are used to establish transfer prices.

There are several reasons for data that are inconsistent with the theory presented here, one of which is in the interpretation of the categories on the questionnaire. For example, it is entirely possible for substantial negotiation to be involved in establishing full cost transfers. Another problem is that respondents in some cases may have interpreted "most common" as most important. Companies do not have uniform strategies when there are many profit centers. Thus, the most important policy could be for inter–profit center relationships involving large volumes of transfers that were atypical for the company as a whole. For example, two profit centers in an unrelated business firm might transfer on a full cost basis while all the rest of the profit centers had absolutely no transfers between them. A closely related issue is how concentrated or dispersed the total extent of transfers was in the company. In this hypothetical example, a measure of 3 percent for extent of internal transfer might represent 30 percent or more of the output of one selling profit center. Questionnaire surveys are crude measuring devices, and the one used by Vancil was not able to pick up such refinements.

A third problem, which relates to survey methodology and the complexity of the task Vancil set for himself, is that data reported by a financial executive were used to identify each firm's strategic type. It is possible that this resulted in a misclassification in some cases.[24] With more detailed data collected by an outsider, firms might have been placed in different strategic categories. Furthermore, Vancil was interested in corporate strategy, and his data thus do not include substrategies at the group or division level.

A final problem is that some companies simply may have used policies contrary to what this theory suggests. In some cases, they may have experienced significant problems and thus could be considered to be "doing it wrong." In other cases, they may have adjusted to the "wrong policy" for reasons not included in this theory—for example, if strategy changed but, because managers had learned to use a particular policy, the costs of changing were perceived to be greater than the benefits from changing. Or some companies may have used a uniform policy for purposes of administrative simplicity even though, in theory, general policies were required. Also, there is always the possibility that the extent of internal transfers was so small that, as a practical matter, any policy would be acceptable.

Although Vancil did not directly ask whether or not internal transactions were mandated in the questionnaire that addressed transfer pricing policy, in a separate "autonomy questionnaire" completed by one to three profit center managers, he did ask questions concerning how various types of decisions were made. One of the decisions cited was "buying from an outside vendor when the items required could be supplied by another unit in your corporation." For the managers who answered this questionnaire, it is impossible to know what transfer pricing policy they used.[25] However, the assertion that the degree of decision-making authority is related to strategy as reflected in transfer pricing policy can be subject to a limited test.

Table 4–4 reports Vancil's findings for our revised strategic typology on an ordered ranking of degree of decision-making authority, from most ("my initiative and decision") to least ("initiated by others"). As expected, profit center managers in single business vertical integration firms reported the least authority on this decision, with less than 30 percent initiating and making this decision on their own and 20 percent requiring a decision from the corporate level. In contrast, 50 percent of the managers in unrelated businesses firms made this decision on their own, and only 3 percent required a corporate decision. Distinct businesses vertical integration firms were intermediate in the extent of authority given to profit center managers; only 35 percent of the managers in these firms reported that they could initiate and make this decision on their own.[26]

The Role of Administrative Process

The theory presented here is incomplete; it tells only half the story. This chapter has addressed the question of what transfer pricing policy should be used and has offered an answer based on two key strategic questions. The other half of the issue is how this policy should be implemented. This is the role of administrative process, which can be described in terms of five elements. The first element is how the transfer price is set. At one extreme is pure negotiation, whereby the trading managers establish their own rules for setting the transfer price. At the other extreme are established corporate rules and procedures, such as list price less 10 percent or standard full cost plus 25 percent. Borrowing from March and Simon (1958), this dimension can be described as a range between unprogrammed and programmed decision making.

The second element is who is involved in setting the transfer price. Many different possibilities exist, including, most commonly, managers in the selling profit center only, managers in both the selling and the buying profit centers only, these managers and corporate-level managers (including both general and finan-

Table 4–4
Profit Center Managers' Authority to Choose between Internal and External Vendors, by Strategic Type

Authority	*Single Business Vertical Integration*		*Distinct Businesses Vertical Integration*		*Unrelated Businesses*		*Total*	
My initiative and decision	29.2%	(19)	35.0%	(43)	50.5%	(48)	38.9%	(110)
My initiative and two-person decision	20.0%	(13)	26.0%	(32)	22.1%	(21)	23.3%	(66)
My initiative and multiple-person decision	26.2%	(17)	17.9%	(22)	14.7%	(14)	18.7%	(53)
My initiative and corporate decision	20.0%	(13)	11.4%	(14)			10.6%	(30)
Initiated by others	4.6%	(3)	9.8%	(12)	9.5%	(9)	8.5%	(24)
Total	100.0%	(65)	100.0%	(123)	100.0%	(95)	100.0%	(283)

Chi-square = 20.822; sig = .008; df = 8.

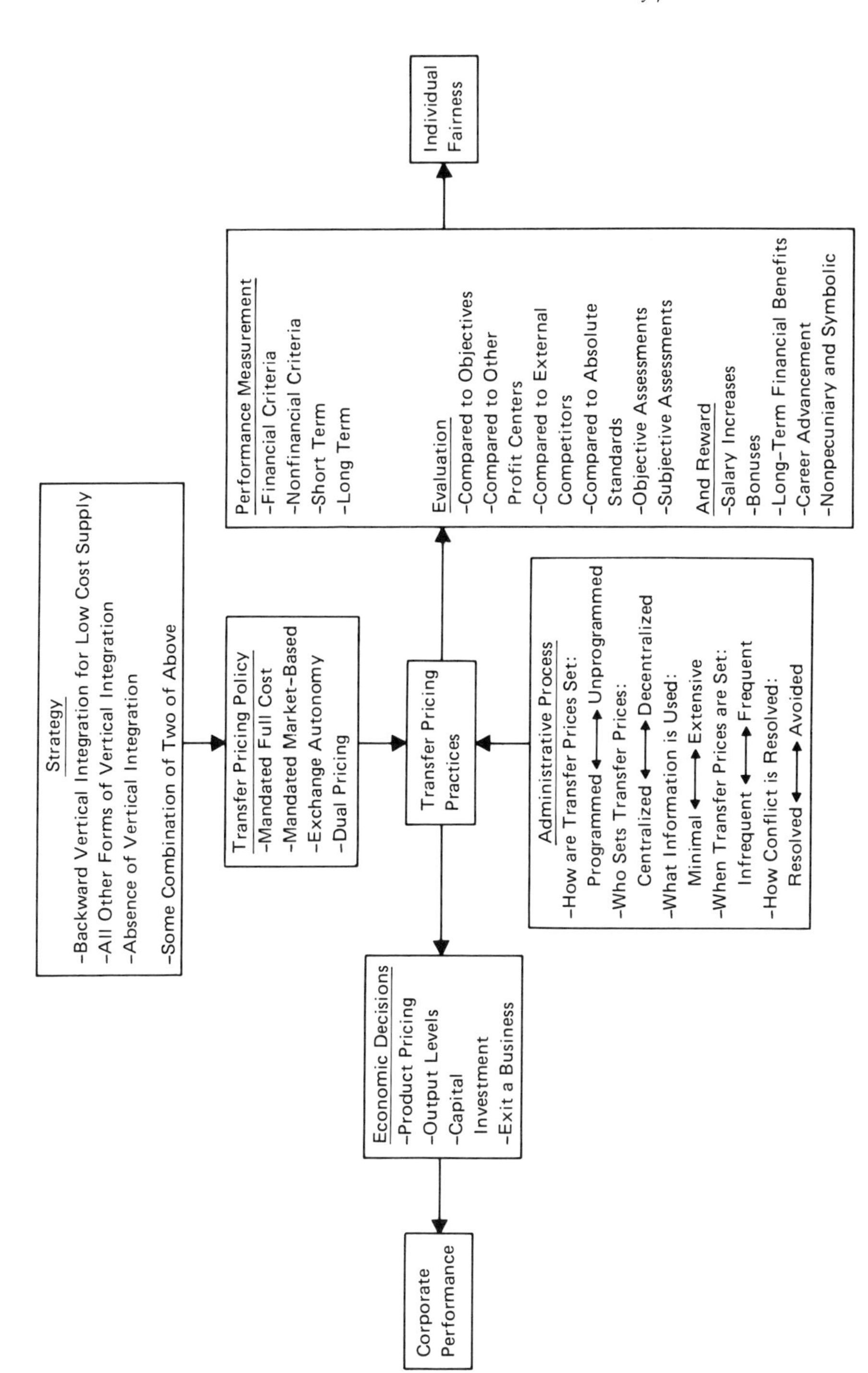

Figure 4–6. A Theory of Transfer Pricing

cial managers), and corporate-level managers only. This element can be characterized in terms of centralized versus decentralized.

Third, the managers who set transfer prices can use many different types of information in doing so, including data on costs, on market prices of the selling profit center, and on market prices of competitors of the selling profit center. This element varies from minimal to extensive.

The fourth element is one of timing—when transfer prices are set. The timing can be periodic, such as quarterly or annually, or it can be episodic and tied to other events, such as changes in costs or market prices. The timing may also provide for retroactive adjustments. The continuum of this element is from frequent to infrequent.

The fifth and final element of administrative process is how conflict is managed, which includes who is involved, what information is used, and the type of conflict resolution process that is used. Lawrence and Lorsch (1967) identified four principal mechanisms for resolving conflict: bargaining, forcing, smoothing, and problem solving.[27] Also at issue is the extent to which efforts are made to resolve the conflict in the first place. This element is the most complex to describe and the most difficult to manage in practice, but it can be described in terms of a complex dimension that ranges from conflict avoidance through forcing and smoothing to conflict resolution through bargaining and problem solving.

Figure 4–6 diagrams the role of administrative process in transfer pricing in terms of the theory presented in this chapter. The next four chapters address the problem of how to manage transfer pricing once a policy has been selected. These chapters identify the common problems inherent in each of the three basic policies and the fourth hybrid policy, dual pricing, and offer some suggestions about how to manage these problems. Some examples will also be given of the problems that can arise from the use of a transfer pricing policy that implies a different strategy than the one it is being used to implement. These chapters on managing transfer pricing will show that transfer pricing is not a problem that is solved once and for all, but one that needs constant management attention.

5
Exchange Autonomy: Pricing in a Market Context

There are two principal ways in which transfer prices can be set when profit center managers have exchange autonomy. The first and most decentralized way is simply to let the managers of the trading profit centers attempt to establish a price that is acceptable to both before the exchange can be consummated. In this case, the transfer price can be truly thought of as a market price, since it is determined by the profit centers acting in their roles as buyers and sellers in a market context. Since higher levels of management are not involved, the organizational hierarchy plays no role in setting these prices. This version of exchange autonomy will be called *pure market price*. It is used when profit center managers have exceptionally high levels of authority and responsibility.

When profit center managers determine the transfer price themselves, a certain amount of negotiaton is involved. Negotiation is often criticized by accounting theorists because it determines a transfer price that is best for the better negotiator, but may not be best for company profit maximization. This narrow technical view fails to recognize that negotiating skills are important to the overall effectiveness of general managers. There are benefits to be obtained from a transfer pricing process that enables them to develop these skills and that provides information to top management about which lower-level general managers are the most able negotiators.[1]

Milton: The Use of Pure Market Price Transfers

Milton was an example of a company that used a policy of exchange autonomy based on pure market prices for transfers between groups. The corporate office played no role in these intergroup transfers. Group general managers, who carried the title of group president, had the authority to use whatever policy they chose for transfers between divisions within their groups; all three basic policies were used. One manager explained the approach taken by these managers:

> The group presidents optimize their empires. They establish by fiat the transfer prices which will optimize resources within their empire.

The five group presidents at Milton had even greater authority and responsibility than the division general managers at Bacon & Bentham did. The group president of the Electronics Group described the company's organization:

> The groups are different and operate like separate companies except for central banking and a few other things. The groups tend to get organized the way the group executive feels is appropriate.

From the perspective of division general managers, internal transfers that crossed groups were done primarily on the basis of pure market prices, although in some instances group general managers might play a minor role in facilitating these exchanges. The group president of the Computer Group explained how divisions in his group purchased semiconductors from divisions in two other groups:

> Prices for these semiconductors are derived by negotiation, essentially on an arm's-length basis between the selling division and my buying division, with a little push here and there from us [the group presidents] if necessary. We could buy on the outside, but I think it's good for the corporation. Internal sellers are becoming more supportive.

He believed that this process was working reasonably well:

> I see potential cost and technological advantages. As we work together, I see cost and performance benefits from working in-house and retaining exclusivity for some time.

One potential problem with this approach, noted by another group president, sometimes occurred when buying divisions solicited outside bids as a way of obtaining information on market prices to be used in the negotiation process. This manager observed: "There is a tendency for people to take an occasional low outside price from unusual circumstances and argue that this is the market price." Because of this, although this practice was occasionally used, "We wouldn't normally do this on every order."

The second and more centralized way transfer prices can be set is for higher-level management—such as the general managers of the profit center managers or corporate financial executives, such as the controller or chief financial officer—to establish a rule for determining transfer prices that is based on prices to external customers. Some common examples are (1) price to distributors; (2) best price to an outside customer during a specified period (which may be for high volumes, but internal customers receive this price even if their volumes are lower); (3) list price less some discount to reflect presumably lower transaction costs because of reduced sales and marketing expenses, no carrying costs for accounts receivable, and no credit risk; and (4) market price determined in some other way less a discount. Because transfer prices in such cases are established under guidelines established by higher-level managers, this version of exchange autonomy will be called *adjusted market price*. Its use reduces the authority of profit center managers to determine transfer prices themselves.

Bacon & Bentham: The Use of Adjusted Market Price Transfers

Bacon & Bentham (described in more detail in the preceding chapter), where division general managers were described as "kings in their little fiefdoms," used adjusted market price transfers for nearly all intergroup transfers and for many intragroup transfers. Semiconductors, for example, were sold at the same discount from list price that a major distributor would receive, regardless of the size of the internal purchase. This could amount to a 35 to 40 percent discount. Discounts for external buyers who were granted "most favored customer" status but who were not distributors ranged from 10 to 15 percent off list price. Transfer prices based on these external market prices were thus higher than those based on prices to distributors.

Transfer Pricing as External Pricing

Whether pure market pricing or adjusted market pricing is used, the transfer pricing problem under exchange autonomy is basically a problem in industrial marketing from the perspective of the selling profit center and a problem in industrial purchasing from the perspective of the buying profit center. The central question is how external prices are established. These activities of marketing and purchasing comprise most of the administrative process in terms of how the price is set, who is involved, what information is used, the timing, and conflict resolution. It is difficult to generalize about process, since it is affected by product, industry, and company characteristics. Nevertheless, the literature from industrial marketing and purchasing can be used to gain some insights into the process aspect of transfer pricing through exchange autonomy.

From the perspective of the seller, marketing involves (1) organizing field sales activity, (2) servicing the product, (3) working with customers on technical development, and (4) dealing with customers' customers (Corey, 1976, p. 348). All of these activities are relevant to the selling profit center with respect to the buying profit center, which is simply one of many customers making claims on the limited resources of the seller. It is easier to maintain a mutually beneficial relationship with some customers than with others, and this is taken into account, especially when demand is high.

From the perspective of the buyer, purchasing involves (1) choosing the type of supplier, (2) determining how many suppliers to have, and (3) establishing the roles each will play (Corey, 1978, p. 34). Vendors have different strengths and weaknesses, and buyers need to obtain a mix so that their needs for delivery, long-term supplies, technical service, and product development support—to name only some of the major concerns—are met. Typically, a number of vendors will be required to satisfy the multiple objectives of a buyer. Corey (1978), in discussing the problem of determining how many suppliers are needed, concluded that "(1) there should not be so many that the buying company is no longer perceived by each supplier as an important customer; (2) there should not be so few that price-and-service competition among suppliers diminishes" (p. 35). The buying profit center views the selling profit center simply as one of many potential vendors with which it seeks to establish a relationship; its characteristics are determined within the context of all the other vendor relationships of the buying profit center.

Bacon & Bentham: A Mismatch on Marketing and Purchasing

An example of how the marketing objectives of the selling profit center and the purchasing objectives of the buying profit center can fail to align occurred at Bacon & Bentham. This example is especially ironic because the product in question, semiconductors, was originally added to the company's activities as an intermediate good in a backward integration strategy.

In the early 1960s, the company decided to make its own semiconductors—a special type difficult to obtain from external sources. When the company integrated backward into semiconductors, it found that it had substantial capacity in excess of internal needs and began selling to external customers. The easiest way to get costs down was to sell high volumes of standard products, although internal needs were for highly specialized products. Some managers believed that the higher manufacturing and engineering costs for these internal sales had resulted in lower priority being given to internal customers.

This tension between the different management approaches appropriate for internal and external business was exacerbated when semiconductors were put into a separate division in the mid-1960s. During this period, when the company was making a number of acquisitions, it adopted its philosophy of highly decentralized responsibility and authority for division general managers. Managers in the Semiconductor Group used this authority to reject internal business, on the grounds that "the overhead on it was too high." Volumes on internal orders were too small to give the Semiconductor Group low enough manufacturing costs to make a profit, given the price of these products. Since buying divisions were unwilling to pay higher prices, the Semiconductor Group had no incentive to become a supplier to internal users. Thus, although the company had originally installed semiconductor capacity as part of a vertical integration decision, the pressures for divisional performance forced buying divisions to return to the external market for their semiconductor needs. They were able to do so since, by this time, external suppliers had emerged that could satisfy their needs.

Ken Gould, vice-president of technology in the Semiconductor Group, believed that the situation was still about the same:

> They know what our products are, but they aren't skilled in their latest use. They don't know enough to ask the right questions. They don't know the parameters of our business. They will ask for things like products which are too complex since the volume is so small. We're competing with the rest of the world. Helping them is not where our paycheck comes from.

Even though he believed internal sales could be increased to 5 to 7 percent of total sales with a great deal of effort, the objective was to stay *below* that volume:

> We would resist going over this very strongly. It would put us at a disadvantage. We try to keep from going over 5 percent of our output to any single customer.

When internal customers did make purchases, they were given no priority over external customers. Winthrop Hector, controller of the Semiconductor Products Division (one of two divisions in the Semiconductor Group), explained how internal and external sales were treated:

> We can be hard-nosed. We have a $100 million backlog and are not looking for business. We don't give many discounts, even on the outside. Right now we have limited capacity and are asking for $70 million to increase our capacity. We tell internal customers that if they're willing to pay the price, we'll put them in the backlog and they can wait their turn.

It can by no means be assumed that the marketing objectives of the selling profit center and the purchasing objectives of the buying profit center will lead to an internal exchange. At the heart of this issue, of course, is the price of the product. This price is evaluated in terms of expectations and promises about quality, delivery, service, technical support, and warranties. If the price is acceptable to both parties, the exchange is consummated.

The problem of product pricing for external sales is also extremely complex, and the literature on it is vast. For our purposes, one of the values of this literature is that it emphasizes the importance of strategic thinking at the product level and the role of process.[2] Webster (1979) noted that "price strategy should be seen as an adjunct to product strategy" and that it is simply one element of the marketing mix of product planning, pricing, distribution, advertising and promotion, and selling. Corey (1976) stated that "the pricing process must be viewed as a dynamic one in which moves are made, responses are analyzed, and further action is taken." Oxenfeldt (1975) also emphasized that pricing is a process and that prices cannot simply be calculated through the use of formulas.

This literature is also valuable in identifying three different procedures—what Corey (1976) called "pricing conventions"—for pricing products.[3] In Corey's terminology, the three major conventions are contract, list price (including discounts), and competitive bidding. These correspond to the three basic ways in which buyers select sources and establish prices (Corey, 1978): cost-based pricing, market-based pricing, and competitive bidding. These pricing conventions elaborate two elements of process: what information is used and who is involved. For all pricing conventions or methods, information from three parties is relevant in the determination of a price, although the importance of the information from each party varies according to pricing convention. Information on *supplier costs* is especially relevant in cost-based pricing; information on *competitor's prices* is most relevant in market-based pricing; and information on *customer value* is most relevant in competitive bidding.

The objectives of the seller in cost-based price negotiations, in which the seller gets a markup on cost to cover overhead and to provide a margin of profit, are to get a fair return and to minimize cost-factor risks. For the buyer, the objectives are to negotiate a fair price and to benefit from vendor cost reductions Corey (1978) described the situations in which this method is used:

> The *cost-based price model* is the basis for a close working relationship, typically symbiotic in nature, between vendor and customer. The salient features of the strategy initially are: (1) a single supplier; (2) a single item being developed and purchased; (3) a time-and-materials pricing arrangement; and (4) contracts initially negotiated for short duration and limited quantities. (p. 7)

Clearly, such an approach can be applied in a transfer pricing situation.

Cost-plus contracts often evolve into fixed price contracts once costs are known and the production process is well established. This transition may also occur in transfer pricing situations, but sometimes the outcome of the negotiations is to retain a cost-plus contract. The contract may also have incentive arrangements—such as when both parties share profits if costs are lower than anticipated. In cost-plus pricing, the source is determined first—for instance, on the basis of technical competence—and then a price is determined through negotiation and the use of calculations. Thus, this pricing method is a combination of programmed and unprogrammed decision making. Both market prices of similar products and customer value can influence what is determined to be a fair markup on costs. Cost information can include both present costs (full, variable, and opportunity) and future costs to account for learning curve and inflation effects.

The cost-plus pricing convention is often used to establish the transfer prices of proprietary products. The problem here is to determine a fair markup to add to costs. Who is involved in this determination, the information used, and resolution of disputes are especially important process concerns, because these products are, by definition, unique.

Market-based pricing is used when products are relatively undifferentiated and market forces determine price levels, signaled by published list prices, either because the market approximates that of perfect competition with many small buyers and sellers or because the supplying industry is oligopolistic and prices are determined by the actions of one price leader. When these conditions exist, buyers use multiple vendors and allocate their total purchases across these vendors according to the objectives of (1) ensuring long-run availability of the resource, (2) ensuring suitable quality, and (3) obtaining the lowest price, although prices are established more by forces at the industry level than by those at the firm level. In this convention, the price is determined before the source is selected.

Market-based pricing tends to be done through a programmed process, although there is opportunity for negotiation. The outcome is a price expressed as either list price or some discount from list price to recognize quantity or trade discounts. Supplier costs and customer value are of relatively little importance compared to competitors' prices in determining the price. When market-based pricing is used, the existence of a market price makes this the easiest situation in which to determine a transfer price.

The third pricing convention, competitive bidding, can be the most complex. As Corey (1978) noted: "When suppliers do not willingly arrive at prices through discussions of their costs with customers and when, on the other hand, prices are not purely market-determined, competitive bidding is likely to be the mechanism by which prices are set" (p. 54). Forms of competitive bidding include sealed bids, open bids, and negotiated bidding. These vary in the extent to which they define programmed versus unprogrammed processes, although the latter best describe this pricing method. Price and source are determined more or less simultaneously.

Competitive bidding is often used when there are differentiated products. This makes customer value especially important, since the customer may be willing to pay more for a higher-quality product. The seller must also consider its own costs and estimate the prices that will be offered by competitors. The buyer, in turn, is able to estimate the "market price level" by soliciting bids from a number of potential vendors. The seller attempts to have the price reflect all the considerations that are relevant to the buyer, such as technical support and service. The importance of relating pricing to the other elements of the marketing mix is especially acute in competitive bidding.[4]

Competitive bidding in transfer pricing is effective only when buying profit centers can choose external sources. A common observation by managers is that without this freedom, "it is difficult to make the market work." If outside suppliers are dubious about their chances of actually obtaining business, they may quote extremely high prices to indicate that they know they are being used for setting a price or to indicate their disinterest in the game. Or they may submit extremely low bids, perhaps in the hope of actually getting some business on which they might raise prices later or as another way of signaling their displeasure.

Even when buying profit centers can source externally, disputes can arise about external bids—such as when inside suppliers are given a preference if they meet outside prices. There can be problems with this procedure, however, when these outside prices are unusually low or unusually high. The former can occur when a supplier has substantial spare capacity, when a supplier is new to a market and wants to establish a position, or when a supplier is simply uninformed about its costs or industry conventions. The last reason can also explain unusually high prices.

When pure market price exchange autonomy is used, the transfer pricing process will correspond to one of these three basic pricing conventions. The variables that determine which convention is used are the same ones that determine which convention is used for external transactions. When adjusted market price exchange autonomy is used, the transfer pricing process is based on one of these three pricing conventions but includes some adjustment. How programmed or unprogrammed, centralized or decentralized, minimal or extensive, and frequent or infrequent the transfer pricing process is depends to a large extent on how these process characteristics describe the external product pricing process.

For both variations of exchange autonomy, it could be argued that the transfer pricing problem should not be so difficult, since management practices already exist for handling it—external product pricing.[5] In fact, however, some special difficulties arise because these internal transactions, though established by profit centers in their market roles, take place within an organizational hierarchy. This introduces some important variations in the transfer pricing process as compared to the external product pricing process.

Disincentives to Trade Internally

The most difficult problem under a policy of exchange autonomy for a manager of two or more profit centers that have the potential to trade with each other is overcoming disincentives for these profit center managers to trade internally. Because of these disincentives, since managers have exchange autonomy they may actually trade less internally than would be desirable from a corporate point of view by giving external transactions priority over internal ones. There are four major disincentives to internal trading: (1) those that result from a mismatch between marketing objectives of the selling profit center and purchasing objectives of the buying profit center, as discussed earlier; (2) those that exist for the selling profit center when adjusted market prices are used, thus giving it lower revenues than it would receive from a comparable unit volume of external transactions (an incentive to the buying profit center is thus a disincentive to the selling profit center); (3) those that exist because the transaction takes place within an organizational hierarchy; and (4) those that result from government regulations on certain types of government contracts.

The root cause of these disincentives is that when exchange autonomy is used, performance is measured, evaluated, and rewarded primarily on the basis of individual profit center results, and little provision is made to recognize efforts that help other profit centers, especially at the expense of one's own. The challenge for higher-level managers is to find ways to overcome these disincentives and thus improve economic decisions without negatively affecting other economic decisions and without causing perceptions of unfairness on the part of the managers involved. In particular, profit center managers are likely to believe that they are being treated unfairly by upper management when top management reduces the profit center managers' authority, thereby interfering with their ability to achieve their objectives.

Lost opportunities for internal sales can hurt corporate performance in two ways. The first—most commonly cited in the theoretical literature—is that buying profit centers may source externally when spare capacity exists internally. When this occurs, the price to the company of the external purchase is the outside price plus some portion of the unused fixed capacity, which causes overall corporate profits to be lower than they would be if the buying profit center sourced internally. The second consequence, which is more difficult to quantify, is the failure of profit centers to coordinate product development and design efforts. For example, if the buying profit center works only with outside suppliers to develop new component parts, internal suppliers may not develop the technology or skill for making these components and will lose some potential business. This consequence involves lost competitive advantages through proprietary technology more than lost cost economies.

How much these lost opportunities affect corporate performance depends on how significant they are. In many situations of exchange autonomy their effects are not great; if they are, a strategy of vertical integration is called for. However, even when the consequences are small for the total corporation, they can be large for a particular product line or even for a division. For this reason, companies that use exchange autonomy sometimes make exceptions for particular products.

Milton: Lost Opportunities of Small Consequence

Milton, Inc.—the company whose group presidents had extremely high levels of authority and responsibility—furnishes a good example of why disincentives exist for internal transfers under a policy of exchange autonomy, although at Milton the general perception was that any lost opportunities were fairly small. Roland Bergman, vice-president of strategic planning, said that internal transfers occurred only for two reasons:

> We only buy internally for strategic or huge cost reduction reasons. Strategy can make a huge difference to internal transfers.

A number of managers felt that internal sales could be increased but that the volume was not significant. The group director of research and development in the Semiconductor Group, Bill Jevon, estimated that if his group got all possible internal business, it would only double, because "there just isn't that much." A major reason for the low volume of internal sales was that other groups could not use the products in the Semiconductor Group, even though they purchased semiconductors from external suppliers.

Jevon gave as another reason for the low volume of internal transfers the lack of formal incentives for doing so. At Milton, sizable bonuses for group and division general managers (up to 50 percent of base salary) were awarded on the basis of group financial performance. The performance measurement, evaluation, and reward system did not recognize contributions to the performance of other groups.

Managers saw some very real advantages for preserving exchange autonomy. David Dergola, president of the Retail Electronics Group, which purchased internally some products that were available from external suppliers, admitted that "I get banged by my engineering and procurement people that we could get better prices and turnaround outside." In fact, he had evidence of the advantages of external suppliers, which was recognized by the president of the Semiconductor Group:

> Dergola's group has been one of Intel's best customers for the past five to six years. Dergola, the president, and I talk. I say "As long as Intel's product line is more comfortable and they will jump through hoops to give you good quality, then it is in the corporation's interest to stay with them."
>
> When given the option, I've recommended against adding the volume to my sales in order to keep Intel working for us. And this amounts to between $4 million and $6 million in additional sales for me.

Just as buying profit centers sometimes preferred external suppliers, so did selling profit centers sometimes prefer external customers. As one manager explained: "If we have excess capacity, we are more likely to do business internally. If we are at full capacity, we want to sell outside for more."

Another significant disincentive was the perception that internal transactions were harder to manage than external ones—either because internal customers or suppliers were treated less well than external ones or, somewhat conversely, because internal parties were treated as well but were more difficult to please. A group president believed that the latter problem was a fairly general one, based on his experience at Milton and other companies: "The internal guy, whether as supplier or as user, is never treated as well. I've been on both sides. It's sad but understandable."

This same manager noted the exacerbating problem that was a consequence of these poor internal relationships:

> An in-house guy may say not to supply for three weeks. He would be much more careful to do this with an outsider due to cancellation charges. Conversely, an in-house guy may say he needs more, and if he doesn't get them he complains to his boss. Guys will say they could be doing better if the other guy was doing better. Hence, people are reluctant to do business in-house.

Another group president at this company agreed: "In my kind of business emotions can run high. If things screw up, they run up the line. You don't have this sensitivity in dealing outside."

The vice-president of strategic planning remarked: "If managers sell inside, they are only doing what they are supposed to. If they screw up, they get in trouble." A group financial executive of the company agreed that "internal divisions are under more pressure. The first missed step could be heard about by the president."

A group financial executive also believed that internal relationships were more difficult to manage than external ones. He cited as a reason the fact that the emphasis on individual profit center results leads to competitive comparisons:

> In my experience, sister divisions are more antagonistic to each other than to outsiders. Basically, this is due to competition as to who is the best performer. There is the suspicion that other divisions are doing something to get more than their share, especially when a product is forced on a division.

Despite the lost opportunities for internal sales as a result of various disincentives, little if any sentiment existed to reduce the authority of profit center managers to select their vendors and customers. One manager summarized the attitude at the company about this problem: "The view here is 'Okay, we know we're losing out on some decisions, but we don't want to step on the general managers' toes.'"

The disincentive to trade internally that results from such exchanges occurring in the context of an organizational hierarchy is the most complicated and interesting of the four disincentives cited. Although transactions in a policy of exchange autonomy closely model external market transactions, in the end they are not identical, because they are between units that are part of the same organization. The problems that emerge from this difference result from the fact that these transactions can be viewed from two perspectives—as market transactions and as hierarchical ones. If either or both profit centers become dissatisfied with their market relationship, they can always resort to hierarchical channels for a redress of grievances.

When internal transactions do take place, problems can arise that are typical of all buyer-seller relationships. The buyer's complaints include (1) lack of sales attention, (2) lack of technical support, (3) lack of service, (4) low-quality product, (5) slow deliveries, and (6) difficulties in getting problems resolved. The seller's complaints include (1) short lead times, (2) abruptly canceled orders, (3) excessive quality requirements, (4) lack of technical cooperation, and (5) unreasonable expectations that can never be satisfied. These problems are greatest when sellers view internal buyers as a last resort or when buyers so view internal sellers, and when prices are not adjusted (perhaps because top management has intervened in product pricing) to reflect differences in volume, quality, service, and so on, between internal and external sales. Each party may attempt to equate the overall value of internal transactions with external transactions by adjusting other terms of the exchange. As a result, internal transactions may be given lower priority than external ones.

Problems in external transactions are usually resolved by the parties involved. They resort to litigation only rarely because of its expense and because of the prospect that both parties might be worse off than if they had reached an agreement between themselves.[6] External transactions are also less visible to top management, unless they are major transactions or have extremely severe problems. Most problems can be resolved without top management's knowledge of them, which preserves the autonomy of profit center managers.

When problems arise in internal transactions, there is always the temptation to appeal to higher levels of management, which is easier and less expensive than resorting to litigation. In fact, the efficiency of a hierarchy in resolving disputes has been cited by some economists as a major reason for vertical integration.[7] Managers' lack of certain types of negotiating leverage on internal transactions furthers the temptation to appeal to top management. For example, payments on many internal transfers are recorded as bookkeeping entries at the end of the month, but this practice prevents the buying profit center from withholding payment as a means of getting the seller to attend to complaints.[8]

The temptation to appeal to higher management levels for resolution of problems in internal transactions becomes greater when these transactions represent a greater proportion of the selling profit center's revenues and the buying profit center's costs, since in these circumstances they have a greater effect on measures of financial performance. Since both profit centers are part of the same organization, they are able to compare their performance with each other and they can perceive the situation as one in which gains to one party are losses to another. Comparative profitability with external suppliers or customers is less important, particularly when they are in different industries. Within one company, however, the comparative profitability of profit centers is very important, even when they are in different industries, because they compete for capital and other resources. In general, higher-performing profit centers receive a greater share of resources, particularly when some form of portfolio planning is used in making resource allocation decisions, unless they are being "milked" as "cash cows."[9]

Complaining to top management about problems with internal transactions is a double-edged sword.[10] It draws attention to the general manager's operations, over which he or she has been given substantial decision-making authority. Frequent complaints that require top management involvement may ultimately reduce the general manager's authority or raise questions about his or her ability to balance cooperative/competitive relationships with peers and to run his or her business. Thus, a manager must be careful in choosing when to escalate concerns up the hierarchy of authority. On the other hand, if the other manager complains, the first manager's decision not to complain may be seen as accepting the other's complaint as legitimate.

Internal transactions under exchange autonomy have the characteristics of the "prisoner's dilemma."[11] If neither manager complains and they resolve disputes between themselves, they are able to keep the problem from the attention of top management (which could be their mutual boss), just as they are able to do with external transactions. Both parties benefit when this can be accomplished. However, if one manager complains, the other's failure to do so can result in an unfavorable resolution by a higher authority. This is an incentive for the second manager to complain as well, but that would only increase top management's attention to profit center operations and still might not lead to a favorable resolution for either party.

Thus, each manager has an incentive to be the first to complain to top management. If the other does not respond, the first manager can win a favorable settlement. But if the other is first to complain, there is no clearly favorable payoff for the best response, which is to complain as well. How much of a dilemma this is depends on how much financial performance is emphasized, how much internal transactions affect performance, the perceived probability of winning a favorable settlement in a dispute, top management's response to these disputes, and the mechanisms for adjudicating them. The presence of this dilemma creates the irony of a strong incentive to choose external transactions over internal ones. The potential negative consequences of inter–profit center conflict may result in increased involvement by higher-level management in profit center operations, which reduces the authority and autonomy of the profit center general managers. A logical response by these managers is simply to avoid this conflict by avoiding internal transactions.

Of course, conflict can also exist in external relationships as a result of competition between the parties to secure the best deal. On external transactions, however, advantages accruing from long-term relationships help keep the competition over short-term results from becoming detrimental to longer-term performance. Similar incentives on internal transactions exist only to the extent that there is a mutual desire for a longer-term relationship—and the existence of the "prisoner's dilemma" is a constraint on this desire. Comparative profitability with external suppliers or customers may also be less important than comparative profitability with sister profit centers when it may have consequences for short-term financial rewards and longer-term career prospects. Furthermore, an emphasis on individual profit center performance in measuring, evaluating, and rewarding performance leads to competition between profit center managers, because they can compare their contributions to total corporate sales and profits with each other.

Hume Fabrication Company: The Agony of an Internal Transaction

A vivid example of the kinds of problems that can arise in internal transactions under exchange autonomy occurred at Hume Fabrication Company. Although the company's transfer pricing policy did not grant autonomy to both buyer and seller, the buyers were allowed to choose between internal and external sources. A dispute arose when the Foundry Division voluntarily purchased a piece of equipment from the Manufacturing Equipment Division. The company's vice-president of finance summarized the dispute:

> The equipment supplied to the foundry didn't work. This started a two-year argument about who would pay for what. It involved vice-presidents and the president of the company. Both sides had good points. But it got to the point that each management got completely turned off from the other.

One source of the problem was a lack of agreement about the terms of the transaction:

> The buying division thought it had a turnkey arrangement. The selling division said the standard terms are to provide equipment only with no performance guarantees.

Although the selling division's point was valid, the vice-president of finance believed that since the internal transaction was a one-time purchase, the Foundry Division was treated differently from a major external customer:

> Now the equipment is normally sold this way, but if an installation is sold to Ford and it doesn't work, they go out of their way to make it right. In this case they didn't feel the same obligation to their brother, the foundry. It was an inside sale and a one-time deal.

One of the vice-presidents who was involved in adjudicating the dispute believed that both parties had a legitimate argument and that, in the end, the dispute had hurt the company overall:

> If you talk to people in the foundry, they will tell you that Manufacturing Equipment caused them great suffering. If you talk to the Manufacturing Equipment people, they will tell you there was a problem and they fixed it. Both are right.
>
> The purchase was about $100,000. Frankly, I would say Manufacturing Equipment screwed up their calculations in installing the equipment and this was the cause of the problems. They worked hard to fix the machine, but the problem kept reappearing. They ended up rebuilding the machine at a cost of $50,000 to $60,000.
>
> The foundry had every reason to be upset, but Manufacturing Equipment went full out and rebuilt the machine. Both sides were coming to me and my only goal was to get the problem resolved. It went on at a lot of expense to the company. That's what gripes me. It went on for many months. The managers involved both smile sweetly at each other but think the other is a no-good so-and-so.

Although this was a fairly expensive purchase, it was a small part of the Foundry Division's costs and the Manufacturing Equipment Division's sales. No doubt, both sides would have preferred this equipment to have been purchased externally, given the problems that ensued.

The fourth disincentive for selling profit centers to trade internally comes about in some cases when the buying profit center is sourcing components for a product being made under a government cost-plus contract. Anthony and Dearden (1980) explained this government regulation of internal transfers:

> Government regulations state that transfers from other divisions, subsidiaries, or affiliates will be at cost except under the following conditions:
>
> 1. The transfer price is based on an established catalogue or market price of commercial items sold in substantial quantities to the general public.
> 2. It is the result of adequate price competition and is the price at which an award was made to an affiliated organization after obtaining quotations on an equal basis from such organizations and one or more outside sources which normally produce the item or its equivalent in significant quantities.

> The price calculated above must not be in excess of the selling division's current price to its most favored customer. Also, the transfer price should be adjusted, when appropriate, to reflect the quantities being procured and may be adjusted for the actual costs of any modifications required by the contract. (p.245)

Bacon & Bentham: Preferences for External Sources

Bacon & Bentham faced the constraint of the government regulation because its Government Systems Division did a significant amount of cost-plus contract work for the government. It used custom-developed semiconductors in its products, and it sourced them externally, because external suppliers could receive a profit whereas internal suppliers did not. Although some incentive could have been provided to the profit center selling semiconductors by sharing the profits earned, this would have reduced the profits of the Government Systems Division. Several managers did note, however, that selling profit centers might be willing to do work at cost if it helped fund the development of a product that would later be commercially successful. At the same time, personnel in Government Systems had another reason to prefer external sources, according to one manager, because the engineers in this division were better able to retain total responsibility for design of the devices with external suppliers than with internal ones.

Bacon & Bentham experienced the same problem as Milton Electronics—profit center managers preferring external transactions over viable internal ones. One view was noted by a division controller, who remarked: "Sister divisions suck hind tit. I've seen it happen here."[12] The vice-president and group general manager of the Semiconductor Group cited another reason— the consequences of conflict:

> It is more difficult to work inside than externally. In the smallest impasse, a guy can go up the line. Nobody wants to have his boss coming and telling him he's not cooperating. It is always difficult, so you need a financial incentive or something else such as recognition for being a good corporate citizen.

There are three ways for managers to address the problem of disincentives to trade internally: (1) to make greater use of the hierarchy by restricting the exchange autonomy of profit center managers; (2) to emphasize the relationship between the profit centers in their market context; and (3) dual pricing. Each of these solutions can be effective, but each has some inherent problems that must also be managed. Since there are problems in each approach, management needs to be explicitly aware of the competitive advantages it is seeking in increasing the level of internal sales. Some of the most important advantages include (1) giving the buying profit center access to proprietary technology in the selling profit center; (2) not contributing to the market share of competitors of the selling profit center; (3) achieving cost reductions in the buying profit center because of increased volume; (4) achieving cost reductions in the buying profit center because of cheaper component parts or raw materials; (5) increasing knowledge in the selling profit center about the markets in which it sells, which enables it to market to external customers more effectively; and (6) increasing knowledge in the buying profit center about the parts and raw materials it purchases, which enables it to purchase from outside suppliers more effectively.

Incentives Through the Management Hierarchy

Perhaps the most obvious solution to the problem of profit centers refusing to trade internally—even when it would be in the corporation's best interest—is for higher-level management to encourage them to do so. This encouragement can take a variety of forms, all of which involve some restriction in authority. It has already been noted that adjusted market prices are an incentive to the buying profit center but not necessarily to the selling profit center. Top management can encourage selling profit centers to accept this business or, in the extreme case, can require them to do so, as occurred at Hume Fabrication Company. Another way to encourage internal sales is to restrict exchange autonomy by giving internal suppliers the opportunity to meet outside prices or by requiring buying profit centers to purchase internally if the prices of internal suppliers are within a certain percentage of the best outside price. Finally, objectives for internal sales and purchases can be included in the plans of both profit centers.

There is a range of intermediate possibilities between complete exchange autonomy and absolutely mandated internal transactions. In its most extreme form, restriction on exchange autonomy results in a different transfer pricing policy—mandated market-based transfers. The exercise of higher-level management's authority to encourage internal sales and purchases interferes with the authority of profit center managers to make their own purchasing and marketing decisions. This can create problems of perceived unfairness if lower-level managers believe that these restrictions interfere with their ability to achieve the financial objectives for which they are responsible. Top management must consider whether the economic and strategic advantages justify the increased conflict that is likely to result.

Bacon & Bentham and Milton: The Use of Hierarchical Encouragement

---

Bacon & Bentham and Milton both used a transfer pricing policy of exchange autonomy, and both companies were aware that a consequence of this policy was lost opportunities for internal sales. Although both companies were committed to decentralized authority and responsibility, each was struggling with the problem of finding a way to encourage more internal sales, particularly on a few key products, such as semiconductors, which could yield competitive advantages. Also, managers in both companies recognized that the solution to this problem created another one—increased conflict.

Karl Hardman, vice-president and group general manager of the Semiconductor Group at Bacon & Bentham, emphasized the importance of top management's attitude in determining the extent of internal coordination and cooperation.

> We are not getting the leverage we should out of our $250 million capital investment in semiconductors. We need to design it into products of other divisions. Inside sales are about 1.2 percent of total sales. In the past, people tried to work with Semiconductor and were rebuffed. Much of this was due to the attitude of my predecessor.

Other managers agreed that his predecessor had actively discouraged internal trading. One of the legacies of this attitude was that buying divisions ended up sourcing company products from distributors, rather than directly through their sister divisions. Their small volume of purchases was another reason Semiconductor was unenthusiastic about selling to them. Hardman believed that opportunities were being missed:

> The internal opportunities are immense. Other divisions could be more profitable and could command a higher price because their products would have unique features.

When internal transfers are based on proprietary technology, buying divisions can become captive customers, even though, in theory, they have autonomy to choose their sources. Mason Robinson, vice-president and general manager of the Programs Division in the Semiconductor Group, believed that "there is increasing recognition by our sister divisions that we can help them" through proprietary technology but that "they feel they are screwed if they are captive customers." As a result, "they can make life difficult for me by going to my boss." He made his books available in negotiating prices so that the other divisions would know his costs, but disputes still arose. "Complaints go on, but business continues," Robinson said.

Robinson echoed the importance of top management's attitude in encouraging internal transfers, but he added that the attitudes of the division general managers were also important:

> If the top executive doesn't want internal transfers to happen, there is no way they will. I saw this happen in a previous company I worked for. If he does want them, a lot depends on relationships at the working level.

On his own initiative, Robinson worked at improving relationships with buying divisions, because he felt that over the long run, it could benefit him as well: "I get a kick helping a sister division win a contract. One hand washes the other. Times can get tough for me some day." In the final analysis, encouragement of internal transactions by higher-level management is most effective when profit center managers themselves see the advantages of the transactions.

Milton had also addressed the problem of how to increase internal sales. In this case, the president was attempting to do so through the planning process—as explained by the general manager of the Computer Group:

> The president has made a policy statement that the component businesses are to direct their efforts to help and support assembly businesses.

> He's convinced of added value and synergism. He rejected Semiconductor's preliminary plan because it was not sufficiently supportive of Computer's divisions. It is conceivable that there will be more hassle on negotiations, since there will be more pressure for internal transfers.

Despite this expected hassle, he remained confident that this change in policy could be implemented:

> I think you can make any one of a number of policies work. They have to be understood and well applied, and the measurement system has to be considered.

A possible response by lower-level managers to "encouraged" internal transactions that they would not have entered into if they had complete choice is to seek compensation for any perceived inequities. For example, if the buying profit center believes that the price is too high for the level of quality of the internally purchased intermediate good, it may make stringent demands regarding deliveries or technical service to get value for the price being paid. From the perspective of the selling profit center, if the price is lower than it believes it could get externally, it may give the buying profit center lower priority on deliveries or lower-quality product. The result can be a vicious cycle in which the attempts of each profit center manager to compensate for perceived inequities in the exchange become the source of what the other profit center manager is also attempting to compensate for. It is even possible that both managers will tacitly enter this cycle of increasing conflict in an attempt to convince upper management that these "encouraged" internal transactions create more problems than they are worth.

Although these problems are grounded in perception—and it is not always easy to determine which profit center is in some sense "right," given the complexity and uncertainty of this problem—the perceptions are often based on genuine economic and strategic concerns. Exchange autonomy is granted in the first place because top management believes that lower-level profit center managers are in a better position to make what can be very complex marketing and purchasing decisions. By interfering with their authority to make these decisions, top management may actually cause decisions that are suboptimal for the corporation as a whole, since they do not have as much information as those lower down in the hierarchy. For example, intervention by top management may improve short-term results at the expense of longer-term strategic objectives being pursued by the profit centers.

Top management should be aware that in restricting exchange autonomy, it may be substituting one set of problems for another. The new problems concern both fairness and economic decision making. A possible irony in the use of the management hierarchy is that in attempting to prevent one profit center from achieving its objectives at the expense of another—a win/lose situation—top management may inhibit the ability of both profit centers to achieve their objectives—a lose/lose situation.

Hobbes Instrument Company: Problems from Restricting Exchange Autonomy

Hobbes Instrument Company experienced problems in both fairness and economic decision making as a result of restrictions placed on the authority of profit center managers who bought and sold semiconductors. Top management had economic and strategic reasons for imposing these restrictions, but they interfered with the economic and strategic objectives of the profit centers. It is difficult to know whether the gains outweighed the losses. In contrast, no restrictions were placed on buying and selling of printed circuit boards, and managers who bought and sold this product were satisfied with the arrangements they reached.

The company was organized into two major groups, Electronics and Semiconductors, each of which contained a number of divisions. The company had entered the semiconductor business in the early 1960s. Ed Fales, a manager in one of the Electronics Group's divisions, was a bench engineer at the time. He recalled being urged to use Hobbes semiconductors even if they were inferior to some that were available from external suppliers. He vividly remembered the transactions:

> We would have coordination meetings. These were knock-down, drag-out fights. We'd beat them over the head and threaten them with outside suppliers. These were blood-and-guts negotiations and were not based on economic or financial considerations.

Over time, the quality of the Semiconductors Group's products had improved, as had its ability to address specific internal needs. Intracompany sales of semiconductors had grown from $1 million in the early 1960s to $30 million in 1981. Pressures for internal sourcing waxed and waned. One form this pressure took was a measurement of the amount of semiconductor needs satisfied internally. Since the Electronics Group was a large purchaser of semiconductors, there was some concern about the contribution its external purchases made to the market shares of Semiconductors' competitors. However, sourcing inside did not necessarily help the Electronics Group achieve its sales, cost, and profit targets.

According to Fales, internal transactions were no easier now than they had been in the past:

> These are hard-headed negotiations with much saber rattling. We sit down on an annual basis with Semiconductors and negotiate prices. There is no formal policy. Corporate management doesn't get too involved, although the president likes to see us buy from Semiconductors. He monitors this and there are gentle urgings to do business internally. I have heard guidelines that if Hobbes is within 10 percent of a competitor's price, they should get the majority of the business.

He disagreed with the principle of exerting pressure on divisions in the Electronics Group to purchase internally, since it could result in subsidizing businesses in which the company was uncompetitive and using capital that could be better invested elsewhere in the company:

> There are plenty of opportunities for investing resources. We shouldn't subsidize businesses unless there are critical strategic reasons, and even in this case it should be absorbed higher up, not by the buying division.

Fales thought that Semiconductors was as unhappy with pressures to trade internally as Electronics was.

These tensions had recently escalated in transactions between Advanced Systems, a division in the Electronics Group, and Semiconductors. A year ago, the president had instituted the policy that if the economy was in a recessionary period, internal buyers would have to source their semiconductors internally for a substantial percentage of their total purchases, at prices close to competitive prices. No precise definitions were given for "substantial percentage" or "close to competitive prices." In nonrecessionary periods, the old policy of getting both internal and external quotes and choosing between them was to apply.

Eric Berke, vice-president and general manager of Advanced Systems, commented on the current situation with a wry smile:

> I think we're still in a recessionary period. They raised prices a lot and were willing to lose a share of their business with us. The president deemed the prices should hold and that we had to order inside. They aren't happy and we aren't either. They'd rather make investments in other areas which are more profitable for them and growing faster, rather than continue to invest in areas to support our products.

He cited examples of semiconductor markets that were growing at the rate of 100 percent per year and were a much more attractive use of resources than maintaining products to support internal use. Thus, both buyer and seller in this case would have preferred external transactions. Top management may or may not have been aware of the economic consequences of interfering with profit center autonomy. If it was not, this illustrates the need for caution when doing so. If it was aware of these consequences, the offsetting benefits were not apparent to lower-level managers.

This company also experienced some of the problems that can arise once these internal transactions are established. One type of problem was experienced by the Electronics Group over some proprietary semiconductors that had been developed for them by the Semiconductors Group. The Semiconductors Group sold some of these devices to external competitors of Electronics, thereby reducing the Electronics Group's competitive advantage. This behavior was to be expected, given the incentives for the Semiconductors Group to achieve high performance levels. Its argument was that these external sales were necessary to obtain sufficient volume to lower costs. However, Fales saw it "as a question of leverage—the $1,000 system versus the $10 semiconductor device." Although he acknowledged a similar risk with outside suppliers, he thought better guidelines existed for managing this problem. As it was, even when the Electronics Group sourced internally to gain competitive advantages, the failure by top management to prevent the Semiconductors Group from selling these components to external competitors of the Electronics Group reduced this advantage. Top management's uneven restriction of purchasing autonomy in the buying profit center and marketing autonomy in the selling profit center resulted in potentially suboptimal decisions by the latter, which interfered with attempts by the former to enhance its own and the corporation's performance.

This was especially frustrating to the Electronics Group because of another problem that emerged with respect to proprietary semiconductors. The Semiconductors Group had raised the prices of these sole-sourced products. The Advanced Systems Division in the Electronics Group solicited outside bids, but Semiconductors rejected their validity and continued to charge the existing price. Advanced Systems could not persuade Semiconductors to accept this pricing basis or to change the transfer price. This was all the more irritating to managers in Advanced Systems when they learned that if Semiconductors had decided to invest more in these products, the prices would not have gone up.

These examples of restrictions on exchange autonomy for semiconductors at Hobbes Instrument Company illustrate that such restrictions can lead to a number of other problems, such as lost opportunities for both profit centers that might be better for total corporate performance than the internal transaction, actions by one profit center that interfere with the objectives of another when the latter has lost the option to source externally, and disagreements over what the transfer price should be. These problems must be managed to prevent them from overwhelming the advantages sought from restrictions in exchange autonomy.

The underlying cause of problems that emerge when restrictions are placed on exchange autonomy is that performance measurement, evaluation, and reward are based primarily on the financial outcomes of the individual profit centers when this policy is used. There are no incentives for profit center managers to make sacrifices in the interest of each other. As restrictions on exchange autonomy increase, it will be necessary to change the criteria for performance measurement, evaluation, and reward, especially if one or both profit centers perceive that they are making sacrifices. The ultimate result of such restrictions—mandated market-based transactions—represents a shift in transfer pricing policy, which accompanies a shift in strategy. This shift in strategy must also be recognized in other implementation aspects.

Incentives Through Market Mechanisms

In some instances, an increased level of internal sales and purchases can be beneficial to both the buying and the selling profit centers, and corporate optimization does not imply any sacrifice by either profit center. Presumably, each profit center, in pursuing its own self-interest, would be motivated to trade more internally, since this would improve its performance. Resorting to hierarchical authority to encourage these transactions may be too crude an approach, since perceptions of unfairness because of restrictions on exchange autonomy may cloud the very real benefits that can be achieved through increased internal cooperation. Ideally, each profit center would come to see these advantages for itself and would make the decision to trade more internally of its own free will. When this happens, decentralized authority and responsibility are preserved while, at the same time, corporate performance is improved.

This can be accomplished when efforts are made by each profit center to deal with the other as much as possible as it would deal with external parties. This somewhat counterintuitive recommendation is entirely consistent with decentralized authority and responsibility, and it avoids the problems that can emerge when hierarchical authority is used to restrict exchange autonomy. Selling profit centers can develop explicit marketing objectives directed toward internal customers—even assigning salespeople to internal accounts. Buying profit centers can develop explicit purchasing objectives to enable them to take full advantage of internal capabilities. If profit centers on both sides of the transaction find the advantages to themselves of trading internally, they will have an especially strong incentive to make these relationships work. This can be done by each profit center educating the other on its capabilities, needs, and objectives—for example, through presentations and seminars similar to those sponsored for outsiders.

The obvious weakness of using market mechanisms is that it can lead to an increase in transaction costs, whereas reduced transaction costs are often given as a reason for using adjusted market prices. These transaction costs must be compared to the costs of using hierarchical authority—such as increased transaction costs because of increased conflict—and the costs of lost opportunities. Furthermore, in many cases, resources will not have to be added, since these efforts can use already existing marketing and purchasing capacity.

Milton and Bacon & Bentham: Efforts to Use Market Mechanisms

Milton and Bacon & Bentham had both made attempts to use market mechanisms to improve internal coordination, with varying degrees of success. The situations in which these efforts were successful were when inter–profit center transactions very closely approximated external transactions. This occurred in some instances at Milton. These efforts were less successful—as in some instances at Bacon & Bentham—when there was a dilution in clarity about the purposes of these mechanisms to reproduce market relationships.

Michael Mead, president of the Semiconductor Group at Milton, had explicitly assigned salespeople to call on internal customers and maintain relationships, just as other salespeople did with external customers. This was especially important, since price was not the major criterion of buyers for his group's products:

> In our relationships with other groups, factors other than price are more important. Since the product life cycle is so short, applications technology is important. If you want to increase sales, you have to increase applications support. You need to show them how to substitute integrated circuits for traditional transistors. We recently did this for one division, which saved them costs on making their product.

Mead believed that internal customers were likely to be serviced better than external customers, because his group wanted to develop a reputation for being responsive. He also believed that special attention was paid to quality, so that his group would have a reputation inside the company for being a quality producer. But even with all of these efforts, "there are times when others are happy with our performance, and there are times when they're unhappy."

Similar attempts to improve interdivisional relations were made at Bacon &

Bentham. Selling divisions sent people to buying divisions to help them make semiconductor purchases, whether from internal or external sources. A special laboratory with a very fast turnaround capability had been installed to service the Government Systems Division. Seminars were held to help educate buying divisions about the products available internally and how they could be used. The Products Division in the Semiconductor Group had assigned a sales representative two years ago who was supposed to call only on internal accounts. However, the controller of this division believed that "he has not been all that successful, probably because he has been used on other things."

The key to using these market mechanisms is for top management to have minimum involvement and for the profit center managers to resist any temptation to appeal to higher levels for adjudication of disputes. Top management can contribute to this by refusing to become involved. Market mechanisms can be an effective method of improving internal coordination through increased sales when the hierarchical roles of the profit centers are almost completely suppressed.

Incentives Through Dual Pricing

The third incentive available to upper-level management to improve the level of internal sales is dual pricing. When dual pricing is used with exchange autonomy, it can be considered a variation on the adjusted market price approach whereby top management specifies the transfer price to the buying profit center as full cost and to the selling profit center as market price. Top management may or may not be involved in the determination of these two transfer prices.

In using dual pricing with exchange autonomy, top management hopes that the lower transfer price will be an incentive to the buying profit center to source more internally. This will occur only if budgeted objectives are not revised to reflect that the buying profit center is paying less for a raw material or component. At the same time, top management hopes that the selling profit center will be willing to accept internal orders. It is more likely to do so when it has spare capacity—especially if its budgeted objectives are based on full cost transfer prices. When budgeted objectives for each profit center are set on the transfer price to the other, each has a kind of "fudge factor" or head start on achieving its objectives by increasing its level of internal transactions.

How much of an incentive dual pricing provides the buying profit center depends on the importance of price as a consideration in sourcing the intermediate good and on how much more readily the profit center can meet its financial objectives with internal sourcing. If price is of less concern than quality, service, technical support, and so on, receiving the intermediate good at cost is not a major incentive to source internally, especially if this good represents a small portion of the total costs of the final good. Furthermore, if top management adjusts financial objectives by increasing the buying profit center's profit targets to reflect the full cost transfer (as it does when mandated full cost transfers are used), the incentive to source internally disappears.

The extent to which dual pricing provides an incentive to the buying profit center to source internally greatly affects the incentive of the selling profit center to sell internally. For example, less work goes into negotiating the sale if the buying profit center is enthusiastic about sourcing internally. Internal sales are attractive to the selling profit center when buying profit centers initiate requests for product and are willing to improve internal cooperation, such as through design coordination. Greater cooperativeness and the buying profit center's desire to source internally lower the selling profit center's barriers against selling internally. It is also unlikely that the buying profit center will complain when it is paying much below market price; if it does, top management is unlikely to be very sympathetic.

Although dual pricing would appear to be a mechanism by which everybody wins, it too has problems—besides the fact that it simply may not be such a large incentive for the reasons stated earlier. One problem is that disagreements can arise about what the market price portion of the transfer price should be. Another problem is that in some cases, market price is less than full cost. This can happen in products such as semiconductors, which are priced externally through "forward pricing" based on average costs over the entire product life cycle, since there is a strong learning curve effect. At the beginning of the product life cycle, costs are much higher than they will be at the end, and they are higher than market price.

Finally, there is the problem that profits earned on internal sales by the selling profit center may be considered "second-class" profits both by that profit center's managers and by managers in other profit centers. Managers are fully aware that dual pricing cannot create something from nothing and that it results in reported profits in the profit centers that sum to more than total corporate profits. Thus, these profits are less real than profits earned on other transactions. This accounting sleight of hand ends up fooling no one—except, perhaps, higher-level management.

Milton and Bacon & Bentham: Efforts to Use Dual Pricing

Both Milton and Bacon & Bentham had attempted to use dual pricing with exchange autonomy as a way of increasing incentives for internal sales. Because of the problems they had experienced with it, opinion varied in both companies regarding how useful a policy it had been. At Milton, the divisions negotiated the market price portion of the transfer; at Bacon & Bentham, corporate management specified it as "most favored customer" status. This policy was used for three to five years in each company before the policy of exchange autonomy was reinstated.

Milton used actual full manufacturing costs for the cost portion of the transfer price. Herbert Litten, president of the Electronics Group, explained why the company had instituted a "corporate billing" policy, so-called because the profit earned by the selling division that was not included in the full cost transfer price was "billed" to corporate headquarters:

> In order to encourage internal trading, the policy of actual full costs and corporate billing was set up in the early 1970s. This was done by the current president. Several senior managers worked out this system. The difference between market price and full cost was shown in an invoice to the corporation.

Litten noted that disagreements had existed about the market price portion of the transfer price:

> One of the problems was disagreements on what was market price. This was due to large volume purchases or items especially manufactured for one division by another.

Nevertheless, he felt that "it did get more transfers going so it was the right move at the time." The president of the Computer Group thought that when the corporate billing policy was implemented, "intracompany business took off." However, the president and group general manager of the Semiconductor Group stated that this policy "didn't work too well." Since it had been abandoned in the mid-1970s, managers were again concerned about lost opportunities for internal trading as a consequence of the policy of exchange autonomy.

The reason for adopting a dual pricing policy at Bacon & Bentham was similar—as explained by Mark Overhold, vice-president and controller:

> We had decentralized so much that each division was acting as a separate company with its own marketing, design, manufacturing, and so on. They had no incentive to help other divisions meet their objectives, but only to meet their own. They gave orders to competitors of inside divisions, which made it awkward when customers wondered why we didn't use our own products.

He believed that dual pricing had increased the amount of internal business and that it had had some positive lasting effects, even though it was discontinued after several years.

Besides using dual pricing with exchange autonomy as a way of providing an incentive for all intracompany transfers, it can be used with a policy of mandated transactions for one or a few key products for which management has established specific objectives. When dual pricing is used with mandated transactions in a company where all other internal transfers are under a policy of exchange autonomy, it is less of an incentive to trade internally than it is a way of compensating managers in the buying profit center for this restriction in their authority. This compensation is in the form of increased profits, although how important this is and how real the profits are considered to be depends on the particular situation, as discussed earlier.

When the selling profit center gains by having its products as mandated purchases by internal customers, it does not need to be compensated beyond receiving a market price for the transfer. When the mandated transaction primarily benefits the buying profit center, there is no obvious way to give a special compensation to the seller in return for this restriction in its authority. Perhaps the only way is an especially generous market price, such as one that does not involve volume discounts.

Bacon & Bentham: Mandated Dual Pricing

The use of dual pricing for computers at Bacon & Bentham is an example of how dual pricing is used for mandated internal transactions in a company practicing exchange autonomy. Implementation of dual pricing for this product was the impetus for using the policy for the company as a whole, although internal transactions were mandated only for computers. Top management made this change in policy to support the strategy of the Computer Division.

The Computer Division was based on an acquisition in 1973 of a small company that manufactured a minicomputer. It became the foundation of the Information Systems Group, which also contained the Controls Division. By 1980, the Controls Division was the largest customer of the Computer Division but the smallest division in the company. Originally, Controls had been reluctant to source from the newly created Computer Division. Its external supplier had a reputation for providing a high-quality, reliable product and the computer component was a large portion of the cost of the final product and played a crucial role in product performance. Richard Dennis, controller of the Information Systems Group, explained the problem:

> There appears to be somewhat of a resistance for divisions to deal with each other. There's some difficulty in doing it. It is hard to imagine a division taking a look at products of a new division, especially if it has a good external supplier.

Bacon & Bentham's CEO believed that the Controls Division's reliance on sourcing from a competitor of his company inhibited the Computer Division's ability to establish a stronger position for itself externally. If internal customers did not want the product, why should external ones want it? He also saw that enlarging the volume of internal sales could help reduce unit costs in the Computer Division. Finally, internal sales also provided an opportunity to identify technical problems that could be fixed to improve product quality.

The CEO decided to mandate internal transactions and use a dual pricing policy. He believed that receiving the computer at full cost would compensate managers in the buying divisions for having their autonomy reduced in this way. He determined the market price portion of the transfer price. The increased volume of internal sales at market price built up profits for the Computer Division, which had been sustaining a loss when it was first acquired.

The Controls Division had been very dissatisfied with this policy at first. As one manager commented: "In general, the divisions resent being dictated to. On occasion it happens, but mostly not." This dissatisfaction wore off as the quality of the computer improved and the selling division became an effective supplier. After several years, the dual pricing policy was eliminated, but the Controls Division continued to source internally now that its own product was designed around Computer's.

The Computer Division negotiated agreements with internal customers in the Controls Division and other divisions on an annual basis at market prices varying between the "most favored customer" price (10 to 15 percent off list price) and the distributor price (35 to 40 percent off list price). Dennis attributed the level of cooperation between the Computer and Controls divisions to their experience during the period of dual pricing and to reinforcement by the current group general manager, who was perceived as fair in his management of interdivisional relationships. Nevertheless, Dennis commented that transfer pricing still involved an element of friction between the divisions:

> Transfer pricing is working. It takes its share of time. It's something we continue to look at. Rarely do both sides feel like they are getting a good deal.

The CEO's mandate that buying divisions source from the Computer Division had extended to purchases that were considered capital assets; in this case, the computer was treated as an asset in managing the division, rather than as a product sold in external markets. A dual pricing policy continued to be used for capital asset purchases. Ken Gould, vice-president of technology in the Semiconductor Group, recalled a time when the CEO had heard that Semiconductor was going to buy a computer from an external supplier:

> Three years ago we were going to buy a scientific computer. We looked at a lot of vendors and it was clear that Prime Computer was the best. This was the boss's month for looking at these things. The chairman went through the roof when he heard about this. He said, "Buy Bacon & Bentham." We had experience with our computers in the past and had experienced lots of agony. It turns out this was primarily because we had used them for the wrong application.

Gould emphasized that the CEO had admonished both sides for the failure to trade internally.

> The chairman said, "I have personally talked to forty-two customers. They're all happy except for you jerks." The chairman also kicked ass on Computer, telling them, "If you can't satisfy internal customers, how will you satisfy external ones?" We bought the computer internally, and it worked great since we were using it for the right application.

Dual Pricing as a Limited and Temporary Solution

Although it is possible to use dual pricing for a specific product for a sustained period of time, it is unlikely that the policy can be used for all of a company's products beyond a limited time frame—probably three to five years. None of the companies in my study that had a large amount of internal transfers ever used dual pricing for all intracompany transactions; the two companies discussed in this chapter who did use this policy for all internal transactions ended it after several years.

There are two major reasons why dual pricing does not offer a long-term solution to the transfer pricing problem for all intracompany sales—both based on the fact that an elimination of the double-counted profits is necessary. The first reason is simply that, with this policy, the whole can be less than the sum of the parts. The second reason is that in certain circumstances, it is especially difficult to forecast the required level of eliminations; as a result, top management often discovers that the company is doing worse than expected. Obviously, the magnitude of these problems increases with the volume of internal sales.

An example will illustrate the importance of the first reason—that it is quite possible for all profit centers to be showing a profit while the company as a whole is losing money. Assume that a company has one selling profit center and one buying profit center. The selling profit center's full costs are $100 per unit, and its general and administrative costs are $80,000 for a period. This profit center sells half of its output externally and half internally at a market price of $150 per unit. The buying profit center adds another $200 per unit in direct costs to the $100 per unit paid to the selling profit center and also has an overhead of $80,000. It sells its product for $400 per unit. Table 5–1 shows the profit center income statements and the consolidated statement after the elimination of double counting for a period in which the selling profit center sold 2,000 units and the buying profit center sold 1,000 units.

The consequences of dual pricing can be seen by comparing these statements with those that would result from the use of full cost and market-based transfer prices. With full cost transfer prices, the sales of the selling profit center would be only $250,000 and it would show a $30,000 loss, which, offset by the $20,000 profit in the buying profit center, equals the corporate loss of $10,000. Similarly, using market transfer prices, the buying profit center's direct costs would be $350,000 and it would show the $30,000 loss. Under dual pricing, the simple sum of profit center profits suggests a corporate profit of $40,000, when in fact the company has a loss of $10,000.

This problem of the whole being less than the simple sum of the parts is greatest when there are many internal transfers, when the difference between the cost and the market price of the intermediate good is large, and when the gross profit margin of the buying profit center is small. When the elimination is sub-

Table 5–1
The Effects of Dual Pricing on a Consolidated Income Statement

	Selling Profit Center	*Buying Profit Center*	*Consolidated*
Sales	$300,000	$400,000	$550,000
Direct costs	200,000	300,000	400,000
Overhead	80,000	80,000	160,000
Profit	20,000	20,000	(10,000)

stantial, it undermines the integrity of the company's management control systems. This is especially critical when the company has low profits or losses.

In the foregoing example, which profit center is responsible for the $10,000 loss being suffered by the company as a whole? The selling profit center can argue that the buying profit center is responsible, since it should pay the same market price for the intermediate good that external customers pay—$150. Thus, a market-based transfer pricing policy would more accurately pinpoint responsibility for corporate losses. In response, the buying profit center might argue that all of its competitors are vertically integrated and receive the intermediate good at $100 per unit, and that the selling profit center gets $150 only by selling this good into a market that has a different use for it. The buying profit center might also argue that the selling profit center could not sell its total output externally. From this perspective, transfers at full cost best pinpoint responsibility for the loss on the selling profit center.

Dual pricing creates two perceptions of the role of the selling profit center in corporate strategy. Disagreements about sharing responsibility for corporate performance are really disagreements about the selling profit center's role, which is ambiguous in dual pricing. This policy makes it impossible for profit centers to calculate their proportional contribution to corporate profits as they do with market-based transfers, which define the selling profit center as a business in its own right. Dual pricing also makes it impossible to hold the buying profit center responsible for the total profitability and return on investment of the assets devoted to its business, as is done with full cost transfers, which define a portion of the selling profit center as a manufacturing unit for the buying profit center.

The second reason dual pricing does not offer a general solution to the transfer pricing problem is that it is difficult to forecast accurately the magnitude of the elimination of double-counted profits. In particular, this elimination is likely to be greater than expected when the company can least afford it. If the buying profit center is having trouble meeting its profit objectives, it can increase internal purchases at cost as a way of increasing its gross margins. It may do this even when internally supplied products do not suit its requirements as well as those supplied externally. If this results in lower product performance, it will hurt longer-term performance. Selling profit centers also have an incentive to sell more internally when they are having difficulty meeting profit targets, especially when buying profit centers have performance problems that make them willing customers.

An increase in internal trading arising from external conditions that make it difficult for profit centers to meet profit objectives increases the required elimination. These external conditions can also affect the company as a whole and can decrease total profits. The higher-than-expected elimination on the lower-than-expected profits makes the surprise especially unpleasant.

A greater-than-expected elimination can result from both higher internal sales on a unit basis and a higher price on the market-based portion of the transfer price. The dual pricing method reduces the incentive of the buying profit center to negotiate for the best price possible from the selling profit center, since no matter what this price is, the buying profit center only pays full cost. This may enable the selling profit center to keep the price higher on internal sales than on external sales when the market is softening, thereby earning greater profits on internal sales. Limitations can be placed on such practices if top management is more actively involved in setting the market-based portion of the transfer price, but this can create its own set of problems when dual pricing is used with exchange autonomy.

Bacon & Bentham and Milton: The Ultimate End of Dual Pricing

The problems of measuring divisional performance and forecasting eliminations caused both Milton and Bacon & Bentham to stop using the dual pricing method. At Bacon & Bentham, dual pricing became an "accounting nightmare" as the volume of internal sales increased and bonuses were affected. The corporate controller stated that this method had "too much flexibility." One year, the elimination was much higher than expected, and the effects were especially severe since it was a year in which corporate performance as a whole was down. The corporate controller concluded: "We've matured and outgrown this system now that we know how to transfer products inside and get the side benefits, such as using inside sales for testing our products."

Milton experienced all of these problems with dual pricing and did away with the dual pricing policy after four years. Herbert Litten, president of the Electronics Group, noted that "the bookkeeping system didn't have the ability to handle it." He also remarked:

> Dual pricing sort of died of its own complexity and conflict. There were some situations where divisions could get something internally that didn't exactly fit their needs, but went ahead and did it since actual full cost was so much less than market price.

One group president thought the divisions had taken advantage of this method:

> There were a lot of problems. Who was going to audit the market prices? Some divisions had rather large corporate charges, and these were higher when they were doing poorly.

When dual pricing was first implemented, the president of the Semiconductor Group had requested and received an exception to being bound by the policy, since actual full cost was greater than market price for many of his products. Although some managers thought dual pricing had been useful for increasing internal coordination and cooperation, others were less sure. The vice-president for strategic planning concluded that this problem had never been solved.

Managing Disincentives

As a way of summarizing the key conclusions of this chapter on exchange autonomy four hypotheses can be added to the twenty-three that were generated in the examination of transfer pricing practices at Alfarabi Chemicals (see chapter 3).

> **Hypothesis 24:** When a policy of exchange autonomy is used, managers have a disincentive to trade internally, so internal transfers will be less than what is optimal for the corporation.
>
> **Hypothesis 25:** The use of hierarchical authority to overcome these disincentives will result in perceptions of unfairness, which will result in conflict.
>
> **Hypothesis 26:** The use of market mechanisms to overcome these disincentives will be more effective and will produce less conflict than the use of hierarchical authority.
>
> **Hypothesis 27:** Dual pricing for all intracompany transfers can be used only for a limited period of time.

These hypotheses, which are subject to empirical test by other researchers, have important implications for managers. First, managers should be aware that if a policy of exchange autonomy is chosen, there is a likelihood that profit centers will trade with each other less than is best for the total company. At the same time, this policy is the least burdensome to higher-level management since it creates less conflict—largely because of the small amount of interaction between the profit centers. This policy is also the most consistent with profit center managers having high levels of authority and responsibility.

Higher-level managers will often be aware of lost opportunities because of the failure of profit centers to work together to develop internal business. Of the three possible solutions to the problem of overcoming disincentives, market mechanisms are most consistent with preserving the authority of profit center managers and treating these internal exchanges in their market context. A dilemma is involved, however, regarding whether or not top management should exercise its authority by requiring that profit centers establish these market mechanisms for internal sales. The best approach is for top management to exercise very gentle persuasion or to create opportunities for internal transactions, such as by increasing the budgets of the profit centers to enable them to devote resources specifically to internal business.

The use of the management hierarchy to overcome disincentives is most problematic in that, at some point, a fine line is crossed between encouraging internal transfers and mandating them. Once this line is crossed, a new transfer pricing policy is in place without being explicitly recognized. Giving only the illusion of decentralized authority can be worse than explicitly taking it away, and when the competitive advantages of internal transactions are significant, it is best to establish an explicit strategy of vertical integration with a policy of mandated internal transactions.

Although dual pricing does not represent a long-term solution to the transfer pricing problem on all internal transactions, it can be used to help profit centers learn to work together. Once they develop an awareness of the advantages of doing so, dual pricing can be replaced by market mechanisms. Dual pricing can also be used when exchange autonomy is replaced by mandated transactions, as a way of compensating the profit centers for a restriction on their authority. In such cases, the use of dual pricing can also be a clear signal that the particular transaction is an exception to the general policy of exchange autonomy.

Effective management of transfer pricing under a policy of exchange autonomy depends on how skillfully the profit center managers and their bosses use administrative processes to implement the policy. How something is done can be of equal or greater importance than *what* is done. Whether hierarchical authority, market mechanisms, dual pricing, or some combination of the three is used, the effectiveness of the approach will depend on managers' awareness that they must establish the five elements of process that are most appropriate given the business context and the managers involved. Because of the large number of variables that must be considered, the managers involved in the transfer pricing situation are in the best position to develop a process that meets their needs. It is especially crucial to recognize that transfer pricing is a general management problem, because it is based on strategy, and that it cannot be resolved by financial executives alone, however important their input may be to the total, general perspective.

6

Mandated Full Cost: Measuring the Cost of Production

There are two principal ways in which transfer prices can be set when a policy of mandated full cost transfers is used: (1) what it actually costs the selling profit center to make the products purchased by the buying profit centers—what is called *actual cost;* and (2) what it should cost the selling profit center to manufacture these products given a set of assumptions—what is called *standard cost*. Between these two measures is a range of possibilities defined by who pays for any differences between what it should have cost to make the product and what it really did cost. When a policy of mandated full cost transfers is used, the transfer pricing problem becomes one of measuring the cost of production for the intermediate good.

Measuring Standard and Actual Costs

Standard costs are what the unit costs of a product should be for a given volume when labor and materials are used efficiently. They are often set by engineering studies that determine what the ratio of inputs to outputs should be in a well-managed plant. It is common to use *practical full capacity*—the volume of output that is possible when the plant is operating at full capacity, with provision for maintenance and unexpected down time (usually 10 to 15 percent less). Standard costs include fixed costs (overhead, plant, and equipment) and variable costs (direct labor and materials). Actual costs for a period are the total of fixed and variable costs actually used. Fixed costs are assessed on a period basis, and as volume increases, the fixed cost portion of unit cost decreases. For the most part, variable costs do not change with changes in volume.[1]

The performance of a cost center is measured by comparing actual costs for the number of units produced with standard costs for the volume that was produced. By convention, actual costs are subtracted from standard costs. Positive variances occur when actual costs are lower; negative variances occur when actual costs are greater.

There are many reasons for variances. Volume may be greater or lower than the volume used in standard cost calculations. These *volume variances* can be distinguished from *efficiency variances* (also called *manufacturing variances*), which reflect relative management efficiencies or inefficiencies on the basis of assumptions made in setting standard costs. Efficiency variances, in turn, can be distinguished from *purchasing variances,* which result from higher or lower prices than those assumed in standard cost calculations for raw materials, energy, labor, and other inputs to the production process.[2]

Standard costs are used as the basis for measuring the performance of the manufacturing function.[3] Vancil (1973) defined such standard cost centers:

> *Standard cost centers* are exemplified by a production department in a factory. The standard quantities of direct labor and materials required for each unit of output are specified. The foreman's objective is to minimize the variance between actual costs and standard costs. (p. 77)

He distinguished them from profit centers, although we have shown that, in practice, organizational units can have both of these roles when internal transfers are on a mandated full cost basis.

Setting standard costs and measuring actual costs can be a very complex procedure. In many cases, no single, obviously correct answer can be determined by technical criteria and accounting conventions alone. Plant and equipment costs must be allocated among all products that are manufactured using the same assets. This allocation can be especially complex for joint and by-products. Kaplan (1982) noted that "the allocation of joint costs gets the accountant involved in some of the more arbitrary and difficult-to-defend decisions associated with the profession."[4] Another controversial problem is determining what overhead and capital costs should also be charged to the product. Overhead costs are incurred at both the factory and profit center level. Capital costs exist for both fixed resources and working capital. Decisions regarding which overhead and capital costs to allocate among products are matters of management judgment and thus are subject to dispute.[5]

Paine Chemical Company: A Problem in Cost Allocation

An example of the kind of problems that can occur with cost allocations occurred at Paine Chemical Company. The product in question was transferred by a mandated market-based transfer policy, and both profit center managers believed that the transfer price was fair. The dispute between them was over how the selling profit center manager allocated joint costs between the transferred product and a product that was sold externally. Nicholas Pappas, business center manager of Organic Specialty Chemicals, purchased a cellulose resin from Jason Welch, business center manager of Specialty Chemicals. Pappas was concerned that Welch's allocation of costs across products understated his own profits on internal sales, which could be used to justify not investing in capacity to fulfill internal needs.

The production of this cellulose resin yielded two forms, mono and poly, in the ratio of nine to one. Pappas purchased 70 percent of his 1.5 million pounds of polycellulose resin (PCR) requirements from Welch and the rest externally. Only two U.S. producers and some Japanese and Chilean producers made PCR for the merchant market. Paine's output of PCR was determined by the maximum quantity it could produce without reinvesting in the business, since demand for monocellulose resin (MCR) was not growing.

List price for PCR was $1.00 per pound. Pappas purchased from a foreign external supplier at American list price plus freight ($1.08 per pound), since the U.S. producers were reluctant to sell to him. The internal transfer price of $.95 per pound made internal sourcing attractive, and Pappas wanted to meet as much of his needs internally as possible. However, he was concerned that although his needs were increasing, the amount of PCR available from Specialty Chemicals would not increase, because it was not investing in new capacity.

Pappas attributed the problem to Welch's assignment of costs:

> I'm not happy with the way he assigns costs inside his manufacturing facility. When it is transferred at list less 5 percent, it is assumed a guy makes money on the transfer. But Welch allocates 50 percent of the fixed costs to PCR, even though it is only 10 percent of output based on pounds. This inflates PCR costs. By heavily weighting costs onto a captive customer, it makes my profit contribution to his business look worse. Then nobody can justify building more PCR capacity. It looks like I will have to go outside for more.

Pappas talked with Welch, who had argued that equipment and maintenance costs were higher for the PCR portion of the facility. To add insult to injury, Pappas believed that this cost allocation scheme understated MCR's costs, which enabled Welch to price it lower but achieve the same profit margins.

The Need for Strategic Clarity

A policy of mandated full cost transfers cannot work if each profit center's role in the corporate strategy is not clear. Such clarity must be reinforced by the ways in which performance is measured, evaluated, and rewarded. There are two reasons why this clarity can be difficult to achieve. First, with mandated full cost transfers, selling profit centers do not earn the same profits or losses on internal transfers as they would if market prices were used. This needs to be taken into account in measuring, evaluating, and rewarding performance.

Second, mandated full cost transfers create interdependencies between the profit centers, which can cause the actions and outcomes of one to affect the performance measures of the other. The extent of this interdependence depends on the particular variation of the full cost transfer price that is used. It is also affected by whether buying profit center managers have the authority to choose the particular plant from which it will source when several make the same product. Restrictions on this authority increase the extent of interdependence.

Full cost transfer prices that closely tie the performance measures of the two profit centers together are most appropriate when their businesses are intimately related, either technologically or in terms of external markets. In these cases, it is especially important for top management to make it explicitly clear to profit center managers that it is aware of the effects profit centers can have on the performance measures of other profit centers, and to evaluate and reward them accordingly. This requires the exercise of subjective judgment to assess the contribution of each profit center to corporate performance.

The interdependence of performance measures between the selling and the buying profit centers is greatest when actual full cost transfer prices are used. Thus, the transfer price is an effective way for top management to emphasize how closely the fate of each profit center is tied to that of the other. Many accountants fail to see the value of this strategic purpose in their many criticisms about the use of this transfer pricing policy. Common criticisms are that it inhibits measurement of performance and that it can lead to improper capital investment decisions.

When the method of actual full cost is used for transfers, the costs incurred in a production period (typically, a month) are distributed among all users of the product in proportion to their share of the total output. Positive and negative volume, efficiency, and purchasing variances are shared among all users of the product. The financial responsibility of profit center managers is much greater on paper than their authority to fulfill this responsibility. For example, the unit costs of a product that the selling profit center sells externally will fluctuate for a given volume as the volume of the buying profit center fluctuates. Thus, if the external volume of the buying profit center is so high that actual unit costs are below standard costs, the selling profit center will pay less than expected for the product it uses for its own needs, and vice versa.

Similarly, unit costs to buying profit centers will fluctuate as the total volume of the selling profit center fluctuates with changes in external sales or changes in demand from other buying profit centers. Because actions by and outcomes of both buying and selling profit centers affect the results of each other, both positively and negatively, this type of transfer price emphasizes their shared responsibility for joint outcomes. There is direct interdependence between selling and buying profit centers and indirect interdependence between buying profit centers that source from the same selling profit center.

A distinctive characteristic of actual full cost transfer prices is that the price is not known until after the exchange has taken place. This is in sharp contrast to the prevailing view in economic and accounting theory—that prices are information for making resource allocation decisions. Production-level decisions and external product-pricing decisions by both buying and selling profit centers are made before the period commences, but the unit costs—the transfer prices—are not known until after the period has ended. If previous period transfer prices are used in making production-level and pricing decisions, these will fluctuate as well, thereby leading to changes in these decisions for the next period. The result will be constant oscillation or a continuing spiral, which will hurt the performance of both profit centers.

For example, if the volume of the selling profit center is high in period 1, the unit costs for the transferred good will be low. This will encourage buying profit centers to order large quantities (probably for period 3, since they will not have the results for period 1 until some time in period 2, after the books have been closed) and price the final product very competitively because of the cheap raw material or component part. The selling profit center will also have an incentive to produce as much of this final good for the external market as possible and to price very competitively. One resulting problem could be constraints on capacity and the need to allocate the transferred good—a further restriction on the authority of the profit center managers.

Another problem could be that demand fails to materialize, unit costs are higher than expected, losses are incurred from competitive pricing, and profit centers reduce their demand for a later period and/or raise their prices. Obviously, instabilities in output levels and prices will hurt performance through manufacturing inefficiencies and marketing ineffectiveness. These problems occur, however, only when pricing and production-level decisions are made on the basis described here.

In practice, these decisions are not made in this simplistic fashion. They typically involve higher-level managers who provide guidance to ensure that the efforts of both buying and selling profit centers are coordinated. Such "guidance" may include centralized decision making on prices and production levels, which is consistent with the restriction on profit center managers' decision-making authority when mandated actual full cost transfers are used. In this situation, profit center managers have much less responsibility for financial outcomes and less authority to achieve them than when exchange autonomy exists.

Aquinas Chemicals Company: The Viability of Actual Full Cost Transfers

Those who take a narrow perspective on the transfer pricing problem sometimes argue that actual full cost transfers are used only by companies with unsophisticated management control systems. Aquinas Chemicals, a successful multibillion-dollar diversified specialty chemical company with a very sophisticated management information and control system, is a counterexample to this claim. It vividly illustrates how actual full cost transfer prices can be used effectively when there are high levels of interdependence between profit centers. A key component was the extensive use of subjective judgment in evaluating and rewarding performance. In this and a number of other ways, Aquinas was similar to Rousseau Chemical Corporation, which also used full cost transfers.

Aquinas was organized into a matrix structure based on geographic areas and worldwide product lines. The geographic dimension focused on short-term, annual plans. The product dimension was concerned with longer-term performance and was responsible for R&D and capital investments. Extensive interdependencies existed between product lines and geographic areas. Business directors had a product line boss and a geographic area boss, both of whom participated in evaluating their performance and determining their raises and bonuses. Business directors were measured on the basis of net profits after tax and return on net assets (RONA). Coordination of interdependencies required extensive negotiation among managers and a high degree of centralization of authority.

Nearly all of the internal transfers were made on an actual full cost basis. (The exception was by-products, which were transferred to other profit centers at 90 percent of market price and then sold externally.) Profit center managers' sourcing autonomy was especially restricted, since they were told which plant to source from. Matching internal buyers with sellers was a complex decision that involved balancing transportation costs and optimal plant loadings; it could only be made at a high level in the organization. Since costs varied according to plant, this decision had a substantial effect on the business directors' financial results. And since actual full cost transfer prices were used, the results were also affected by changes in demand by other business directors who sourced from the same plant.

Investments at Aquinas were allocated as low as the level above the business directors to measure return on net assets. This sometimes caused problems, as the company's controller, Paul Donnelly acknowledged. He also said that more complaints about variances arose at levels below the business director. At that level and above, they tended to even out, given the number of plants and products involved:

> At a more refined level we have more problems. Most of the problems are in the problem businesses. A guy here watches his numbers very carefully. It is easier to fuss about that than to look at the fundamental problems with the business.
>
> People think they are getting hosed but I don't think so. I don't know how much of the complaints are from the finance guys who have to explain the numbers or from business managers who have genuine questions.

Although they expressed some concern about transfer prices, most managers did not believe that their evaluations and rewards were unfair. Nor was there much support for changing the current method. Donnelly explained that this was partly because transfer prices were not perceived as affecting product-pricing, production-level, or capital-investment decisions:

> The alternatives are worse than what we have, such as using market-based pricing or keeping track of who gets favorable and unfavorable variances. Financial information is important, but it doesn't provide yes or no decisions for managers. We still pay them to run the business.

Donnelly believed that, despite the problems, managers were accustomed to using actual full cost transfers. He thought that bad experiences in the past were the main reason for resistance to market-based transfer prices. "People throw up a psychological block," he said. "A lot is history and how people have been trained to look at information." At Aquinas Chemicals, managers had learned to run their businesses using actual full cost transfer prices, and they saw no major reason to change.

The close relationship between strategy and transfer pricing policy is further illustrated by the fact that actual full cost transfers are sometimes used in companies where they are an exception to the general policy. This often occurs when one profit center is subdivided into two or more. There are a number of reasons why management may want to make such a subdivision, including creating opportunities by increasing the number of general manager positions, increased diversity of product lines, and increased complexity in the external markets. For all of these reasons, corporate performance may be enhanced by refining the company's definition of the businesses in which it competes.

Even when this approach promises advantages, the fact remains that the new profit centers are created from a common technological base. It may not be possible to make each profit center self-sufficient in manufacturing capacity because of economies of scale (for example, three small plants making the same product may not be as efficient as one large one) or because the technology simply is not separable (for example, a chemical by-product can only be produced at the same time as another chemical product; of course, which chemical is the by-product can be a matter of definition and depends on how the company defines the businesses it is in). The result will be a high degree of interdependence, reflected in substantial transfers between profit centers. Actual full cost transfers are a way of reinforcing this interdependence to counterbalance any temptations that may emerge to place the interests of one's own profit center above those of the corporation.

In some cases, the ultimate objective may be to use standard full cost or even market-based transfer prices. However, since it is not always possible to implement these policies immediately, actual full cost transfers are an interim policy. This situation may exist, for example, when standard costs have not been established for a particular product or when no obvious external market prices exist. In the past, it may not have been necessary to establish standard costs for a particular component used within a single profit center. For certain by-products, there is no external market and thus no market price.

Exception Examples of Actual Full Cost Transfers

The role of strategy in determining transfer pricing policy, illustrated from a corporate perspective in the case of Aquinas Chemicals, can be further emphasized with some examples of the use of actual full cost transfers in companies that primarily used mandated market-based and/or exchange autonomy policies. These examples show how subunit strategies can lead to a transfer pricing policy that is different from the policy commonly used in the company if these subunit strategies vary from the more general corporate strategy. The first two examples, from Paine Chemical Company (which primarily used mandated market-based transfers) and Hobbes Instrument Company (which primarily used mandated market-based and exchange autonomy transfers), were cases in which this policy was working well. In the third case, at Bacon & Bentham (which primarily used exchange autonomy transfers), this policy was in the process of being replaced because it did not support the strategies of the two profit centers.

At Paine Chemical Company, the Organic Chemicals Division had been subdivided into three profit centers—called business centers—when the company reorganized from a multidivisional to a product/function matrix structure. The Organic Chemicals Business Center, under Bernard Michels, supplied the basic raw material to itself and to Organic Specialty Chemicals, under Nicholas Pappas, and Paper Chemicals, under David Winter. Pappas explained why this method worked:

> You must have individuals who have as their priorities the corporate goals. They must be able to justify bonuses and pats on the back in achieving corporate, not divisional goals. The first question we always ask is: "Is this good for the corporation?" If the answer is yes, one business center makes a sacrifice for another with no questions asked.

This emphasis on optimizing the performance of all three business centers was facilitated by the fact that all three managers knew each of the businesses well—having worked in them in the past when they were all in one division. Furthermore, Pappas had previously worked for Michels, and Michels had worked for Winter for many years. Pappas noted the importance of these relationships and the fact that all three men had been appointed just recently to general manager positions:

> Bernard, David and I are business friends. I respect their abilities. A lot of this is working because the three of us have been in the others' shoes. We're all new to this level. It is not in our interest to fight amongst ourselves.

He compared their working relationships and business approach to that of a family:

> We all understand the other business centers' needs pretty clearly. We all believe each business plays a role in the family. If the course for the family is clearly understood, we will make decisions in the interest of the total family.

At Hobbes Instrument Company, the Systems Division in the Electronics Group had been similarly split into three divisions: Advanced Systems, Basic Systems, and Intermediate Systems. Advanced Systems sold very little to the other two divisions but was highly interdependent with Basic Systems as one of its largest customers. Basic Systems and Intermediate Systems did not trade with each other, but Intermediate Systems had some sales to Advanced Systems. Al Webster, group director of financial analysis, doubted that the actual full cost transfer method that these subdivisions used would be changed:

> The autonomy hasn't been there with the Systems Division, so we don't expect to change the transfer basis. Each is so interdependent they are not trying to get profits out of the other. These divisions are used to being together.

The general manager of the Advanced Systems Division agreed with him and believed that "we need some refinements on internal sales in terms of how it's handled, but basically the procedure is working okay."

Actual full cost transfers were used even at Bacon & Bentham, a company that generally relied on a policy of exchange autonomy because of its strong emphasis on decentralized authority and responsibility. Special circumstances made an exception of the two semiconductor divisions—Products and Programs. The Products Division, which sold catalog devices that could be bought through distributors, was about five times the size of the Programs Division, which made special devices for individual customers. Both types of semiconductors had been made in a single division until four years earlier. The subdivision implemented at that time was incomplete, however, since both divisions were on the same set of books, and their general managers shared a bonus pool.

The two divisions had a capacity-sharing program, with Products sourcing from Programs. On small, one-time orders, Products would manufacture according to a shop order and charge what was for all practical purposes actual direct labor and materials costs. For larger orders, a markup to cover overhead was included. Although some thought was given to including a markup for profit to make these transfers similar to all others in the company, this had been rejected as too complicated.

Actions were being taken that were likely to lessen this interdependence. Each division was to have its own set of books the following year, and the bonus pool would be separated. Winthrop Hector, controller of the larger division, anticipated that Mason Robinson, general manager of Programs, would want a markup to include profit. He noted that Programs advocated greater separation:

> Every meeting we go to now, Programs says it's getting screwed. They say that if they were stand-alone they would have lower overhead so they could be more competitive and get more business.

In turn, Products criticized Programs for having inefficient manufacturing methods and preferred not to source there even on the current occasional basis. This was agreeable to Programs, which wanted all of its capacity for its own use. Actual full cost transfers had been appropriate in a situation of high interdependence, but the situation was contrary to Bacon & Bentham's overall management approach of emphasizing divisional autonomy. Once this situation changed to one more consistent with the company's corporate strategy, so would the transfer pricing method policy.

The use of standard full cost transfer prices makes it possible to reduce the extent to which the performance of one profit center affects the performance measures of others. Since standard costs are set and known before the period begins, buying profit centers know the transfer price before the exchange takes place, in contrast to actual full cost transfer prices. Since they are paying the cost for which the selling profit center is supposed to be able to manufacture the product—given certain assumptions about volume, production efficiencies, and raw materials and other costs—buyers are not affected by conditions beyond their control that influence the performance of the selling profit center. This makes it posssible to place more emphasis on financial measures in measuring, evaluating, and rewarding the performance of buying profit centers. Thus, the use of standard cost transfer prices is a way of producing performance measures that reflect responsibility more commensurate with the authority of the buying profit center managers.

One variation of standard cost transfers is to allocate a portion of the investment in the selling profit center to users of the product on a basis proportional to their stake in the total output. If a buying profit center takes 30 percent of the output, it will be allocated 30 percent of the investment. Allocating investments in this way emphasizes the cost center role of the selling profit center in internal transfers, as if it were a manufacturing unit of the buying profit center that is responsible for its return on investment. The ROI for the selling profit center is then calculated on the basis of investment applied to external sales as well as profits earned. The ROI for the buying profit center is calculated on an investment base, which includes its stake in the selling profit center's assets as if these assets were located in the buying profit center itself.

Although the use of standard cost transfers partially resolves the interdependence of performance measures, it does not change the fact that the selling profit center does not receive the same profits or losses on internal sales as it would with market prices. If the selling profit center does not accept its cost center role, the use of standard cost transfers can exacerbate the situation, since standard cost transfers more clearly pinpoint financial responsibility than actual cost transfers do. With actual cost transfers, there is an understanding among the managers involved that measures of financial performance are interrelated, which makes it more difficult to compare them across profit centers. Standard cost transfers make this comparison more meaningful while at the same time denying the selling profit center the opportunity to earn profits on internal transactions.

Locke Chemical Company: Problems from Ambiguity in Role Definition

Locke Chemical Company was an example of a company that experienced severe problems with standard full cost transfer pricing because of the failure of the selling profit center to accept its role as a manufacturing unit on internal sales. Even though the performance measures of the buying and the selling profit centers affected each other much less than was the case at Aquinas Chemicals, disagreements about transfer prices were much greater. This was because there was less clarity at Locke than at Aquinas about how all of the profit centers fit into the corporate strategy.

Locke was a multibillion-dollar, highly vertically integrated chemical company that produced raw materials, intermediate products, and end products through production processes that involved two to four steps. In production technology and strategy, it was similar to Aquinas and Rousseau, and it made capital investment decisions in a similar way. Locke used a form of portfolio planning in evaluating business investment proposals and had to take account of their impact on all stages of the production process. Scott Wakefield, corporate controller, emphasized that although studies of investment decisions were based on calculations of the consequences for relevant products, "we don't run this business simply by the numbers—we do it by long-term strategic consequences."

As a marketing-oriented company, Locke emphasized to investors that its businesses were those of its end products, including consumer chemicals, plastics, and molded products. Since 1972, it had been organized into four reasonably self-contained divisions, each of which had all the necessary functional resources to run a business, although a substantial number of products were transferred internally. These mandated internal transfers were on a market price basis. The division general managers were all respected senior executives who carried the title of corporate vice-president and were members of the board of directors. Corporate involvement in divisional operations was minimal, and these general managers had substantial decision-making autonomy to manage their businesses as they thought best. However, internal transactions were mandated.

The primary performance measure for these divisions was called performance income (PI), which was similar to pretax net profits for the company as a whole and included a charge for working capital. Asset management was also important in evaluating a division general manager's performance. Performance income and asset management measures were the basis for determining a division general manager's bonus, with an adjustment to reflect other factors, such as decisions affecting other divisions. Although more emphasis was placed on individual profit center performance than at Rousseau, it was not as great as at Bacon & Bentham or Milton Electronics. Arthur Lipkin, vice-president and general manager of the Plastics Division, noted: "you have to keep in mind that there is a culture here that if an individual is caught maximizing his self-interest at the expense of the corporation, he is in deep trouble." Nevertheless, Nathan Farber, controller of the Molding Division, believed that "it has become increasingly hard to think of oneself as a Locke employee first when incentives are largely based on the Molding Division's results." This was one of the reasons that the bonus plan "had been buffeted" ever since its installation in 1974.

Another aspect of the company's culture was a higher level of conflict than existed at Rousseau Chemical Corporation. At one time, the practice had been to avoid this conflict through "pork barrel trading." This was changed by David Cartman, a CEO who had been brought in from outside the company and still occupied this position. He had worked at developing an atmosphere in which conflict could be aired more openly; opinion varied about how successful he had been. One manager expressed his view:

> There aren't many disputes at the division general manager level. We strive for a degree of consensus that is unwarranted and don't like open disputes. To really take on somebody else is not the style here. Cartman has done a lot to try to overcome this tendency to avoid conflict.

Paul Hayden, vice-president and general manager of the Molding Division, disagreed:

> Conflict is handled pretty damn openly. We are not afraid to air our disagreements to try to come to a consensus or agreement. Despite Cartman's strong and domineering characteristics, he encourages others to speak out beforehand. He has fostered a group of people willing to disagree with him.

Formation of the Basic Chemicals Division

One issue on which conflict had been apparent and open was the formation of the Basic Chemicals Division in 1976. The idea of creating this fifth division out of products from the other four was initiated by one of the executive vice-presidents. He wanted to combine all raw material or "building-block" chemicals that were the foundation of the company's end products into a single division. This was similar to an idea that had been rejected at Rousseau Chemical Corporation. His reasoning was that combining all of the chemicals whose production processes were based on large-scale, capital-intensive process technology would make it possible to apply the company's best process manufacturing skills to developing improvements that would drive costs down. This change was implemented on January 1, 1977.

The Basic Chemicals Division contained businesses that manufactured seven basic products. (An eighth building-block product was retained in the Consumer Division for some special reasons.) Five criteria were used to identify these building-block products: (1) further expansion would be only for internal use; (2) the company satisfied all its internal needs for this product; (3) the product was not available in the external market at the quantities needed by the company; (4) whether transfer prices were full cost or market price could affect downstream business decisions; and (5) transfers at cost instead of market price would improve outsiders' interpretations of line of business results. The eight building-block chemicals were all transferred on a standard full cost transfer price that was referred to as cost plus investment (C&I), since investment in the new division was allocated to the buying divisions in calculating ROI. Depending on the product, between 30 percent and 95 percent of the output was used internally, and the rest was traded externally. The Basic Chemicals Division was also responsible for another thirty products that it sold primarily in the external marketplace and for which it received market price on internal transfers.

Ambiguity about Cost and Profit Center Roles

For strategic reasons, top management had split the Basic Chemicals Division into cost and profit center roles. This caused problems from the very beginning. One of the most vocal opponents had been Ed Jakowsky, general manager of manufacturing of the Basic Chemicals Division, who was responsible for over $2 billion in plant and equipment and 6,000 people. He recalled giving his opinion to Don Falk, the general manager of the newly created division, and to Cartman, the CEO:

> I went to Falk and expressed what I thought about C&I. I told him I was concerned from both a manufacturing and a company standpoint. How do we measure ourselves and keep motivation? The word "marketing" wasn't in our charter. Instead we had manufacturing, technology, and commercial departments. We had a hell of a morale problem coming right off the bat. Falk agreed with me.
>
> Within thirty minutes I was in Cartman's office with the top ten people. He said, "Mr. Jakowsky, I understand you have some concerns." Shields [vice-president of finance] rebutted. I said, "I appreciate the opportunity to be heard," and walked out.
>
> I haven't changed my mind one damn bit.

The problem of how to measure the performance of the Basic Chemicals Division was the underlying cause of many managers' dissatisfaction in this division.

Performance income was used as the primary measure, just as it was for the other divisions. Like Jakowsky, other managers were concerned that their division had a different status from the others and that this caused a morale problem. However, no one stated that this morale problem had led to performance problems.

Profit center status was important, because a great deal of emphasis had been placed on the importance of the division general manager's role when the other divisions had been set up five years before the formation of Basic Chemicals. Managers in other divisions felt that giving the new division marketing capabilities (if not the name) had confused their charter. Instead, they felt that other divisions should have been given responsibility for marketing products sold externally, which would have emphasized Basic Chemicals' role as a corporate manufacturing cost center that supplied raw materials to all divisions.

Don Falk, the first general manager of Basic Chemicals, had experience and seniority that gave him higher status than the general managers of the divisions that bought from him. Managers within his division and in the buying divisions believed that he had put more emphasis on profits than on lowering costs. Because of his competence and personality, "Falk was inclined to throw his weight around. He would intimidate whenever he could." Don Falk thus exacerbated the ambiguity about the role of Basic Chemicals.

Hayden recognized the effect of Falk's behavior and how others reacted to him:

> Falk wanted to run the best manufacturing division possible. He also wanted it to be a profit center, as he had run one before. He believed in doing an outstanding job at anything you gave him. But the aura of trust around him was not as great as around others.

This view was confirmed by Leo Derby, who had been controller of the division at the time:

> Having been at Basic Chemicals, I know we were striving to fulfill the intended mission. Falk's main concern was the cost side of the ledger. He put a lot of pressure on manufacturing people to drive down costs. He also emphasized profits quite a bit.

Others outside the division thought that profits received the greatest emphasis. Farber commented, "At the first top management meeting, Basic Chemicals pushed for more profitable orders—this from a division whose charter was to minimize costs."

Falk was replaced at the end of 1977, and his successor was replaced in the middle of 1979. With each succession, the cost and profit center roles of the Basic Chemicals Division became clearer. Derby commented that, over time, there had been "a steady improvement in an attitude of emphasizing process and step-change technological improvements to drive costs down." (The term *step-change technological improvements* was used at the company to refer to major changes in process technology that made nonincremental reductions in manufacturing costs.)

The current general manager had been most explicit in making this emphasis. However, some problems still remained from using performance income as a measure of Basic Chemicals' performance. Victor Vallon, vice-president and general manager of General Chemicals, agreed that the latest general manager of Basic Chemicals had placed a strong emphasis on lowering costs, but he remained skeptical about how completely that division would accept its role. He noted that in the top management meeting held every Monday, "the bulk of Basic Chemicals' briefings are devoted to profitability."

The failure to determine how to measure the performance of Basic Chemicals inhibited its ability to maintain both cost and profit center roles. This failure resulted partly from emphasizing objective quantitative measures for the division, to which financial rewards were tied. Other division general managers were also evaluated in this way, and the incentive for conflict became apparent in disputes over the standard cost transfer prices.

Problems in Allocating Variances

The other major problem with full cost transfers, closely related to but distinct from maintaining strategic clarity, is that variances from standard costs can be caused by actions and outcomes of both buying and selling profit centers. Although standard full cost transfer prices insulate buying centers from events that affect the performance of the selling profit centers and other buying profit centers, they do not insulate selling profit centers from events that affect the performance of buying profit centers. As a result, variances are reported in the selling profit center, and they affect both its performance as a cost center on internal sales and its performance as a profit center on external sales.

The consequence of retaining all variances in the selling profit centers is that they obtain all of the advantages reflected in positive variances and all of the disadvantages reflected in negative variances of events beyond their control. They also receive positive and negative variances because of events that are considered to be under their control—although the control can be very limited, such as control over general business conditions or fluctuations in raw material costs. Buying profit centers are protected from the negative consequences of their own and others' actions, but they do not have the opportunity to benefit by them. Obviously, both profit centers have an incentive to be able to establish what variances they deserve credit (or blame) for as distinguished from those for which others deserve blame (or credit).

The manner in which variances are allocated identifies which profit center is responsible for better or worse production costs than expected. This is especially important when a great deal of emphasis is placed on measuring the selling profit center as a standard cost center on internal sales. Even when both profit centers accept a full cost transfer pricing policy, there are likely to be disputes over variances, since they affect measures of cost control and profitability. The greater the emphasis on profit center financial results in measuring, evaluating, and rewarding performance, the greater will be the conflict over how standard costs are established and how variances are allocated.

When variances are allocated, the transfer price is some number between actual full cost and standard full cost. As a result, the selling and buying profit centers do not know the ultimate price of the transaction until after it has occurred, the bookkeeping period has closed, and the variances have been calculated and allocated. This final price is likely to differ from the expected price—that is, the standard cost.

Although, in theory, the three types of variances (volume, efficiency, and purchasing) can be separated in terms of which profit center is responsible for them, in practice there is always some ambiguity. The selling profit center does not have much influence on the volume of internal sales, which is determined largely by the needs of the buying profit center, and it is not usually considered responsible for volume variances. However, it is certainly more responsible for volume variances resulting from external sales, although it does not completely control the external events that produce those variances. Since the selling profit center has more control over efficiency and purchasing variances, it is usually held responsible for them. However, the complexities of interdependence make it difficult to assign responsibility for a variance unambiguously to one profit center or the other. A buying profit center that requests products that require interruptions in planned long production runs in the selling profit center may cause negative manufacturing variances. Similarly, problems or bottlenecks in the production process caused by the selling profit center may lead to lower-than-anticipated levels of output and negative volume variances.

There is further ambiguity regarding whether or not standard costs are "what they should be." If they are "too tight," the selling profit center manager may argue that negative variances are caused by unreasonable expectations about capacity utilization, manufacturing efficiencies, and costs of raw materials and other inputs. Conversely, managers in the buying profit center may argue that positive variances result from "too high" standard costs that are caused by incorrect assumptions about volume, manufacturing efficiency, and the cost of input factors.

Since variances are a measure of performance for the selling profit center as a cost center and also affect the profitability of the buying profit center, they create incentives for gaming on the part of both managers for which formal management systems provide no technical solutions. For example, management in the buying profit center may suspect that management in the selling profit center is setting standard costs too high to guarantee a positive variance and thus "good performance." One response to this is to evaluate performance on the basis of the absolute value of the total variance, which may be small. This can lower the incentive to decrease costs; instead, the actual costs may be "managed" to come as close as possible to standard costs, even if this entails some suboptimal use of resources.

Similar opportunities for gaming exist when investments are also allocated. Investments are often allocated on the basis of calculations, made during the budgeting cycle, of the proportion a buying profit center will take of the total output. This gives a buyer the opportunity to consciously underestimate its total requirements at budget time. If this estimate is not changed to reflect actual results, and if underestimating the quantity of a product required has not prevented the buying profit center from obtaining what it actually needs, the buying profit center is held responsible for a lower investment base, and its ROI is higher than it would be if it were calculated on its actual use of resources.

Locke Chemical Company: The Difficulty of Allocating Variances

Locke Chemical Company used a standard cost transfer price for the building-block chemicals in the Basic Chemicals Division and allocated all variances and investments in an attempt to measure the total financial responsibility of buying profit center managers. The company experienced severe problems with these allocations, since buying profit center managers often felt that they were being charged for variances that were beyond their control. At the root of this problem was the manner in which standard costs were set. The problem was exacerbated by the lack of strategic clarity about the role of the Basic Chemicals Division and criteria for performance measurement, evaluation, and reward, which were largely based on divisional financial results. As a result, although a continuing series of adjustments were made in how the transfer price was calculated, no real improvement was achieved until some clarification in the role of this division was established and changes were made in the process for setting standard costs.

Calculation of Transfer Prices

The original policy developed when the Basic Chemicals Division was created in 1977 was that transfer prices of building-block chemicals were calculated as inventory standard cost at capacity, plus packaging and shipping costs, plus a fixed budgeted product surcharge to cover start-up, obsolescence, and marketing, administration, and technical (MAT) expenses. Inventories were allocated to buying divisions, and they paid a finance charge on them to the corporate level. Variances were not allocated for raw material and utility costs. Several difficulties immediately arose with this policy. The product surcharge was originally set at 5 percent of inventory costs for all products, but buying divisions complained that this was too high for some products. After several years, the surcharge was calculated for each product separately and ranged from 1 percent to 6 percent.

The MAT portion of this surcharge had proved very difficult to determine; it was calculated by allocating these costs in proportion to the share of total investment that a product represented. In spite of these technical efforts to refine the MAT calculation, it remained controversial. In one division, the controller noted that the division received 60 percent of these expenses for one building-block chemical, even though Basic Chemicals incurred no marketing costs on these internal sales. Nearly all these marketing expenses came from external sales. He also noted that Basic Chemicals had undertaken some technical programs that never would have been undertaken if his division had been responsible, because it would have treated the product as a cash cow. Nevertheless, the buying division was charged 60 percent of these expenses.

Locke Chemical's policy included investment allocations and a take-or-pay provision. A buying division was charged for the amount requested in the budget and the proportionate investment, even if it ended up taking less. This incentive to keep divisions from purposely underestimating their needs and to hold them responsible for negative volume variances was strengthened by charging them spot market prices for demand greater than anticipated. Tom Hewitt, assistant controller of corporate accounting, recalled how controversial this portion of the policy had been:

> The issue of volume variances has driven everybody crazy. The initial policy was that if the receiving division took less than planned, it got a negative variance. If it took more, it paid market price for the difference. The downstream divisions said that the policy was a lose/lose situation for them, since there was only one point where they could break even.

Disputes over Variances

Another effect of this policy was that in some instances, the buying division was charged a negative volume variance but the product was sold externally. Basic Chemicals was, in effect, paid twice for the same product, which contributed to its profits and further confused its cost center role. To resolve these problems, the policy was changed so that a fixed cost penalty was assessed only if idle capacity was not used for another internal or external buyer, and buying divisions paid spot market prices for demand in excess of that requested in the budget only if there was no capacity. This policy was applied on a by-source-location basis so that buying divisions that sourced a product from several plants could not balance out positive and negative deviations from plan. Volume commitments could be changed during the year through negotiations between the selling and buying division general managers.

Inventories were allocated according to the percentage of actual volume taken by the buying divisions, and a working capital charge of 14 percent was calculated and included in the transfer price. As with fixed costs in actual full cost transfers, buying divisions could end up with higher or lower capital charges for the same volume if the total output of the selling division was less or greater than expected, respectively. Managers in the buying division often complained that allocated inventories were too high. According to Leo Derby, assistant controller of financial analysis, "Generally, disputes on inventories are resolved to nobody's satisfaction."

Another complaint about the original cost plus investment (C&I) policy was that raw material and utility variances were not allocated to buying divisions, and these were always positive. This raised the suspicion in the minds of buying division managers that Basic Chemicals estimated raw material and utility prices at levels higher than those at which it could purchase them to ensure itself a positive variance. Since January 1, 1980, this portion of the policy had been changed so that both positive and negative raw material and utility variances were allocated to buying divisions on a monthly basis according to year-to-date quantities. Resolution of this problem had required many meetings and studies and a series of recommendations. Tom Hewitt, who had been deeply involved in this controversy, expressed his view about how such transfer pricing disputes were managed:

> At my level we spend a hell of a lot of time trying to iron out disputes. Cartman [the CEO] spends no time. The top fifteen or twenty people think it is working okay.

> The pattern I've seen is someone comes in and bitches. A task force does a study and makes a recommendation that is not exactly what the aggrieved party wants but doesn't please the accused either. Everybody is pissed. The dust settles for six months and then starts again.

Problems in Determining Standard Costs

Although problems with the surcharge, the take-or-pay provision, and the treatment of raw materials and utility variances had consumed a great deal of management time and attention, they were secondary issues compared to the problem of setting standard costs. This was the source of the greatest controversy about transfer prices; buying divisions suspected Basic Chemicals of setting standard costs it knew were higher than actual costs would be. In the process by which standard costs were set, there was no involvement by the buying divisions or corporate staff. This problem was exacerbated by a lack of trust among buying division general managers in the general manager of Basic Chemicals, who they believed had not accepted his division's role as a cost center on internal sales.

Ron Shields, vice-president for finance, understood why there had been so much controversy:

> All of the problems we ran into were due to questions about the integrity of standard costs. It is here that games can really be played. They should have been reviewed by the corporate controller and corporate vice-president for manufacturing. As it was, they were determined by the general manager of Basic Chemicals. There have always been nice, positive variances from them. A suspicious mind would think they were set too soft. All of the problems have centered on standard costs.

This problem had been greatest when the new division was first established and Don Falk was its general manager. Only minimal improvement occurred during the time Falk's successor, Martin Imholz, was general manager. Although Imholz was considered to be a manager of high integrity, he communicated poorly. One manager explained:

> He was not a poor communicator with the intent to use it to his advantage, like Falk. His attitude was more "I'm running things well so don't step into my territory." He was very rational, with a strong manufacturing background.

Imholz's lack of communication with other divisions did not allay suspicions about the standard costs, although he did make some improvements and tightened them up a bit.

The suspicions were sustained by the fact that Basic Chemicals continued to show positive variances. The same manager continued:

> During this time Basic Chemicals still had a habit of beating standard costs. There were some great disparities. They did this on purpose so they could show a profit. I never got this resolved with Martin Imholz. He felt that beating standards was a good motivational tool. Corporate elected not to audit Basic Chemicals' standards. However, Imholz thought that some of the other changes made in the C&I policy were fair.

Many managers thought that top management recognized that the standard costs were very conservative, but transfer prices still affected bonuses, which were based on actual results compared to budget as a result of the take-or-pay provision, which charged them fixed costs on unsold products. A further frustration was that at the time, market prices were less than full cost.

Improvements in the Transfer Pricing Process

It was only when Imholz was replaced by Earl Shindell in late 1979 that real progress was made in resolving the conflict over transfer prices. Shindell accepted Basic Chemicals' cost center role more completely and shared more information with the buying divisions. Shindell recalled his first actions upon taking this position:

> When I came to this job I spent 50 percent of my time in the first three months arguing with General Chemicals, Molding, and Plastics. They didn't trust the standards, and I didn't blame them. There was no check-and-balance system. They were written by manufacturing people and set too high. In 1979 they got an extra $12–$15 million out of Molding, which missed bonuses from not getting the required profits.

Shindell substantially tightened up standard costs and eliminated the large positive variances that had previously existed. If he found a way to lower standard costs, the change was made the next quarter to pass on savings to buying divisions as quickly as possible.

Adam Sheldon, controller for the Molding Division from 1968 to 1974 and the recently appointed controller of Basic Chemicals, recalled what Shindell had told him when he first took the job in March of 1981:

> My instructions from Shindell were to understand the problems of the downstream customers. Everything was to be an open book. My impression is that today relationships have improved. The accounting departments and general managers have come clean with information. The mystique has gone out of transfers. It is neat and tidy except for problems of the marketplace—for example, somebody selling for below full cost. But general managers can't take this opportunity and buy outside.

The emphasis on openness with information and high levels of communication had substantially improved Basic Chemicals' especially strained relationship with the Molding Division. Shindell noted:

> Sheldon copies Madigan [controller of the Molding Division] on all reports. There is good communication between these two. My books are open. Imholz kept them closed.

Paul Hayden, vice-president and general manager of the Molding Division, believed that communication was the key to making a transfer pricing policy work, since constantly changing conditions necessitated changes in transfer prices:

> You can never make enough adjustments in the system if you don't have enough communication. You always have changing conditions. Situations never develop exactly as you predict.

He agreed that Shindell had been instrumental in resolving the conflict over standard full cost transfer prices:

> The last of the problems were resolved by Earl Shindell. He had a strong manufacturing background in a variety of products. He is an open communicator, very logical and precise. He is also much more outgoing than Imholz or Falk. He has an inordinate sense of fair play. If you have to pick someone to run that operation, he fits the bill in just about every way.

Hayden saw Shindell's acceptance of Basic Chemicals' cost center role as the basis for the improvement:

> What Earl said when he came in was, "It's our goal to reduce costs. I'll measure my people on this. It is not our goal to set standards which can be beaten." This was a big change in philosophy.

Equally important, he was able to gain acceptance for this among many of his managers:

> Shindell is an excellent motivator. He sold his people that their mission and goals should be aligned to true cost reduction. This has been communicated throughout his organization. If Shindell were initially in charge of Basic Chemicals, things would have sorted themselves out more quickly.

Shindell's efforts were supported by a change made in 1981 to measure the Basic Chemicals Division primarily on the basis of technical effort (cost reduction) and manufacturing effort (cost control), rather than on performance income, as it had been for the past four years. Increased clarity about Basic Chemicals' role in corporate strategy, criteria for performance measurement more consistent with this role, and improvements in the process for setting standard costs all contributed to reduced conflict over transfer prices.

No system is perfect. When standard cost transfer prices are used, disputes about who is responsible for variances and the existence of gaming behavior reflect the fact that there are no definitive answers to the questions of what "true" standard costs are and how much of the capacity in the selling profit center buyers should be held responsible for. For every attempted technical solution to gaming behavior, there is a gaming response. For example, a take-or-pay provision implemented to prevent buying profit centers from making claims on capacity in the selling profit center that are greater than their expected needs as a form of insurance, causing the selling center to forgo external opportunities, can result in buying profit center managers underestimating their needs. If the response to this is to charge them an especially high transfer price for requirements over expectations, thereby placing all of the burden for uncertainty on them, they may negotiate conservative objectives that are less ambitious but less risky. Take-or-pay provisions also give the selling profit center the opportunity to be reimbursed twice—by internal customers for some fixed costs and by external customers at a market price for the same capacity.

However much technical effort goes into determining which profit center is responsible for which variances and how the investment is split between the buying and the selling profit centers, the reality is that mandated transfers create a strong interdependence. Consequently, actions and outcomes of each profit center will affect performance measures of the other. It is impossible to generate measures of performance that completely separate the effects of this interdependence by dividing up the responsibility for financial results with complete certainty. When performance evaluation and reward are based primarily on individual profit center financial results, conflict will be inevitable.

Rousseau Chemical Corporation: The Viability of Not Allocating Variances

Rousseau Chemical Corporation also used standard full cost transfer prices, but it did not attempt to allocate variances to the buying profit centers. Although they were measured, both positive and negative variances were reported in the financial results of the selling profit center, even when they were clearly caused by buying profit centers. Yet very little conflict arose over these transfer prices. Unlike Locke Chemical, at Rousseau there was strategic clarity about the roles of the selling profit centers, and performance measurement, evaluation, and reward were based on subjective judgment that recognized the effects that one profit center had on the results of others. Managers' satisfaction with the company's transfer pricing policy was evident in the fact that little sentiment existed to change it, either by allocating variances or by using market prices.

Standard full cost transfer prices were established on an annual basis and were not adjusted if market prices moved below standard full cost. However, if internal capacity could not fulfill internal needs and external sources were used, these sourcing costs were combined with the internal standard costs. The standard costs were set by managers in production control, accounting, and general management. Company policy permitted transfers at other than standard full cost if the business managers involved could reach an agreement, but this occurred in only a few cases.

As at Aquinas Chemicals, buying divisions were instructed on which plants to source from. This high-level decision aimed at an optimal use of resources by considering such factors as transportation costs, plant loadings, and balancing product and by-product outputs. Higher-level management also made allocation decisions, both between profit centers and between internal and external customers when necessary. Standard costs varied according to the plant in which the product was manufactured.

Rejection of Market-Based Transfer Prices

In the 1960s, a task force was appointed to review standard full cost transfer prices in response to complaints about the existing system. At that time, decentralized profit responsibility had just been established through the new matrix structure, so there was strong support for using market-based transfers to represent each product line as a business. The executive vice-president was opposed to any change. Steve Lampert, director of strategic planning, gave this view of the EVP's position in a hypothetical statement:

> I like the current system. I won't say we aren't inflating downstream profits. I know that and the president knows that. But I want to see volume variances on a few key raw materials all in one place. When I seem them in one place, I can tell how the whole company is doing by looking at the volume variances for them. This would be harder to do if the variances were flowed to a number of products.

Mike Adams, group administrative vice-president, also recalled that the task force had recommended market prices but that the president had rejected this policy: "He just told them not to worry about the report card. It has always been this way."

The practice of not allocating variances had continued. As a result, financial responsibility was greater than authority, but this was taken into account in evaluating and rewarding performance. The EVP's unwillingness to change the transfer pricing method illustrates how he and the president utilized this particular method to manage the company and communicate corporate strategy. By not "flowing" variances, financial reports of the primarily cost center businesses were especially useful to them in obtaining a quick understanding of how the entire company was doing. With today's computer technology, it would be easier to produce reports and continue to flow variances, but at that time a choice was made. Since unallocated variances did not inhibit the ability to evaluate downstream businesses and reward general managers, no major problems were created by this decision.

Lack of Incentives for Change

Standard cost transfer prices with unallocated variances had been used at Rousseau for nearly twenty years. During this time, the company's strategy had remained fairly constant. In 1981, little incentive existed to change Rousseau's transfer pricing practices. Adams observed:

> It's been around so long no one questions it. I've never really wanted to change it. We've looked at rolling variances forward, but we figured it would cost too much.

A financial manager who had studied the possibility of allocating variances had estimated that it would cost $2 million to $4 million to make the necessary systems changes. Lampert also rejected the idea of allocating variances: "I always felt that this is a complicated system."

The fact that standard full cost transfer prices had been used for so many years and were well understood was the major reason managers cited for not making any changes. Alfred Meston, group manufacturing vice-president, did not see any major advantages in change: "Every system has problems. I don't think it really makes any difference which system you use."

Joel Kanter, group marketing vice-president, was also basically positive about the current method but noted one problem with it:

> At worst, people get resigned to a transfer pricing system. At best, you can get them to like it, as we have done here. One problem is that there is a strong feeling that the simple transfer pricing system we are using does not put any pressure on the guy who doesn't have capital. If he goes into a product that doesn't work out, he can walk away from the business. The upstream guy is stuck with eating the variances.

This problem could have been eliminated if investments had been allocated to buying businesses and if greater emphasis had been placed on financial measures of performance. Kanter did not believe that the problem he mentioned was serious, and for this reason any advantages in making the change would have been offset by its likely disadvantages in creating more competitive relationships between interdependent businesses.

Market-based transfer prices were also considered as another main alternative to the policy of standard full cost with unallocated variances. A business director believed that this alternative was not necessary at Rousseau:

> If you're in a conglomerate, you need market prices because you can only evaluate people on numbers. For our purposes, with the way we've grown up and with our structure, the standard cost system serves our needs.

Lampert, director of strategic planning, believed that most of the support for market-based transfer prices was among profit center managers who sold most of their product internally. His view of this method was similar to the business director's:

> There is a lot of merit to a market price system. It focuses in an accounting document the relative contributions to profits of the individual products. If we were to evaluate people on this basis, we would have a better way of showing their contributions.

Meston favored a market-based approach but recognized that one of its major problems was in how to determine a market price:

> I'd just as soon go to market price, but we'd spend a lot more time talking about what market price is. An argument in favor of using market price is that it shows you how a business looks. But what is market price for the products in which we are a dominant producer and most of our output is used internally? Another problem is when there is a chemical which many of our competitors make for themselves. We have one now where the posted market price has been unrealistically high for some time. And what about intermediate chemicals for which there is no market?

Meston believed that these problems were significant enough to discourage most people from switching to a market-based approach. Adams expressed this view:

> We would only use market prices if we really gained something. It is a big pain to establish market price. Market prices fluctuate and everybody ends up having a big argument.

Meston also believed that even if this change were made, the businesses would continue to be evaluated on the basis of standard cost transfer prices as well. Kanter, like several other managers, was a staunch advocate of the importance of historical comparability:

> If you start jiggling with transfer pricing, you run into problems, since you lose the basis of comparison. I say we should stay just exactly where we are. Our people are comfortable and they know how to do it.

He also expressed some concern about the effects of such a change on the pricing of final products:

> If we change the transfer pricing system, people downstream who will then have lower margins will say, "Everybody knows that this is a 60 percent margin business. I have to raise prices." This will hurt our market share.
>
> I tend to be a very simpleminded individual. We know what we're doing, so let's not jiggle with that.

It is clear that managers at Rousseau Chemicals regarded a change to market-based transfer prices as a very significant decision. A group department vice-president articulated what would be required to make this change and some of its consequences:

> A market price system would require a lot of work and a reeducation of values. The upstream businesses would end up looking more profitable, the downstream less.

Thus, a change in transfer pricing policy would change the way management looked at the businesses the company was in and the roles they played in corporate strategy. Since corporate strategy was clear and was supported by standard full cost transfer prices, the arguments for change were insufficiently compelling, given the difficulties that would be invovled.

Managing Costs and Variances

The key issues concerning the mandated full cost policy can be summarized in terms of four more hypotheses to be added to our growing list:

> **Hypothesis 28:** The less the strategic clarity about the cost center role of the selling profit center on internal sales, the higher the level of conflict.
>
> **Hypothesis 29:** The greater the emphasis on individual profit center financial results in measuring, evaluating, and rewarding performance, the higher the level of conflict when actual full cost transfer prices are used.

> **Hypothesis 30:** The greater the emphasis on individual profit center financial results in measuring, evaluating, and rewarding performance, the higher the level of conflict over variances when standard full cost transfer prices are used.

> **Hypothesis 31:** The greater the emphasis on individual profit center financial results in measuring, evaluating, and rewarding performance, the higher the level of conflict over investment allocations when these are made.

The importance of establishing strategic clarity and taking account of interdependence in measuring, evaluating, and rewarding performance has already been emphasized. The effectiveness of a mandated full cost transfer pricing policy is also influenced by the process through which costs are calculated. This includes the calculation of actual costs and the determination of standard costs, which together determine variances.

The underlying difficulty in determining actual costs is that some judgment must be exercised about such issues as joint and by-product cost allocations. The underlying difficulty in determining standard costs is that some judgment must be exercised in making the assumptions that become the basis of calculating these standards. For both of these difficulties, there are no purely technical solutions that will be accepted by all parties involved. In each case, the solution is to be found only by establishing a process that will result in solutions that are reasonably acceptable to all parties. It is unrealistic to hope for unanimous and enthusiastic acceptance that will be sustained over an extended period of time.

Compared to exchange autonomy, full cost transfer prices are determined in a more programmed way. Although some room exists for negotiation—such as over cost allocations in calculating actual costs and over assumptions used in calculating standard costs—existing management information and control systems largely determine the procedure by which these transfer prices are determined. They also largely determine the information that is used, which is primarily costs incurred by the company, results of engineering studies, estimates of future costs (such as for raw materials and energy), and other types of information used in calculating standard costs.

The most crucial issue in the process is who is involved. Problems are likely to emerge when only the selling profit center has access to information on its costs and can determine by itself what standard costs should be. Involvement in both of these procedures by corporate financial and even general managers and by financial and general managers in the buying profit center can go a long way in alleviating perceptions that judgments are being made in the selling profit center that unfairly disadvantage the buying profit centers. Without this involvement, questions can arise, even when buying profit center managers would find the decisions made in the selling profit center reasonable if they knew about them.

Actual costs are calculated on a monthly basis, thus determining the frequency with which transfer prices are established under this policy. It is conceivable that costs could vary from month to month. Because of time and effort involved in establishing standard costs, few if any companies calculate them as frequently as once per month. Instead, they are typically calculated on an annual or quarterly basis. How frequently these calculations should be done depends on how long the assumptions on which they are based remain valid. In some cases, it may be best to change them on an as-needed basis, when other information indicates that they should be changed. For example, rapidly increasing raw material costs that are not expected to go back down and improvements in process technology that improve manufacturing efficiency are legitimate reasons for changing standard costs, and these do not necessarily occur at any given frequency.

Typically, conflict is a result of three major and closely related causes: (1) lack of strategic clarity; (2) performance measurement, evaluation, and reward criteria that emphasize individual profit center financial results; and (3) inadequacies in the process by which transfer prices are determined. Each of these factors must be addressed in the context of the others. For example, a process for setting standard costs that always yields positive variances confuses strategic clarity, since positive variances are formally identical to profits, which makes the selling profit center look like a profit center on both internal and external sales. Another example is when buying profit centers are charged for inventories in measuring their performance but cannot control the level of inventory for which they are charged, which affects the transfer price.

Resolving these conflicts requires a willingness on the part of the profit center managers involved to reach an agreement; if this cannot be done, higher management must get involved if they do not want it to continue. Whether high-level management simply issues an edict to resolve the conflict or works with the parties involved to help them reach an agreement depends, among other things, on the management style of those involved, the manner in which conflict is generally resolved in the company, and the significance of the issue to the company and to the managers involved. A strong reason for resolving this conflict by fiat if necessary—rather than simply ignoring it and letting it continue—is that it can threaten the legitimacy of a company's accounting system and lead to problems on other issues.

7
Mandated Market-Based: Searching for the Just Price

There are two principal ways in which transfer prices can be set when mandated market-based transfers are used: (1) to use market prices of external transactions—what will be called *external market-based prices;* and (2) to add a markup to full cost for overhead and profit—what will be called *cost plus markup*. Both variations on this policy attempt to establish a fair or just transfer price in the sense that it is the price that would be paid to or received from an external supplier or customer. This is the central problem that must be managed when a mandated market-based transfer policy is used.

When a buyer can choose its vendor, market price, by definition, is the price acceptable to both parties, since the exchange occurs in the marketplace. Either party feels free to pursue better alternatives, and new relationships define new market prices. Thus, a buyer may replace one seller by another that has a lower price, the same price but better quality and service, or even a higher price if quality and service are much better. Similarly, a seller may elect to stop supplying a customer if others will pay higher prices or are easier to work with. Both buyers and sellers can use other exchange relationships, either actual or potential, as bargaining leverage in a given relationship. When internal trading is mandated, prices are not set by market transactions, and the bargaining leverage from other relationships is limited, since the internal relationship cannot be severed. This often makes it extremely difficult to determine the market price of an internal transaction. As a result, the problem is very much a search for the just price.[1]

Mandated market-based transfers are similar to standard full cost transfers in that they attempt to identify individual responsibility for financial outcomes within the constraints of interdependence. There is an essential difference between these two methods, however, in that mandated market-based transfers are used when the selling profit center is defined to be a business in its own right. It does not have the role of a manufacturing unit for internal transfers but is expected to earn a profit on both internal and external transactions. As a profit center on all transactions (despite some restrictions on its marketing autonomy), its performance is measured in the same way as the buying profit center's—profitability and return on investment. This makes it possible to compare the performance of both profit centers directly, which is not possible when internal transfers are on a full cost basis; in the latter case, it is understood that low profits and return on investment for the selling profit center as a whole result from profits being assigned to the buying profit center.

The validity of direct performance comparison results in a strong sense of competition between the two profit centers, which manifests itself in conflict. Since transfers are mandated, this conflict cannot be avoided by refusing to trade internally, as can be done under a policy of exchange autonomy. This conflict reflects the tension of competing on an individual profit center basis, while at the same time cooperating for mutual benefit, which is the purpose of a vertical integration strategy. Although conflict can develop with full cost transfer prices—since the transaction affects the performance measures of both profit centers—it is ubiquitous when market-based transfer prices are used, since the units have equal profit responsibility. Similarity of roles makes the effects of transfer prices on performance measures much more apparent.

Even if both profit center managers believe that top management is evaluating and rewarding their performance properly despite inaccurate transfer prices, other reasons for conflict exist. One is that general managers of other profit centers or corporate staff, who may not have the same depth of understanding, will use reported financial outcomes as the basis for comparing the two general managers' performance and management ability. The same is true for new top managers, who can substantially affect the careers of profit center managers. Furthermore, market-based transfers enable each general manager to calculate the proportion of corporate sales and profits for which his of her profit center is responsible. When relative contributions are important determinants of status, general managers will be especially concerned about transfer prices, both for themselves and for other managers in the profit center. This also explains managers' concern about transfer prices even when their profit objectives are adjusted for transfer prices that are "too high" or "too low."

Dewey & Burke: From Manufacturing Unit to Distinct Business

The use of both external market-based pricing and cost plus markup pricing can be illustrated by the transfer pricing policy for printed circuit (PC) boards developed at Dewey & Burke. This example illustrates how transfer pricing policy changes from mandated full cost to mandated market-based when a cost center devoted entirely to internal needs becomes a distinct business in its own right, as indicated by its entering the external market and using market-based transfer prices. The experience at Dewey & Burke also illustrates the competitive dynamics that are involved when a mandated market-based policy is used, including the special problems of internal transactions experienced under a policy of exchange autonomy and the difficulties that can exist in attempting to determine a just price.

Dewey & Burke had been producing PC boards exclusively for internal use for a number of years. Divisions were encouraged to design their products around the boards available internally. At one point, 40 percent of their PC board needs had been sourced internally, and the CEO had wanted this increased to 60 percent. However, this emphasis on internal sourcing and the lack of external PC board sales had led to new problems. R&D money had been spent on developing boards, resulting in some final product designs that prevented the company from taking advantage of technical advances in outside boards. The company also found that it was not cost-competitive on commodity products.

In 1980, the president decided that the company would enter the external market as a supplier of PC boards. Furthermore, he wanted to be able to view PC boards as a distinct business when making investment decisions. A manager was hired who had experience in PC boards, and the product was established as a separate division. He instituted a new policy that internal divisions should source boards externally when they could and should resort to internal sourcing only for boards that gave buying divisions a significant competitive advantage. R&D spending was to be split evenly between products for internal and external customers.

With the change in emphasis on the PC board business from a cost center to a profit center, top management changed the policy of transfer pricing from full cost to a price that included a margin for profit. This was done to emphasize the division's new role as a profit center and to demonstrate its commitment to being an external supplier, which some had questioned. For products sold externally, the transfer price was market price less a 5 percent discount. Ken Malbert, general manager of the Printed Circuit Board Division, explained that the discount was for the supposed lack of costs on internal sales:

> For products also sold on the outside, we give a 5 percent discount when we sell them inside, since we don't have to "sell." But we really do. In fact, we should charge an extra 5 percent due to the nuisance factor. On internal business, there are no communications channels as with outside customers, where lots of people are involved. What's a small matter becomes a big deal.

In fact, two sales representatives were assigned specifically to internal accounts. Their responsibilities were to tell these customers where PC board technology was going and how it might be applied to their products and to find out what products their customers were thinking about so that PC boards could be designed to fill their needs.

Malbert was aware of the tension involved in serving both internal and external customers in roughly equal amounts. He knew that sophisticated planning might be required to determine and balance their needs. The tension was increased by the perception that external customers were easier to work with than internal ones. He commented that when his division first started selling externally, "there was a reaction of 'Gee, these outside guys are easy to deal with.' " Malbert also believed that being able to sell externally had had a more positive effect on the people in his division beyond what could have been achieved by simply turning it into a profit center that did not have external sales:

> We went outside a year earlier than I thought we would. This has generated a lot of spirit in our people. If you just have an internal P&L, how do you win? If your profit is bigger than the people you sell it to, they want to fight.

Malbert had found it more difficult to establish transfer prices for products made only for internal use. Since PC boards represented between 5 percent and 30 percent of product costs, transfer prices could have a noticeable effect on the profits of the buying divisions. Top management did not want profits transferred out of the buying divisions to the Printed Circuit Board Division, but at the same time, they wanted that division to earn a fair profit on internal transfers. Malbert adopted an approach of adding a markup to full cost that yielded a return on assets of 21 percent:

> I think the right thing to do is what is a good financial deal. What I have done is set prices to get a reasonable return on assets (ROA). This is cost-based pricing with a margin for an adequate ROA. I have evolved to cost plus 21 percent. This gives us an ROA which is outstanding in the printed circuit board industry, when it is as profitable as it ever was in 1979.

He saw his main alternative as value-based pricing—or what the customer would be willing to spend for these boards. This had been rejected, since it would have transferred profits from the buying divisions to the Printed Circuit Board Division. Malbert also observed that when "you price on value, you irritate everybody."

External Market-Based Pricing

For products that are traded both internally and externally, the market prices of the external transactions are often the basis of the internal transfer price. Chapter 5 discussed the three basic procedures for determining product prices. When a product is traded both internally and externally, competitive bidding and market bidding are the most likely procedures, since it is not a proprietary good. These procedures cannot be used for mandated internal transactions, however, as they can for situations in which managers have exchange autonomy. Instead, the transfer pricing process begins with the prices of the external transactions, as established by one of these two pricing procedures.

Using external prices to set transfer prices is not always a simple process, especially when volumes of internal sales are extremely large or when internally transferred products differ in some way from the products sold externally. The amount of internal transfers is often large when a vertical integration strategy exists. When the selling profit center is one of the largest producers in its industry and the buying profit center is one of its largest customers, there may be no external sales of equivalent volume for comparison. Since many industrial goods markets are oligopolistic, market prices would be affected if this large quantity were made available on the external market, which makes it difficult to determine what an external price would be. It is possible that this quantity could not even be sold externally to one or many buyers. Similarly, the quantity required by internal buyers may not be available from external suppliers as a basis for determining the transfer price.

When internal transactions have been mandated for many years, the production processes of the two profit centers can become highly interdependent. As a result, the product transferred internally is not exactly the same as that sold externally. Internal buyers may be able to take the product in less finished form because it does not have to be transported. Even when product specifications for internal transfers differ only slightly from those of products sold externally, it is difficult to determine a fair market price for these internal transfers, because no realistic bids can be obtained from outside suppliers.

A wide variety of processes are used in setting transfer prices on the basis of external prices. The process is very programmed when top management's policy is to set transfer prices with a straightforward calculation using only unambiguous information, such as a list price less a 10 percent discount. Typically, transfer prices are specified as some discount on market price (however defined) to reflect the assumed lower transaction costs on internal exchanges. The process is very unprogrammed when corporate policy simply states that internal transfers should be at market price and lets the profit center general managers determine how to establish what that price is through negotiation.

Top management, management in the selling profit center, and management in the buying profit center can all be involved in setting transfer prices. In extreme examples, only one party sets the price. More frequently, managers in the buying and selling profit centers negotiate the transfer price according to some corporate policy guidelines. Top management's input is often low, but it can play a relatively major role.

A great deal of information is used in setting transfer prices, especially when it is a largely unprogrammed process involving only managers in the profit centers. The selling profit center has information on the price of external transactions. The buying profit center may have prices on external transactions when internal vendors are one of several sources. Otherwise, it may have information about what its competitors are paying or may solicit bids from outside vendors. These bids may be very high if outside vendors think that they are simply being used for information and are not likely to obtain any business. Unrealistically high quotes are a way of signaling disinterest or displeasure. However, if these vendors think they do have a chance, they may offer extremely low prices as a way of getting a foot in the door, after which they plan to raise prices. The internal selling profit center may argue that these prices are irrelevant to setting a transfer price.

Information on costs can also be involved in setting the transfer price, particularly when corporate policy requires a discount to reflect the lack of certain expenses on internal sales or the lower production costs for internal transactions. For example, the portion of the discount that reflects the selling profit center's lack of marketing expenses may seem too high if such expenses *are* incurred on internal sales, such as a sales representative who coordinates deliveries and service. The buying profit center may think that the discount is not high enough—

for instance, if it does not receive the technical support that is furnished to external customers. Information on costs is relevant in determining whether the discount is the right amount. Cost information may also be relevant if the selling profit center incurs higher or lower production costs for internal transfers, perhaps because of the volume or the degree of finish on the product. When production costs are higher or lower for internal than for external transactions, an argument can be made that the transfer price should be higher or lower.

When transfer prices are based on market prices to external customers, they are often set simultaneously. If contracts with external customers are negotiated on an annual basis, with a price that applies for the entire year, this can also be done for transfer prices. Similarly, provisions for changing external prices can also be applied to transfer prices. External customers often have greater leverage in enforcing provisions for changes in their favor and for resisting changes not in their favor (such as penalties for orders below a certain volume) than internal customers who cannot replace the internal vendor.[2]

External conditions put pressures on transfer prices. If demand becomes greater than expected and external customers are clamoring for product at almost any price, the selling profit center will want to raise transfer prices on the grounds that market prices to external customers are the opportunity cost of having to trade with internal customers. The selling profit center would be cautious about raising prices to external customers, however, since this could jeopardize the relationship over the longer term. If the selling profit center does not raise prices to external customers even when it is in a position to do so, the external customers may retain that seller as a vendor at contract prices even when market prices fall below those prices. The selling profit center does not have to be so cautious about internal transactions, since buying profit centers have no choice about sourcing internally.

Paine Chemical Company: Limitations in Using External Market Prices

Paine Chemical Company used a transfer pricing policy of mandated external market-based transfers on plastic resins. It experienced great difficulties in doing so for a number of reasons. First, the two major internal customers for this product were the largest two customers of the selling profit center, which raised the question of volume discounts. Second, one of the buying profit centers took the product in a less finished form than was sold externally, which raised the question of what discount to give for this difference. Third, there were many variations of this product, and the internal customers purchased a number of them that were custom-made and not sold externally. Fourth, the buying profit centers sometimes believed that the price they paid was excessive, given the quality of the product they received.

All of these problems were exacerbated by the process used to establish the transfer price. The price was set by the general manager of the selling profit center and was changed only when he thought it was appropriate. The buying profit center managers had little influence on the price and, as a result, often believed that it was unfair, although they were relatively unconcerned about the effects of transfer prices on performance measurement, evaluation, and reward and on the economic decisions that were made. Their concern was more involved with status and their own personal perceptions about what was a just price.

Paine had entered the plastic resins business in 1961 and had soon integrated forward into rigid packaging and flexible packaging. Larry Johnson, president and chief executive officer, explained why the company had adopted this strategy:

> In two other chemicals we had been middlemen and had been driven out of the business by suppliers forward integrating and customers backward integrating. We did not want to make this same mistake with plastic resins. We decided to establish our own pull-through capacity. We made an acquisition to get us into the rigid packaging business and, through a joint venture, got into the flexible packaging business.

Paine was organized into a product/function matrix. Business center managers were in charge of product lines, for which they had profit and loss responsibility. Plastic Resins was under the direction of Vincent Flaherty; Rigid Packaging was under the direction of Helmut Rennke; and Flexible Packaging was under the direction of John Dolan. The company's sixteen business centers were grouped under three senior vice-presidents who reported to Johnson. At that time, Plastic Resins was under Aaron Thornton and the two packaging business centers were under George Mahan.

Business center managers' performance was evaluated annually by Johnson and the appropriate senior vice-president. Bonuses were tied to objectives and could substantially affect total compensation. With no precise formula for evaluation, both long-term strategy and current performance were important. High-level managers also participated in long-term incentive plans based on stock options. The managers of the Plastic Resins and packaging business centers believed that Johnson fairly evaluated and rewarded them. One reason for this was that he had a thorough understanding of all three businesses, since he had worked in them and had later been in charge of them.

The plastic resins product was manufactured in particle form by a unique process at Paine. The processes of Paine's competitors yielded the product in liquid form, which could not be used or shipped until it was further processed into pellets. An advantage of the particle form was that it cost less to manufacture than pellets. Nevertheless, in external sales, Paine had not been successful in establishing a market price differential. Vincent Flaherty, business center manager (BCM) of Plastic Resins, explained why:

> Every time you establish a large differential, those who can't supply particles match their pellet price to the particle price. The only way we have been successful selling particles is when there is a technical advantage to using the product in this form, as is the case with rigid packaging, where particles give you processing advantages.

Low-grade and high-grade resins were produced in both particles and pellets. With many different variations in quality and properties, Paine sold more than 350 types of plastic resins to its customers.

Paine was among the world's largest producers of certain plastic resins. Nearly 40 percent of the company's assets were devoted to this production. Plastic Resins' sales were a bit more than the combined annual sales of the Rigid and Flexible Packaging business centers combined. Plastic Resins had a market share of slightly more than 20 percent of domestic sales and about 25 percent of worldwide sales. The Rigid Packaging Business Center was its single largest customer, taking about 160 million pounds annually, and the Flexible Packing Business Center was its next largest customer, taking about 130 million pounds annually. These two divisions together accounted for between 20 percent and 30 percent of Plastic Resins' output. Transfer prices were to be at market price less a 5 percent discount. As a result of the large amount of internal transfers, John Dolan, business center manager for Flexible Packaging, noted:

> In a sold-out market, Rennke and I account for 12 percent of his [Flaherty's] worldwide profits and 20 percent of his domestic profits. When the market for plastic resins is soft, we can account for as much as 40 percent of his worldwide profits and 50 percent of his domestic profits.

Disputes over the transfer price of plastic resins had continued for many years. These disagreements were over whether or not a volume discount should be given for internal transfers and what the price differential should be for plastic resins sold in particle form. As a large user of plastic resins in the pellet form—the form in which product was sold externally—Dolan believed that he should receive a volume discount, just as he did on products he sourced externally. But, he noted, "Flaherty will tell you he has to make specialty resins of very high quality as one reason for not giving us a discount." Dolan also believed that the packaging business centers received less R&D support than external customers did: "R&D spending costs money, so why do it for internal customers who are captive?" Dolan's concerns about the lack of a volume discount were accentuated by the fact that other suppliers of plastic resins were selling at lower prices. Although Johnson was aware of this, he insisted that all purchases of plastic resin be made internally, with the exception of a small amount for a specialty grade not made by Plastic Resins.

Even if internal purchases were not mandated, Dolan would have been forced to buy from Flaherty in some cases. Flexible Packaging used a sophisticated process technology, and many of its products were based on resins supplied by Plastic Resins and not available externally. For plastic resins that could be bought externally, Dolan suspected he might find better quality from outside suppliers, but he knew it would be difficult to do so even if company policy permitted choosing external suppliers (which it did not):

> No matter how closely you define specifications, it takes time to learn how to work together. We've tailored our processes to fit Flaherty's plastic resins.

The large volume of internal purchases by Flexible Packaging, the dependence on plastic resins not available externally, and the inability to source from external suppliers because of corporate transfer pricing policy and the process technologies adapted for internal sourcing made it extremely difficult to determine the market price from which the 5 percent discount would be taken to arrive at a transfer price. Chris Shaw, vice-president for strategic planning, acknowledged this difficulty with the corporate transfer pricing policy:

> It is hard to tell what market price is, particularly when you are a dominant factor in the marketplace. If we offered to purchase 100 million

> pounds of plastic resins from the market, people would stumble all over themselves for this business, unless they thought you weren't serious and were only getting prices.

Although Dolan believed he was paying too much for plastic resins, his business was quite profitable and had brighter growth prospects and larger capital investment commitments than the other two business centers. This mitigated the effects of transfer prices on his business. In contrast, the Rigid Packaging Business Center was suffering severe performance problems. For nearly eight years, with many chemical companies integrating forward into rigid packaging manufacturing, this business had suffered from overcapacity. This was a serious problem, since it was a highly capital-intensive business and plastic resins represented 45 percent of total manufacturing costs. Transfer prices thus had a significant effect on the financial performance of Rigid Packaging.

Helmut Rennke, business center manager for Rigid Packaging, was also concerned about the lack of volume discounts:

> The Plastic Resins people set the transfer price by analogy kind of thinking. They take the pellet base price, subtract a few cents, and take 95 percent of this. We have complained that this is all well and good, but it fails to recognize quantity. They say there are no volume discounts, but a 45-million-pound customer is getting below-list prices. All of this makes for very interesting discussion and great acrimony.

Rennke used about 160 million pounds annually and believed he should receive a volume discount in recognition of this. He was also concerned that he did not receive a high enough discount for taking the product in particle rather than pellet form. The "few cents" subtracted from the price of pellets was the only adjustment for the plastic resins being transferred in particle form. Rigid Packaging purchased the particle form to give better uniformity to its products. Since Plastic Resins could produce it at 60 percent of the investment required to produce in pellet form, Rennke believed he should receive a larger discount than he was currently getting. Establishing what this discount should be was difficult, inasmuch as the particle form was not sold externally. Rennke compared his situation with Dolan's:

> The Flexible Packaging people use pellets in certain products which could be obtained from outside suppliers, so there is some basis for setting market price for some of the material they use, but not in all cases. Even they have some uncertainty on price. But for us there is no market comparison.

Determining the transfer price to Rigid Packaging was further complicated by the fact that Plastic Resins also sold resins to its competitors. Rennke believed that some of them received volume discounts for even smaller purchases than he made, but Flaherty said this was not true. Furthermore, the same plastic resin had different prices according to the markets in which it was sold. For some nonrigid packaging markets, a discount from list price was given that was not given to competitors of Rigid Packaging. Transfer prices were being calculated on the basis of list price. Rennke argued that the true market price was the discounted list price, since these competitors made a much lower quality product that was not really directly competitive with his.

Disagreements—about volume discounts, about which external sales should be used to define the market price, and about how much of a discount should be given for internal transfers being in particle form—made for continuing conflict between Flaherty and Rennke. It was aggravated by the performance problems in Rigid Packaging and by a strained interpersonal relationship between Flaherty and Rennke. Despite the conflict, Rennke did not believe that transfer prices had been detrimental to capital investment decisions in his business or that they had hurt his ability to compete externally. He stated: "We always price for the best we can get in the market and say 'to hell with transfer prices.' Sometimes we take it on the chin in terms of profits." Rennke considered that the vertical integration strategy gave him and Dolan responsibility for moving plastic resins as profitably as possible:

> Our purpose is to add value through downstream integration and avoiding sales expenses. . . . We try to ignore the rash of shit we get from Flaherty and use as much plastic resins as profitably as we can.

Rennke thought that Johnson, his CEO, had fairly evaluated and rewarded his performance. Nevertheless, he was concerned that others in the company might be deceived by company records and less inclined to emphasize his business. This was made worse by the poor performance of Rigid Packaging, which others perceived as hurting total company results:

> We're an easy target, even though we've done reasonably well compared to the market as a whole. The attitude in the company is "screw Rigid Packaging." When you're in Rigid Packaging, you really have to look out for yourself.

Rennke was also concerned about the effects of transfer prices on the morale of people who worked for Rigid Packaging, since these prices made bad financial performance measures even worse. He also noted that these measures could "hurt you indirectly" in terms of "how you advance in the company."

Cost Plus Markup Pricing

The alternative to using prices of external transactions as the basis for setting transfer prices when the selling profit center is regarded as a business in its own right is to add a markup to the cost of the transferred good to cover overhead and profit. Cost plus markup pricing is one of the three basic pricing processes for external transactions. It is often used for proprietary goods when there is a single supplier, since there is no real market for such goods. It is also used to price products sold externally to many customers when a company uses fairly simple pricing practices. Transfer prices can be determined by adjusting these external prices for lower internal transactions costs, higher volume, and so on. In some cases, however, transfer prices are determined directly by adding markups to cost, either actual or standard, to cover overhead and profit.

A cost plus markup pricing policy is often used when the traded good is a unique product that is not available in the external marketplace, when outside suppliers are not producing it although they may have the capability, and when the selling profit center does not sell it externally (which would establish a market price). It is also used when the differences between the characteristics of internal and external transactions, related to volume and product differentiation, are so great that market-based transfer pricing becomes impossible. The process for determining the markup can range from a corporate policy specifying how it is to be calculated to negotiations between the managers involved in the trade. In both cases, common approaches are (1) some arrangement for sharing the profits on the sale of the final good between the two profit centers, (2) a fixed percentage, (3) a markup that yields the same gross margin as a similar class of products sold externally by the selling profit center, (4) a markup that yields a gross margin equal to the average profit center or corporate gross margin, (5) a markup that yields the same return on investment (or a similar measure of asset usage) as a similar class of products sold externally by the selling profit center, and (6) a markup that yields the average profit center or corporate return on investment.

Unlike the case of market-based transfer pricing, in which the buying profit center may or may not be aware of the costs of the selling profit center, it typically will have this information in cost plus markup transfer pricing, just as buyers insist on it when they sign purchasing agreements on this basis. This creates the potential for disagreements over product costing as well as disagreements over what the markup should be. If top management does not determine the markup by corporate policy or direct intervention, there can be substantial conflict in determining what is a "fair" profit for the selling profit center to earn on the transaction. Even when there is a corporate policy, lower-level conflict can arise over its interpretation and application.

A mechanism sometimes used to determine the markup indirectly is for the buying profit center to solicit outside bids from external suppliers. The markup is then calculated by subtracting internal costs from this price and dividing the difference by the costs. There are some constraints on using this approach, however. Besides the problem of determining how realistic external suppliers' bids are when they doubt they will really get any business, the company may have to make information available about proprietary technology, which could impair its competitive advantages if it is not kept confidential. For example, in getting the information necessary to make a bid, an external supplier may learn how to make a proprietary product and may enter into competition with the selling profit center.

The cost plus markup method makes very apparent to both profit centers how much profit the selling profit center is making on the internal transaction. Very often, the selling profit center also has information about the profit being earned by the buying profit center on the final good it sells externally. Thus, the proportion of the profits earned on the final good each profit center is contributing to the company becomes obvious. The competitive dynamics that are generated by comparing proportional contribution on a profit center basis can be focused on a particular product when cost plus markup transfer pricing is used. When market-based transfer pricing is used, such information is less readily available, and the conflict over individual products will not be great if the transfer price has only a slight effect on total profit center performance. However, the use of cost plus markup transfer pricing focuses attention on the proportionate contribution to profits of individual products, thus increasing the degree of conflict even for transfers that do not substantially affect total profit center results.

Although the potential for conflict is great, cost plus markup transfer pricing is usually used in situations that require a great deal of coordination and cooperation between profit centers. Both profit centers must work together in designing proprietary technology that will give the buying profit center competitive advantages. At the same time, the selling profit center must agree not to use this technology for products sold externally. If the conflict over transfer prices becomes too great, both profit centers will have an incentive to avoid such situations, especially if internal transactions are mandated once they are established. Both will seek to establish external relationships they can claim were developed because internal ones were unavailable, blaming the other for any lost internal opportunities. Thus, the buying profit center may claim that the selling profit center does not have adequate technological capabilities. Similarly, the selling profit center may claim that it is not given the opportunity to submit proposals for proprietary products to the buying profit center.

Either profit center can take the initiative to establish internal relationships based on proprietary intermediate products, and either can furnish the designs for such products, but both must work together on the actual transactions. Conflict over transfer prices can inhibit both parties significantly and can impair the implementation of the vertical integration strategy.

On external transactions, cost plus markup pricing often is changed to a fixed price once the design of the traded good is well established and production costs can be accurately estimated. This approach may also be beneficial with internal transactions. As the selling profit center gains experience in manufacturing the transferred good, it becomes possible to establish accurate standard production costs. Prior to this, the transfer price is often a markup on actual or estimated standard costs. A common complaint of a buying profit center is that the selling profit center has no incentive to be efficient. By adding markups to a standard cost figure, the selling profit center is penalized for any inefficiencies that raise costs beyond standards. However, unless there are pressures to drive standard costs down, the selling profit center has no incentive to lower them, especially if the markup is a percentage of full cost.[3] Even if the selling profit center is achieving cost reductions, the buying profit center may believe that the transfer price is unfair if standard costs are not lowered frequently enough.

Hobbes Instrument Company: Limitations in Using Markups on Cost

A high level of disagreement existed at Hobbes Instrument Company over the transfer prices for proprietary components, which were determined by a cost plus markup policy. Neither the selling profit center, which had formerly been a cost center, nor the buying profit centers were satisfied that the transfer prices were fair. The percentage markup was established by corporate policy, which did not give either a say in determining the transfer price. The buying profit centers were further frustrated by the way the selling profit center established product costs. The selling profit center managers maintained that the transfer price understated their profits, whereas the buying profit center managers were concerned about their ability to earn their required profit margins given the cost of these components to them. Attempts to determine what a just price should be by getting bids from external suppliers had been inconclusive. The concern about the competitive implications of transfer prices had persisted, even when the percentage markup had been lowered by corporate edict. Disputes over the transfer prices of these components were exacerbated by the fact that a high level of conflict existed in the company generally. However, in terms of these transfer prices, there were no mechanisms for resolving conflict, and so it persisted.

The Components Division at Hobbes was subdivided into four subdivisions, including Internal Products, which sold electrical components to the three subdivisions of the Systems Division (Advanced Systems, Intermediate Systems, and Basic Systems). About 80 percent of Internal Products' output was sold internally, and much of that was proprietary products. Part of the strategy of the Electronics Group (which contained the Components and Systems divisions) was to increase the use of proprietary components. Internal Products, originally a cost center, had been changed into a profit center in the mid-1960s, when the current president, then in charge of the Electronics Group, had instituted the product management structure with an emphasis on entrepreneurship and conflict.

Internal Products was made into a profit center by adding a markup designed to give a 10 percent pretax profit, which was the profit goal for the Components Division. The president expected that this would increase total profits to the company by forcing buying divisions to price higher to meet their profit objectives. A number of problems had developed with this method. Systems (which at that time was one division) had obtained outside bids in an effort to determine whether transfer prices were competitive. Systems was able to source externally if products were available and if the outside prices were lower after Internal Products was given the opportunity to meet them. Although it was possible to source outside for nonproprietary components, it was more difficult to do so for the products that were proprietary. Some managers believed that with the complexities of calculating costs and getting external prices for components, the profit margins on transferred goods ended up two to three times higher than agreed upon.

Some managers believed that the markup on components, when added to the markup on the final product, created competitive problems. Eric Berke, vice-president and general manager of Advanced Systems, recalled this problem:

> It was felt that a significant cost burden was being put on us. There was dual profit-taking by Components and us. There was also the concern that if the transfer price was high, we might be making the wrong design decision; for example, we would approach the design in a way so that we could use other, cheaper components.

As a way of avoiding internal sourcing, buying divisions could design products so that they did not use internal proprietary technology, thereby avoiding what they perceived as too expensive internally supplied components. But in doing so, they would risk losing competitive advantages.

In response to these problems, the transfer pricing policy was changed so that proprietary products were priced at a markup that gave Internal Products a maximum 5 percent net profit margin after taxes. In no case was it allowed to receive a higher price than an external supplier would be paid, which sometimes made this profit margin even less. For commodity products, such as printed circuit boards, buying divisions had to source internally if Internal Products was within 10 percent of the lowest outside bid. Higher-level management encouraged greater use of proprietary products to obtain competitive advantages in the final product, and it maintained certain component capabilities in Internal Products to ensure a source of supply.

John Coulter, vice-president and director of business management of the Electronics Group, explained why the 5 percent rule was adopted:

> We tell the Internal Products operation, "You may only make a 5 percent margin or less if it is a proprietary product." He has a cornered market, so he could charge anything and look good. Now he has to publish a statement which everybody sees, including the product managers who use his components.
>
> A lot of the engineers in the Systems Division look at various components and say, "I can design and produce these myself for one-half the cost, so the hell with them." That's why we put the 5 percent maximum on profits.

Top management did not want to interfere with the authority of the buying general managers to make the decision to manufacture components for themselves, but they preferred to use a single facility for manufacturing. Thus, they wanted a transfer price that did not provide an incentive for buying divisions to make components for themselves rather than buying from Internal Products. It was generally perceived that Internal Products made high-quality components at competitive prices.

Buying divisions were allowed to solicit bids for proprietary products when they were first designed and before Internal Products began to manufacture them. Internal Products was given the opportunity to match these outside prices and sometimes did, even when it resulted in a net profit after tax of less than 5 percent. In some cases, buying divisions ended up sourcing externally, although this happened infrequently because of Internal Products' competitive strength in this product line.

Berke noted that the 5 percent figure had not been arrived at by any precise economic rationale:

> The cost-plus prescribed margin of 5 percent was arrived at intuitively. It was kept at a level which seemed reasonable enough to motivate the components people and low enough for buyers to think it a reasonable price.

Although this made it obvious how profits were allocated across divisions, Berke also believed that numbers alone were not the basis of performance evaluation:

> Higher levels should be able to recognize our contribution even if it is not reflected in the measurement system. They've done so in the past, and I hope they'll continue to do so.

Conflict still existed in the relationship between Internal Products and its internal customers over determining the product costs to which the markup was added. Internal cost information and external prices were used in negotiations about what to include in costs. One source of dispute was the overhead markup applied to material costs, since it was included in product costs. George Patterson, vice-president and director of operations in Internal Products, described these negotiations as "pure blood." He was also frustrated at not being allowed to sell some of these proprietary products externally.

Another concern was the relationship between transfer prices on components and final product prices. While managers in Internal Products believed that they were not earning enough profits on transfers, managers in buying divisions believed that Internal Products was earning too much. Ed Fales, director of planning and staffing in the Advanced Systems Division, explained a consequence of this conflict over profits:

> They complain that we beat them over the head and put them through the hoops and make them gouge outside customers to keep profits up. If we raise prices, they automatically do, too. This is suspect and leads to constant battles. Why should their costs rise as ours do? It leads to a kind of ratchet effect.

He thought that group-level management might have had a reason for allowing Internal Products to increase transfer prices, as long as the 5 percent maximum net profit margin was not exceeded and even if costs had not increased, since group level management had to approve increases in transfer prices:

> It may be a tactic to build a little profit pile. The end-product departments push harder for more sales or to offset costs to make up for higher prices paid to Internal Products and still meet profit targets.

Although Fales could see some advantages in using transfer prices to ensure that the group as a whole got its maximum profit margin on products sold externally, he also thought some problems arose from uncompetitive costs in the final product:

> What are the negatives? We are letting an inefficient operation artificially inflate our costs. Since we build proprietary relationships, it prevents us from going outside.

A response of the buying divisions to this problem was to continue to look for ways to keep from sourcing internally. The entrepreneurial emphasis in the company provided an incentive to meet profit objectives, but Fales recognized that this could be suboptimal for the company as a whole:

> I go along with the premise that the entrepreneurial spirit is positive. But there are also some negatives. If people are parochial, they may do things that are not in the best interests of the corporation.

Fales thought that in response to efforts of buying divisions to become less dependent on Internal Products, Internal Products was attempting to develop components that could not be sourced externally and that performed some of the functions added in the assembly of the final product. The result was a struggle between the selling and buying divisions over technological responsibility:

> If Internal Products had a smart manager, he would push for designs that can't be done outside to increase entanglement. I see indications of this happening. They keep pushing more functions into the components they supply. There is a pull and a tug to change demarcation lines in the vertical relationship. We push them away and say, "Just give us a widget."

A different set of problems surrounded transfers of other components. External suppliers could provide for the company's needs, but the policy that buying divisions must source internally if Internal Products' prices were within 10 percent of the outside price constrained them. Fales noted that this rule had been invoked in the past, but that the emphasis on internal sourcing "kind of waxes and wanes depending on the issue and who gets involved." Buying divisions were not eager to source these other components internally, since, unlike electrical components, they perceived the quality to be lower and the prices to be higher from Internal Products than from external suppliers. One manager remarked that although Hobbes had been in this business since the early 1970s, "this is a failure of ours. Our quality is not as good as outsiders."

Patterson, the director of operations, disagreed with the assessments of internal buyers. He thought that external suppliers "low-balled" their bids to get the business, after which they would raise prices. He also believed that his deliveries and quality were better, but by virtue of being an internal supplier, he had to meet higher expectations and be more responsible: "Buyers expect more from me. They can get me on the phone and jerk me around on schedules." In general, Patterson was dissatisfied with his relationships with the buying divisions. Some managers believed that his problems had resulted from the policy of treating Internal Products as a profit center, even though 80 percent of its output was traded internally, and they suggested that it should be redefined as a cost center.

Managing the Ambiguity of Price

Transfer prices in a mandated market-based policy present an interesting contrast to prices in economic theory. In economic theory, prices are unambiguously given by "the market" and serve as the basis of economic decision making. In many academic theories of transfer pricing, transfer prices are intended to play the same role within the organization. Although these theories recognize that determination of transfer prices can be very difficult, they tend to underestimate the complexity of the problem.

In many instances in practice, the problem is not so much how to determine the transfer price that will lead to profit-maximizing decisions as it is how to determine a transfer price that both buyer and seller will regard as fair. Three considerations are especially important for achieving this goal.

The first is to ensure that the criteria for performance measurement, evaluation, and reward are flexible enough to take account of ambiguities in the transfer price. This can be accomplished by not basing rewards strictly on financial measures of individual profit center performance. Profits of both profit centers should be considered, since they are tied together by an underlying strategy of vertical integration. To do this and to take account of other performance measures—such as actions that are beneficial to the corporation over the long term, including joint R&D and product development—subjective judgment must be exercised. When bonuses and other rewards are determined by formulas based on individual profit center results, conflict resulting from perceptions of unfairness will be inevitable because of the ambiguity regarding what is a just transfer price in a mandated market-based policy. This can be restated as a formal hypothesis:

> **Hypothesis 32:** The greater the emphasis on individual profit center results in measuring, evaluating, and rewarding performance, the higher the level of conflict when mandated market-based transfer prices (both external market price and cost plus markup) are used.

The second consideration involves recognizing that there are many facets of an internal transaction besides the transfer price, including quality, delivery, service, technical support, and R&D for future products. All these other aspects are bundled into the transfer price. Because transfer prices represent the value of all facets of a transaction, they will often be the source of dispute when problems arise in an inter–profit center relationship. For example, the buying profit center may argue that the transfer price is too high, given the quality of the product it receives, and that it should be lower or—sometimes more implicitly—that the quality should be improved. Resolution of the problem of what a just price is requires a comprehensive view of the entire transaction and its context. By taking this view, incentives can be built into the transfer pricing process that address the concerns of both profit centers and result in each one receiving a fair value in the exchange.

Hume Fabrication Company: Improved Cooperation Through Transfer Pricing

A cost plus markup transfer pricing policy was used as part of an effort to improve the overall level of cooperation and effectiveness of two divisions at Hume Fabrication Company. This policy provided financial incentives to the selling division to ensure that the quality needs of the buying division were met. The product in question was a component called a mechanical flotation device (MFD), which was sold by the Equipment Assembly Division to the Pollution Controls, Inc. (PCI) subsidiary. Pollution Controls had once been a part of the Equipment Assembly Division but had been made a separate subsidiary in 1969. Manufacturing the MFD used about 45 percent of Equipment Assembly's capacity and contributed substantially to manufacturing efficiencies for its other products.

Since the MFD was a proprietary product, and since there was no patent on it, Hume did not want competitors to learn how to make it. Therefore, Pollution Controls sourced all of its needs internally, although it used outside subcontractors extensively for other components. PCI had only a few competitors and was very profitable. Even though many of its nonstandard needs had standard equivalents, PCI had traditionally submitted custom drawings. Eric Chudnoff, controller of PCI, attributed this practice to a lack of manufacturing discipline. It had increased Equipment Assembly's manufacturing costs, and for a number of years the division had lost money because the internal transfer had been on a fixed price basis. Equipment Assembly had been unwilling to respond to problems with the component once it was installed, and a backcharge system was used to reimburse its losses, thus providing an incentive for it to service the product.

When Eric Chudnoff became controller of PCI, he decided that he could improve interdivisional cooperation by changing the transfer pricing policy. Part of this change involved standardizing many of the drawings PCI would have to submit to Equipment Assembly:

> They insisted that we modify our drawings to fit into their computerized production control system. I was happy with this. This was good discipline for us, although it has been expensive.

The transfer price guaranteed a minimum volume of $6 million in factory costs and a 21 percent return on $400,000 of the $900,000 in assets used to make the MFD. The 21 percent was chosen since it was the figure required at Hume to justify new investments. Another 7 percent was paid to cover the corporate charge assessed against assets. Finally, individuals were identified whose costs were not included in the factory burden for work on the MFD, and PCI paid for them as well. These total costs equaled $540,000 at full capacity. PCI committed to paying a minimum of $450,000 whatever the volume.

No provision was made in the $450,000 minimum markup for backcharges that were the fault of Equipment Assembly. To address the problem of quality in the field, Chudnoff established an additional 1 percent markup as a reserve for field errors. Any charge incurred for fixing problems in the field was charged to this account. Whenever this reserve exceeded a cutoff point, it was split evenly between the two divisions. Since this new method had been installed, there had been only one $500 charge.

Chudnoff was extremely pleased with this transfer pricing policy and with his division's relations with Equipment Assembly in general. A major reason was that the two divisions shared information openly:

> We have the right to send an inspector to their plant to look at their operations and be critical and reject shipments. It has worked well. There are no problems. Costs are down. There have virtually been no squabbles. They have given us permission for our computer to read into theirs so that we know their costs.

He contrasted this with PCI's relationship with the Components Division. Equipment Assembly obtained materials to make the MFD from the Components Division, which in turn got its raw materials from the Foundry Division. Equipment Assembly paid market price for the material it got from Components, but since this was included in PCI's costs, the transfer price was largely Chudnoff's concern. However, he noted that Components never gave him information on costs:

> We never see the costs. I won't be happy until I do. We're all brothers and sisters. The only reason not to show costs is that they're ashamed of what they are.

Chudnoff thought that knowing costs would enable his division to make better external pricing decisions: "Another reason for knowing costs is so that we know what latitude we have in the marketplace on selling the item."

The third consideration in transfer pricing is the process used to determine the transfer price. Although many variables must be considered—including product characteristics, company characteristics, and external conditions—making it difficult to state any strong recommendations, at least one thing is clear: those who must use the process should participate in its design if one of the objectives of top management is to reduce the time and energy spent on conflict over transfer pricing. A process imposed by higher-level management is almost certain to lead to conflict, since either or both parties will be dissatisfied with the transfer price.

When the profit center managers themselves design the process, they are negotiating all five elements of it. Although this process will involve various managers in the profit centers, such as the controller and the head of manufacturing, it is the general managers who will have to reach ultimate agreement on the transfer price. In some cases, the result will be a strict formula; in others, it will more closely resemble the negotiations they engage in with external firms. In general, full and open disclosure of all information—including costs of the selling profit center, prices it is getting from external customers, and prices being paid for the intermediate good by competitors of the buying profit center—will facilitate the determination of what will be perceived as a just price. How frequently the price must be changed will depend on how frequently costs and external prices change, balanced against administrative difficulties in changing transfer prices. Finally, conflict over transfer prices may be an indication that the transfer pricing process needs to be redesigned, which can be done by the managers who designed the process in the first place. In some cases, the redesigning can be done by the profit center managers themselves; in others, their boss and other higher-level managers will also be involved.

Paine Chemical Company: A Process Resolution of the Plastic Resins Problem

---

The dispute at Paine Chemical Company over the transfer price of plastic resins was finally resolved. The manner in which this was accomplished illustrates how critically important the process is in determining the transfer price, given the inherent ambiguities of what the price should be in a transaction between two profit centers that are tied together by a strategy of vertical integration. The process that was implemented at Paine was very programmed (since it was based on a formula), it involved the profit center managers and their boss, it used both cost and market information, it provided for quarterly adjustments to the transfer price, and conflict was resolved by the profit center managers, with their boss playing a strong role.

The conflict over the transfer prices of plastic resins at Paine Chemical Company continued for several years, with the president refusing to resolve it. Agreement on a fair transfer price was not reached until Helmut Rennke, formerly business center manager of Rigid Packaging, was given responsibility for plastic resins, rigid packaging, and flexible packaging. As a result of this reorganization, Vincent Flaherty, formerly business center manager of Plastic Resins, was moved to a different business, which was not involved with plastic resins. Lee Austin, manager of business planning for Plastic Resins, was given responsibility for that business under Rennke.

Rennke and Austin had known each other for years and had a good working relationship. This facilitated a cooperative effort on their part to design a process for determining the transfer price of plastic resins that was acceptable to them and to the new managers in charge of the rigid packaging and flexible packaging businesses. Resolution of this dispute was also facilitated by the fact that Rennke had responsibility for all three businesses and had the authority to do so. Formerly, this issue would have had to go to the president for resolution had he been inclined to do so.

Rennke's approach to the problem was to "develop a system that wouldn't require a hell of a lot of subjective judgment and that depended only on data in the company." He and Austin "carried on disarmament talks for six months," during which time the transfer price of plastic resins did not change, to develop a formula approach to determining the transfer price. This approach was based on classifying all plastic resins into one of three categories (commodity low-grade, specialty low-grade, and high-grade). For each of these categories, the average gross margin was calculated on a quarterly basis. The transfer price of any particular plastic resin was determined by calculating a markup using the gross margin from the category of which it was a member, adding this markup to actual full costs (determined by allocating variances to standard costs on a poundage basis, given the difficulty in measuring actual costs because one plant could make many plastic resins, which created a monumental joint cost allocation problem), and deducting 5 percent from the total. Thus, the process combined both external market-based and cost plus markup policies. The transfer price was based on the gross margin from the previous quarter. Some thought had been given to determining the prices monthly, but there had been opposition to this because of the greater time and effort that would have been necessary for calculating transfer prices.

Rennke found that "people were disposed to go along with this, and the arguments quit. We agreed to stop screwing around and use the goddamned formula." The general satisfaction with this solution dramatically illustrates the importance of process in determining a transfer price. From a strictly technical perspective, there is no reason to think that the transfer prices resulting from this formula were any more accurate as estimates of what the "real transfer price" was than the price the previous approach had yielded.

In fact, the new formula had some peculiar properties. Transfer prices always lagged external prices by one quarter. For example, if costs increased during quarter one, thereby decreasing gross margins, or if external prices declined during quarter one, also decreasing gross margin, these changes would not result in a lower transfer price until quarter two. Measures of financial performance in the Rigid Packaging and Flexible Packaging business centers were always better or worse than they would have been on the basis of more current information when gross margins of plastic resins were increasing or decreasing.

Another peculiar property of this formula was that in one quarter, the Plastic Resins business center actually owed a credit to the buying business centers, since in the previous quarter gross margins on external sales had been negative as a result of extraordinarily high costs of the raw material used in manufacturing plastic resins. A credit was due because the transfer price was less than full cost. Although the president had been highly displeased with this result, Rennke believed that it was appropriate: "If you're evaluating your business fairly, why lose money outside and make money inside?" Even in this situation, Austin remained satisfied with the new approach:

> We did not scream. Everybody was glad to have a formula. People recognized that it was an absolute waste of time for the corporation when people argued about transfer prices. We wanted to get on with running the business.

Competitive Problems Resulting from Market-Based Transfers

The other major problem that must be managed when a mandated market-based policy is used—although it is not as common or as difficult as the problem of determining a just price—is that in some instances, this policy inhibits competitive effectiveness on the final good sold by the buying profit center to the external market. This inhibition takes two forms. The first is when the buying profit center cannot earn the required margins on the final good, given the transfer price, and so forgoes some business that would be profitable for the company as a whole. This is most likely to occur when individual profit center financial results are very important in measuring, evaluating, and rewarding performance. A variation on this problem is when the final good is priced so high that the business attracts competitors, either because they are willing to earn lower margins since they can manufacture the good for less and earn an attractive profit margin or because they price on a full cost transfer basis so that the profits of the profit center selling the final good equal the total profits earned by the company. In any case, the company's market share can be eroded, ultimately forcing it to accept lower profit margins anyway.

Paine Chemical Company: Problems of Weakened Competitive Position

---

Some examples of market-based transfer prices inhibiting the company's ability to compete effectively in the marketplace were thought to have occurred at Paine Chemical Company. The president, Larry Johnson, cited as one example a lost opportunity in the late 1960s and early 1970s to develop technology for transferring plastic resins in particle form to Flexible Packaging, thereby saving on capital costs:

> We wanted the Flexible Packaging people to use it [plastic resins] in particle form. They would have solved the technical problems required to take it in this form if they had been given a sufficient price incentive. This never happened.

He also suggested that market price transfers had resulted in prices of flexible packaging that made the business attractive enough for competitors of Plastic Resins to integrate forward into this business:

> Another lost opportunity is related to the fact that Flexible Packaging's markets work on replacement. It has been argued that if they had attacked more aggressively in terms of pricing, we wouldn't have Integrated Petroleum as a competitor today. There was no major packaging competitor at that time.

More recently, another internal customer of Plastic Resins—Consumer Products—had experienced problems with the use of market price transfers and the small price differential between particles and pellets. This business center was a miscellany of businesses acquired over the last twenty-five years, many of which used plastic resins, with total purchases of 25 million pounds per year. Those businesses that did not use plastic resins were being divested. Some of the businesses that used plastic resins had products that could use scrap-quality or "regrind" plastic resin. Since many of their competitors used this much cheaper raw material, the temptation existed to source this form of plastic resin externally. Robert Decker, the Consumer Products business center manager, recalled that his predecessor had succumbed to this temptation but that higher-level management had reversed the decision when it found out about it. Decker saw this as a problem with market price transfers:

> You have to decide what your objective is. If it is to use plastic resin, maybe it should be transferred at cost. This was a classic case where the transfer price got in the way of the right decision.

Decker believed that his competitive position was hurt by not having sufficient incentive to purchase plastic resins in particle form. He received a one-cent-per-pound discount for particles, but he thought that the true differential in manufacturing costs was nine cents. Other data from the Rigid Packaging business center estimated this differential as two to four cents. In any case, Decker stated: "We have a higher total cost than our competitors, and we are not getting the position in the market that we should."

The second inhibition on competitive effectiveness is due to a failure of either profit center manager to do what is necessary to maintain the competitive strength of the final product. This can occur, for example, when the selling profit center fails to invest in R&D because it believes that the transfer price is too low and that the profits it is earning on internal transfers do not justify this investment. A similar example is when the buying profit center fails to invest in R&D for the final good or is less aggressive about marketing it than it could be because the profits it is earning on the good are low or negative. Although, in the short term, the buying profit center may be selling an amount that is optimal for the company as a whole, because of higher-level pressure to do so, because less emphasis is placed on individual profit center financial performance, or because the product represents a small proportion of its total revenues, its competitive position may be eroded over the long term. Here, the buying profit center manager has little incentive to give this product high priority when allocating scarce capital and human resources, and it will simply wither as a result of neglect.

Locke Chemical Company: Conditions for the Erosion of Competitive Position

There were some instances at Locke Chemical Company when transfer prices had created disincentives to support products for the long term, although it was not thought that, in the short term, any decisions had been made that were suboptimal for the company as a whole. The products in question were made by the Fine Chemicals Department—under general manager Jake Hackman—which was in the General Chemicals Division. Fine Chemicals purchased MNB from the Consumer Division at market price as a raw material for a product called PNB. MNB was used by Consumer to make a mature product whose total sales were gradually tapering off, leaving the Consumer Division with excess capacity in MNB. The principal raw material for MNB was Building Block C, which Consumer obtained from the Basic Chemicals Division. Five years ago, Fine Chemicals had developed PNB, which could use MNB as a material, although it could also use substitutes.

A new plant was built to manufacture PNB, and costs turned out to be higher than expected. The principal competitor used a different and cheaper raw material, which it manufactured for itself. To keep its market share, this competitor had been keeping prices of PNB low. This prevented Fine Chemicals from raising prices to achieve its anticipated profits on top of the higher-than-expected costs. The only way to improve the profitability of PNB was to reduce costs, such as those for MNB. The transfer price on MNB was about twice full cost.

Although the external market for MNB was thin, it could be obtained from another chemical company at a 10 percent "co-manufacturer's discount" below the price currently being paid to the Consumer Division. Fine Chemicals had this in writing from the supplier and presented it to the Consumer Division. Bryan Roderick, controller of the General Chemicals Division, described Consumer's response:

> They said, "No, you shouldn't get the co-manufacturer's discount since we are the ones that make MNB." We went to the director of purchasing and he ruled for Consumer. Neither one of us wants to go to the president.

Roderick estimated that Fine Chemicals lost $1 million per year on PNB, whereas Consumer made nearly $4 million per year on its product that used MNB. Because of this, "there is no motivation for our line managers in General to secure additional volume on PNB, since for every pound we sell, we lose more money."

This created a dilemma for Hackman. He had spent the past four months trying to determine a strategy for PNB. About 18 percent of his R&D was devoted to this product, but his projections showed that on the basis of the current transfer price, cumulative cash flow would be negative until 1990, when the product would only show a 5 percent gross margin. As Hackman expressed it: "It's not very motivating to see I can never make anybody smile about the PNB business." Although this was a strong incentive to exit this business, he knew that that would penalize other Locke businesses. Locke had the "world's best cost position in Building Block C," but PNB was one of the few products with a better than average growth rate that used this building block. Hackman believed that with the right price incentives on MNB, internal demand for Building Block C could be increased through increased volume of PNB. He thought the opportunities would be there if more competitive pricing of PNB put a few of the "weak sister" competitors out of business.

Although Hackman saw the advantages to the company of using more MNB, he could not escape the fact that doing so hurt his performance measures:

> From a corporate point of view, I'm under self-imposed pressure to stay in PNB. And it would never serve the corporate interest to let me buy outside. However, if I keep selling more PNB, I just lose more money and it negatively impacts my performance income. When it comes time to decide how to allocate resources, I wonder why I should put people on PNB. Why shoud I spend a hell of a lot of money on it? I remind my boss constantly and he says, "Wear your corporate hat."

His boss, Victor Vallon, vice-president and general manager of the General Chemicals Division, doubted if his exhortations would be decisive over the long term: "If we are making money on a see-through basis and the end marketer doesn't make any money, he'll turn his interest to other, more profitable products." One of Hackman's longer-term concerns was what would happen if Consumer withdrew from the business that used MNB. He speculated that it might even try to transfer the MNB facility to him to avoid having to write it off if the decision was made to exit the business that used MNB.

Roderick was involved in a similar situation with a product called DAL, which he purchased from the Basic Chemicals Division to make a product called Malor. Basic Chemicals was phasing out of DAL and putting minimal capital into the facilities, which were operating at about 30 to 40 percent of capacity. DAL was transferred at a market price that was about twice the full cost. The external market for DAL was fairly thin, because there was not much demand for it. Fine Chemicals was losing $1 million per year on Malor, while Basic Chemicals was making $3 million per year on DAL. Hackman was unhappy with this arrangement: "They won't give us any profit, so our managers have no motivation to push this, but neither line manager wants to admit to the president that they can't resolve this."

Hackman thought that prices in the Malor market were extremely low because his three major competitors in this slow-growth market "don't have any sense in how they price." He had concluded from a financial analysis that he should withdraw from the Malor business, but other considerations prevented him from doing so:

> By spending $1 million to reduce Malor costs, I still end up losing money, but from a corporate perspective, there is a 13-month payout. So I had to put my corporate hat on. I told one of my peers in Basic Chemicals that I

needed relief on the transfer price of DAL. I just wanted to break even. He told me to wear my corporate hat.

Hackman was further aggrieved that Basic Chemicals was not soliciting additional external business, which would lower the external market price and thereby lower the transfer price. Hackman said that situations such as this were annoying, but "I don't know of a major decision made against the corporate interest by a general manager." Other managers were not so sure; some believed that this kind of transfer pricing problem had led to suboptimal corporate performance, because some businesses had not been pursued aggressively enough.

It can be very difficult for top management to determine whether transfer prices are leading to problems in the pricing of the final good or are being used as excuses for poor performance that is due to other reasons. In fact, it can be very difficult for the profit center managers themselves to untangle the various causes of poor performance. The validity of the claim that market-based transfer prices or excessively high transfer prices are hurting performance depends on a number of variables, some of which can be difficult to determine. These variables include how the final good is priced, how competitors price the final good, the extent to which competitors are vertically integrated backward into the intermediate good and how they price internal transfers, the relationship between full cost and market price of the transferred good, and how profit targets are set in the budgeting process.

An obvious solution to the problem of an uncompetitively priced final good would be to lower profit objectives for the profit center that sells it. Top management may be unwilling to do this for many reasons: it may not have sufficient information about competitors' cost structures to justify such a move, or it may prefer to retain an incentive for aggressive marketing efforts to encourage the profit center to drop this product. In fact, the effectiveness of market-based transfers in forcing general managers to drop unprofitable product lines is sometimes cited as a major reason for using this method.[4] Another obvious solution—using a mandated full cost policy—implies a change in strategy that may be inconsistent with the way in which top management has defined the company's businesses.

The use of market-based transfers does not create competitive problems in pricing the final good when competitors are paying the same price for the intermediate good, either because they also transfer on this basis or because they source externally. This problem is also less acute when customers are less price sensitive and care more about a high-quality product that the company can provide. Finally, concerns about market-based transfer prices will be small when this intermediate good represents a small proportion of the total cost of the final good.

Top management may or may not have the information necessary to make a decision about how transfer prices affect a product's price competitiveness; if it does not have such information, it may or may not want it. The more top management gets involved in internal transactions, the less complete is the authority of the profit center general managers. Top management involvement can include determination of the transfer price, lowering of profit expectations on a product in light of market-based transfer prices and external conditions, or participation in the pricing of the final product. In any of these instances, profit center managers may argue that top management interference has inhibited their ability to achieve their objectives. This is particularly likely when such involvement results in a decision with which profit center management does not agree. Top management must take a number of variables into account and must consider potential effects of its intervention. Caution should be exercised in making these interventions, because conflict over transfer prices is often a result of other aspects of the interdivisional relationship, as discussed in the preceding section.

The Dual Pricing Solution

Dual pricing offers a solution to the problem of an uncompetitively priced final good when mandated market-based transfer prices are used that satisfies the needs of both profit centers. Since the buying profit center only pays full cost, it can lower the external price of the final good while maintaining or improving its profit margins in either percentage or absolute terms. At the same time, since the selling profit center continues to receive a market price, its profit margins are not affected, nor is its profit center status diluted. Thus, dual pricing could also be a solution to the problem of full cost transfer prices not being accepted by the selling profit center, while preserving a strategy of backward integration for low-cost raw material from the perspective of the buying profit center.

As the analysis in chapter 5 demonstrated, dual pricing is not a solution that can be applied to all intracompany transfers for a long period of time. It clearly can be used in only a limited number of instances in a company that uses either of the mandated transfer pricing policies. The problems of double counting and budgeting for elimination would be especially severe in such companies, since a vertical integration strategy results in a large volume of internal transfers. Nevertheless, an implicit policy of dual pricing is sometimes used when profit center managers report financial results to higher-level management that uses both full cost and market price transfer prices, as a way of demonstrating the profits their profit centers are contributing to the corporation.

Dual pricing has another related use when corporate policy requires that profit centers generate their own funds for new products, R&D, or even capital investment. Changing from mandated market-based to mandated full cost or vice versa, to solve the problems of final goods that are priced too high or too low, respectively, can lead to conflict, because such a change will affect these types of funding decisions. By using dual pricing, both profit centers will show profits on the transaction, which they can use to fund projects. Of course, not all companies require profit centers to be self-financing in this fashion, and in reality profits are only being earned once. This use of dual pricing is simply a way of manipulating the company's own systems to enable decisions to be made according to policy. The alternative to dual pricing in this situation would simply be to fund some of these projects from a corporate resource pool. Top management may have reasons for not wanting to use this approach, however, if it is aware that dual pricing is only an artificial way of adhering to investment policy.

Hobbes Instrument Company: Dual Pricing for Antennae

Managers at Hobbes Instrument Company used dual pricing to solve the problem of uncompetitive pricing on the final good caused by the transfer price of the intermediate good. The problems this company experienced illustrate how complex this problem can be, since it often involves technological developments, company reorganizations, and changes in industry structure. All of these factors contributed to the implementation of dual pricing, which was thought to have solved the problem. However, management was very specific about using dual pricing for this one situation. Although managers in both the buying and selling profit centers were satisfied with this arrangement, and although the manager of the selling profit center strongly advocated the use of this method for all of his products sold internally, no support existed for broadening the coverage of the dual pricing policy. It was not seen as a general solution for all of the other products that had disputed transfer prices.

At Hobbes Instrument Company, dual pricing was implemented for antennae transferred between the Internal Products Division and the Parts Division on a mandated basis. Antennae were also transferred to other divisions, primarily Intermediate Systems, on a cost-plus basis, with a markup calculated to yield the corporate average return on net assets. John Coulter, vice-president and director of business management in the Electronics Group, observed: "Antennae was one of the all-time great management problems we had." The reasons for this problem were based on the complex evolution of the Internal Products–Parts trading relationship.

A number of years earlier, Intermediate Systems had sourced antennae from an external supplier. As a component in its product, the antennae represented a fairly large portion of total product costs. When Intermediate Systems could not find a supplier willing to devote enough engineering effort to develop a special antenna for a new product, the division acquired the technology from a company that was not then a supplier. It used this technology to develop a proprietary antenna designed to give it a strategic advantage.

The original antenna development work was done by engineers in Intermediate Systems whose time was costed to this effort to keep from overstating development costs of end products. Eventually, a product manager for antennae was named, and the antenna was sold to other product managers at an estimated market price. One reason for transferring at market price was to generate profits for the antenna product line that could be used to fund further development. This was also consistent with measuring product managers in terms of financial outcomes.

A replacement market existed for all antennae contained in Intermediate Systems' products. The Parts Division served this market, and for a time it continued to source from external suppliers for the antennae that Intermediate Systems had originally purchased externally. However, it had to source proprietary antennae internally. Intermediate Systems also began to manufacture nonproprietary antennae, now that it had the technology, as another source of revenue for the product manager. Gradually, the external sources lost interest in supplying the Parts Division. The original transfer price to the Parts Division was the same price charged to other product managers in Intermediate Systems. However, prices to Parts were soon raised to reflect the markup charged by Parts, which was higher than the markup implicit in the total price of the end product.

In 1976, the antenna product line was transferred to the Internal Products Division, which had a better understanding of the process technology for manufacturing this product. Because Intermediate Systems had paid for the development work, which was almost complete, Internal Products was told that it could not raise prices to this division for two years. However, it raised prices to the Parts Division, so that Parts was paying 50 percent more than Intermediate Systems. Although George Patterson, director of operations in Internal Products, made money on the 20 percent of his antenna output sold to Parts, he lost money on the 70 percent sold to Intermediate Systems. Coulter explained the problem that sales to Intermediate Systems created for Patterson:

> Patterson was losing money on sales to Intermediate Systems and he was under heavy profit pressure. As he shipped more, it hurt his P&L. He wanted to cut his development budget, but there were pressures on him not to do this. He wasn't being motivated properly.

Patterson raised prices to Intermediate Systems when the two-year constraint ended, claiming that additional development work had been done. Top management remained involved, however, since the cost of the antenna had a significant effect on the price of the final product.

During the period when prices were being raised on antennae transferred to the Parts Division, a new manager, who had a marketing background and who came from the Systems Division, took over Parts. Parts was part of the larger Distribution Division, which was under a manager who emphasized strategy in terms of market share, something the new Parts manager was very comfortable with. This manager was also aware of the full potential of the replacement market and the difference in price being paid by Intermediate Systems and Parts. The new Parts manager argued that because of the high transfer price, his division had lost market share in the antenna replacement market; strong profit pressures placed on the division by its financial objectives had led it to price by marking up cost. Coulter recalled the consequences of this situation:

> Parts found out they were paying a lot more than Intermediate Systems. They were also under tremendous profit pressure. This started a hate war. They began to look around to buy from outside vendors. They came up with a strategy to argue that they were losing market share to force the issue on transfer prices. But I didn't believe it. They really didn't know what their market share was. We went out to measure it.

All three divisions worked together, pooling information, to determine whether market share had in fact been lost. Charles Tretter, controller of Intermediate Systems at that time, said, "We were able to peg pretty well that we did lose share and that transfer pricing was part of the problem." Some estimates placed this loss as high as twenty points. One cause of the loss was that former suppliers to Parts had entered the replacement market directly, even with the proprietary antennae they had learned to manufacture.

The decision was made to implement a dual pricing policy for antennae sold to Parts by charging inventory cost and crediting Internal Products with the profits made on external sales by Parts. For sales to Intermediate Systems, Internal Products earned a profit equal to the corporate average return on net assets. Since this price was nearly the same as the market price for these antennae, Intermediate Systems was satisfied with the arrangement.

Both Internal Products and Parts considered that the dual pricing policy had solved the problems between them. Parts was able to price more competitively, and Internal Products earned profits on sales to both Intermediate Systems and Parts. Its profits on antennae were higher than the rest of its profits for all other products combined. Patterson was more pleased with this arrangement than with the cost plus profit markup method used on components sold to Parts, even though the profits on these transfers were higher than those on transfers of components to the three systems divisions. Patterson believed that the dual pricing method used for antennae produced "much better cooperation" with Parts than they had had on components. Patterson wanted to use the dual pricing method on all of his products sold internally.

There was no general support for a more general application of dual pricing, despite management's satisfaction with its use for transfers of antennae. One reason was that a bonus program was being implemented that could result in bonuses being paid on profits counted twice. Although this problem could be addressed by accurate forecasts of the elimination that would be necessary to establish profit targets for bonus purposes, historically the company had experienced difficulty in making these forecasts. In discussing the problem of establishing profit targets adjusted for the effects of dual pricing, a group financial executive stated, "I haven't figured out what to do."

A Remaining Question

One of the consequences of dual pricing is that it reduces—and in some cases entirely eliminates—conflict between the two profit centers over the transfer price of the intermediate good. Other ways of reducing conflict in mandated market-based transfer pricing include (1) making changes in the transfer pricing process and (2) establishing criteria for performance measurement, evaluation, and reward that take account of the fundamental interdependence between profit centers in a strategy of vertical integration. Both of these approaches—and clarifying the role of the selling profit center—also apply when a mandated full-cost policy is used.

Although I have made a number of suggestions about how to reduce conflict and have pointed out some of its dysfunctional consequences, I have never argued here that conflict resolution should always be higher-level management's objective. The question remains whether a lack of conflict is an indication of effective transfer pricing practices. For some of the companies in this study—such as Alfarabi Chemicals, Aquinas Chemicals, and Rousseau Chemical Corporation—that was in fact the case. All of these companies had cultures that valued conflict negatively. There were other companies, however—such as Hobbes Instrument Company and Paine Chemical Company—where conflict was allowed to continue. Was this because they could not resolve it, because they did not believe it was a problem worth addressing, or because they believed that it had positive consequences?

Evidence has already been reported that managers at Hobbes Instrument Company regarded conflict as healthy and as an important part of the company's management style. If this is true, the logical next question is how conflict can be useful to the profit center managers, to their bosses, or to both. Since mandated internal transfers have a built-in potential for conflict, a complete understanding of how to manage both full cost and market-based policies requires a more complete discussion of conflict. This is an extremely important practical concern for managers who are involved in transfer pricing. It is also an issue about which there is a great deal of misunderstanding because of a failure to look at transfer pricing from the perspective of the top-level managers who oversee the internal transactions between profit centers.

8
Managing Conflict for Information and Control

Interdependence between buying and selling profit centers can result in conflict between them, because it gives each some power over the other. The inability of either profit center to substitute an external transaction for the internal one makes conflict nearly inevitable. If the buying profit center is not happy with the transfer price, deliveries, product quality, service, or technical support, it is nevertheless a captive customer, and the selling profit center has much less incentive to be responsive to internal customers than to external ones. At the same time, the selling profit center cannot replace internal buyers with outside customers that may be willing to pay more or that are more cooperative and easier to work with.

There are two basic types of interdependence: activity interdependence and outcome interdependence.[1] The *activities* of one profit center affect those of another when, for example, the selling profit center is late in supplying the intermediate good and the buying profit center has to make adjustments. Conversely, if the buying profit center delays taking delivery or places an order with a short lead time, the activities of the selling division are affected. In both cases, conflict can lead to improved performance by making one profit center more responsive to the needs of the other.

The *outcomes* of one profit center can affect those of another in two ways. Their interdependence is *competitive* when the outcomes for one profit center are gained at the expense of the other's outcomes. This can happen when conservative standard costs are set and the buying profit center does not benefit from positive variances. It also occurs with market-based transfer prices, since the higher the transfer price, the greater the profits are in the selling profit center, at the expense of profits in the buying profit center.

The interdependence is *symbiotic* when either gains or losses in the outcomes of one profit center result in gains or losses for the other. This occurs, for example, when standard cost transfers are used and volume variances are not allocated. If the buying profit center is experiencing reduced demand for the final good, it uses less of the intermediate good, which affects the performance of the selling profit center. Another example is with actual full cost transfers, when all positive and negative variances are shared between the selling and buying profit centers. Here, the indirect interdependence between buying profit centers that purchase from the same selling profit center is also symbiotic.

Although activity and outcome interdependence are conceptually distinct, in practice they are often related. The activities of one profit center can affect the activities of another in ways that also affect the other's outcomes—for example, when orders with short lead time interrupt production runs and result in negative efficiency variances. Conversely, outcomes can affect activities when the buying profit center faces strong demand for the final good and the selling profit center gives its orders high priority, since they require long production runs, which contribute to manufacturing efficiency.

The Conflict Dynamics of Interdependence

By definition, in a situation of interdependence, each profit center is dependent upon the other. Pfeffer and Salancik (1978) identified three critical factors that determine the degree of dependence: (1) the importance of the resource provided to a party for its continued operation and survival, (2) the extent to which the other party has discretion over how this resource is allocated and used, and (3) the extent to which alternatives exist for this resource. When internal transactions are mandated, discretion over resource allocation is limited and alternatives are restricted. This creates a situation of high dependence for both profit centers. The degree of dependence thus depends on the first factor and on the type of transfer pricing policy that is used. Concerns about the fairness of transfer prices and the importance of process are greatest when either or both divisions are highly dependent on each other. The amount of conflict in internal transactions is also directly related to the degree of interdependence.

The importance of a traded good to the selling profit center depends on (1) the percentage of this good that is traded internally (product materiality), (2) the percentage of total output represented by this good (profit center materiality), (3) current performance of the product and the profit center, and (4) the extent to which performance is evaluated and rewarded on the basis of financial outcomes. If most of a product is traded internally, the selling profit center is highly dependent on the actions of buying profit centers. This a minor matter when the product is a small proportion of the selling profit center's output for all products taken together, but it is a major matter when it is a substantial proportion of total profit center output. If profit center and product performance are good, this mitigates the dependence; if it is poor, however, the dependence is strongly felt.

External conditions have strong effects on profit center performance. For example, when external demand is strong, actual costs will be lower than when it is weak.[2] This mitigates the effects of less-than-expected internal demand, especially when external buyers can be found for all output. Finally, the more emphasis that is placed on evaluating and rewarding the management of the selling profit center on the basis of financial outcomes alone, the more concern there will be about the effect of internal dependencies on these measures.

The importance of a traded good to a buying profit center depends on (1) the percentage of total costs this good represents for the products in which it is used, (2) the percentage of total output represented by these products, (3) current performance of the product and the profit center, and (4) the extent to which performance is evaluated and rewarded on the basis of financial outcomes. If the transferred good represents a high proportion of total costs of a product, the transfer price will have a strong effect on the profitability of this product. This is especially important when the product accounts for a high proportion of the profit center's total sales and profits. When the buying profit center is doing well financially, the effects of transfer prices on profits are less significant than when profits are low or when the profit center is experiencing a loss on a product or total basis.

External conditions, such as the relationship between supply and demand in the industry and the general state of the economy, are important determinants of financial performance. If a competitor of the selling profit center adds a large new plant, there may be a temporary state of industry overcapacity, which will drive prices and profits down on the intermediate good. This can substantially benefit the buying profit center when a mandated market-based policy is used. But if a standard full cost policy is used and market price falls below full cost, the buying profit center may think that the transfer price is unfair. From its perspective, the role of the selling profit center is to provide low-cost intermediate goods. When market price is less than full cost, this role is no longer being fulfilled.

Conversely, if a competitor of the buying profit center adds a large new plant, prices and profits on the final good will go down. This will make this profit center even more sensitive to transfer prices, since they now have a larger proportional effect on its profitability. The buying profit center will be especially sensitive to this if the plant is built by a new competitor that has been a competitor on the intermediate good and is suspected of transferring it on a full cost basis.

Effective management of both types of mandated transfer pricing policies requires an awareness of how much one profit center's dependence on the other affects its response to transfer prices. The greater the dependence, the greater will be the concern about whether or not the transfer price is an accurate measure of market price or production costs and about how transfer prices affect performance evaluation and reward. Even when clarity and consensus exist about corporate strategy and each profit center's role in it, and even when the transfer pricing policy is accepted as the proper one, given the strategy, conflict over transfer prices can occur if dependencies are high. When internal transfers represent a large proportion of the selling profit center's total output and also represent a large proportion of the buying profit center's costs, and when either profit center is suffering performance problems, conflict is likely. This is because transfer pricing can have a strong effect on the profit center's performance measures—in many cases, more so than any other single action or renegotiation of any single external relationship.

Locke Chemical Company: Examples of High and Low Interdependence

Locke Chemical Company experienced a number of problems when it implemented a mandated full cost transfer pricing policy for the so-called building-block chemicals in the Basic Chemicals Division. This division objected to the policy because its top management had not accepted the new role it had been given in the corporate strategy. The buying divisions were extremely concerned about how standard costs were set and about the take-or-pay provision. The extent to which these divisions complained about this policy was directly related to how dependent they were on the Basic Chemicals Division and how well their business was doing.

The Molding Division had the most difficulties with transfer pricing. It was a very large user of building-block products, and its financial performance was quite weak. The Plastics Division was also a large user, but less so than the Molding Division, and its financial performance was better; it complained less about transfer prices. The General Chemicals Division was also a large user, but its financial performance was quite good, so it was relatively unconcerned about transfer prices. Finally, the Consumer Division was both the smallest user of products from the Basic Chemicals Division and the most profitable division in the company. Its management was totally unconcerned about transfer prices. In cases where there was concern, it was exacerbated by the effect transfer prices had on bonuses, since they were based primarily on divisional results.

The Molding Division

The Molding Division's business was very different from Locke's other chemical businesses. One manager described the selling environment for molded products as a "jungle." The differences between molded products and the other businesses exacerbated problems of interdivisional relations. Concerns about transfer prices were also exacerbated by Molding's poor financial performance over the past several years. In the past year, the bonuses for its managers had averaged less than half of those received by managers with equivalent positions in other divisions and the same individual performance ratings. Paul Hayden, vice-president and general manager of the Molding Division, estimated that transfer prices had cost him $30,000 to $35,000 in bonuses over the past two years.

Nathan Farber, the division controller, admitted that managers in Molding were "the biggest bitchers about corporate transfers," and he believed that "the day the cost plus investment policy was adopted was the day my troubles began." He recounted some actions he and Hayden had taken to address their problems with transfer pricing:

> I have had a long and frustrating experience with this current transfer pricing policy and its major deficiencies. I have had a lack of success in getting it changed. Paul Hayden has shared my frustration and brought it

> up when I gave up. He works it into quarterly reviews and budget forecasts. We are persona non grata at corporate headquarters. But it has significantly impacted our results reported to the outside world, as well as our incentive compensation.

In one of these reviews, Hayden had presented tables showing that in 1979, the standard full cost transfer prices he had paid exceeded actual costs by $20 million. Even worse, he showed that the full cost transfer prices exceeded the market price valuation by $12 million to $17 million. This was especially irksome to him, since outside customers of Basic Chemicals that were his competitors were receiving the product at the lower market price. In 1980, the excess costs were $12 million and the difference between standard full cost and market price was $18 million. Hayden summarized the basis of his dispute:

> When the using division that takes the product has bonus opportunities and appraisals for the year tied into bottom line income, it requires a great deal of confidence that transfers are done on a fair basis.

Most of Molding's purchases from Basic Chemicals were for Building Block A and Building Block E; the first product was used to make the second. Molding absorbed about 80 percent of Basic Chemicals' output of Building Block A—about half of it directly and the other half through its purchases of Building Block E, of which it consumed about 95 percent of Basic Chemicals' output. Building Block A had only recently become available in the external marketplace, and Locke was the largest producer of this chemical. Building Block E, which was not an item of commerce, had been manufactured by Molding before the Basic Chemicals Division was established. Thus, the reorganization created a new and major interdivisional interdependency. Tom Hewitt, assistant controller of corporate accounting, believed that this reorganization was one cause of Molding's dissatisfaction with the current transfer pricing policy:

> Molding was vociferously opposed to the new structure. It was the first real time they lost pieces of plant on a nonvoluntary basis. It rubbed them the wrong way. They have consistently been the strongest critic of the program.

His recommendation was to put production of Building Block E back into the Molding Division:

> If I were in Mr. Cartman's [the CEO] boots, I would take away from Mr. Hayden every internal reason he has for why he is not performing well. So I'd give him back Building Block E so he'd have one less excuse for poor performance.

The transfer price of Building Block E was especially controversial, since Molding's management believed that standard costs were set so high on this product that they made Molding's annual profits $10 million to $15 million lower than they should have been. Molding's management further believed that Basic Chemicals did not have enough experience in manufacturing Building Block E to run these plants efficiently.

There was some question of whether security analysts who looked at the molding business knew how profits were being affected by transfer prices. The problem of getting security analysts to understand reported figures was a reason some managers gave for not changing the transfer pricing policy to a market price basis. Jason Walker, director of planning and administration, spoke of his dilemma in wanting to preserve comparability with past records while at the same time not wanting current reports to be inaccurate measures of performance:

> I'd hate to see them change the son of a bitch again. It would make it hard for me to explain the figures to the outside world. We spend an enormous amount of time trying to explain misperceptions. That doesn't make anybody any money. But you don't want to look worse than you already are.

Walker also believed that perceptions of other managers in the company were another reason why Molding was so concerned with transfer prices:

> Internally, people see us as the biggest bunch of bastards in the company. In 1968 we made $72 million in profits and the whole company made $117 million. We have gone through a hell of a situation since 1973 of overcapacity, accelerating costs, and an inability to pass on price increases. Things will improve, although we will never get the same growth as before.

Transfer pricing was an especially sensitive issue to Molding, since its recent performance had been poor. Hewitt regarded this decline in Molding's performance as one reason its managers were such vocal critics of transfer pricing:

> If you look at Locke historically, the guys bringing home the bacon have a degree of independence which is much greater than the rest of the crowd. Molding was this way for many years until the mid-1970s, when they hit a time of low profitability. Plastics never had that stature, so they didn't lose as much.

For this reason, he believed that Molding managers' claims that transfer prices were hurting their reported financial performance were exaggerated:

> Molding is a $1 billion company and a shitty business. You can't do anything for them to make them look good. This is a problem I have with Mr. Hayden. The most we can change the numbers is about $50 million.

The Plastics Division

Arthur Lipkin, vice-president and general manager of the Plastics Division, also linked poor performance with complaints about transfer prices:

> There is a pretty close relationship between how well a business is doing and complaints about transfer prices. If you are in trouble, you do whatever you can that's legal and moral to get charges out of your division.

Lipkin said he was not completely satisfied with the current policy: "I think I should get product at C&I or market price—whatever is lowest"; but he believed that "it doesn't do any good to argue these issues." He had less incentive to argue than Hayden; although he was a large user, his division was not suffering performance problems. He also thought that one reason transfer pricing often proved to be very difficult to manage was that "in my experience, the problem with internal transfers is that too often it's viewed as an accounting problem and not as a behavioral problem."

The General Chemicals Division

Victor Vallon, vice-president and general manager of the General Chemicals Division, was even less concerned with transfer pricing:

> I don't have great problems with transfer pricing. It's an overworked problem in this company. I don't expect a perfect solution. There is always some problem with any system. I've always thought that transfer pricing was a much dramatized thing.

Although this division purchased about one-third of its raw materials from Basic Chemicals, it was the second most profitable division in the company, which reduced the concerns of General Chemicals' management with transfer pricing.

One particular transfer, however, had been a fairly significant problem for several years. When the Basic Chemicals Division had been created, Building Block G had been moved from General Chemicals to the new division. General Chemicals purchased some $100 million worth of the product on a C&I basis—about 97 percent of total output. The new division's manufacturing personnel did not have experience with the production technology for this chemical, and personnel had been transferred in. Basic Chemicals had adopted its own strategy for this chemical, which had created problems for General Chemicals. As Vallon explained:

> Basic Chemicals runs the Building Block G plants differently than we ran them. We were milking them. The strategy in this product is to maximize cash flow. They started putting more dollars into maintenance and capital. On one of our products our major competitor signed a firm pricing agreement with our customers for 18 months, so we couldn't increase selling prices. During this time our margins got squeezed.

The pressure on margins caused by increased investment in Building Block G facilities was more intense because Locke had been a higher-cost producer of this chemical in the first place.

Within the past two years, the situation had improved somewhat. One reason was Earl Shindell's appointment as general manager of Basic Chemicals. Shindell had a great deal of experience with Building Block G from assignments earlier in his career. Interdivisional coordination was also improved when the general manager of the profit center in General Chemicals that was the major purchaser of Building Block G was brought in to become head of the department that manufactured it in Basic Chemicals. This individual had good relationships with his former colleagues in General Chemicals, which facilitated positive interdivisional relationships.

The Consumer Division

Managers in the Consumer Division were least concerned about transfer prices because their internal purchases were small and the division was currently extremely profitable. Unlike those of the other divisions, Consumer's products were high-margin products whose value was unrelated to cost. The division was much more marketing-oriented than the others, and being a low-cost producer was not a major element of its strategy. Henry Firth, the division's controller, summarized his attitude toward transfer prices:

> We have not been impacted much by internal transfer policies. Maybe one-half of a percent of our total costs are purchased internally. On internal purchases we don't care whether it's at C&I or market. We don't use much of these products, and we're making a lot of money.

Thus, this division was in exactly the opposite situation to the Molding Division, which made substantial internal purchases and was suffering very low financial performance. These differences explained the differences in degree of conflict over transfer pricing.

Another reason why interdependence leads to conflict is based on an irony of vertical integration: internal transactions are most attractive to one profit center when they are least attractive to the other. This irony is most apparent when mandated market-based transfer prices are used, because internal and external transactions are more comparable under this policy. However, it also exists when mandated full cost transfer prices are used, especially when the selling profit center has not accepted its cost center role on internal transactions.

When demand for the intermediate good is strong, prices are high. Outside customers will then be especially attractive to the selling profit center because they will be willing to pay high prices for large volumes. Under these conditions, however, the advantages of vertical integration to the buying profit center are most apparent, since it has a guaranteed supply. Unless the buying profit center pays the same price as could be obtained externally, the selling profit center will perceive internal sales as inhibiting its ability to increase its profitability. This will be especially irksome when the vertical integration strategy of giving priority to internal customers jeopardizes longer-term relationships with external customers, which may conclude that the selling profit center is not a totally reliable supplier.

Conversely, when supply of the intermediate good is high relative to demand, external suppliers look most attractive to the buying profit center. These suppliers may be willing to sell at a price above variable cost to keep their plants operating close to capacity, and this price may be much lower than the transfer price being paid to the selling profit center. In these circumstances, however, captive internal customers that take a large volume of the intermediate good at prices above market price are very much appreciated by the selling profit center. If the buying profit center sources both internally and externally and is forced to reduce its external purchases, it may find external suppliers unwilling to give it high priority when demand for the intermediate good becomes strong. The buying profit center is then especially dependent on the selling profit center, which is facing very attractive external opportunities.

In both of these situations, the irony of the vertical integration strategy being most advantageous to one profit center when it is least advantageous to the other will result in conflict over transfer prices. The obvious solution is to use a transfer pricing process that is flexible enough to allow transfer prices to change as market prices change. However, this can reduce other advantages of a vertical integration strategy. For example, the buying profit center can be more competitive on the final product when it pays less for the intermediate good than is paid by its competitors who purchase it externally. This depends on how strong the demand is for the final good. Even when the demand for the intermediate good is strong, demand for the final good can be relatively weak if the intermediate good is used in other final goods that do face strong demand.

Furthermore, long-term contracts are often written for external relationships to protect the buying profit center from price increases or the selling profit center from price decreases. Although similar frustrations can be felt when external conditions change, both parties accept the fact that they entered these contracts of their own free will, as opposed to mandated internal contracts. It is also common for external contracts to be renegotiated in the interest of the longer-term relationship, since either party can dissolve it when the contract expires.[3] This provides an incentive for flexibility in enforcing contract terms that does not apply to internal transactions. When internal transfers are mandated, both profit centers are free to attempt to aggressively renegotiate the transfer price when it is to the advantage of either party to do so. If the transfer pricing process does not provide for renegotiating frequently enough, either profit center may initiate efforts to change the process, which can result in conflict.

How Top Management Can Use Conflict

The use of conflict for generating information and facilitating control is virtually ignored in the literature on transfer pricing. Instead, conflict is typically regarded as a problem and a sign that changes need to be made in people or in transfer pricing policies.[4] Similarly, negotiation—a term for conflict resolution—is typically considered to create problems, since the best negotiator will get the best price.[5] These interpretations of the role of conflict and negotiation in transfer pricing are not based on a general management perspective. For higher-level managers, conflict between lower-level general mangers (and functional managers, for that matter) can be used to generate information and facilitate control. This conflict usually includes negotiation between these lower-level managers, which provides the additional benefit of giving them training in an important general mangement skill.

When conflict over the transfer price generates information, the role of price is very different from its role in economic theory, where it captures all the information necessary for making resource allocation decisions. In contrast, prices as information generators can play a very minor role in resource allocation. This finding from practice is the basis for an important formal hypothesis:

> **Hypothesis 33:** Conflict can be used by top management to generate information and exercise control.

Since conflict increases the transaction costs of the exchange in terms of the time and energy spent on it, the fact that it has positive consequences presents a challenge to the new institutional economics (Williamson, 1975), which fails to recognize that in a strategy of vertical integration, it is difficult to instill discipline in both parties to the transaction, since exchanges are mandated. When exchanges are not mandated, nonperformance can be dealt with by the discipline of the market, through replacing one relationship with another. Conflict is a way of ensuring such discipline when the market mechanism is not present—both directly, as discussed earlier, and indirectly, through its information and control benefits to higher-level management.

Williamson (1975) cited reduced transaction costs and the greater efficiency of a hierarchy for revolving disputes as major reasons for vertical integration. He claimed: "Since the aggressive pursuit of individual interest redounds to the disadvantage of the system, and as present and prospective compensation (including promotions) can be easily varied by the general office to reflect noncooperation, simple requests to adopt a cooperative mode are apt to be heeded" (p. 29). In practice, however, these "simple requests" either are not made by top management or are often heeded in only a partial and temporary way. Experience in practice also belies Williamson's assertion that "finally, internal organization is not beset with the same kinds of difficulties that autonomous contracting experiences when disputes arise between the parties" (p. 30). Managers often find that resolution of disputes is easier with external transactions than with internal ones, as discussed in chapter 5 in regard to exchange autonomy. Arguing that these internal relationships are maintained because their greater transaction costs do not overwhelm efficiencies from economies of scale both oversimplifies the problem and denies the central thesis of the new institutional economics, which emphasizes the importance of transaction costs over economies of scale.

The positive benefits of conflict have been identified by organizational sociologists such as Lawrence and Lorsch (1967), Pondy (1967), and Walton and Dutton (1969). For Lawrence and Lorsch, conflict resolution is synonymous with joint decision making between different units of an organization, since the decision requires resolution of differences regarding what actions to take. Pondy noted that organizational performance involves productivity, stability, and adaptability. He argued that conflict could simultaneously facilitate some of these performance criteria and inhibit others, since it is difficult to promote productivity, stability, and adaptability all at the same time. Whether or not conflict contributes to performance depends on the extent to which gains from competitive behavior outweigh its losses (Walton and Dutton, 1969).

The effects of conflict on performance must be assessed in each particular situation. It is important to make this assessment from the perspective of top management, since neither of the profit center managers may be in a position to see that the conflict is producing net benefits to the company as a whole. Evidence that top management finds conflict useful and does not perceive it as hurting organizational performance is suggested by the fact that in many conflict situations, top management refrains from resolving the conflict either through the exercise of hierarchical authority or through some other mode. Instead, it lets the conflict continue, even though managers in both profit centers are dissatisfied with the transfer price.

There are two major benefits in this conflict from the perspective of top management. First, it is a useful source of information. When top management prefers not to intervene in profit center operations (beyond mandating internal transactions) to emphasize the authority and responsibility of lower-level general managers, conflict is one way of obtaining information freely supplied by these managers themselves. For example, if the selling profit center thinks that the transfer price is too low, it may supply top management with information about its contracts with external customers and about the prices its competitors are obtaining. Similarly, if the buying profit center thinks that the price is too high, it may supply top management with information about contracts the selling profit center has with external customers, about bids it has received from external suppliers, and about prices being paid by its competitors either to the selling profit center or to other suppliers.

Second, conflict enables top management to use each profit center to exercise some control over the other by monitoring its performance. Rather than intervening directly to ensure that a profit center is taking steps to achieve agreed-upon objectives, top management can let transfer pricing policies provide an incentive for other profit centers to do so. Conflict between profit centers is a way for top management to use each profit center to monitor the actions of the other to ensure that both are using resources as efficiently and effectively as possible. Since all aspects of the inter–profit center relationship are ultimately related to the transfer price, this makes transfer pricing policy a kind of universal tool for monitoring and indirectly controlling each profit center.

For example, if transfer prices include a provision for R&D support by the selling profit center to the buying profit center, the latter will have a strong incentive to make sure that money is being spent on R&D to support its products. Or if transfer prices are on a cost plus markup basis, the buying profit center will have an incentive to monitor the costs of the selling profit center to ensure that it is producing the intermediate good as efficiently as possible. A final example is when conflict illuminates any tendency of the management in the selling profit center to get conservative standard costs that always yield a positive variance.

If top management is disturbed by conflict or finds that its usefulness for information and control is outweighed by the disadvantages of a lack of inter–profit center coordination and cooperation, it can make adjustments in the transfer pricing process or become involved in adjudicating the dispute. In doing so, however, it must be aware that it is impossible to achieve any ultimate resolution, especially when either or both profit centers are suffering poor performance. There is also the danger that lower-level general managers may simply keep the conflict from the attention of top management while continuing to engage in it. This can result in mutual efforts to hurt each other's performance—efforts about which top management remains unaware. In general, it is better to have any conflict out in the open so that top management can determine its net consequences. The elimination of conflict is an unrealistic and sometimes unproductive goal for mandated transactions.

Paine Chemical Company: Using Conflict for Information and Control

The disputes over the transfer prices of plastic resins at Paine Chemical Company, which continued for several years, are a good example of how a CEO used conflict for generating information and obtaining control. Upon becoming CEO on January 1, 1978, Larry Johnson faced a number of significant challenges, since the company's performance had been suffering in recent years. In fact, this poor performance had been the impetus to put Johnson in this position because of his reputation as a tough and disciplined executive. One of his first acts was to implement a reorganization that placed the plastic resins businesses under profit center managers two levels down in the organization. However, because these businesses were crucial to his plans to turn the company around, he needed to ensure that he had sufficient information about them and sufficient control over them. At the same time, he did not want to achieve this information and control in a way that interfered with his efforts to decentralize responsibility. The information and control made possible by conflict over transfer prices enabled him to implement the reorganization while reducing any risk of lower-level decisions that hurt company performance.

Johnson reorganized the company from a multidivisional structure to a product/function matrix in which business center managers reported to one of three senior vice-presidents. The senior vice-presidents were former division general managers who were soon to retire and who were associated with the company's performance problems. Chris Shaw, vice-president for strategic planning, described how the organization really worked:

> There was a potential concern with giving them [the senior vice-presidents] this responsibility, given problems from the past. This has not turned out to be too big a problem. The investment community dismisses the reporting responsibilities shown in the organization chart. They know that Johnson is in charge.

Another manager described the structure as one in which "Johnson centralized power and authority and decentralized responsibility."

Johnson was especially concerned with the three major plastic resins businesses, since they represented about 40 percent of the company's assets. The Plastic Resins Business Center was under the direction of Vincent Flaherty, who reported to Aaron Thornton, senior vice-president. Reporting to the other senior vice-president, George Mahan, were the business center managers of Flexible Packaging, John Dolan, and Rigid Packaging, Helmut Rennke. Thus, these three businesses were split between two senior vice-presidents and were one level removed from Johnson, who at one time had been directly in charge of all three.

The Transfer Price of Plastic Resins

When Johnson had been given responsibility for these three businesses some ten years earlier, he had changed the transfer price from market price less a 5 percent discount to a cost plus investment policy, similar to that used at Locke Chemical Company. Rigid Packaging and Flexible Packaging were charged standard costs and were assessed assets based on their volume as a percentage of total actual output for the purposes of measuring return on total operating assets (RTOA). Johnson's reason for making this change in transfer pricing policy was that the emphasis at the time was on building volume in the packaging businesses. By transferring at cost, these businesses could build volume through lower prices.

He also believed that this policy more accurately reflected Plastic Resins' role as a manufacturing unit for the packaging businesses, given the large volume of internal transfers:

> This worked to give the packaging people an inducement. We were trying to build volume in these businesses, not in Plastics. When I took over Plastics, 50 percent of its output was consumed by the packaging businesses, and Plastics made 90 percent of its profits from the internal business. Its whole business was being sustained on internal pass-throughs at artificially high prices.

Johnson believed that some other positive effects of this change were that it forced Plastic Resins to pursue outside business more aggressively to increase profits and that it improved the motivation in the packaging businesses, since they now showed a profit. In general, Johnson advocated using a transfer pricing policy that was consistent with strategy:

> The question is, "What is the business you're characterizing—what business are you trying to push?" Transfer pricing is a matter of internal strategy. If people say that market less 5 percent is the only way, I think they are narrow-minded. One of the most important aspects of transfer pricing is motivation. If your strategy is one to encourage people to move forward, set your transfer pricing strategy to encourage that.

Shaw agreed with him:

> Transfer pricing is not something you just have fixed. It depends upon the strategy of the business, which requires you to set up ways of measuring performance based on return on capital. You set up your approach to transfer pricing based on this strategy. I reject the virtues of a uniform and equitable policy. That idea is bullshit.

Some managers believed that one of the reasons Johnson had made this change was to show greater profits in the packaging businesses as part of his efforts to get top management to increase its investment in them. Johnson admitted that "in making this change, I was accused of all kinds of hanky-panky." Although the managers in all three businesses were not completely satisfied with this policy, they all knew that they were evaluated by Johnson on the basis of total divisional performance. The policy was retained when Johnson was transferred to another division at the end of 1973.

Johnson changed the transfer pricing policy back to market price less 5 percent when the matrix structure was implemented on January 1, 1978—the date he took over as CEO. By splitting the plastic resins businesses between two senior vice-presidents, Johnson prevented any one executive below him from having total control over all three businesses. Changing back to a market-based policy was also consistent with the increased emphasis on decentralized profit responsibility. It also led to continuous conflict, which provided him with information about the selling business center. Thornton noted that when disputes existed about the transfer price, "we tend to let the business managers haggle." The market-based transfer price was especially effective in keeping Johnson informed about these businesses, since they were split across two senior vice-presidents. Johnson noted that if these businesses were put under one executive, "consolidating them will give the transfer pricing problem more visibility to the senior vice-president. He'll have to solve it."

The Dispute over Transfer Prices

The current structure did not resolve the problem, however, and for two and a half years the dispute over transfer prices raged on, with Johnson refusing to get involved. During this time, Rennke and Dolan reported financial results on both a market and cost-plus basis in their presentations to top management and the board of directors. Throughout this dispute, a great deal of information was made available to Johnson and the senior vice-presidents, including the prices Plastic Resins received in external markets and from specific customers, the volume of sales by Plastic Resins to external markets and to specific competitors of Rigid Packaging, standard cost differentials between particle and pellet manufacturing costs, cost allocations made for product costing, the indirect costs of Plastic Resins that were allocated to other business centers, and the prices being paid by competitors of Rigid Packaging to competitors of Plastic Resins.

Rennke was most concerned about transfer prices, since they had such a large effect on his reported profits, although he was not concerned that these transfer prices were affecting Johnson's evaluation of his performance. Rather, he was concerned about their effect on business center morale and on personnel in the functions working for Rigid Packaging, as expressed in a memorandum of February 13, 1978:

> It is recognized that we will all be judged by our performance versus our promises (forecasts). However, if strictly internal accounting procedures result in undesirable absolute apparent levels of profitability, it is hard to believe that this will not have some negative effects, particularly on the attitudes and efforts of people in the line areas of marketing, operations, and development, who have been working since last summer on a com-

> prehensive plan to make major improvements in the Rigid Packaging business along the same lines the entire company is now following.

Rennke thought his transfer prices were too high because he was given no discount for large volume, because his deduction for taking plastic resins in particle rather than pellet form was too low, and because the market prices used as the basis for determining transfer prices did not include prices to all markets in which plastic resins were sold. By his calculations, transfer prices were roughly 20 percent higher than they should have been. In September 1979, he calculated that this amounted to overpayments in gross profits of $1.8 million to Plastic Resins over a 19-month period, as a result of which, he said, "Rigid Packaging will be permanently damaged in company records" unless an adjustment was made. To make this adjustment, he proposed that Rigid Packaging be "paid back" these profits over the next 19 months, with an adjustment for inflation.

Rennke also argued that although external prices had been declining steadily throughout 1978, corresponding adjustments had not been made on transfer prices. Flaherty alone established the transfer prices for plastic resins, and he had not made any changes. Given the problem of deriving transfer prices from market prices, Rennke proposed that they be set as markups on cost. He suggested that the average gross profit margins of Plastic Resins' total domestic sales of the type of plastic resins sold to Rigid Packaging be used, and he noted that Plastic Resins was earning higher gross margins on internal sales. Flaherty rejected all of Rennke's charges and his recommendation for a change in policy.

Escalation of the Dispute

The conflict escalated in April 1980, when Plastic Resins announced a large price increase due to rapidly increasing raw material costs. Although the increase did not hold on external sales, Flaherty maintained it on internal transactions, arguing that not only had past transfer prices not been too high, they had actually been too low, and that this price increase simply restored them to what they should be. Lee Austin, manager of business planning in Plastic Resins, described what happened:

> The market was really strong and feedstock prices were going crazy. We were frantically trying to restore our margins. We bit the bullet and said, "We've got to lead an enormous price increase." Everybody followed. But then the market started to weaken and the price didn't hold. Rennke and Dolan started raising hell. Mahan perceived Rennke as probably right and raised hell with Thornton. Thornton came to me and said, "Put yourself in a totally objective position and make a recommendation."

Thornton's request put Austin in an awkward position. He was a personal friend of Rennke's, although he worked for Flaherty, and Rennke had helped advance his career. Austin established four objectives for developing a method that would yield a good measure of the market value of internal transactions: (1) to minimize subjective input, (2) to apply one system to all inter–business center transactions, (3) to use readily available data requiring minimal calculations, and (4) to be fair to all parties. He proposed a cost plus markup approach to determine a market price from which the 5 percent discount would be taken, although it was slightly different from the one proposed by Rennke. For example, in light of objective (2), he included all types of plastic resins in determining what the gross margin percentage should be, including some that had high margins but were not bought by Rigid Packaging (although they were purchased by Flexible Packaging). Austin also argued that the product costing system understated the costs of plastic resins sold to Rigid Packaging and would have to be changed. Finally, he presented data designed to show that external marketing costs were less than 5 percent of sales, and he thereby argued that the discount should be only 3 percent.

The effects of Austin's proposal were more salutary for Flexible Packaging than for Rigid Packaging. Rennke agreed in principle with Austin's recommendations but wanted some adjustments, such as eliminating some types of plastic resin in the determination of the gross profit margin percentage markup. Austin submitted his proposal in May 1980, but had heard nothing back as of the end of July. He was discouraged by this and said that despite all his efforts, since he had received no support on this proposal, "we are sticking with the old method."

Dolan gave his view of why Johnson had not become involved:

> Johnson just doesn't feel strongly about getting involved in these situations. For him they aren't important enough to haggle about.

However, he expected some reduction soon in transfer prices, because his senior vice-president felt strongly about it and "Flaherty has gone too far. He can't support it." Although Dolan thought that he was paying too much for plastic resin, he did not believe that it had negatively affected his performance evaluation or reward:

> I don't worry about the fact that I'm giving Flaherty an extra $4.5 million in profits. It bothers me more from an ego standpoint than salary compensation.

Also, although it did not seem to have hurt his competitive position in general, he noted that it had affected some product mix decisions. For example, he had refused outside business from one customer for a particular product because the transfer price prevented him from making the gross profit he needed.

Mahan, the senior vice-president who was Rennke's and Dolan's boss, thought that Flaherty was overcharging them, but he noted that Larry Johnson did not seem concerned:

> I really think Dolan and Rennke have bent over backwards to be good corporate citizens. I think it's Flaherty who's the problem. This has gone on for two years. Larry didn't think it made any difference. I think he knew and made a mental adjustment. Thornton and I have talked about it, but I like to try to let people work it out among themselves first.

Mahan had gone to Johnson because Flaherty had claimed that Johnson approved of the current transfer prices. Johnson had confirmed the importance of the downstream businesses, but at the same time he stressed the importance of Plastic Resins. As Mahan described it:

> I went to talk to Larry since Flaherty thought he had Larry's blessing on transfer prices. Larry said we're a downstream company. He said to get it straightened out, but not to get a formula which penalizes Flaherty.

Mahan reasoned that this could be done by simply lowering the profit margin objectives of Plastic Resins if the transfer price was lowered.

The Controller's Proposal

At the same time as the price increase was announced in April 1980, the new corporate controller, hired from another company, had asked one of his managers to take a "short and sweet survey" on transfer pricing methods at Paine. He was not satisfied with what he found out, and although he was not sure what new method would be proposed, he was sure about how it should be implemented:

> We will get guys to agree on a pricing system and then we will take it away from them. I would be very nervous letting business center managers calculate price. And whatever we do, not everybody is going to be happy.
>
> We're going to keep score. We'll get senior management to approve this. Then the business center managers can get as mad at us as they want.

Given Johnson's view about the dispute, it was unlikely that the controller would get his way. As Johnson expressed it:

> I'm not going to step into this thing. I let problems come to me. I create my own problems to solve. They're negotiating about what the true market price ought to be. It is best to let the business center managers decide. I don't think controllers have the knowledge of the marketplace. The customer regulates the selling price. The vice-president of marketing is in a better position to adjudicate, but he's too smart to get involved in this.

In August, Flaherty announced reductions in the transfer prices, although Rennke did not think they were great enough. In September, Johnson reaffirmed his unwillingness to resolve these disputes. Upon receiving the controller's recommendations, he stated that he wanted results reported using both market-based and cost plus investment methods, in effect resolving nothing. By maintaining the ambiguity of what the "true" transfer price was and how it should be derived, he guaranteed that the conflict would continue.

Johnson's "nondecision" decision was seen by several managers as consistent with his management style. Rennke observed:

> Johnson tries to make other people make decisions. He signals things. He operates on the basis of creating dissension and conflict, which he has openly stated. He pits people against each other on the theory that this gets a better overall response by getting consideration of all the different angles. This works if everybody approaches it as a statesman.

Shaw described Johnson as an "intuitive manager" and noted that this type of manager "frequently lacks that clean, decisive set of actions. He gives the appearance of being indecisive and not taking positions." Shaw also agreed that conflict was an important part of Johnson's management style:

> Johnson is a conflict-oriented person. He thinks it's useful and desirable and can be in favor of perpetuating it if he sees no obvious and destruc-

tive impact on the corporation. He feels that the right decisions and the right people emerge out of conflict.

Evaluating the Benefits of Conflict

The mere existence of conflict over transfer prices does not guarantee that it is being used as a mechanism of information generation and control by top management. Whether or not conflict serves such a purpose depends on how top management uses it. At a minimum, there must be a toleration of a certain level of conflict. Some managers use conflict as an important part of their management style, whereas others go to great lengths to eliminate it. If a manager does not know how to use conflict constructively and how to determine when the gains exceed the costs, conflict will only create problems that hurt company performance.

It is important to distinguish between conflict over the transfer pricing policy being used and conflict over the transfer price itself, even when there is consensus on the policy. Conflict over the policy is useful only if it helps resolve ambiguities about strategy. It has a negative value if it results from disagreements about a strategy that higher-level management is committed to pursuing. When there is agreement about strategy, and thus agreement about transfer pricing policy, conflict will be useful if the benefits from information and control exceed its costs—that is, lower levels of cooperation and coordination, which hurt company performance.

It is difficult to balance the positive and negative consequences of conflict, since the source of conflict is the perception of either or both profit center managers that there is something unfair about the exchange. For conflict to have primarily positive consequences, these managers must not also believe that they are being treated unfairly in terms of their performance measurement, evaluation, and reward. To make profit center managers believe that they are being treated fairly in terms of their relationship with the total company—even though there may be aspects of unfairness in their relationships with other profit centers—higher-level management must be able to exercise subjective judgment and demonstrate an understanding of an individual's contribution that goes beyond reported financial results. Thus, perceptions of unfairness on internal exchange relationships must be compensated by the perception of fairness in the individual's relationship with the company.

The degree or level of conflict must be considered in evaluating its net consequences to the company. It has already been shown that the level of conflict is directly related to the degree of interdependence. In some situations, it is likely that the level of conflict exceeds what is necessary for generating information and maintaining control—such as when a substantial portion of a buying profit center's costs is made up of internally purchased items and the profit center is suffering poor performance. It is important that top management recognize when this is the case, since there is no easy way to reduce the level of conflict by changing either policy or process. Instead, efforts should be directed toward ensuring that there are no substantial negative consequences of this conflict.

Finally, conflict in inter–profit center relationships may have a large interpersonal component. When there are personal animosities between lower-level general managers or when they are engaged in a power struggle, transfer pricing becomes a substantive issue through which this conflict is conducted. In most companies, it is far more legitimate to argue about transfer prices than to engage in mutual character defamation. When general managers are in competition for status and advancement, the substantive and emotional issues become inextricably intertwined.

There is a "chicken and egg" property to transfer pricing conflict when substantive disagreements become the basis for emotional issues that in turn reinforce the substantive issues. These disagreements can be very difficult to untangle, especially if the conflict has accumulated over a long period of time. Replacing the managers involved is certainly a solution, but this should be a last resort, because so many other factors need to be considered in choosing general managers. In any case, it is important for top management to be aware of the possibility that transfer pricing disputes might have a large emotional content, based primarily on personal animosities between the managers involved.

Paine Chemical Company: Power Politics in Transfer Pricing

Disputes over the transfer price of hydrocarbon resin at Paine Chemical Company were largely based on a power struggle between the two profit center managers that was part of a conflict that had existed for a number of years. Although little personal animosity was involved, the buying profit center manager, who acknowledged that the transfer price was unfair in his favor, had not attempted to get it changed. There were no obvious positive or negative consequences of the conflict that existed. It was simply a situation in which the current transfer price was the issue on which this struggle was fought.

Some of the products that John Dolan, business center manager of the Flexible Packaging Business Center, bought from the Plastic Resins Business Center used an organic resin made by the Organic Chemicals Business Center, which was under Bernard Michels. Plastic Resins received this hydrocarbon resin from Organic Chemicals at full cost, which was currently $.85 per pound. Flexible Packaging paid Organic Chemicals $.20 per pound for overhead and profit. The transfer price had been set on this basis for eight years. Flexible Packaging was currently purchasing 4 million pounds of this product annually.

Organic Chemicals was not satisfied with the present arrangement. Dolan said that they claimed they could not pursue external opportunities when they were forced to sell internally, but he denied the validity of this argument, since these external markets valued the product at less than full cost:

> They have said, "We guarantee you a supply, so we can't develop new markets which would be more profitable." The markets they could get are only worth $.50 per pound. They couldn't make it cheaply enough to be cost competitive.

In spite of this, Dolan acknowledged that the transfer price was unfair, because the markup of $.20 per pound became a smaller percentage of full cost as costs continued to rise. "Clearly, it's unfair to have this margin continue to deteriorate. If I were Michels, I'd argue that we should determine a fair margin." Dolan thought that Michels was probably reluctant to do this because if the price went too high, Flexible Packaging could install its own capacity:

> Another thing that scares Michels is that we could propose to make it ourselves and save on freight. To develop our own capacity would only cost about $400,000.

Another constraint was that Michels had only recently become a business center manager and did not really have enough power to enforce a change. He had been involved in the original negotiations eight years before, when Flexible Packaging had thought it had been treated unfairly by Organic Chemicals. Before the policy of full cost plus $.20 per pound was implemented, Flexible Packaging had purchased hydrocarbon resin for $.44 plus $.10 per pound profit. Ed Clifford, then general manager of Organic Chemicals, had unilaterally raised the profit to $.20. Flexible Packaging went to the Forest Chemical Company, the only external supplier of this product, and negotiated an arrangement. When Clifford was told about this, he asked Flexible Packaging not to change sources and promised to keep the transfer price at $.54 per pound. Within a few months. Organic Chemicals acquired Forest Chemicals, eliminating Flexible Packaging's opportunity to source externally, and Clifford changed the policy to cost plus $.20 per pound. Flexible Packaging was able to renegotiate this to cost plus $.20 per pound and not to exceed $.64 per pound, to avoid absorbing any manufacturing inefficiencies.

In 1975, Organic Chemicals suffered severe performance problems. In 1976, it claimed not to have made a $.20 per pound profit on hydrocarbon resin, and so it added divisional overhead into product costs as a way of increasing the transfer price. This set the transfer pricing policy at full cost including overhead plus a $.20 per pound profit. According to Dolan:

> They changed the ground rules and sent through the paperwork. We had no choice. They stuck us retroactively to 1975. Now Michels wants to change because he is at a disadvantage. There's always a sticker and a stickee.

Dolan took some pleasure in this twist of events:

> Michels was a junior guy back then, a product manager. It is harder for him to deal with me, business manager to business manager, because he's new in the job. Michels has just been a business manager since January. You don't get instant equality. He will have to get it over time.

Dolan was reluctant to negotiate a percentage markup on cost, both because of what had happened in the past and because of the problems it could create in the future:

> There is no way to establish a market price on this product. We asked them to make this for us, but they screwed us, so now we'll screw them. Once I say they can get a fixed margin, they can run a sloppy business, and since I'm paying a fixed percent they can screw me. I can't control his cost allocation, but he doesn't have options with this equipment.

Michel's view of hydrocarbon transfer pricing minimized its importance:

> The transfer price on hydrocarbon resin is cost plus $.20 per pound. This is based on historical reasons involving general managers who didn't get along having a buying/selling relationship. I'm not satisfied with this, since there isn't enough margin. Neither is my internal buyer, since he takes cost swings. But we haven't had time to renegotiate.

In this situation, the product was not large enough as a sale to Organic Chemicals or as a purchase to Flexible Packaging to materially affect either business. However, there were no obvious criteria for establishing a fair transfer price for this product.

Implications for Dual Pricing

The fact that conflict can have positive benefits is another reason why dual pricing has limitations as a solution to the transfer pricing problem, since it reduces or eliminates conflict between profit centers. When dual pricing is used with mandated internal transactions, each profit center has less incentive to monitor the performance of the other. Since the buying profit center is only paying full cost, it is less concerned that the overall value of the relationship be accurately reflected in the market price the selling profit center is receiving. This is especially true when the difference between market price and full cost is large. Even if the buying profit center is receiving lower-quality product or poor service, it may rationalize this in terms of the lower transfer price it is paying. It may also invest less energy in ensuring that the selling profit center is investing in R&D to support the final good. Over time, this may inhibit the performance of the final good.

The buying profit center also has no incentive to bargain hard on the market price portion of the transfer price, since it does not affect its reported profits. This can reduce the incentive of the selling profit center to drive down costs, since it has a comfortable profit margin.[6] Thus, although dual pricing may eliminate conflict over transfer prices, it also thereby eliminates some of its positive benefits. Top management would be sacrificing substantial opportunities for generating information and exercising control if it were to implement dual pricing for all intracompany transfers.

Dual pricing decouples the transfer price to the one profit center from the performance measurement of the other. In doing so, it creates a great deal of slack in the organization, since two sets of measures exist, each of which is most favorable to one profit center, thus eliminating the competitive aspects of inter–profit center relationships. Since the effects of interdependence are reduced under a dual pricing policy, each profit center has a diminished incentive to ensure that gains in the other are not being achieved at its expense.

Hypothesis 34: Dual pricing with mandated transactions reduces the positive benefits of conflict.

9
Pressures for Endless Change

The principal focus of this book so far has been on how to manage a particular transfer pricing policy that has been selected for implementing a particular strategy, and a number of examples have been given of how changes in strategy have led to changes in transfer pricing policy. There are many reasons why strategies change, including (1) changes in the characteristics of the product, (2) changes in the characteristics of the market, (3) changes in technology, (4) changes in competitors' strategies (which may cause them to change their transfer pricing policies), (5) changes in the balance of internal and external sales, and (6) changes in the management of the profit center. In some cases, management might change transfer pricing policies as a way of signaling and preparing for changes in strategy.

Changes can also be made in the specifics of a transfer pricing policy without changing the policy itself. Adjustments in the process might be made to accommodate adjustments in a basic strategy that otherwise remains constant. Again, these adjustments might be made first as a way of reshaping a strategy.

Whether basic changes or simply adjustments are made in policy, there is a trade-off between the advantages expected from the change and the costs incurred in making it. In some cases, managers cite these costs as an explanation for why changes in policy were not made, even though, in some sense, they would have been appropriate.[1] Advantages of not changing include having comparable historical records available for performance evaluation and the fact that managers are familiar with existing policies and know how to use them. These arguments were made at Rousseau and Aquinas Chemicals to explain why they had not changed their transfer pricing policies.

This chapter explores some important topics related to change. First, the concept of the product/process life cycle is used to show how some of the underlying evolutionary forces exert pressures to adapt transfer pricing policies to a particular set of conditions. Second, the problem of implementing transfer pricing for the first time is explored. Third, the problem of changing transfer pricing policy because of a change in structure that was made to implement a change in strategy is examined. The fourth topic concerns the trade-offs that are necessary in having one uniform policy versus having many different policies. Finally, the chapter concludes with a brief discussion of a particular use of transfer pricing that illustrates how the act of change itself can help management achieve certain objectives.

The Product/Process Life Cycle

Environmental conditions, such as industry structure, and product characteristics, such as whether or not the product is a proprietary good, have been shown to influence both the choice of transfer pricing policy and the set of problems that must be managed for any given policy. Many variables are relevant, and the concept of the product/process life cycle can be helpful in developing a simple framework for understanding how these variables create pressures on transfer pricing. Because the product/process life cycle demonstrates the evolution of environmental and technological conditions for a product, this concept provides a perspective on how pressures on transfer pricing change over time.

Porter (1980) has called the product life cycle "the grandfather of concepts for predicting the probable course of industry evolution" (p. 157). Hayes and Wheelwright (1979a, 1979b) have shown how manufacturing process technology varies according to the stage of the product life cycle. Each stage of the product/process life cycle is associated with environmental and technological characteristics that affect transfer pricing policy. Figure 9–1 summarizes the product, process technology, environment, transaction, and best overall strategy characteristics for the four phases of the product/process life cycle: introduction, growth, maturity, and decline. The implications of the product/process life cycle can be examined from the perspective of both the selling profit center and the buying profit center.

The Selling Profit Center

From the perspective of the selling profit center, the simplifying assumption is made that it prefers market-based transfers, since as a profit center it has a strong need to earn a profit on the intermediate good. Although selling profit center managers can accept a cost center role for internal transactions, they rarely advocate this role in practice, because decentralization emphasizes the importance of profit responsibility. For the selling profit center, the issue is how the intermediate good is priced and whether or not internal transactions are mandated.

When the intermediate good is in the introduction phase of the product/process life cycle, the product is a custom design manufactured by a job shop production process. Engineering and R&D are key functions in this phase. Buyers are not price-sensitive, but profit margins are still low because of high production and marketing costs. It takes a great deal of effort and education to get customers

	INTRODUCTION	GROWTH	MATURITY	DECLINE
PRODUCT	-Product design and development key -Many different product variations; no standards -Frequent design changes -Basic product designs emerge -Custom design	-Products have technical and performance differentiation -Reliability key for complex products -Competitive product improvements	-Less product differentiation -Standardization -Less rapid product changes; more minor annual model changes	-Little product differentiation
PROCESS TECHNOLOGY	-Jumbled flow (job shop) -Overcapacity -Short production runs -High-skilled labor content -High production costs	-Disconnected line flow (batch) -Undercapacity	-Connected line flow (assembly line) -Optimum capacity or some overcapacity -Increasing stability of manufacturing process -Lower labor skills -Long production runs with stable techniques -Capital intensive	-Continous flow -Substantial overcapacity -Mass production -Vertical integration -Capital intensive

Figure 9–1. Characteristics of the Phases of the Product/Process Life Cycle

	INTRODUCTION	GROWTH	MATURITY	DECLINE
ENVIRONMENT	-High income purchaser -Buyer inertia -Buyers must be convinced to try product -Few competitors	-Widening buyer group -Consumer will accept uneven quality -Entry of other firms -Many competitors -Lots of mergers and casualties	-Mass market -Saturation -Repeat buying -Choosing among brands is the rule -Price competition -Shake out -Increase in private brands	-Customers are sophisticated buyers -Exits -Fewer competitors
TRANSACTION	-Very high advertising/sales -Creaming price strategy -High marketing costs -High prices and margins -Low profits -Price elasticity to individual seller not as great as in maturity	-High advertising but lower percent of sales than in Introduction -High or highest profits -Fairly high prices but lower than in Introduction -Recession resistant	-Market segmentation -Service and deals more prevalent -Lower advertising/sales -Falling prices -Lower or lowest profits -Lower or lowest margins -Increased stability of price structure	-Low advertising/sales and other marketing -Low prices and margins -Falling prices; might rise in late decline

	INTRODUCTION	GROWTH	MATURITY	DECLINE
BEST OVERALL STRATEGY	-Best period to increase market share -R & D and engineering are key functions	-Practical to change price or quality image -Marketing the key function	-Bad time to increase market share; particularly if low share company -Having competitive costs becomes key -Bad time to change price image or quality image -"Marketing Effectiveness" key	-Cost control key

*Adapted from Competitive Strategy by Michael E. Porter, 1980, Figure 8-2, pp. 159-161 to try the new product. Since competitors are few, it is a good time to build market share.

During the introduction phase, the selling profit center receives very tangible benefits if buying profit centers are required to source internally. This enables the selling profit center to increase volume, thus lowering production costs, and to use internal buyers to identify flaws in the product design and application. By saving on marketing and advertising costs, the selling profit center increases its profit margin on internal sales as compared to external sales at the same price. Establishing a transfer price is difficult, since the few competitors use different designs for their product. A cost plus markup method must be used, which is how products sold externally are priced. Proprietary products have many of the characteristics of products in the introduction phase.

The job shop technology and the existence of overcapacity make it difficult to determine the costs of the product on either an actual or a standard basis. It is also difficult to determine what a "fair" markup is for overhead and profit and how much of a discount, if any, should be given to reflect any reduction in marketing costs on internal sales. Disputes about the transfer price will intensify when buying profit centers are required to source internally, given the problems with the product at this stage and possible preferences for designs that are developed externally. Thus, although mandated internal transactions are advantageous to the selling profit center, the buying profit center may have strong objections to them.

When the product enters the growth phase, a dominant design has emerged and most of the problems have been fixed. It is much easier now to measure product costs. Also, with the use of batch production technology, it is much easier to establish standard costs. Although there are many competitors, a widening buyer group creates a strong demand—more than the selling profit center can satisfy, even operating at full capacity. Extremely high profits make external sales especially attractive. The selling profit center's preference for mandated internal transactions now shifts to a desire for exchange autonomy, thus creating pressures for a change in transfer pricing policy. These pressures will be extremely strong if the selling profit center needs all of its capacity to maintain or build its share in the external marketplace.

Although the selling profit center may be willing to sell internally, it will expect to receive the same profits on internal sales as it receives on external sales. In this growth phase, determining the transfer price is relatively easy. The market is not oligopolistic, and prices can be obtained from competitors that produce a product similar enough to that made by the selling profit center. This creates pressures to change from a cost plus markup policy to one that is based on external market prices. Fewer complaints will emerge from the selling profit center with a policy of exchange autonomy than with one that mandates internal transactions. However, the strong demand may make it difficult for the buying profit center to obtain the product, and it may prefer mandated internal transactions for an assured supply of the intermediate good. Again, the preference of one profit center may be contrary to that of the other.

As the product enters the maturity phase, repeat customers account for much of its business. Products are standardized, and only minor design changes take place—although market segmentation and brand identification begin to receive more emphasis. As the market reaches a saturation point, prices begin to fall, which puts pressures on profits. This price competition can lead to a shakeout in the market, eliminating some competitors. Marketing expenses are not as high as they were in the previous two phases, but service and special deals become increasingly important. The use of an assembly-line production technology makes it important to continue operating at full capacity, with long production runs to keep costs low, especially as prices fall. However, overcapacity can emerge during this phase, which makes it difficult to operate at full capacity.

In a period of market saturation and overcapacity, internal customers are more attractive to the selling profit center than they were in the growth phase. It may now prefer mandated internal transactions rather than exchange autonomy. Product standardization should simplify the use of market prices to set transfer prices, but segmentation by brands and markets leads to different prices for the same product. When internal transactions have been customary, the buying profit center will be quick to complain if transfer prices are not reduced as fast as prices fall in the marketplace.

Another complication in determining the transfer price is the comparative levels of service and special deals offered to external customers by outside suppliers or by the selling profit center. The selling profit center's efforts to keep transfer prices up, combined with the buying profit center's efforts to get them reduced, will be complicated by attractive offers to the buying profit center from external suppliers. The buying profit center's preference for sourcing autonomy thus will conflict with the selling profit center's preference for guaranteed internal sales.

Pressures on transfer pricing policies that are characteristic of the maturity phase become more extreme in the decline phase. There are fewer competitors, but by now customers are extremely sophisticated and some have integrated backward. Extreme pressure on prices reduces profit margins and makes cost control critically important. Low manufacturing costs are obtained through capital-intensive continuous-flow technology, if it is used at full capacity, which contributes to pressure on prices as competitors also attempt to operate at close to full capacity. This can be difficult if a condition of chronic overcapacity develops in the industry. The product is highly standardized now, and buyers can switch to other suppliers. The fact that it is standardized also contributes to low marketing expenditures.

During the decline phase, guaranteed internal customers play an important role in helping the selling profit center operate close to full capacity to keep unit costs down. However, buying profit centers may be able to find extremely attractive external offers because of overcapacity in the industry, particularly in times of economic recession. As a sophisticated buyer, the buying profit center will be able to compare the total product packages offered by internal and external suppliers. Nevertheless, determining a transfer price from market prices may be complex. Disputes can arise about what kind of discount to allow for high-volume purchases by internal customers and about how market prices would be affected if the selling profit center tried to sell the same amount of product externally. Disputes can also concern discounts for the lack of marketing expenses, which are not very high on external sales during this phase. On the other hand, R&D expenditures for process technology improvements are important, and the buying profit center will want to ensure that R&D efforts are being made.

If the volume of internal transfers is large and the product form has evolved differently from that sold externally, the problems of product pricing that were found in the introduction phase or for proprietary products will recur. This can create pressures for cost plus markup transfer pricing, a policy that is particularly attractive to the selling profit center if it guarantees profits when market prices are continuing to fall. At the same time, the buying profit center may argue that it should have autonomy to accept attractive external offers or, if internal transactions are mandated, that they should be full cost or market price, whichever is lower. When full cost is lower than market price, the buying profit center will argue that its vertically integrated competitors are receiving the intermediate good on this basis and that unless it does, too, its pricing will be uncompetitive. The selling profit center, however, will want to earn a profit on the transfer. However, when market price falls below full cost during times of severe overcapacity, the buying profit center will prefer market price as the basis of a transfer price—just when the selling profit center would be happy to settle for full cost.

The vertical integration that is common in the decline phase—forward by suppliers and backward by customers—creates strong pressures to regard the selling profit center as a cost center for internal sales. Maintaining its profit center status will inevitably lead to high levels of conflict, particularly when internal transactions are mandated. The change from profit center to cost center may be perceived as a reduction in status unless it is carefully managed. There are no easy answers to transfer pricing problems in the decline phase.

The Buying Profit Center

The product/process life cycle is also relevant to the buying profit center's preferences for transfer pricing policies and to how these preferences change over time. Just as the selling profit center has a general preference for market-based transfers, so does the buying profit center have a preference for full cost transfers, assuming that full cost is less than market price. However, unless the selling profit center is regarded as a manufacturing unit for the buying profit center, the latter expects to pay the selling profit center a transfer price that includes a margin for profit. The assumption will be that when the final good is in its maturity and decline phases, the buying profit center will shift its strategy toward treating the selling profit center as a manufacturing unit. In the introduction and growth phases, it will be more willing to pay market-based transfer prices.

When the final good is in the introduction phase, the buying profit center will have a strong preference for exchange autonomy, which will enable it to source from suppliers the components that best meet its needs, and suppliers may change as the design evolves. Profit margins are low and there may even be losses in this product phase, but buying cheaply is less important than buying properly and being able to firmly establish the prices of component parts for better control over product costs. The buying profit center will thus be willing to pay market price, although the price may be established through a cost plus markup policy if the component is especially designed for the final good.

The buying profit center has the greatest reason to prefer mandated internal transactions in the growth phase, when the intermediate good is a constraint on its ability to keep up with demand. Since its competitors are also increasing in size, a failure to satisfy demand can result in a loss of market share. Guaranteed internal suppliers can offer an important competitive advantage by eliminating sourcing bottlenecks for the intermediate good. Also, since the buying profit center is making a great deal of money during this phase, it is not especially sensitive to the price of the intermediate good.

As the final good enters the maturity phase, the transfer price becomes more important. The buying profit center will have a strong preference to obtain the intermediate good at cost, especially if internal transactions are mandated. If they are not, it will prefer sourcing autonomy to obtain the best deal and to keep costs low. Should it have trouble getting product from external sources, however, it will want to have internal capacity available to maintain long production runs and operate as closely as possible to full capacity.

The strong preference for full cost transfers is most extreme when the final good is in the decline phase and low-cost production is key to being competitive. When market price is less than full cost, the buying profit center will want that to be the transfer price unless it can source externally. Also, as in the maturity phase, the buying profit center will want a priority on the selling profit center's internal capacity if it cannot meet its needs externally.

Both Profit Centers

Since both the intermediate and the final good go through the four phases of the product/process life cycle, sixteen situations can be identified, as shown in figure 9–2. The figure illustrates how a profit center's preferences in transfer pricing policy change over time and change with the tension inherent in the inter–profit center relationship. In terms of sourcing policy, the selling profit center's preferences begin with mandated transactions, change to exchange autonomy, and

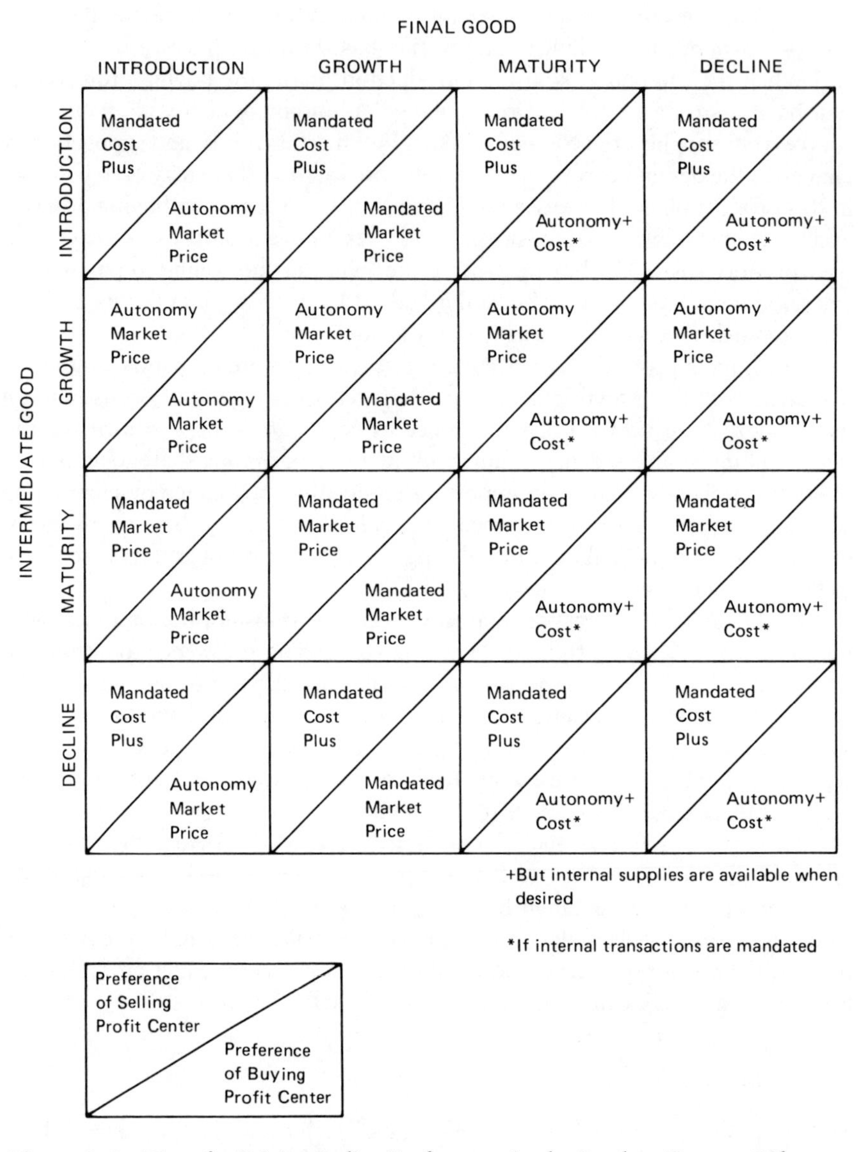

Figure 9–2. Transfer Pricing Policy Preferences in the Product/Process Life Cycle

change back to mandated transactions. In contrast, the preferences of the buying profit center begin with exchange autonomy, change to mandated transactions, and change back to exchange autonomy. The preferences match in only six of the sixteen situations. In terms of pricing policy, the buying profit center is most willing to pay a transfer price that includes a profit to the selling profit center when the final good is in the introduction and growth phases. When it is in the maturity and decline phases, competitive pressures and vertical integration by competitors create strong pressures for a preference to receive the intermediate good at cost or to be able to source externally at market price if it is lower.

Considering both sourcing and pricing decisions, there are only four situations in which preferences of both profit centers are reasonably well aligned: (1) when the intermediate good is in the introduction phase and the final good is in the growth phase, (2) when the intermediate good is in the growth phase and the final good is in the introduction phase, (3) when the intermediate good is in the maturity phase and the final good is in the growth phase, and (4) when the intermediate good is in the decline phase and the final good is in the growth phase. In all other situations, the tension between the two profit centers on sourcing and pricing policy will create pressures for change. The desired direction of the change will itself change as the intermediate and final goods move through the product/process life cycle. Managers need to be aware of these pressures to understand the conflict that arises over transfer pricing when changed conditions strain current strategies and transfer pricing policies. As products move through the life cycle, appropriate strategy will change and so, too, will the appropriate transfer pricing policy.

> **Hypothesis 35:** Transfer pricing policy is affected by the phases in the product/process life cycle of the intermediate and the final good.

Of course, the preferences shown in figure 9–2 are by no means without exceptions. One important qualification that must be made is based on the very fact that there are limitations in the concept of the product life cycle.[2] It is not completely inexorable for all products, and reverse movements can occur. Furthermore, Hayes and Wheelwright (1979a, 1979b) have shown that although there tends to be a relationship between stage of the product life cycle and type of process technology used, variations on this relationship are possible. They cited as an example Rolls-Royce Motors, Ltd., which "still makes a limited product line of motor cars using a process that is more like a job shop than an assembly line," as is typical for nearly all other automobile manufacturers. Although deviating from the process technology most appropriate for the stage of the product life cycle can lead to problems if the reasons for the deviation are not understood, it can also be a means of gaining competitive advantage. Thus, Rolls-Royce sells a very small number of extremely high-quality and expensive cars to a particular market niche.[3]

If either profit center chooses to compete with a process technology that is atypical of most other competitors, it will have a strategy that is more characteristic of other phases of the product life cycle. The result will be a different set of preferences for transfer pricing policy. A hypothetical example can be given by comparing Rolls-Royce with a more typical auto manufacturer. If Rolls-Royce had two profit centers—one producing engines and the other assembling the car—the buying profit center would be willing to pay market price, since it does not compete on price. This would be entirely consistent with the preference of the selling profit center, which might also have external sales of engines to achieve economies of scale, given the low level of internal demand. In contrast, the assembly (buying) profit center of a manufacturer of compact economy cars that competes primarily on the basis of price would prefer to obtain internally supplied engines at full cost. The strategy of Rolls-Royce places the final good in the introduction or growth phases in terms of the characteristics shown in figure 9–2, whereas the final good of the economy car manufacturer is located in the maturity or decline phase.

The Introduction of Transfer Pricing

Transfer pricing is sometimes introduced into a company for the first time when the company's structure and systems are changed from a functional to a multidivisional or matrix form. Unless the divisional or matrix profit centers are independent of each other, transfer prices will become an issue. When the transactions are substantial, top management is likely to mandate them, at least for a time, to avoid some serious potential problems of suboptimization, such as buying profit centers sourcing externally when selling profit centers have a great deal of spare capacity. Transfer prices must be established for these exchanges to measure the revenue to the selling profit center and the cost to the buying profit center.

Implementing the change to a multiple profit center organization is a difficult and complex task, and the problem of transfer pricing is often underestimated.

> **Hypothesis 36:** When a company implements a multiple profit center structure for the first time, transfer pricing will be a major problem in implementing the new organizational form.

The focus of top management's attention is on redesigning the organizational structure to give general managers responsibility for resources that affect both revenues and costs and on designing the management control systems and performance measurement and evaluation criteria to control and reward these lower-level general managers. In such situations, transfer pricing is often treated as a technical problem to be resolved by management information and control systems. This approach ignores, however, the central importance of the process elements of transfer pricing.

Managing these process elements is as crucial as establishing a clear strategy, whether a full cost or a market-based policy is chosen. Problems can arise with full cost because transfers that earn no profit for the selling profit center may seem inconsistent with the new philosophy of "decentralization." Thus, top management must be able to distinguish clearly between the cost and profit center roles of the selling profit center when it is setting objectives and evaluating and rewarding performance. For example, if it emphasizes the comparative profits of the new profit centers as a way of fostering the entrepreneurial spirit attributed to decentralization, the selling profit center will find full cost transfers highly objectionable. It will take time for top management to demonstrate its ability to distinguish clearly between cost and profit center roles; in the meantime, there will be concern about full cost transfers.

Even when top management has established strategic clarity about the two roles of the selling profit center, a difficult problem remains in setting the full cost transfer prices. Structural reorganizations can be implemented fairly rapidly, but it usually takes several years to develop the necessary management information and control systems to support the structure. Measuring the costs of individual products requires a degree of sophistication in a multiple profit center structure that is beyond the experience of functional managers. For example, if most of a product is transferred internally but its coproducts are sold externally by the selling profit center, the question of how costs are allocated between the primary product and its coproducts can be critical and not easy to resolve by simple technical criteria.

In a company that has operated for many years with a functional structure, there will be many examples of persisting cost allocation policies that are no longer adequate for the new structure. Perceptions of fairness in full cost transfers will depend on the process used, especially in terms of who is involved and what information is relied upon to develop the cost allocation rules. If these rules are developed totally within the selling profit center—without being monitored by top management or by the buying profit center—transfer prices will turn out to be highly disputable. A strong emphasis on profit center general manager autonomy is necessary to implement the multiple profit center structure.

The effects that profit centers can have on each other's results when they use full cost transfers are often more important than the details of cost allocation. The situation is different when standard full cost transfers are used and variances are allocated. The process by which these standard costs are set—especially in terms of who is involved, what information is used, and how often the costs are changed—is extremely important to managers' perceptions of fairness in both profit centers. Again, the new emphasis on decentralized authority may keep top management from participating enough in setting standard costs or providing for the buying profit center's involvement. As a result, the buying profit center may harbor suspicions about the standard costs or the reasons for positive variances.

Process issues are also crucial when top management implements a policy of mandated market-based transfers, especially when the volume of internal transfers, or their proprietary nature, makes it difficult to use external transaction prices to establish transfer prices. Implementing market-based transfers is an even greater challenge than implementing full cost transfers. The full cost policy is based on already existing systems (although they may require substantial elaboration) and is already incorporated in transactions within the company—though between functions, not profit centers. Market-based transfers are a new type of internal transaction that must be learned.

Whether corporate policy should program the decision to establish transfer prices or whether the profit centers should be left to negotiate it themselves presents a dilemma for top management. The first approach is consistent with the high degree of hierarchical authority, responsibility, and control exercised by top management in the old functional structure. The other approach is consistent with the new philosophy of decentralized profit responsibility. Too much top management involvement can be seen as a lack of commitment to the new organizational form, but minimal top management involvement can cause problems for profit center managers.

The process elements of deciding what information to use, when to set transfer prices, and how to manage conflict are especially crucial when negotiations are undertaken with little involvement by top management. Profit center managers must establish among themselves the information that is relevant to setting transfer prices and the conditions for their renegotiation. The result can be substantial discord. By intervening, top management may prevent profit center managers from finding out how to manage the inter–profit center relationship. Top management also needs to learn how this conflict can generate information and improve control; it must accept the fact that one of the costs of the new structure will be a potentially higher level of conflict than has existed before.

Blackstone Machinery Company: The Difficulty in Implementing Transfer Pricing

Blackstone Machinery Company is an example of a company that experienced such difficulties in implementing a multiple profit center structure, with transfer pricing one of the most vexing, that it temporarily abandoned its attempt to reorganize. Transfer pricing proved to be a difficult issue largely because the efforts to change the structure and create new systems were not completely coordinated. The new structure was in place before the problem of transfer pricing had been thoroughly thought through. Then transfer pricing was implemented so hastily that it only added to the confusion about the strategy behind the reorganization. The company's poor financial position also contributed to the decision to retreat from the new organizational structure. From its aborted first attempt to create product-based profit centers, the company learned some valuable lessons that it put to good use when it successfully implemented a simpler multidivisional structure several years later.

Blackstone manufactured and sold heavy machinery and machinery components on a worldwide basis. Some twenty operating units (OUs) were scattered throughout the world as legal entities engaged in the manufacture and/or sale of the company's products. One OU, the World Export Organization (WEO), did not manufacture but arranged for the sale of products to countries where no OU was located. An OU that did not manufacture all the products it needed could obtain them from an OU located in another country. Some OUs sold most of their manufactured output to OUs in other countries; components used by one were often manufactured by another. Thus, OUs were highly interdependent for both manufacturing and sales.

For many years, these country-based operating companies were grouped under three regional vice-presidents for North America, Europe, and International (including the WEO). These vice-presidents reported to an authoritarian CEO, who evaluated their performance on a largely subjective basis that apparently had little to do with their results. This attitude extended throughout the company—so much so that a company joke at the time was that nobody ever got fired because of poor performance. The vice-presidents, who had substantial staffs and a great deal of power, were referred to as "barons." The company itself was characterized as based on "tribal nationalism," with "medieval baronies."

This "tribal nationalism" and the minimal relationship between performance evaluation and reported financial results were reinforced by the company's accounting system, based on legal entities, which did little to identify responsibility for performance. It was designed largely to produce reports for external observers. Product line profitability reports, which required collecting numbers from many OUs, were produced through a complicated program that made them late and unreliable. Howard Byrne, senior vice-president for planning and administration, described the company's financial systems:

> The company had been geographically organized and treated itself as a geographic holding company. Accounting was done on a legal entity basis. Financial systems were related to this structure. Banks wanted to see the numbers for OUs in their country, but for the public we had to produce consolidated statements.

During 1978, the company experienced serious financial difficulties as the markets for its products declined. Leo Hart, controller, was named president and CEO. One of his first steps was to eliminate the regional vice-presidents and have all OU managers report to him. He eliminated the regional staffs, pushing some functions down to the OUs and pulling others up into the corporate office. Hart wanted to reduce the power of the regional vice-presidents and also to improve OU–corporate communications. Another step in the reorganization was to transfer Kevin Conley from a centralized corporate engineering function to vice-president of the United States operating unit as of January 1, 1979.

In September 1979, Hart regrouped the OUs under other vice-presidents for operations and physically relocated the centralized engineering staff into various operations offices. Hart was explicit, however, about not recreating the old regional structure. The vice-presidents for operations had no staffs of their own. A controller, engineering personnel, and marketing personnel were physically located in the operations offices but reported to their respective function managers at corporate headquarters.

While still vice-president for engineering, Conley had become interested in introducing profit centers into Blackstone Machinery. As vice-president for the U.S. OU, he quickly took advantage of the opportunity to implement this idea, which was supported by the new U.S. controller. One of Conley's reasons for introducing profit centers was that, in the past, only the regional vice-presidents had been concerned with profits, and even then they had focused almost exclusively on income statement items, ignoring balance sheet measures. Another reason was that one product line—construction machinery—was losing money, while another—industrial machinery—was making money. Conley believed that making each of these product lines a profit center would provide the necessary focus and motivation to improve the performance of the construction machinery product line.

The Responsibility Accounting System

Between December 1978 and February 1979, Conley made three presentations of how he would reorganize the U.S. OU into profit centers. Each succeeding presentation was increasingly detailed, although a number of issues were left unresolved. Hart supported Conley's recommendations, since he saw profit centers as a way of decreasing bureaucracy and increasing the entrepreneurial spirit in the company. He also thought that the move toward profit centers would be consistent with another major change he himself had commissioned.

When he first became CEO, Hart held monthly meetings with all of his direct-reporting managers—about ten OU managers and ten staff managers. During these meetings, he was exposed to a long-continuing dispute between the WEO and the UK OU. The WEO sold a large proportion of the UK OU's output, acting as a sales agent, but it was simply evaluated as an expense center. Although the WEO manager had tried to calculate a "memo profit" to demonstrate his unit's contribution to the firm's profits, few of the other OU managers regarded it as legitimate since all the costs, including those from carrying receivables, were the responsibility of the UK OU.

At one of these meetings, Hart was trying to determine who was responsible for a shortfall in performance. The UK OU manager blamed the WEO OU manager, and vice versa. Hart turned to Howard Byrne, who was then controller, and said, "Damn it, I'm tired of this problem. I want a responsibility accounting system. I want a way to measure responsibility." In this sytem, he wanted a requirement that an OU had to take a product that it ordered. In the past, WEO had canceled orders when demand had not materialized. Hart's attitude was, "Bullshit—you order it, you take it."

Another problem was that many criteria existed for measuring an OU's financial performance. Hart wanted to focus on a few crucial criteria, especially the return on average assets (ROAA). The financial staff was given the responsibility for designing a system that would measure OUs on ROAA. Since this required assigning sales, profits, and assets to each entity, Hart thought that it would enable him to establish responsibility for financial performance. Every OU was to have an income statement and a balance sheet. Some managers believed that Hart, a former controller, hoped that a profit center structure based on product lines would follow the design of a responsibility accounting system.

Allen Furman, director of short-range planning, was given the job of designing the responsibility accounting system. He believed in profit centers and had a "small is beautiful" philosophy. Furman was faced with the problem of designing the accounting system at a time when the structure itself was in a state of flux and there was much ambiguity about what the units of responsibility would be. He was told to design a modular accounting system flexible enough that the pieces could later be reassembled to match the accounting system for the still-to-be-determined organizational structure. He began the project during the first part of 1979, as financial performance continued to deteriorate.

Furman designed a detailed system with seventy-seven responsibility units, each of which would be measured as a profit center. These profit centers included factories, sales units, and product lines. One manager described this approach as being "rather like the search for the elementary particle." Another manager described it as "the electron theory of responsibility accounting."

While Furman was designing an "elementary particle" responsibility accounting system and Conley was working to create a profit center structure in the U.S. OU, the decision was made to reorganize the French OU into profit centers as well. Ed Berkin, director of organizational planning, went to France in June 1979 to begin the implementation of profit centers. Since the French OUs also had construction machinery and industrial machinery product lines, it seemed like the logical next place to introduce profit centers. Both the Franch OU general manager, Dave Short, and the director of personnel and industrial relations, Pierre Veaux, were skeptical about adopting this approach in France, because their manufacturing and sales were highly interdependent with other OUs. They received a large supply of goods from the European Parts OU and the Engines OU (located in Germany), and over 40 percent of their output was sold by other OUs outside of France. The French controller also resisted the profit center concept because he feared he would lose his system for pulling together the legal entity accounts, which were necessary for governmental reporting and banking relationships.

By March 1979, Furman's responsibility accounting design and Conley's efforts to reorganize the U.S. OU were being coordinated to some extent by Carl Stockton, vice-president for organization and employee relations. Paul Danton, his successor, recalled that those designing the new structure had come up against one critical issue that ultimately revealed that they did not properly understand what was involved:

> The earliest symptom of a problem with the profit center structure was a transfer pricing issue—is sales a profit center or a commission center? Conley decided to depart from what Furman wanted to do for the company as a whole and made sales a commission center. This turned out to be the single biggest indicator we had not moved to profit centers. All Conley had done was throw some engineers at manufacturing. This became obvious as things went along.
>
> We should have caught him on this. We worked closely with the planning people but not the systems people. We made an organizational change and then struggled to retain control of management information.

Problems with Transfer Pricing

The lack of coordination in structural and systems changes became apparent when management confronted the transfer pricing problem. By the end of 1979, the responsibility accounting system was nearly completed, except for a policy for handling internal transfers. This was a major issue, since each manufacturing unit typically had between eight and ten internal customers. Byrne recalled: "We still had to settle on transfer prices. This is the biggest bone of contention. It always is."

Several options that were considered included guaranteeing a margin to the buying profit center, paying the buying profit center a commission, using market price, and a using a markup on labor cost. All proposals met strong objections. Guaranteeing a margin to the buying center, and paying the buying center a commission would not motivate it to emphasize the most profitable products. Objections to market prices included the fear that currently depressed market conditions would not leave "enough profit to go around," and for many products it was hard to determine a market price. Furman decided to use a markup on labor policy, since that would be simple and the deadline was fast approaching for finalizing the budget and implementing the responsibility accounting system for the next year.

Under the cost plus markup policy, each factory had a different markup factor, with the objective of giving each some profit so as to show a positive ROAA. No strong justification existed for the particular markups chosen, and managers affected by them had had no input. Another disadvantage was that unless standard labor costs were set properly, a selling profit center could increase its ROAA by manufacturing inefficiently. This was especially serious because there was no information about what proper labor standard costs should be. Furman's intention was to "bootstrap" the standard rates by using the system for one year to gather data that could then be analyzed to calculate these rates. Because of these transfer price problems, profit center managers believed that the numbers reported by the responsibility accounting system were highly artificial and of little use.

The Change Effort Deteriorates

The responsibility accounting system was producing financial reports by early 1980, although there were many disputes about their value. Efforts to establish profit centers in the United States and France continued. Berkin, the director of organizational planning, traveled to France in February 1980 and found the situation chaotic. He conferred with his boss, Danton, and they decided to remove Veaux from his position and make him director of profit center implementation for Europe as of April 1980. Veaux visited corporate headquarters to get all the documentation on U.S. profit centers, assuming that it would provide him with solutions to many of the problems in France. Much to his surprise, he found practically no documentation; instead, he found that the U.S. OU was having as much difficulty as the French OU.

It soon became clear to those involved in the effort to reorganize the company that there was too much confusion about what profit centers were. A project team was set up to study this question, including Veaux, Hart, Berkin, and others. Their mandate was to define a profit center precisely and to suggest what would be required to introduce profit centers into the company. While the team studied the problem, financial performance deteriorated to the point of crisis.

The project team concluded that with such a high degree of interdependence, the company would never be able to create numerous autonomous profit centers that were independent of other parts of the company. Because of this, substantial top management involvement would be required to make pricing decisions for product sold externally, to specify particular sources for intracompany transfers when several existed, and to determine output levels. The team also concluded that, at best, Blackstone Machinery could be organized into "simulated profit centers" engaged in extensive intracompany transfers. A solution to the transfer pricing problem would have to be agreed on to make this work, and the decision was to delay further organizational change. When the company's financial crisis threatened its continued existence, the issues of responsibility accounting and profit center structures became a very secondary concern to top management, and the company announced its decision to delay the implementation of the new structure.

Rethinking the Use of Profit Centers

While Hart concentrated on the company's financial crisis, Byrne, the controller, was promoted to senior vice-president for planning and administration. He was replaced by Michael Satter, controller of the Engines OU—a position formerly held by Hart, in which he had implemented a responsibility accounting system later improved by Satter. Byrne gave Satter the responsibility accounting system to deal with in January 1981.

Satter did not think that previous efforts had been fruitful:

> The person who created the responsibility accounting system had the perception that profit centers were the only way to run a company. He figured the only way to do this was to establish a process called responsibility accounting. He thought that structure would follow this system. This turned out to be a mammoth load of horseshit. Transfer pricing developed into a monster. Nobody regarded it as worth anything.

Satter also doubted that the concept of numerous profit centers could be adopted at Blackstone Machinery because of the interdependence of its current financial systems:

> I believe the application of profit centers at Blackstone Machinery is an absolute waste of time. The company is organizationally and physically a tightly interwoven mesh of operations. When you try to break it apart into profit centers, you run into hassles such as how costs will be allocated. It is a constant battle and a no-win situation.

Satter decided to eliminate the responsibility accounting system. By early 1981, the consensus was that the "elementary particle" approach had resulted in a system that was too segmented and was based on too many artificial and arbitrary numbers. He decided to implement a simpler system, called "accounting for responsibility." Satter reasoned that rather than attempting to move immediately to profit center–based systems, they should take incremental steps. OUs were used to receiving the product of other OUs at variable cost, with no allocation of manufacturing overhead. As a first step, he was implementing a system that allocated manufacturing overhead, but not on a product-by-product basis. From here, he hoped to allocate costs to each product and eventually to allocate all other fixed costs, of which manufacturing overhead was the largest. Satter thought that two separate sets of books were a necessary precondition for profit centers—one for legal entity reporting, which would be needed for statutory reasons, and one for management information and control. He concluded that the company's previous efforts had been a case of trying to run before it could walk. Thus, he pointed out that, currently, ROAA measures were being reported only at the highest level on a regional basis.

Danton agreed with Satter's assessment of why the company had had difficulties reorganizing into profit centers, and he attributed the problems to the need for "simulation" or transfer pricing between interdependent profit centers. He believed that this structure could be implemented only when the company had found a solution to the transfer pricing problem, which in his opinion would be based on market prices:

> The one thing we never really appreciated until the project team's study was that the more simulation you have, the more complications exist. At one point a crossover takes place where the disadvantages outweigh the advantages.
>
> If this company could handle transfer pricing in a very simple and effective way, we could move that crossover point, which would sure be a help. To operate on a profit center basis, we need a simple approach to transfer pricing based on market prices.

Throughout 1981, management continued to study the problem of which type of organizational structure was most appropriate given its strategic direction. The decision was made to implement a multidivisional structure, beginning with a few large divisions that had worldwide responsibility for their product lines. These very large divisions contained the major line functions, such as engineering, manufacturing, and marketing. The finance function reported on a straight-line basis to corporate headquarters and on a dotted-line basis to the division president. This new structure, announced on November 30, 1981, required some decentralization of resources that had formerly been part of the corporate office. Berkin explained that "these divisions would be profit centers and would have a mass of viability that would avoid the problems of the previous effort. We got away from the 'small is beautiful' philosophy."

The implementation of this new structure began in March 1982 with the formation of the Industrial Machinery Division and the Engines Division. Over the next two years, more divisions were created, including the Components Division and the Foundry Division. Management was much more successful in phasing in this new structure, which it regarded as continually evolving through the creation of new divisions, as appropriate, by subdividing existing ones. New divisions were not created, however, until the division out of which they were created was firmly in place.

The multidivisional structure was supported by the creation of management control systems that measured the resources under the authority of the division presidents and the profitability and other financial outcomes they achieved with these resources. Berkin noted that "accounting for responsibility" was much easier to implement given the size of the divisions, since they were "measurable units that made more sense in terms of accountability. We got better control over the business." Evidence of this control was that raw material and work in process inventories for given levels of output were substantially reduced.

In this new structure, Components and Foundry were changed from cost centers to profit centers and were encouraged to sell outside. Although both had done so in the past to a very limited extent—and Engines had to a greater extent—part of the company's strategy was to increase the external sales of all of these divisions. In attempting to do so, the divisions had a rude surprise, since they found that they were far from being competitive in the external market. Typically, if full cost was 100, market prices on Foundry's and Components' products were 70 to 80.

This was especially ironic since the divisions themselves were somewhat responsible for this situation. In the past, as cost centers, they had sold spare capacity to external customers for very low prices, since the purpose was simply to operate as closely as possible to full capacity, rather than to earn profits. In doing so, they had established low levels for market prices, to which external competitors had adapted by becoming very efficient. Thus, whereas the competitors were able to earn a profit at these prices, Foundry and Components incurred losses on their outside sales. The pressures were greatest in Components, and some of its managers argued that it should be regarded as a cost center once again.

With the new multidivisional structure, complaints that had existed for many years about the cost of raw materials and parts escalated with the transformation of both suppliers and buyers into profit centers. The transfer pricing problem resurfaced, since internal transfers were still very high even under this simpler structure. Engines sold 40 percent of its output internally, Components sold 70 percent, and Foundry sold 80 percent. Although the objective was eventually to use market-based prices, top management decided to phase this policy in over a period of time, since to go to it immediately would have "bankrupted" the Components and Foundry divisions. The decision was made to use full cost the first year, with a reduction of 10 percent from full cost each year until the transfer price equaled market price. As part of its effort to decrease the amount of internal interdependence, buying divisions such as Industrial Machinery could, in principle, source from external suppliers. To do so, they had to present their case in terms of price, quality, service, and so on, and even then some lead time had to be provided to enable the selling divisions to find an alternative use of this capacity. Top management hoped that the pressures of market-based transfer prices and exchange autonomy would force the selling divisions to become more efficient, lower-cost suppliers, which would enhance their share in external markets and the competitiveness of the buying divisions.

Several important lessons that can be learned from the experience of Blackstone Machinery Company are important for managers who are attempting to implement transfer pricing for the first time. One lesson is that although it is relatively easy to reorganize a company's structure by simply placing resources under the authority of a lower-level general manager, it is much more difficult to develop the management information and control systems that measure the value of these resources and the outcomes achieved by them. An organizational unit becomes a profit center only when its profits can be measured.

The second, and related, lesson is that it is very difficult to transform a cost center into a profit center. Simply being able to measure profit does not mean that the managers in this unit have adopted the general management perspective needed for running a profit center. Such a perspective takes time to develop, and the discipline of the marketplace can contribute to this learning. Thus, encouraging these new profit centers to sell externally is an important step in making the transformation a concrete reality.

Of course, when internal sales remain substantial, there is the possibility of a split role for the selling profit centers. Although this can be eliminated by instituting a mandated market-based policy or even a policy of exchange autonomy, neither of these policy changes is easy to make immediately. The third lesson is that attempting to do so can create substantial risks. A bloated cost center cannot adapt to the disciplines of the marketplace overnight. Top management must determine the time frame that is appropriate for balancing the advantages instilled by the discipline of trading externally and/or selling at market price internally with the disadvantages of high reported losses in the selling profit center or substantial spare capacity in the selling profit center because internal customers source externally. One situation in which extremely rapid change may be appropriate is when top management wants to make a decision very soon about whether or not to remain in the activity of a selling profit center. If it does not plan to exit this activity, some period for phasing in exchange autonomy or market-based transfer prices must be provided.

Reorganizing Exchange Relationships

Once a company has implemented a multiple profit center organization, it continues to reorganize, either through a continuous process of incremental changes or through less frequent major reorganizations. Continuous incremental change takes place when top management gradually gives lower-level general managers more resources and more authority and at the same time increases their responsibility for financial results. It does this by reducing the role of the corporate office in operating decisions at the profit center level. Major changes include reducing or increasing the number of profit centers or changing the basis of the profit center structure, such as from geographic markets to product lines.

Reorganizing creates pressure for changing transfer pricing policies. For example, as profit center managers gain greater authority and responsibility, they may feel too restricted by mandated transfers and may argue that exchange autonomy would be a more effective policy. Similarly, selling profit centers will be dissatisfied with full cost transfers and will argue for market-based transfers. If actual full cost transfers exist, buying profit center managers will increasingly push for standard full cost transfers.

The transfer pricing policies of actual full cost, standard full cost, mandated market-based, and exchange autonomy can be ordered along a continuum of increasing authority and responsibility for profit center managers. Dual pricing is not part of the continuum, but it represents several points on it, from two

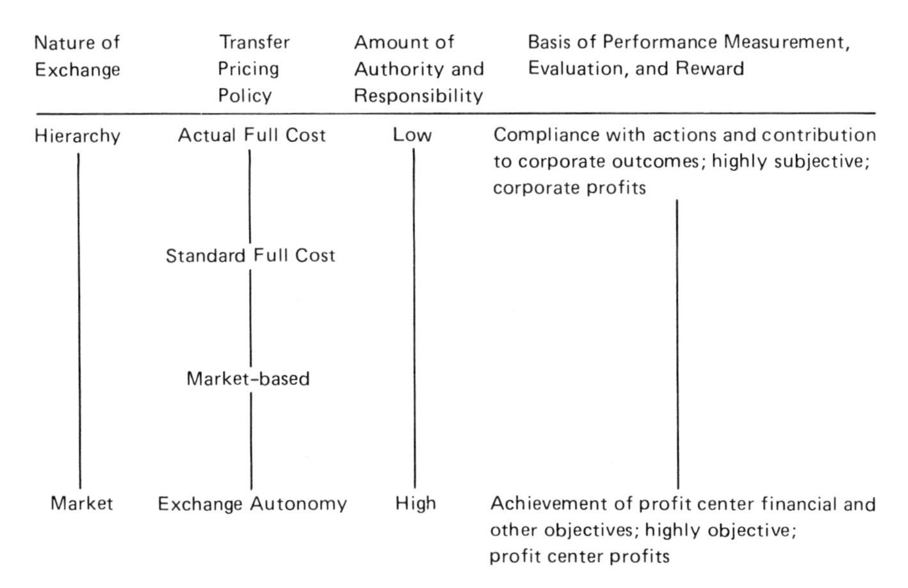

Nature of Exchange
Transfer Pricing Policy
Amount of Authority and Responsibility
Basis of Performance Measurement, Evaluation, and Reward
Hierarchy
Actual Full Cost
Low
Compliance with actions and contribution to corporate outcomes; highly subjective; corporate profits
Standard Full Cost
Market-based
Market
Exchange Autonomy
High
Achievement of profit center financial and other objectives; highly objective; profit center profits

Figure 9–3. A Continuum of Exchange Relationships for Transfer Pricing

different perspectives, combined into one relationship. As the profit center general manager's responsibility for profit center financial outcomes is emphasized more and he or she is given the necessary decision-making authority, the appropriate transfer pricing policy changes from mandated actual full cost to mandated standard full cost to mandated market-based to exchange autonomy, as shown in figure 9–3.

Although discrete transfer pricing policies can be identified, the exchange autonomy continuum extends from none to complete, with intermediate points such as internal suppliers being allowed to meet the lowest outside price. Similarly, a continuum extends from full cost, defined as direct production costs, to market price, with intermediate points such as including profit center overhead (general and administrative) expenses in full product costs.

This continuum matches a more general continuum of exchanges that vary from hierarchical to market forms.[4] In the hierarchical form, internal relationships are established by administrative fiat in which transfer prices play no role. Top management retains substantial authority, and profit responsibility exists at the top of the organization for all practical purposes. At the other extreme, transfer prices determine whether the exchange takes place, just as prices do in market transactions. Here, profit center general managers have substantial profit responsibility, and the role of top management in interdivisional relationships is minimal.

A continuum of fairness is associated with this continuum of exchange relationships defined by transfer pricing policy and the relationship of top management to profit center managers. This continuum of fairness ranges from rewards for compliance with corporate management directives to rewards for achieving profit center financial results. At the hierarchy extreme, subjective judgment plays a much larger role in evaluating performance and matching rewards to performance than it does at the market extreme, where objective criteria are available for evaluating performance and matching rewards to performance.

Incremental change creates pressures for changing the transfer pricing policy in existing exchange relationships, and this change can go in either direction along the continuum. Nonincremental change often leads to new exchange relationships that require new transfer pricing policies. For example, when a product is moved out of one profit center to be manufactured in another, a new inter–profit center relationship is created. Transfer pricing may shift from the intra–profit center "transfer" at mandated full cost to an inter–profit center mandated market-based transfer. Conversely, the transfer pricing problem, strictly defined, disappears when a product involved in an inter–profit center transfer is moved to the buying profit center, unless there are multiple profit centers within this profit center. Thus, one "solution" to the transfer pricing problem found in practice is simply to eliminate the transfer in this way.

In general, the greatest degree of change in transfer pricing policy causes the most difficulty. Profit centers that are used to exchange autonomy will probably resent having internal transactions mandated. Instituting exchange autonomy opens the way for profit center–optimizing decisions that are suboptimal for the company. Changes in policy also create problems for comparing present and past performance, since the score-keeping system changes, too. This can lead to disputes about how the performance measures should be evaluated and rewarded. Finally, different policies require different processes, and problems often arise from giving insufficient attention to the process aspect of transfer pricing. For example, when a company changes from mandated standard full cost transfers—with standard costs set on an annual basis—to mandated market-based transfers, provision has to be made for significant shifts in market prices over short periods. This can create problems if transfer prices are set on an annual basis, but in the meantime external transactions include provisions for adjusting to drastically changed market conditions.

The reorganization of inter–profit center exchange relationships and top management–profit center manager relationships creates pressures for changes in transfer pricing policies. If the policy changes, the transfer pricing process must be changed, and a new system must be developed to evaluate and reward performance fairly. Changes in transfer pricing policies may obviate comparisons with past performance when top management establishes new rules for the game; in this case, profit center managers have a natural concern that these rules apply fairly to everyone.

Locke Chemical Company: The Evolution of a Transfer Pricing Policy

The transfer pricing policy at Locke Chemical Company changed over time with changes in the company's strategy and structure. In some cases, these changes were met with a high degree of acceptance. In other cases—such as the implementation of standard full cost transfers for building-block chemicals—these changes met with resistance. One of the reasons for this resistance was that the managers who were affected had almost no input into the decision to implement this policy. Top management's lack of attention to the change process itself helped create the problems that ensued over ambiguity in the role definition of the Basic Chemicals Division and the setting of standard costs.

Prior to 1972, twelve profit centers had been engaged in substantial transfers, creating a high degree of interdependence. The company's transfer pricing policy was actual full cost, with investments also allocated according to percentage of actual usage to calculate ROI for each profit center. Ron Shields, vice-president for finance, described this policy:

> At that time there was a concept of "we're one big family and so integrated that everybody should share and share alike." A share of investment (SOI) transfer basis was used. Everybody was getting product from everybody else. You had little control over what happened to you. Your profits could go to hell if another guy's plant had trouble.

If internal suppliers could not meet total internal demand, internal customers could make external purchases and add their cost into the total pool of product for calculating actual cost transfers. Internal suppliers complained that they would prefer selling to outside customers that could forecast their needs more accurately. Internal customers complained that they could buy outside for less and that inefficiencies in the manufacturing process were passed on to them.

From Actual Full Cost to Market-Based Transfers

In 1972, the CEO implemented a reorganization designed to set up self-contained profit centers, push decision-making responsibility further down into the organization, and reduce the day-to-day operating responsibility of top management so that it could spend more time on longer-term issues. The twelve profit centers were combined into four large profit centers, and the large functional staffs at corporate headquarters were broken up and placed in these profit centers to give the profit center general managers full authority over the resources needed to achieve divisional objectives. The managers put in charge of these profit centers were highly respected senior executives. They were given the title of vice-president and were made members of the company's board of directors.

Although every effort was made to make each profit center self-contained, the extent of the company's vertical integration made interdivisional transfers inevitable. The decision was made to change from the SOI policy to mandated market-based transfers, with transfer prices set at the lowest price to an outside customer. Dissatisfaction with the old policy was a major reason for this change. Another reason was the looming requirement for Securities and Exchange Commission (SEC) line-of-business reporting, itself a factor behind the structural change.

Earl Shindell, vice-president and general manager, recalled some difficulties the company had experienced in making this change, which centered on the process for determining transfer prices. Unlike the SOI policy of calculating transfer prices, the new policy required that the profit centers agree on what the lowest outside customer price was:

> During the budget season things were wide open. For three months it was hell trying to get prices. Only profit center general managers could negotiate prices, since we knew this couldn't be resolved lower down in the organization.

After this adjustment period, the policy had apparently worked well, despite the "normal amount of bickering"—particularly during budget time, when transfer prices were set. One provision in the policy was that disputes that could not be resolved should be taken to the corporate controller, but this had rarely occurred. Shields thought that all in all, the policy change had contributed to the reorganization effort designed to decentralize authority and responsibility. However, some people complained, no matter what the policy was:

> We had positive businessmen interactions and dispelled most of the issue of managers feeling they did not control their own destiny. Of course, we still had some problems, such as quantity discounts. The same human beings who complained prior to 1972 were the ones who complained under the new system. But in general, this was as positive an environment as we've had on transfer pricing.

Lee Madigan, controller of the Molding Division, recalled this period as a "trouble-free time for the most part." Scott Wakefield, corporate controller, even attributed some of the improvement in the company's per share earnings to the new policy:

> One of the reasons behind the quantum jump in earnings was the shift from SOI to market transfers. Everybody was put on a profit center basis and was responsible for managing the business this way. Since people were responsible for individual numbers, there was an impetus we hadn't had before.

Introduction of Standard Full Cost Transfers

The mandated market-based policy was used for all interdivisional transfers between 1972 and 1976, until the Basic Chemicals Division was established on January 1, 1977. This further reorganization brought about some new interdivisional transfers, since products were assigned from the original four profit centers to Basic Chemicals. Furthermore, transfers—both intradivisional and interdivisional—

that had formerly been market-based were changed to standard full cost if they involved one of the eight building-block chemicals.

A number of difficulties in implementing this change began with the attempt to reach a consensus on how the new profit center could continue to use performance income as its primary measure of performance when a substantial part of its output was "sold" on a standard full cost basis. The first general manager of Basic Chemicals took an attitude that exacerbated this ambiguity, but gradually it lessened. And under Earl Shindell, performance measurement shifted from performance income to cost control and reduction, which helped appreciably in establishing the cost center role of this new division.

Their positive experience with mandated market-based transfers made managers in Basic Chemicals especially reluctant to accept standard full cost. Since theirs were the only products subjected to this policy (except for one product in the Consumer Division), they perceived it as reducing their status. Not only were other divisions profit centers for all of their products, but their reported profits in many cases had benefited by the shift from market-based to standard full cost transfers for the products they purchased internally. Basic Chemicals' negative reaction was matched by buying division managers' doubts concerning how standard costs were set and variances allocated. In implementing this new policy, too little attention had been paid to the process for using standard full cost transfers.

Another reason for the problems the company had in adapting to this change lay in the process of implementing standard full cost transfers. Discussion of the reorganization had included very little attention to the question of transfer prices of products manufactured in Basic Chemicals; as a result, opinion differed about why the new policy was adopted. This, in turn, contributed to the ambiguity of the role of Basic Chemicals in corporate strategy. The change in policy was made too quickly to hold discussions about it with the managers who were affected. At the last minute, top management realized that transfer pricing policy had a significant role in defining the mission of Basic Chemicals and that concentrating on structure alone had provided an inadequate perspective on all that was required to implement this change in strategy. As Shields admitted:

> When we were designing the new structure, I'd have to candidly say that there was little attention given to how we would move products between the divisions. It was one of those restructurings done by a few people at a very senior level. The transfer pricing issue was overlooked or forgotten.

However, transfer pricing policy had a major effect on defining the businesses in which the company considered itself to be competing:

> We found that if we left transfer prices to a market price basis, some portion of the company's profits would be in the Basic Chemicals Division. This told us something about the businesses we were really in. Were we in the molding business or the intermediates business?

Because the company's strategy emphasized the downstream, end-product businesses, management decided that it did not want to report most of its profits in the upstream, intermediate-product businesses.

The decision was made to use a cost plus investment (C&I) policy of charging internal customers standard costs and assigning a portion of the investment on a take-or-pay basis. It was thought that this policy would provide a basis for reporting divisional profits that more accurately reflected the company's definition of its businesses. At the time the change was made, standard full costs were roughly equal to market prices. The C&I policy was also thought to provide appropriate motivation for the Basic Chemicals Division by highlighting manufacturing efficiencies and inefficiencies. Some managers believed that the transfer pricing policy was changed primarily to improve the reported profits of the Molding and Plastics divisions.

Another manager confirmed that the company was somewhat taken by surprise by the impact of market-based transfer prices in the new structure:

> There was some surprise when people were confronted with the fact that given the new organizational structure, market prices might not make sense. So there was a rush after the Basic Chemicals Division was formed to figure out an appropriate transfer price.

Although both internal and external consultants were involved in discussions of what transfer pricing policy should be adopted, time was limited, because a decision had to be made before preparing the budget for the new structure for 1977. Under this time pressure, management was not able to think through completely the process of standard full cost transfer pricing, the way in which the performance of Basic Chemicals was to be evaluated, and the impact of the new policy on performance evaluation and reward of managers in other divisions. Serious disputes about this policy continued for several years.

Experience with Standard Full Cost Transfers

In 1980, managers still expressed significant dissatisfaction with the cost plus investment policy, but a number of them did not recommend changing back to the market-based transfers for the building-block chemicals. Their feeling was that this would create another set of problems, such as explaining to security analysts the impact on divisional reported profits and making current results noncomparable to historical results. Jason Walker, director of planning information and administration in the Molding Division, argued:

> A hell of a lot can be said for a company to get a procedure and keep it. You get a changing perception of operations compared to the outside world. Something is to be said for consistency. When methods change, financial results change, and it is difficult to track the profitability of an operation.

However, he also noted a potential advantage to changing: "Maybe this is good because it confuses others." Earl Shindell, general manager of Basic Chemicals, said that he could "make any of three systems [market, cost, and cost plus investment] work well and live with them," but, like some others, he preferred shifting back to a market-based approach: "I clearly like market best. Don't ask me to defend it. I just like it." One advantage of market-based pricing was that it would reduce the "constant bitching and complaining about transfer pricing." Shindell had a proposal for adjudicating such disputes under a policy of market price:

> Today I'd establish market prices and have a court of appeals composed of the head of purchasing, the head bookkeeper, and one other manager. It would convene once a month for one hour. Presenters would get three minutes to present their cases. Disputes would be settled within one hour.

John Newman, controller in the Plastics Division, also advocated market-based transfer pricing because of the complexity of the cost plus investment policy:

> I think we should be on a market price basis. The C&I policy is like tax law—it has so many ifs, ands, and buts. It is a controllership tribal language. It is difficult for people managing a business to easily, clearly, and readily understand what is happening to them from transfer prices.

Although improvements were made in the cost plus investment policy, its problems were never adequately resolved from top management's perspective. After about five years, the company was reorganized back into a structure similar to what it had before the creation of the Basic Chemicals Division. In this new structure, all internal transfers were market-based.

The experience of Locke Chemical Company illustrates an important principle that can be stated in the form of a hypothesis:

> **Hypothesis 37:** The effectiveness of a new transfer pricing policy depends on the effectiveness of the change process used to implement it.

Exactly how a company should go about implementing changes in transfer pricing policies in terms of such considerations as who is involved in designing the new policy, what information is made available, and how fast the change is implemented depends on many considerations. Too often, problems with a new transfer pricing policy are due to insufficient attention to the process used to implement it. Through the change process, clarity about the new policy and the process for using this policy can be established. Although it is impossible to make precise statements that are applicable in all instances, some general guidelines can be established.

Top management should be clear in its own mind about why it is implementing this change and should anticipate any difficulties that might arise. The reasons for the change and any anticipated difficulties should be clearly communicated to profit center managers. Top management also needs to determine who should participate in the design of the new policy. This can help clarify the strategic reasons behind the change to lower-level general managers. It is also useful to obtain input from lower-level general managers about the process for using a particular policy, since they are the people who are closest to it and who will be most affected by it.

Another important consideration is how the change in policy will affect comparisons with historical records. Profit center managers should feel confident that misperceptions of their performance will not arise because of changes in the "rules of the game." Otherwise, they will resist the new policy by constantly complaining about its inevitable shortcomings.

Uniformity for Administrative Simplicity and Fairness

As a product goes through the product/process life cycle, its strategy changes; in inter–profit center transfers, the transfer pricing policy may change, too. At any point in time, a company's products—both the intermediate and the final good—will be at different stages of the product/process life cycle. As a result, multiple strategies will exist for inter–profit center relationships, requiring managers to resort to multiple transfer pricing policies and processes.

At any point in time also, pressures for uniformity in transfer pricing policies will be based on the advantages of administrative simplicity and concerns about fairness. Unless top management abstains completely from involvement in transfer pricing—as in situations of extreme exchange autonomy—the complexity of its role in these inter–profit center exchanges will increase with the diversity of the transfer pricing practices throughout the company. Different criteria have to be applied in evaluating and rewarding performance. For example, in situations of exchange autonomy, top management can evaluate profit center performance primarily on financial outcomes and can reward its managers accordingly. However, when inter–profit center relationships are affected by a vertical integration strategy, top management will have to consider each profit center's actions as contributing to or detracting from the performance of the other. In this situation, rewards must be based at least partially on the joint outcomes of the profit centers.

Furthermore, top management cannot really become involved in adjudicating disputes without a great deal of prior knowledge about the many different transfer practices. Since the disputes concern not only the policy used but the process by which it is managed, a detailed grasp of these different practices will be needed to determine whether the gains from conflict outweigh its losses or whether further changes should be made in either policy or process.

The diversity of transfer pricing practices can also create concerns about fairness in deciding which policy is most appropriate for a given strategy. Managers may believe that a uniform policy that applies to all inter–profit center exchanges is "fair"—a sentiment most likely to be expressed by those who prefer a policy being used by other profit centers. For example, a profit center general manager who has to source a component part internally may be resentful that another profit center has the autonomy to choose between internal and external suppliers.

In general, being able to compare one's situation with others that are in some way similar is a major element in perceptions of fairness. If profit center general managers do not like the transfer pricing policies assigned to them, it is only natural for them to point out that different ones are being applied to other profit centers and argue that the situation is unfair. At the same time, if other profit center general managers like the policy governing their exchanges, they can argue that the differences in their situations justify different transfer pricing policies.

Thus, a company's transfer pricing practices are subjected to tensions along two dimensions. On the temporal dimension, pressures for change because of changing strategies must be balanced against pressures to retain existing policies. The advantages of changing to support the strategies of the intermediate and the final good must be balanced against the disadvantages of implementing a change—perhaps the loss of historical comparability for performance evaluation or the recurrence of some earlier unsatisfactory experiences with a particular policy.

On the cross-sectional dimension, pressures to adapt transfer pricing policies to strategy must be balanced against pressures to have a uniform policy. If policies are based on strategy, it is possible that different policies can be used for different products exchanged between different profit centers, for different products exchanged between the same profit centers, and even for the same product exchanged between different profit centers. At the same time, for reasons of administrative simplicity and fairness, there are advantages to using the same policy for the same product sold to different profit centers, using the same policy for different products sold to the same profit center, using the same policy for all products bought by a profit center from different profit centers, and even using the same policy for different products exchanged between two different pairs of profit centers. Figure 9–4 diagrams these possibilities.

The simultaneous pressures from both dimensions determine a company's transfer pricing practices and its experience with these practices.

> **Hypothesis 38:** At any given point in time, a company's transfer pricing practices are a result of pressures for uniformity balanced against pressures for diversity.

Since each dimension contains tension between conflicting forces—and a tension exists across the two dimensions—the transfer pricing problem can never be "solved" once and for all for all internal transactions. Instead, the problem must be managed by balancing pressures for constancy and pressures for change with pressures for uniformity and pressures for diversity so as to shape inter–profit center relationships in a way that best contributes to organizational effectiveness. This can be achieved through an administrative perspective on the transfer pricing problem that takes account of strategy, fairness, and process.

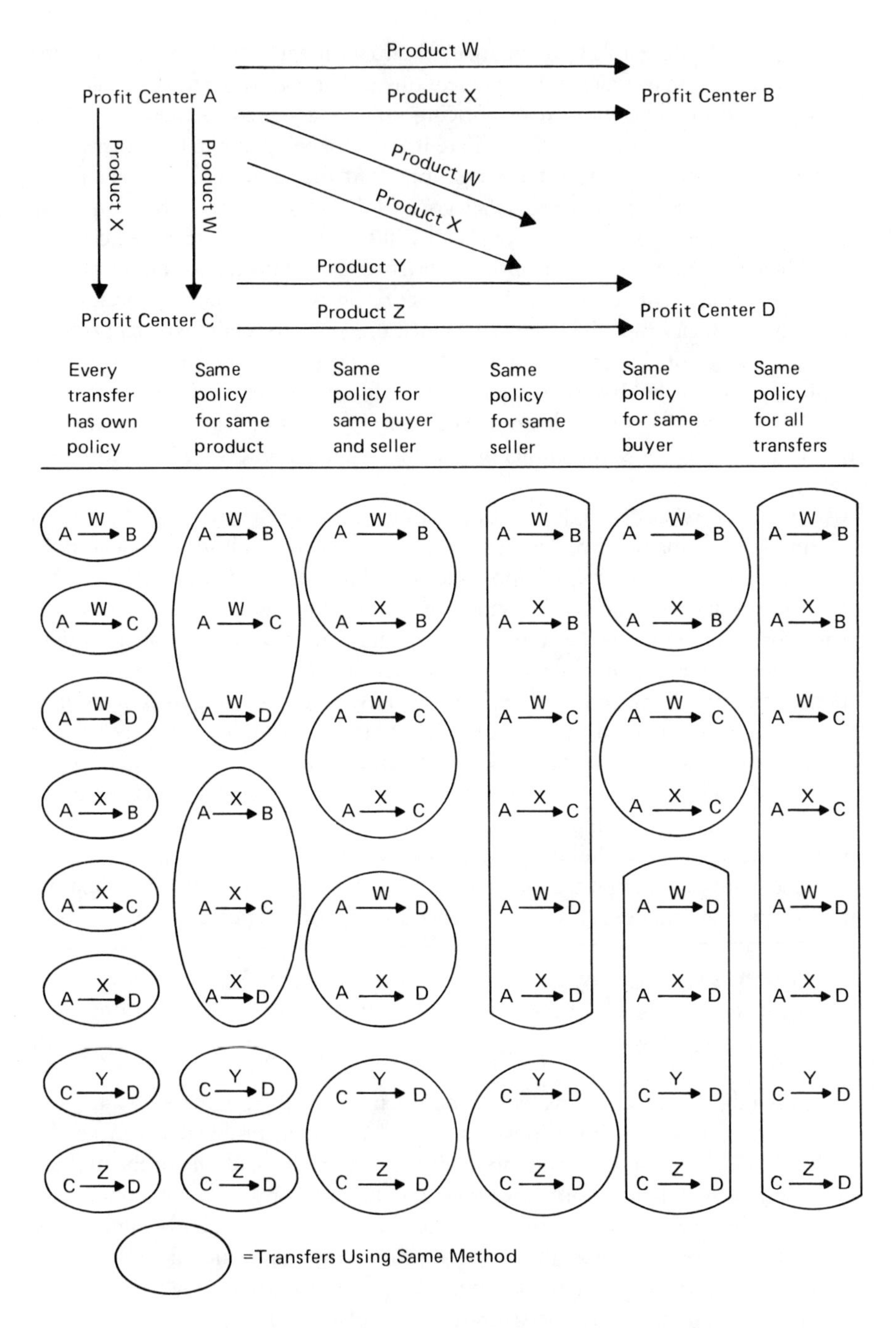

Figure 9–4. Pressures for Diversity and Uniformity

Cicero Systems, Inc.: Balancing Diversity and Uniformity

Cicero Systems, Inc., is a good example of a company that had to face the problem of balancing pressures for diversity with pressures for uniformity. It is also a good example of how a company can manage the trade-offs between constancy and change. Since a great deal of time and attention was given to determining and implementing a new transfer pricing policy, this company's experience also provides some guidelines on managing change. The manager responsible for designing and implementing the new policy was very sensitive to the change process itself. As a result, the managers who were affected understood and, for the most part, accepted the new policy. This example also illustrates how history can affect a company's transfer pricing policy. Like Aquinas Chemicals Co., Cicero Systems had had a negative experience with market-based transfers and did not want to repeat it.

Cicero Systems, Inc., was organized into five profit centers: Components, Systems, Services, Retail, and International. These profit centers were subdivided into thirteen product families, which in turn were subdivided into 105 profit centers. Historically, the division presidents, who were referred to as "barons in their fiefdoms," had functioned in an environment of entrepreneurial autonomy. The chairman, who had been with the company for many years, had a strong belief in letting the division presidents do their own thing. One result of this high degree of autonomy in the past had been some bitter internal disputes and even business competition between Components and Systems.

In 1965, the original team of managers, whose orientation had been primarily technical, was replaced by a group more oriented toward marketing, although technical concerns remained important. By 1974, the company was in serious financial difficulty, and a new president, Roger Peterson, was named. As one manager put it, his appointment marked "the downfall of the technocrats and marketeers." Since Peterson's appointment, a significant improvement in the company's performance had resulted from better financial management and greater internal cooperation and coordination. Peterson still emphasized the importance of the entrepreneurial spirit, but he tempered it by recognizing the necessary constraints of being in a large company with interdependent divisions.

Historically, the company had been weak in asset management. As one manager noted:

> Up to 1974 we were neanderthal in financial matters. We had been a high technology company, and then added an emphasis on marketing. The idea was that we could keep growing no matter what, since we could always get a customer to finance us.

Division presidents were held responsible only for inventories until 1975, when Mal Goldsmith, senior vice-president for operations finance, instituted an asset management program. Balance sheets were made up for each division, and the division managers were held responsible for all balance sheet items. This resulted in a $250 million reduction of the company's $750 million debt, which greatly exceeded its equity.

Goldsmith wanted continued emphasis on asset management, and in 1979 one of his major objectives was to use return on invested capital (ROIC) as a major performance measure for all divisions. At that time, Components was using return on investment and earnings before interest and taxes as its principal performance measures; Systems was using profits and return on revenues; and Services was using return on assets. Goldsmith wanted to institute uniform performance measures for all divisions, at the same time generating measures that would enable the company to compare its divisions' performance with their external competitors. He also believed that the divisions were increasingly comparing their performance with each other. His desire to establish a uniform approach to performance measurement was the basis for reviewing the company's transfer pricing practices. Another reason, according to Goldsmith, was that "it took longer to get internal transfers reconciled than all of the rest of the budget when we were putting budgets together."

History of Transfer Pricing

The company's original transfer pricing policy had been standard cost of manufacturing plus a fully loaded cost (FLC) "adder" for expenses such as R&D and technical support. Each division had a different way of calculating standard costs and the FLC adder. When the original management team left in 1965, a type of market price approach was used, but severe problems because of the company's unsophisticated accounting systems resulted in a double counting of profits, similar to a dual pricing approach. These problems came at a time when the company as a whole was beginning to experience severe financial difficulties. There were times when each division showed a profit but the company as a whole was showing a loss. According to one manager, "We almost sank ourselves with this method"; it was discontinued in 1971.

After that, the company used the following formula for determining transfer prices for several years:

$$\text{Transfer price} = \sqrt{\frac{\text{Selling price} - \text{Cost}}{\text{Cost}}} \times \text{Cost}$$

The selling price was the published list price, and cost was standard full manufacturing cost. This formula was developed by a former McKinsey consultant who was a division controller at the time. One manager recalled that "to implement this method, we hired clerks by the boatload to do invoices on a line-by-line basis."

By 1979, Cicero Systems managers were using thirteen different methods for the forty-six internal product transfers and nineteen different methods for the internal service transfers. The frequency of the most popular method for each category was seventeen and sixteen, respectively. Four product transfer methods and five service transfer methods accounted for 70 percent of the relationships in each category.

Divisional Preferences

Each of the three divisions that were significantly involved with internal transfers—Systems, Components, and Services—had strong preferences for a particular method. Systems, which had been the basis of the company, regarded internal transfers as a way of increasing volume to reduce unit costs, but its primary focus was external sales. Managers in Systems favored standard full cost transfer prices without the FLC adder. Negative volume variances were a minor concern, because constant growth had made them rare. They believed that capital charges or asset allocations were a matter of "splitting hairs." They were also concerned about the effect on technical spending in other divisions. At Cicero Systems, R&D expenses were budgeted as a percentage of total costs. Systems argued that if buying profit centers paid standard cost plus the FLC adder, technical spending would be inflated more than was necessary. Systems also thought that R&D budgets should be based only on external sales.

The Components Division advocated standard full cost plus the FLC adder. They wanted the adder to include R&D, other technical expenses, selling expenses, and cost of capital charges, for several reasons. One was to increase the division's technical spending levels, since paying more for internal transfers would make costs higher. Another was to increase revenues by being able to charge more for products sold internally. Revenue growth was a major objective in this division, as symbolized by the party the managers held when they reached the $1 billion mark. The split of the division's output was roughly even between internal and external sales.

The Services Division advocated the use of market prices based on leases. This was the method its competitors used when they obtained systems and components from external suppliers. A special concern of managers was to be able to compare this division's performance with competitors, and they wanted to establish internal transfers on the same basis. For similar reasons, they did not want transfers that put these products on their books as long-term assets.

The Services Division was based on a 1973 acquisition of a division from another company that had received product on a market price lease basis. Top management believed that immediately changing to standard full cost plus the FLC adder would have been a mistake, because it would have meant windfall profits, which would put pressures on the Services Division to lower external prices to increase its market share. The market price lease method was retained and never changed.

At first, Services had had difficulty convincing Components, its major supplier, of the value of a market price approach. Eventually, Components had developed a favorable attitude, consistent with its desire to increase revenues as quickly as possible. Components had become a good supplier, partly because it received market prices on internal sales to Services and partly out of a desire to give Services a positive opinion of its products and service. Unlike the other divisions, Services was allowed to source externally.

Given the diversity of preferences among these three divisions, Goldsmith established a task force in the fall of 1979 that included representatives from the three divisions (two from Systems), corporate headquarters, and marketing. The chairman was from Systems. Goldsmith recalled that each division president had "an emotional stake" in his preference. He explained his own preference:

> Where I was coming from, and I had convinced Peterson of this, was that it may not be possible to get perfect external comparisons, but we should have a simple way of handling transfer pricing so we didn't have to hire thousands of accountants to keep track of this crap.

As a first step, the task force examined all the methods currently being used in terms of their advantages and disadvantages. A variety of methods were considered and evaluated. In spite of the positive aspects of market price, it was rejected almost immediately; only Ted McCarthy, the Services representative on the task force, favored it. Memories of the company's negative experience with this method in the past and the feeling that it involved "a great deal of accounting pain" were the primary reasons for rejecting it.

Task Force Recommendations

The task force made its first presentation to Goldsmith and the financial planning committee in May 1980. It recommended that every buying division receive a charge for technical expenses, part of the FLC adder. The task force also recommended allocating assets. Goldsmith told the chairman that he wanted a simpler approach, and he made two major points. First, anything that "changed form" would not carry technical expenses. This meant that Services would pay no technical charge, since this division used the product to produce the services it sold externally, as opposed to Systems, which incorporated Components' products into the systems it sold to external customers. Goldsmith believed that this distinction should be made because Services had little influence or effect on Systems' technical spending and so should not be assessed this charge. Components, on the other hand, did affect and was affected by R&D and other technical efforts in Systems. Second, Goldsmith thought that allocating assets would be too complicated, and he wanted a cost of capital charge instead. The chairman was given instructions to work with the members of the task force "to get them to see the light."

In the meantime, Goldsmith spent time preparing Peterson and the division presidents for the change that his work with the task force would produce. He described his role during this period:

> I turned into a PR man to Peterson and the presidents of the divisions. I kept talking to them individually, dealing with them in an informal way to explain to them the reasons for the direction we were taking. I'm relating this in a rambling way, but that's how it happened. From May on I worked hard with each division to see the point by having their financial officers work through the numbers to see the impact on them of the new approach.
>
> The president of Services was the biggest problem. He kept insisting on market price. I had a lot of meetings with him. He understood what we were trying to do and said he could see that it was better for the corporation, but it made it harder for him to compare himself to external competitors. But every time he brought up the external comparison issue, I said, "You're not comparable anyway," since most of his competitors are not supplied internally.

Through his efforts, Goldsmith sought to help these managers understand the reasons for the change and the impact it would have on their reported financial results, and, when necessary, he tried to convince them of the merit of making the change.

Similarly, through the task force, Goldsmith sought to make other managers in the divisions aware of his objectives for transfer pricing and to get them to take a more corporate perspective. Ted McCarthy believed that Goldsmith had been successful in this: "Initially, I felt funny about the direction of the task force. As things went along, I felt better as I understood more the other parts of Cicero Systems and their needs." He also recognized that Goldsmith's objective was to create a uniform policy that was relatively painless to implement:

> One of the objectives of the task force was to have a uniform company-wide policy. We didn't feel that everybody should be left to do their own thing. We needed to impose some accounting discipline. Another one of the objectives of the task force was to develop a policy that could be implemented with the least pain and strain.

The task force made another presentation to Goldsmith and the financial planning committee in July 1980. A month later, when they presented it to Peterson and the top officers, it was accepted completely. Goldsmith commented on its acceptance:

> I'd never given the division presidents bad advice in the past, so I had credibility on transfer pricing recommendations. We knew we couldn't change everybody dramatically because nobody would buy it, but we knew that we had to change it some.

He noted that one difficulty with the change was losing comparability with historical data. And he added: "I would personally fight very hard against going to market price."

In its final presentation, the task force noted that the "difficult and controversial issue" of transfer pricing had become more severe "as increasing attention is paid to product family net profit before taxes, asset levels, and ROIC because of the impact that transfer prices have on these key indicators." The procedure recommended by the task force was based on standard costs plus a monthly FLC adder. This FLC adder differed according to whether the seller was a hardware product family or a software product family, and similarly for buyers. A separate task force would deal with software transfers, but its recommendations would not be available for 1981 budgets. In its presentation, the task force evaluated four different approaches—standard cost, standard cost plus one-time FLC adder, standard cost plus per-product FLC adder, and market price based—in terms of five transfer pricing objectives: (1) goal congruence (promotes rational decision making in the supplying division and in the receiving division), (2) enhancement of product family performance measurement, (3) how systematic, rational, and understandable it was, (4) ease of administration, and (5) conversion costs. Figure 9–5 reproduces a table prepared by the task force on its evaluation of the four policies. A standard cost approach was considered poor for goal congruence and enhancement of product family performance measurement but the easiest to administer and convert to. It also rated high as being systematic, rational, and understandable, as did a market price based approach. On the other four criteria, market price was the opposite of standard full cost. Market price was considered good in terms of goal congruence but most difficult to administer and convert to. The other two methods were in between, with standard cost plus one-time FLC adder most similar to standard cost, and standard cost plus per-product FLC adder most similar to market price. The selected method of standard cost plus one-time FLC adder was second lowest on the first three objectives but second highest on the last two.

The New Policy

In its recommendations, the task force balanced Goldsmith's desire for a uniform policy with pressures for diversity created by product and divisional characteristics. For transfers from hardware product families, of which there were six, the transfer

Comparison of Transfer Pricing Methods

Transfer Pricing Objective	Transfer Pricing Method: Standard Costs	Standard Costs Plus One-Time FLC Adder	Standard Costs Plus per-Product FLC	Market Price Based
Goal Congruence				
Promotes rational decision-making in the supplying division	poor	moderate	better	best
Promotes rational decision-making in the receiving division	poor	better	better	moderate
Enhances product family measurement	worst	moderate	better	best
Systematic, rational, understandable	best	better	moderate	best
Ease of administration	easy	moderate	harder	hardest
Conversion costs	lowest cost	moderate cost	higher cost	highest cost

Figure 9–5. The Task Force's Evaluation of Four Transfer Pricing Methods

price was the approved transfer cost (ATC)—equal to standard manufacturing cost unless approved by Goldsmith—plus a monthly pro rata cost of capital charge to all buying product families, plus a monthly pro rata FLC adder for technical expenses to all buying hardware product families. Assets eligible for inclusion in the cost of capital charge included gross inventory; net plant, property, and equipment; and other direct assets used in the production process. The calculation of the charge was 7 percent of the assets budgeted in the selling division that were allocated to the buying division. The allocation was determined by the ratio of budgeted ATC for products to be sold to the buying division divided by total budgeted costs. A similar allocation approach was used for determining technical effort. Technical expenses could amount to 30 to 40 percent of standard costs. Adjustments were made when actual costs varied from standard costs by more than 10 percent.

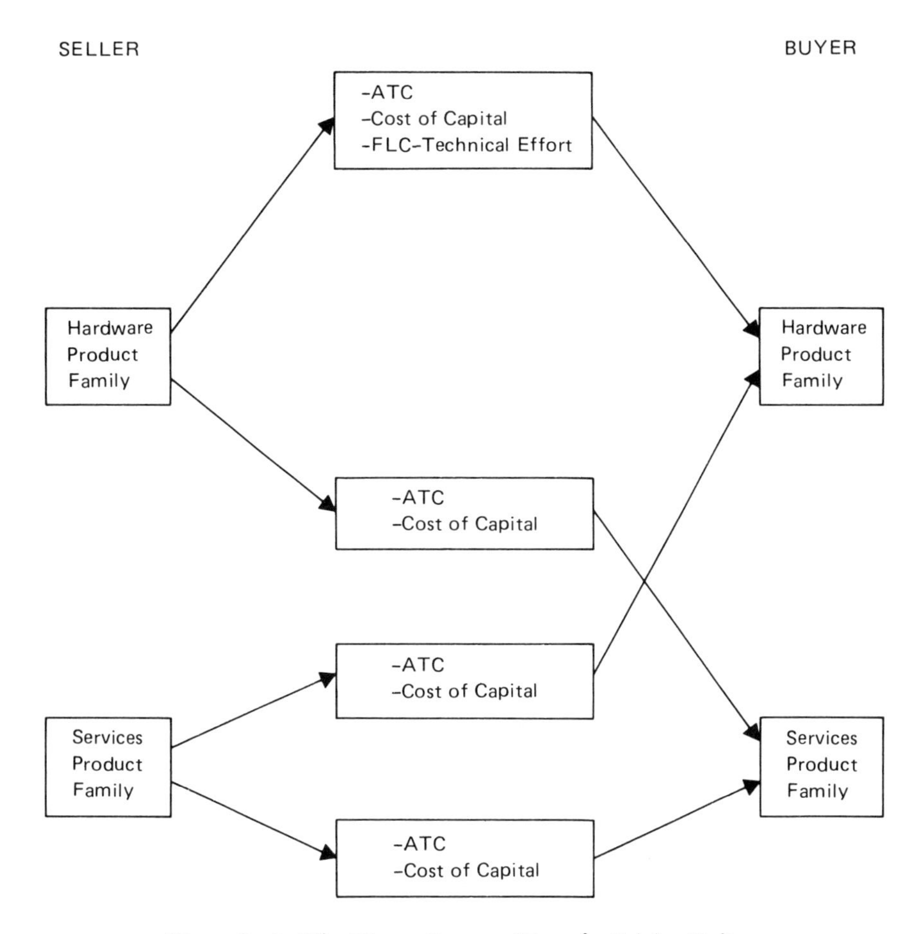

Figure 9–6. The Cicero Systems Transfer Pricing Policy

For service product families, the transfer price was ATC plus a cost of capital charge calculated in the same way it was for hardware product families. There were no technical expense charges for sales from service product families. Figure 9–6 diagrams the proposed—and accepted—policy. As part of its effort, the task force produced a working document to help division managers use this method in preparing the 1981 budget. The new policy contained the provision that "any disputes or disagreements as to interpretation or implementation of this policy will be resolved by Goldsmith." It also stipulated that "requests for deviations from this policy must be specifically approved by Goldsmith."

Although the decision was made to use standard cost plus an FLC adder for all transfers, this method would be phased in for transfers to Services over a two-year period to prevent major discontinuities in reported profits for Components (which would become lower) and Services (which would become higher). This problem was less acute than it would have been five or six years earlier, because hardware costs were a steadily decreasing share of Services' total costs. McCarthy, the Services representative, was reasonably positive about the change.

Goldsmith reported that there were no major negotiations or arguments when it came to using the new policy to prepare the 1981 budget: "Maybe some people didn't like it, but there were not a lot of problems." Another manager was less positive and doubted the long-term viability of the policy. He had misgivings about the balance that had been struck, which made provision for some variations in the uniform policy:

> On the task force each person was trying to represent his boss's point of view. What we wound up with was a bunch of half-ass compromises. It is simpler, so by definition it is good, but in the long run I'm not sure how it will work. My guess is it will not hold.

The Inherent Value of Change

Just as there are advantages to retaining a transfer pricing policy, so are there advantages to changing a transfer pricing policy. There are a number of ways in which change can be useful for its own sake. For example, over time, managers will learn various ways to "game" any given policy, and this may keep some information from top management that it would find useful. This gaming may also reduce top management's control. By changing the transfer pricing policy, top management can create conflict that will increase the flow of information and improve its control. Furthermore, if both profit center managers are dissatisfied with a given policy, changing it may mollify them, at least for some period of time.

Finally, since every policy has particular advantages and disadvantages, a change in policy can help overcome some of the disadvantages of the previous policy.[5] Thus, the lack of internal transfers because of a policy of exchange autonomy can be overcome by a policy of dual pricing, with or without mandated internal transactions. Eventually, however, new disadvantages arise and the advantages of the old policy are lost, which creates an incentive to change yet again.

I found a special case of this kind of change after the formal data collection phase of this project had ended. It was identified in conversations with managers at three different companies. In each company, management was contemplating turning some cost centers into profit centers to drive down costs. The thinking in these companies was that over time, the costs of manufacturing, data processing, and other staff functions had become excessive and had exceeded market prices for these products or services. (Recall that Blackstone Machinery experienced this problem with the new Components and Foundry divisions.) In all of these companies, managers of these cost centers had been under some pressure to control costs, but top management believed that it had become impossible to determine which cost levels really were appropriate for a given quantity of product or service because of limited external sales by supplying cost centers and limited external purchases by buying profit centers.[6]

As noted, all three companies were considering proposals to change these cost centers into profit centers. They were considering the change implemented at Blackstone Machinery Company—and for the same reasons. The change would include charging market price for internal transfers, giving buying profit centers some limited autonomy to source externally in the beginning that would increase over time, and in some cases permitting the selling profit centers to sell externally if they were not already doing so. Top management hoped that by creating these competitive internal relationships based on the discipline of the market, incentives would exist for the selling profit centers to find ways to reduce their costs.

There is a certain irony to this way of thinking when it is contrasted with the experience of other companies when a change is made from market price to full cost transfers to obtain the same objectives. In the latter case the reasons typically given are that full cost transfers are less than market price and that if the selling profit center is not given a profit on internal transfers, it will focus more on reducing costs rather than trying to maximize its profits by emphasizing external sales and negotiating for high internal transfer prices. Larry Johnson at Paine Chemical Company gave this argument as a reason for changing the transfer price of plastic resins from market price less 5 percent to full cost when he had responsibility for the three plastic resins businesses.

Companies may make different changes in transfer pricing policies to accomplish the same objectives if they start out in different situations. Conversely, they may make similar changes to accomplish different objectives. This finding emphasizes the fact that transfer pricing is a tool for top management to use in implementing strategy. How this tool is used and what it is used for depends on the context of its application, as determined by a company's history, strategy, and organizational characteristics.

10
The Manager's Analytical Plane

The five preceding chapters have shown that a number of variables, in addition to strategy and process, must be considered in developing a thorough understanding of how to manage transfer pricing. Nevertheless, managers could use a robust but simple framework that would enable them to assess transfer pricing quickly in their own organization, whether it is a total company or a lower-level profit center, such as a group or a division. This assessment could be done by specifying the type of transfer pricing policy that should be used for a given strategy and the organizational characteristics (structure, systems, and processes) that are both a result and a determinant of strategy.[1] Such a "first cut" analysis would, of course, have to be supplemented by other considerations, such as history and administrative simplicity, which have been discussed in previous chapters.

This final chapter presents a concept I call the Manager's Analytical Plane (MAP). It is so named because it is based on a plane defined by two dimensions of strategy—vertical integration and diversification—that managers can use to analyze their company's or profit center's strategy and its organizational characteristics, or what will be called the "implementation mode." Transfer pricing policy is included in the implementation mode. However, the MAP has more general uses in helping managers think about their current and future strategy and their current and future implementation mode.

Strategy and Its Implementation

Figure 10–1 presents a simple model of strategy implementation. Although it is similar to models proposed by others—such as in the relationships shown between strategy, structure, and systems—it has some distinctive characteristics.[2] First, it emphasizes processes as the crucial management variable. Here, the term *process* will be used in a more general way than it has been so far to refer to patterns of behavior that emerge from the activities and interactions of people in a company.[3] Processes are especially important for determining how conflict is

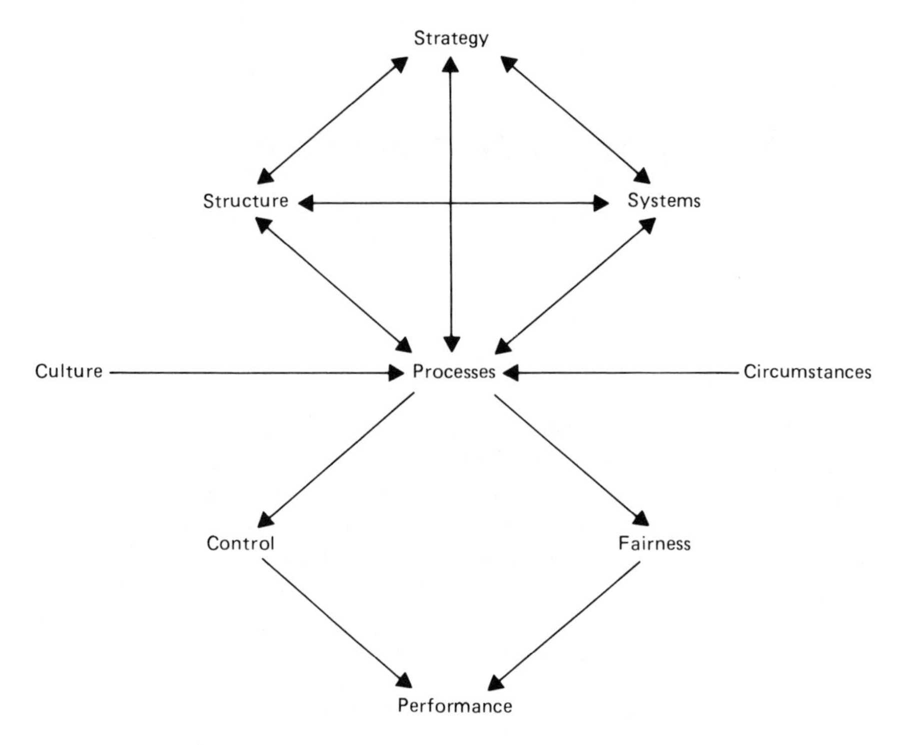

Figure 10–1. A Model of Strategy Implementation

resolved in an organization. Structure and systems are the foundation on which processes are built, but processes are also affected by company culture (norms, values, beliefs, attitudes, rituals, and myths) and circumstances (such as a change in management, a strong or weak economy, technological innovation, and the like).

The second distinctive aspect of this model is that it emphasizes how processes determine fairness and control, which in turn determine performance. *Fairness* is used in the same way it has been throughout this book—managers believe they are being treated fairly when they receive rewards that they believe are commensurate with their contribution to the company. At the same time, the company needs control over the actions of and outcomes by managers to ensure that their pursuit of personal and subunit objectives is supportive of corporate objectives. Obviously, there can be some tension in simultaneously ensuring control while preserving fairness. For example, the intervention by higher-level management in the actions of profit center managers, such as requiring them to trade internally, is an exercise of control that may be in the best interests of the company but may be perceived as unfair by the profit center managers. Over the long

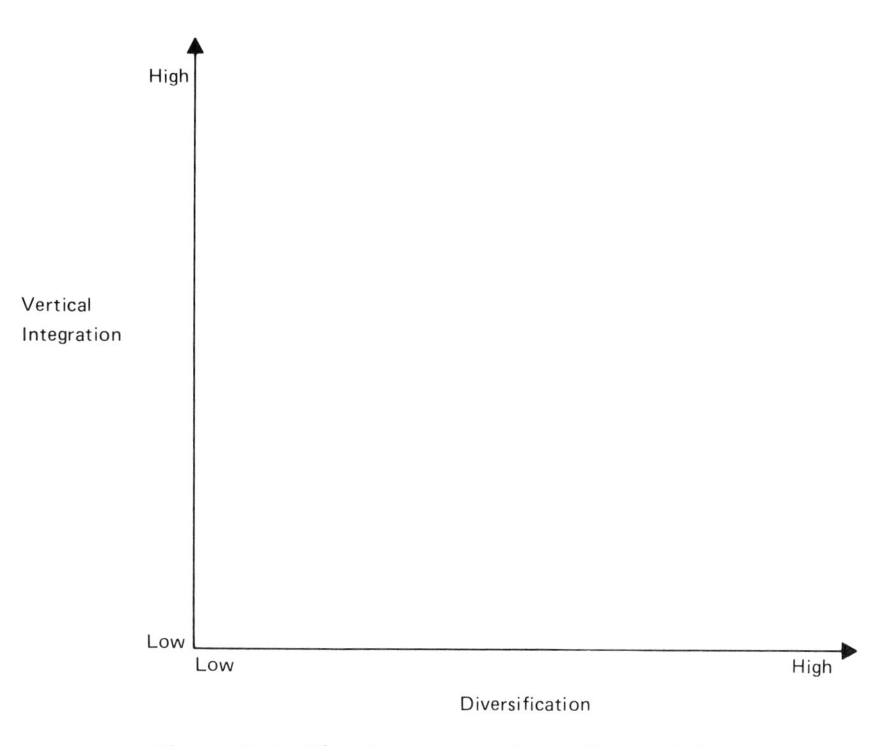

Figure 10–2. The Manager's Analytical Plane (MAP)

term, this can hurt performance. The challenge of management is to balance fairness and control within the organization to obtain the best possible performance.

The third distinctive aspect of this model of strategy implementation is that it treats vertical integration and diversification as two independent dimensions of strategy—as shown in the diagram of the Manager's Analytical Plane in figure 10–2. Both of these dimensions have received extensive discussion in the literature on business policy and strategic planning, but there has generally been a failure to recognize that these dimensions are independent. For example, an electronics company that integrates backward into semiconductors that it uses only for internal needs is vertically integrating without diversifying. A machinery company that acquires a semiconductor company to enter a growth market but has no internal needs for semiconductors is diversifying without vertically integrating. However, if the electronics company in the first case also sold its semiconductors in the external marketplace, it would be diversifying as well. Similarly, if the machinery company used some semiconductors internally, it would also be vertically integrating.

A continuum of strategy is of much less analytical utility than a plane. This is one of the reasons Vancil (1978) had trouble analyzing the data from his decentralization study. He used a well-known typology of corporate strategy developed by Rumelt (1974), who built on earlier work by Wrigley (1970). Rumelt's typology is based on nine categories arranged along a single diversification dimension based on combining relatedness (proportion of a firm's revenues derived from its largest single group of related businesses) and specialization (proportion of a firm's revenues derived from its largest single business). His development of a one-dimensional typology—typically aggregated into four types (single business, dominant business, related businesses, and unrelated businesses)—is somewhat ironic, since he noted that "vertically integrated firms often did not seem to belong in any of the categories defined," and he concluded that they were "sufficiently different from other firms to warrant an entirely separate set of categories to describe their diversification postures" (pp. 20, 22). He did not develop this separate set of categories, because he thought the result would be an overly complex classification scheme.

At least two other students of business policy have recognized the importance of identifying two dimensions. Bower and Doz (1979), using the terms *variety* and *interdependence* in the same general way as Rumelt used *diversification* and *vertical integration,* respectively, argued that "variety and interdependence are not extremes on the same linear scale. Rather, they are orthogonal notions" (p. 164). Although many different definitions exist for the terms *vertical integration* and *diversification,* they will be used here in a broad and general way that incorporates most specific definitions, since the objective is to develop a framework that is of practical use.

Vertical integration will be used to refer to the inclusion of activities within the firm that could be obtained externally, such as component parts, distribution channels, and staff services (legal, advertising, electronic data processing, and so on).[4] Vertical integration creates interdependencies between functions, between profit centers, and between profit centers and corporate line and staff functions, which is why Bower and Doz's label of "interdependence" for this dimension is equally appropriate.

The extent of interdependence depends on where the boundaries of the firm are drawn through many make-or-buy decisions—the "concrete" aspect of vertical integration—and on how management designs the organization. For example, there is a higher level of interdependence when all of the company's legal resources are centralized at corporate headquarters than when they are distributed in the various profit centers. Thus, companies that are equal on the concrete aspect of vertical integration may vary on the "design" aspect.

The term *diversification* will be used to refer to the number of different businesses in which the company competes and to how different these businesses are from each other. This definition is consistent with the one suggested by Salter and Weinhold (1979), who used the term to refer to both product and market diversification. The larger the number of products and markets in which a company competes—the concrete aspect of diversification—the greater is the variety of its businesses; again, the label used by Bower and Doz is equally applicable. The decision regarding the products and markets in which to compete is analogous to the decision regarding which activities to incorporate within the firm.

Similarly, just as there is a design aspect to the vertical integration dimension, there is a design aspect to the diversification dimension. Management decides how to define the businesses in which it competes; as Abell and Hammond (1979) put it, "Business definition is a creative decision in its own right" (p. 390). For example, a company increases its extent of diversification or variety when it segments a product into two businesses based on different markets, such as large customers and small customers, and treats these market segments as distinct businesses for which separate plans are made and performance measurements are taken. Again, companies with the same concrete aspect of diversification may vary on the design aspect.

Four Pure Organizational Types

Managers can use the plane in figure 10–2 to map the location of their company (or group or division) according to its current strategy, as well as its expected future location if this strategy is expected to change. The utility of this plane, however, comes from recognizing that each location in the plane is associated with a particular implementation mode. Although continuous variation in strategy is possible, four pure organizatonal types can be identified that correspond to the four "corners" of the plane. Each of these types is an equilibrium configuration based on an internally consistent set of characteristics that are appropriate for a given strategy.[5] Figure 10–3 shows each of these four types and, in parentheses, an example of a company of each type, based on data from case studies.[6] Table 10–1 summarizes the implementation modes for each organizational type. Although actual organizations will not conform exactly to any one of these types for a variety of reasons, performance generally will be greatest when the implementation mode matches the strategy. Furthermore, pressures exist that push any organization into one of the four corners of the plane. Also, any actual organization can be composed of several of these types; for example, it might be one type from the perspective of the CEO, while various groups and divisions conform to that and other types. The distinctive nature of each type can be illustrated by a brief description of the key characteristics of all four.

The Collective Organization

The collective organization—low on both vertical integration and diversification—is typical of small and new firms that focus on one or a few functions (for example, the company is either a manufacturer or a distributor) or one or a few products. The term *collective* is used to indicate the lack of formal management

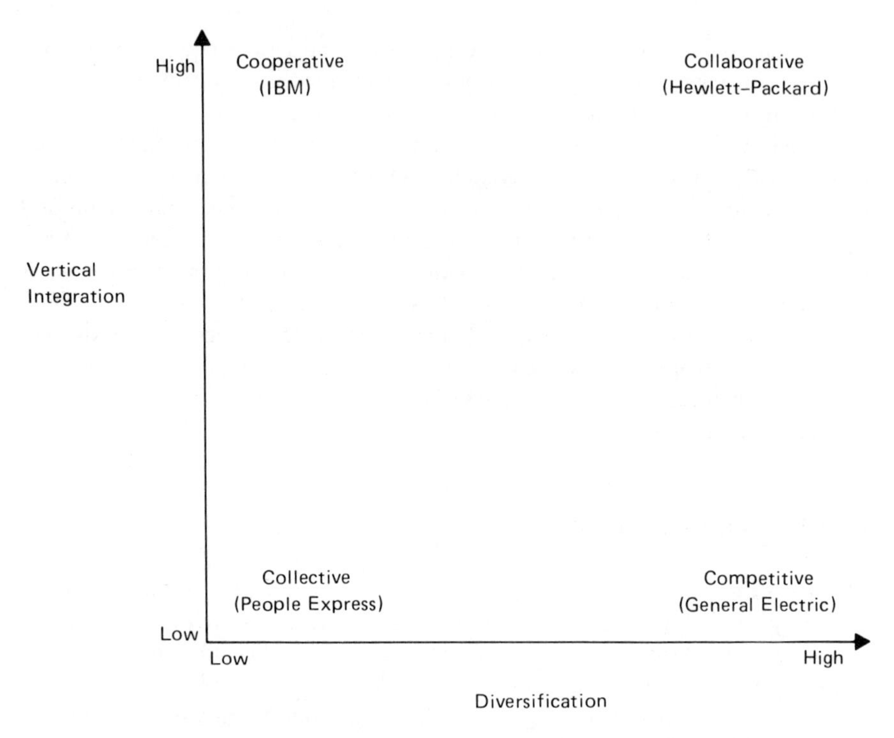

Figure 10–3. Four Pure Organizational Types in the MAP

in the collection of people that make up this organization. The simple strategy of this company is implicit in the vision of the owner/entrepreneur. Small size and/ or newness result in a structure that is nonexistent to rudimentary. Similarly, management systems are nonexistent to very simple.[7]

The processes governing superior–subordinate relationships between the owner and those who work for him or her are directive or top-down. Those between employees are based on personal relationships, and the quality of these interpersonal relationships determines how conflict will be resolved. The owner retains control by his or her *individual involvement* in operations, and employees frequently have more responsibility than authority. Whether or not they feel they are being treated fairly depends on the *personal code* the owner uses in evaluating and rewarding performance. The principal challenge of the collective organization is to grow through vertical integration and/or diversification. In either case, further elaboration of the strategy necessitates increased formalization and complexity in the implementation mode. Making the transition from an informal to a more formal organization is a classic and difficult problem for the small entrepreneurial firm that wishes to grow.

Table 10–1
Implementation Modes of the Four Pure Organizational Types

Implementation Mode	*Collective Organization*	*Cooperative Organization*	*Competitive Organization*	*Collaborative Organization*
Strategy	Implicit in vision of entrepreneur	Total company strategy	Aggregate of division's strategies	Mutually defined total company and profit center perspectives
Structure	Nonexistent to rudimentary specialization	Functional or a few high-level profit centers (basic unit is function)	Multidivisional (basic unit is division)	Matrix (basic units are functions and profit centers) or very complex multidivisional
Systems	Nonexistent to very simple	Costs, revenues, physical measures; internal and historical; subjective	Profits and ROI; budget and external; objective	Combination of financial and physical measures; budget, historical, internal and external; objective and subjective
Processes	Vertical are directive; horizontal are interpersonal	Vertical are top-down; horizontal are integrative bargaining	Vertical are bottom-up; horizontal are distributive bargaining	Vertical are iterative; horizontal are mixed-mode bargaining
Control	Individual involvement	Through structure on actions	Through systems on outcomes	Through processes balancing structure and systems
Fairness	Personal code	Shared fate	Impartial spectator	Rational trust

The Cooperative Organization

The collective organization grows into a cooperative organization, which is high on vertical integration and low on diversification, when it integrates forward and/or backward while retaining its focus on a narrow line of products. This organizational type is often found in mature or capital-intensive industries. The term *cooperative* is used to indicate that the implementation mode of this firm is focused on cooperation among all managers to maximize total company performance.[8]

The strategy for this type of company is a strategy for the company as a whole, with all subunit strategies being expressed in terms of their contribution to it. The narrow product focus results in the company being organized as a single profit center, or at most a few high-level profit centers, some of which are quasi profit centers because of their substantial interdependence with other internal units. Management systems distinguish functional responsibilities in terms of costs, revenues, and physical measures, and authority generally is equal to responsibility. Great emphasis is placed on using internal standards and historical results in evaluating performance. The high interdependence across subunits (for example, manufacturing and sales) requires substantial subjective judgment on the part of the general manager in evaluating performance, since high interdependence makes these measures imperfect.

The vertical processes between superiors and subordinates are very much top-down because of the focus on a narrow range of products and the interdependence across units. Horizontal processes for conflict resolution are characterized by integrative bargaining, which "functions to find common or complementary interests and solve problems confronting both parties" (Walton and McKersie, 1965, p. 8). In other words, units seek to find a solution that is in the best interest of the company as a whole. The term *win/win* is often used to describe this type of process.

Top management exercises control primarily through the organizational *structure* on the actions of lower-level managers. Control over actions is necessitated by the high degree of interdependence caused by vertical integration. It is possible to have such control because of top management's experience in and detailed familiarity with the narrow range of businesses in which the company is engaged. Also, because of the high degree of interdependence, lower-level managers are rewarded in terms of their contribution to the performance of the company as a whole. This is fairness based on *shared fate,* since a manager's rewards depend on how well all other managers in the organization have performed.

The Competitive Organization

The conceptual opposite of the cooperative organization is the competitive organization—high on diversification and low on vertical integration—which is based on many different businesses that do little sharing of such resources as manufacturing facilities or sales forces. This organizational type is exemplified by conglomerates or holding companies. The term *competitive* is used to indicate that the subunits of this organization are profit centers and compete with each other for capital and other resources on the basis of performance, which is comparable across all subunits—unlike the case of the cooperative organization.[9]

Corporate strategy in the competitive firm is largely an aggregation of subunit strategies, such as those of divisions or subsidiaries. Although broad strategic guidelines might exist for the company as a whole, they are not nearly as important in developing subunit strategies as they are in the cooperative organization. Competitive firms employ a multidivisional structure, supplemented by systems that measure the profitability and return on investment of the divisions. Comparisons with the budget, long-range plans, external competitors, and other internal divisions are used to evaluate these performance measures.[10] Both authority and responsibility are highly decentralized in the competitive organization to middle-level general managers, who have authority commensurate with their responsibility.

As a result of the high degree of decentralization of authority and responsibility, vertical processes are bottom-up—initiated by lower-level profit center managers when they want assistance from top management or corporate staff. The horizontal processes of conflict resolution are characterized by distributive bargaining, in which "each party attempts to maximize his own share in the context of fixed-sum payoffs" (Walton and McKersie, 1965, p. 13). In other words, profit centers seek to maximize their own results even at the expense of other profit centers. The term *win/lose* is often used to describe this type of process.

The emphasis on using financial measures to evaluate performance and on the comparability of these measures across subunits makes it possible for top management to exercise control primarily through *systems* on the outcomes of the lower-level general managers. Top management must exert control primarily through the measures of financial outcomes, since it cannot know each of the company's many businesses in sufficient detail to deal more directly with operating concerns. The lower-level general managers are rewarded in terms of the performance of their divisions. This is considered fair when the performance of other divisions or of the total company does not affect their rewards when their own division's objectives have been met. Thus, fairness is similar to the *impartial spectator* of the marketplace in Adam Smith's economic theory, whereby individuals are rewarded according to the extent to which they achieve their own self-interest.

The Collaborative Organization

The collaborative organization—high on both vertical integration and diversification—combines characteristics of the cooperative and competitive types. It is similar to the cooperative organization in that there is a high degree of interdependence across subunits of the company. However, unlike the cooperative organization, these subunits include a number of profit centers, which is more similar to the competitive organization. There is an important difference as well. Whereas the competitive organization has a number of unrelated businesses, the collaborative organization has a number of related businesses. The former emphasizes the concrete aspect of diversification, and the latter emphasizes the design aspect. There is also a strong design aspect of vertical integration, which creates profit center interdependencies, in addition to the concrete aspect, which creates functional interdependencies.

The collaborative organization is a complex organization to manage, since at a purely logical level the cooperative and competitive types have mutually exclusive characteristics on the variables in their implementation modes. Firms of this type are found in project-based industries (such as aerospace and construction) and in industries that define many product/market segments from a common technological base (such as automatic test equipment and other electronics products). The term *collaborative* is used to indicate that subunit managers must both cooperate for the good of the total company and compete with each other for resources and results.[11]

Corporate strategy in the collaborative organization is a result of both a total company strategy and individual profit center strategies—each contributing to the definition of the other in an interactive way. These firms often have matrix structures or very complex multidivisional structures, with an equal emphasis on product profitability and functional efficiency (in the case of a product/function matrix) or on product profitability and geographic profitability (in a product/geography matrix). Systems measure performance according to the specific, functionally based criteria of the cooperative organization, which requires substantial subjective judgment, and according to the more objective financial measures of profitability and return on investment of the competitive organization. The nature of strategy, structure, and systems in this type of organization results in a substantial gap between authority and responsibility.

The complexity of the collaborative organization's strategy, structure, and systems and the excess of responsibility over authority for middle-level general managers are reflected in the complexity and importance of processes. Processes are especially crucial in this type of firm, since the more easily specified and created management tools of structure and systems are insufficient to manage the company. Vertical processes are iterative, combining both top-down and bottom-up elements. Similarly, horizontal processes of conflict resolution are characterized by mixed-mode bargaining, which "is really a complex combination of the two bargaining processes" (Walton and McKersie, 1965, p. 162). In other words, this organizational type contains both win/win and win/lose aspects.

Top management exercises control through these *processes,* which reconcile the conflicting imperatives contained in the company's structure and systems. The conflicting imperatives result in high levels of conflict, which must be constructively managed. However, any attempt to eliminate this conflict by simplifying the organization toward either the cooperative or the competitive type will require a sacrifice of some advantages of diversification or of vertical integration, respectively. As a result of the stress, uncertainty, ambiguity, and conflict found in the collaborative organization, the potential for unfairness is high.

Lower-level managers must have a *rational trust* in top management's ability to evaluate and reward their performance properly. The rational portion of this type of fairness is based on the emphasis on objective, quantitative measures of subunit performance, such as occurs in the competitive organization. The trust portion is based on the ability of top management to exercise subjective judgment in rewarding subunit managers who contribute to total company performance even when doing so hurts the reported financial results of the manager's subunit. Thus, although numbers are important, they are not the only factor that counts.[12]

The MAP and Transfer Pricing

Corporate transfer pricing policies are one aspect of strategy implementation and thus can be understood in terms of the MAP. Figure 10–4 identifies the transfer

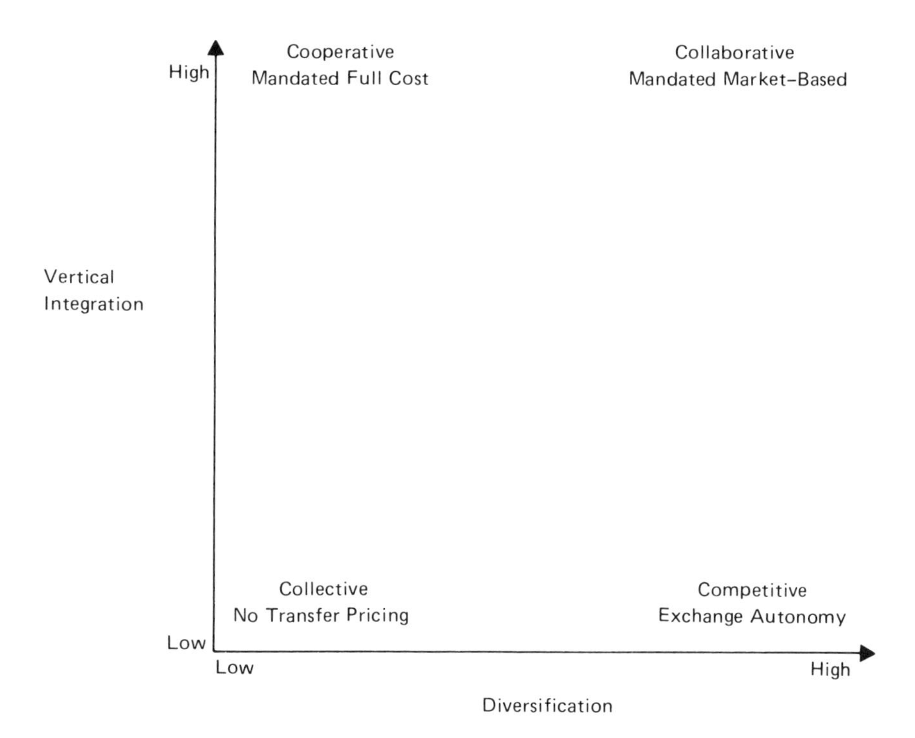

Figure 10–4. Transfer Pricing Policies in the MAP

Table 10–2
Transfer Pricing Policy, by Strategic Type

Transfer Pricing Policy	*Cooperative Organization*		*Collaborative Organization*		*Competitive Organization*		*Total*	
Full cost	48.8%	(20)	23.0%	(29)	15.0%	(12)	24.7%	(61)
Cost plus profit	14.6%	(6)	15.9%	(20)	17.5%	(14)	16.2%	(40)
Market price	22.0%	(9)	35.7%	(45)	25.0%	(20)	30.0%	(74)
Negotiation	12.2%	(5)	16.7%	(21)	33.8%	(27)	21.5%	(53)
Variable cost	0.0%	(0)	5.6%	(7)	5.0%	(4)	4.5%	(11)
Combination	2.4%	(1)	3.2%	(4)	3.8%	(3)	3.2%	(8)
Total	100.0%	(41)	100.0%	(126)	100.0%	(80)	100.0%	(247)

Chi-square = 26.892; sig = .003; df = 10.
Note: Of the 291 firms in the survey 247 answered this question.

pricing policies appropriate for each region in the plane.[13] In the competitive organization region, exchange autonomy is appropriate because of the high degree of diversification and low degree of vertical integration, which results in a substantial delegation of authority and responsibility. The high degree of vertical integration in the cooperative organization region requires mandated transfers, and these are at full cost because the supplying units serve as manufacturing units to the limited number of businesses that compose a strategy of low diversification. Mandated transfers are also required in the collaborative organization region because of the high degree of vertical integration, but here the high degree of diversification requires market-based transfers, since every unit is regarded as a distinct business. There are no inter–profit center transfers in the collective organization because of the simplicity of this type of organization and its lack of a multiple profit center structure.

The analytical power of treating vertical integration and diversification as two independent dimensions of strategy is demonstrated in table 10–2, which is simply a reproduction of table 4–3 (chapter 4) with a change in the labels for strategic type. Thus, what was called "single business vertical integration" is a cooperative organization in MAP terminology, "distinct businesses vertical integration" is a collaborative organization, and "unrelated businesses" is a competitive organization. As shown in this table, full cost is the most popular policy for cooperative organizations, market price is the most popular policy for collaborative organizations, and negotiation (which I have argued is probably associated with exchange autonomy) is the most popular policy for competitive organizations. A similar analysis can be done for the data reporting the extent of internal transfers, shown in the bottom part of table 4–2 (chapter 4). Since both cooperative and collaborative organizations have a high degree of vertical integration, they have a similar extent of inter–profit center transfers—higher than the extent for competitive organizations.

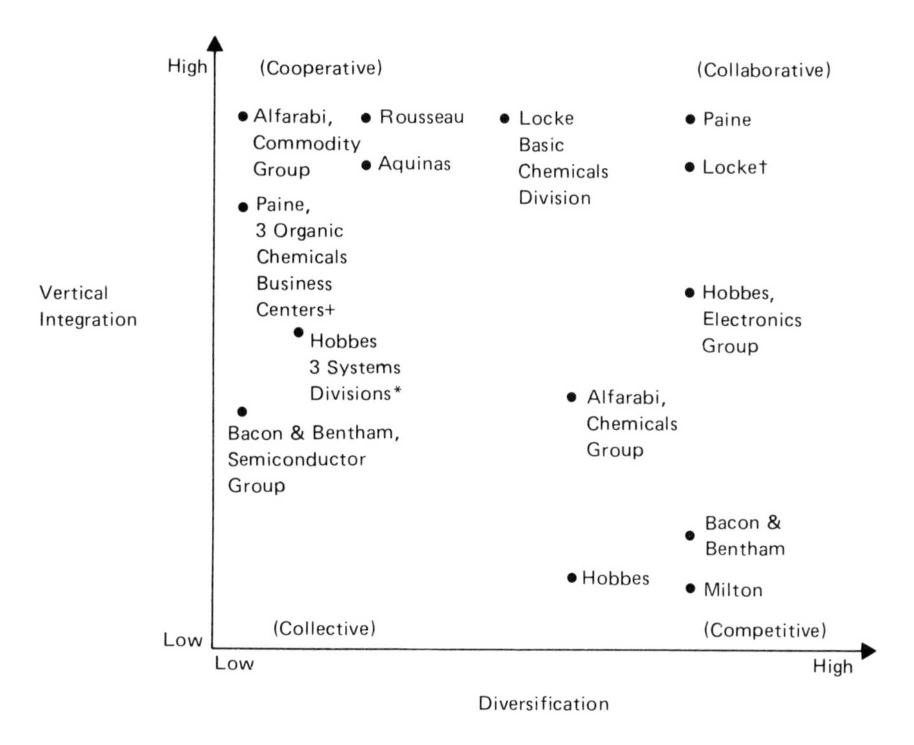

Figure 10–5. Locations of Companies in the MAP

The MAP can be used to provide an overall perspective on the companies used in this research project and discussed in earlier chapters. Figure 10–5 shows a graphic representation of the locations in the MAP of some of these companies and the subunits within them. Obviously, no claim is made regarding the accuracy of the precise locations shown; achieving such precision would require creating metrics for each of these dimensions.[14] Nevertheless, even approximate locations vividly illustrate how the MAP can be used to understand transfer pricing policy.

Mandated Full Cost

In the cooperative region of the plane are Rousseau, Aquinas Chemicals, the Commodity Group at Alfarabi Chemicals, the three organic chemicals business centers at Paine Chemical, the three systems divisions at Hobbes Instrument, and, to a lesser extent, the two divisions in the Semiconductor Group at Bacon

& Bentham. With the exception of the Bacon & Bentham Semiconductor Group, which was in the process of being changed, all of these companies or subunits had a number of things in common. They used either actual full cost transfers or standard full cost transfers, and little effort was made to identify responsibility for variances and allocate them to those responsible. As a result, the performance of each profit center affected and was affected by the performance of others.

The distinctive characteristic of these companies and subunits was the low level of conflict that existed. This was because of the high level of cooperation among the managers involved; all were focusing on objectives at a level higher than their own profit center. In all cases, subjective judgment was important in evaluating and rewarding the performance of these managers, since financial measures were an imperfect indication of their contribution to the company. The reader may wish to review the descriptions of these companies or parts of companies and their transfer pricing practices in chapters 4 and 6 to see how they conform to the characteristics of the cooperative organization.

Mandated Market-Based

Paine Chemical, Locke Chemical (excluding the eight building-block chemicals), the Electronics Group at Hobbes Instrument, and the Chemicals Group at Alfarabi Chemicals are all located in the collaborative region of the plane. In these companies and groups, strategies of vertical integration resulted in high levels of internal transfers. In all cases, however, there was also a great emphasis on treating all subunits as distinct businesses under product managers, business center managers, or division general managers. As a result, mandated market-based transfers were used and other efforts were made to measure these units as distinct businesses, such as through overhead and asset allocations.

The distinctive characteristic of these companies and groups was the high level of conflict that existed. This conflict was inevitable, given the simultaneous emphasis on interdependence and responsibility for subunit outcomes. Although the conflict was generally regarded as constructive, there were always temptations to suboptimize corporate results in favor of subunit results. To prevent the level of conflict from becoming destructive and the temptations to suboptimize from becoming overwhelming, subjective judgment again played an important part in evaluating and rewarding the performance of profit center managers. This tempered the emphasis on measures of financial outcomes that is necessary in pursuing a strategy based on a high degree of diversification. The reader may also wish to review the descriptions of these companies and groups and their transfer pricing practices in chapters 4 and 7 to see how they conform to the characteristics of the collaborative organization.

Analysis of the Problems at Locke Chemical Company

The Basic Chemicals Division at Locke Chemical is shown between the cooperative and collaborative regions in figure 10–5. This placement can help explain the problems the company had in implementing its cost plus investment policy, as described in chapters 6, 8 and 9. Although the rest of the company used a mandated market-based policy, the eight building-block chemicals were transferred at standard full cost, and a great deal of effort was given to identifying responsibility for variances and allocating them to those responsible. This use of full cost transfers emphasized that the buying profit centers were the businesses—and hence the degree of diversification was less than at Paine or in the rest of Locke—but the emphasis on separating financial responsibility more clearly distinguished the internal and external roles of the Basic Chemicals Division, resulting in greater diversification than existed at Rousseau or Aquinas.

Because of the lack of attention to the change process itself in implementing this strategy and the ambiguity that resulted about Basic Chemicals' role—as reflected in the use of performance income to measure its performance—a high level of conflict emerged. This conflict served no obvious purpose once it became clear that there was ambiguity about corporate strategy and that standard costs were set too high. The company ended up with few of the positive benefits of conflict and many of the negatives because of the time and energy that was spent on it. A tentative conclusion that can be drawn from this example is that companies that use standard full cost transfers and emphasize the allocation of variances to those considered to be responsible for them will experience a number of difficulties with transfer pricing, because they are somewhere between the cooperative and collaborative regions, which can result in strategic ambiguity.[15]

Exchange Autonomy

Finally, Bacon & Bentham, Hobbes Instrument (in terms of the relationship between the Electronics Group and the Semiconductor Group), and Milton are located in the competitive region. All of these companies had a strategy of high diversification, as evidenced by the identification of many distinct businesses under group general managers, division general managers, and product managers who had very high levels of financial responsibility. These profit center managers had substantial authority, as evidenced in the transfer pricing policies of exchange autonomy, since little emphasis was placed on vertical integration strategies between profit centers. Milton, which used the pure market price version of exchange autonomy with almost no top management intervention, is shown below Hobbes and Bacon & Bentham, where some informal pressures existed to trade internally. At Bacon & Bentham, for example, some pressure existed to choose internal suppliers when the adjusted market price transfer price, established by corporate policy, was close to outside bids. Similar pressures also ex-

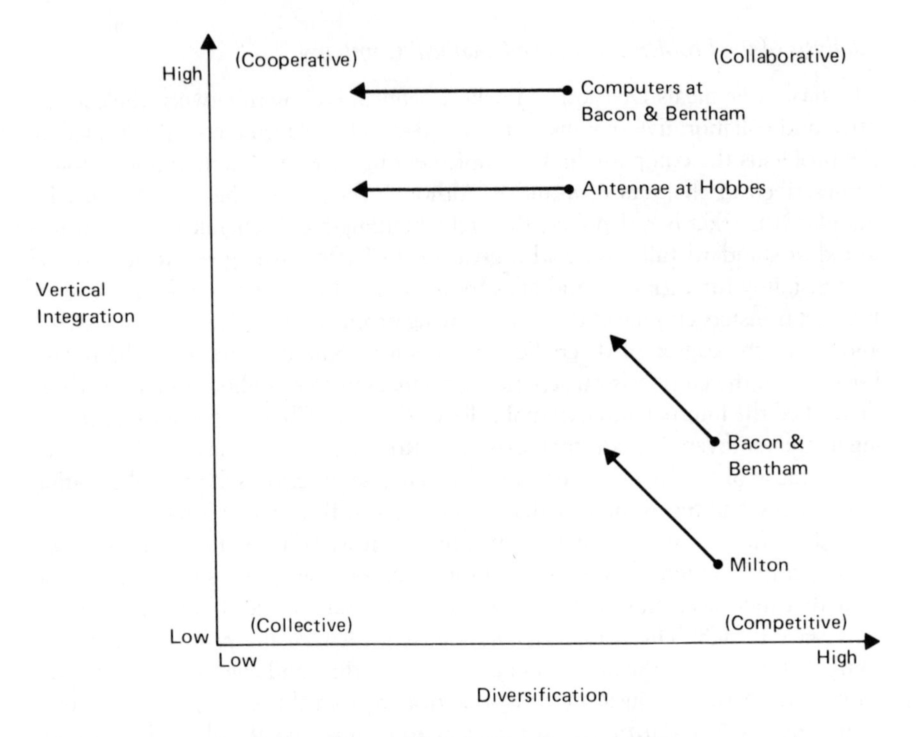

Figure 10–6. Dual Pricing in the MAP

isted at Hobbes, but top management had less involvement, since the pure market price version of exchange autonomy was used.

The distinctive characteristic of the companies in the competitive region was that there were disincentives to trade internally. This problem resulted from the pressures placed on profit center managers to achieve financial objectives and from their awareness of the difficulties internal transfers could create for them in inhibiting their ability and authority to achieve these objectives. Because they were evaluated and rewarded primarily in terms of objective measures of the financial outcomes of their individual profit centers, they had little incentive to cooperate with other profit centers. The reader who wishes to review the descriptions of these companies and their transfer pricing policies is referred to chapters 4 and 5.

Dual Pricing

The fourth hybrid transfer pricing policy—dual pricing—can also be understood in terms of the MAP, as shown in figure 10–6. (Readers can refresh their memories of the examples discussed here by reviewing their descriptions in chapters 5 and 7.) Both Milton and Bacon & Bentham used this policy for several years while preserving exchange autonomy in an effort to improve the cooperation and thus the degree of vertical integration between groups and divisions. In these two companies, dual pricing was used in an attempt to preserve the characteristics of the competitive organization while obtaining some of the advantages of the cooperative organization by having the buying profit centers receive products at full cost. It is no wonder that this policy did not prove to be viable over the long term, since these companies were attempting to occupy two different positions in the MAP simultaneously. Since both buying and selling profit centers retained exchange autonomy, and since the selling profit centers received a market price, half of the dual pricing policy conformed to the competitive region. However, the full cost transfer price to the buying profit center was more appropriate to the cooperative region—though not exactly, because transfers were not mandated.

The dual pricing policy was implemented for computers at Bacon & Bentham when these transfers were mandated, and dual pricing was implemented at Hobbes for antennae on transfers that were already mandated. This use of dual pricing was an attempt to preserve the advantages of a vertical integration strategy between buying and selling profit centers while eliminating its disadvantages to the buying profit center in a way that did not interfere with the status of the selling profit center as a distinct business on all of its sales. In effect, the market price portion of the transfer price preserved the location of the exchange in the collaborative region from the perspective of the selling profit center, while the full cost portion of the transfer price placed the exchange in the cooperative region from the perspective of the buying profit center. Obviously, it would be very difficult for a company to occupy both positions in the plane simultaneously by splitting the perspectives of the buying and selling profit centers; therefore, no use of this policy was found for companies that had a substantial volume of internal transfers.

Changes in Transfer Pricing Policies

The MAP can be used to understand how changes in strategy create pressures for changes in transfer pricing policy. Four examples are shown in figure 10–7. The most dramatic was Blackstone Machinery, which for many years had been a classic cooperative organization (see chapter 9). Its first effort to move into the collaborative region by creating multiple profit centers through recognition of the distinct markets in which the company competed was ultimately aborted because of, among other things, severe difficulties in establishing market-based transfer prices. After retreating back to the cooperative region, the managers in this company developed a more moderate approach based on a small number of profit centers. In the implementation of this new multidivisional structure, they even-

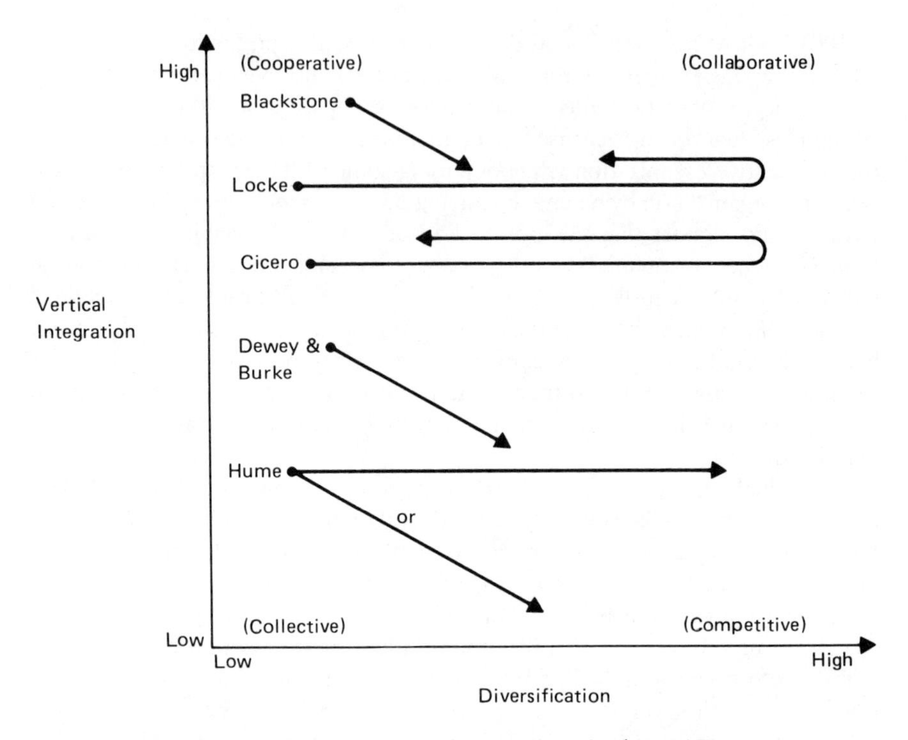

Figure 10–7. Changes in Locations in the MAP

tually hoped to reduce the requirement for internal transfers; thus, the company is shown in figure 10–7 as heading toward the competitive region.

Similar analyses for Locke Chemical, Dewey & Burke, Cicero Systems, and Hume Fabrication are graphically depicted in the same diagram. Over time, Locke had moved from an actual full cost policy to a mandated market-based policy, from which it had partially retreated with the creation of the Basic Chemicals Division and standard full cost transfers for the eight building-block chemicals. Dewey & Burke had shifted from the cooperative region in the direction of the competitive region when it changed from mandated full cost to market-based transfers and when pressure was actually being placed on buying profit centers to do more external sourcing (see chapter 7).

Cicero Systems, which had shifted from mandated full cost transfers to mandated market-based transfers, had met with such disaster it had retreated back in the direction of the cooperative region. It was continuing in this direction because the new policy developed by the task force required that the market-based transfers to the Services Division become full cost transfers within two years (see chapter 9). This company was something of an anomaly according to the theory of transfer pricing presented in this book. In many ways, the company had characteristics of the collaborative organization or even the competitive organization in the few cases where transfers were not mandated because of the emphasis on the responsibility of division presidents for optimizing their own financial outcomes.

According to the theory presented in this book, Cicero should have used market-based transfer prices. It did not, however, because of some peculiar characteristics of the company that were significant enough to create a mismatch between strategy and transfer pricing policy. One of these characteristics was the bad experience the company had had with market-based transfers, which made it unwilling to try this policy again. The other concerned the fact that technical spending budgets were based on total manufacturing costs, and some managers believed that higher transfer prices would unduly inflate this expense. Thus, in particular instances, there may be reasons why a company's transfer pricing policy will vary from the policy that would be most appropriate given its strategy yet will still be effective.

Finally, Hume Fabrication had been experiencing a progressive movement from the cooperative to the collaborative or competitive regions as it moved from full cost transfers that did not include general and administrative costs, to transfers that included these costs, to market-based transfers (see chapters 4 and 7). It is difficult to tell exactly what direction the company was moving in, however, since its sourcing policy was asymmetrical—selling profit centers had to accept internal business but buying profit centers did not. This asymmetry had existed for many years and had led to a number of confusions and problems with the company's transfer pricing policy.

The Terminology of Transfer Pricing

Changes in transfer pricing policy are sometimes accompanied by changes in terminology. Two particularly interesting examples that illustrate how changes in policies influence linguistic conventions came from two companies—not part of my formal research design—with which I became familiar in 1984. The first was a cooperative organizaton that was moving in the direction of the collaborative region. It was thinking of changing its mandated full cost transfers from what were primarily cost centers to mandated market-based transfers. Managers spoke of this proposal as implementing "transfer *pricing*." The emphasis on "pricing" reflected the fact that internal transfers under the new policy would more closely resemble external transactions valued at a market price.

In contrast top management in a competitive organization that was a well-known conglomerate had decided that it was important to encourage greater internal cooperation among the divisions, thereby moving in the direction of the collaborative region. Previously, there had been no concrete policy on internal transfers, and divisions dealt with each other, at most, in terms of their roles as in a market. At other times, they went out of their way to avoid each other. The new policy specified that internal transfers would be at a discount from market price, and various forms of encouragement were exercised to increase the amount of internal transfers. Managers in this company referred to this new policy as "*transfer* pricing." The emphasis on "transfer" reflected the greater emphasis on these internal exchanges as transfers within one company as compared to exchanges established in a market context.

Both of these companies were moving toward the collaborative region, and in both cases this had led to the introduction of the term *transfer pricing* to describe the policy on internal transfers. However, the fact that each company was starting from a different location in the MAP was reflected in a difference in emphasis between the two words that described the new policy.

Managing Change

These examples of changes in transfer pricing policies illustrate one way in which the MAP can be particularly useful to managers. If changes in strategy are being contemplated—whether at the corporate, group, division, or even product level—they can be examined for their transfer pricing implications by diagramming the current and future locations of the organization. Changes in strategy that lead to substantial changes in location in the MAP may very well require changes in transfer pricing policies. Failure to make such changes and implement them effectively, including making the required changes in administrative processes, can inhibit or ultimately prevent the desired change in strategy.

Conversely, managers need to recognize that a change in transfer pricing policy effects a change in strategy that results in a change in location in the MAP. In some cases, managers are explicitly aware of this effect and may even use a change in transfer pricing policy to spearhead a change in strategy that will be accompanied by other changes as well. In some cases, however, managers so concentrate on the details of the change in transfer pricing policy that they fail to recognize its broader repercussions. Because strategy, process, and transfer pricing policy are so intimately related, it is impossible to make changes in one without taking account of its effects on the others.

Other Uses of the MAP

Besides being the basis of a theory relating strategy and its implementation, the MAP is a useful tool for managers that can be applied to many other problems besides transfer pricing.[16] Three such applications will be discussed briefly to illustrate the general utility of the MAP: (1) the general problem of strategy implementation (including some specific examples), (2) capital budgeting, and (3) the distribution and cost allocation of corporate line and staff resources.

Strategy Implementation

The assertion that there are four "pure" organizational types hypothesizes that for a given strategy, there is a certain implementation mode—based on six interrelated variables (strategy, structure, systems, processes, fairness, and control)—that is most appropriate. It follows that a company that has organizational characteristics that are best for another strategy will not be as effective as one that conforms to the theory presented here. For example, it is very difficult to pursue a strategy of vertical integration when profit centers are not required to trade with each other.

One consequence of this hypothesis is that as a company changes its location in the MAP in terms of strategy, it must also change its characteristics, beyond simply changing its transfer pricing practices. The required change can be massive if the shift in strategy is significant, since it may affect all six key variables, any one of which can be very difficult to change by itself. Sometimes, companies find that although the new strategy is a reasonable one, difficulties in implementation prevent them from making the shift.

The implications of the MAP for major strategic shifts can be illustrated in terms of the efforts being made by many large commercial banks in the mid-1980s to become more diversified financial services companies. The vast and rapid changes in the financial services industry—brought about by deregulation, the entrance of new competitors, the introduction of new technology, and the emergence of new products—are presenting unprecedented challenges to managers of commercial banks. For many years, these companies exemplified the cooperative organizational type as evidenced by profit measures at the very top of the organization, functional structures, and the absence of conflict. All of these characteristics will have to change as banks alter their corporate strategies.

Although many approaches are being taken to finding a competitive advantage, they all have one thing in common: a more refined definition of the businesses the bank is in, arrived at through the use of strategic business units and other such concepts. The factors that are contributing to change are also contributing to the emergence of identifiable markets based on specific products. As a result, banks are being forced to unbundle the package of services they provide their customers and charge for each one separately, rather than continuing to deliver a package of services in return for a level of compensating balances for which a revenue is calculated on the basis of assumptions regarding how effectively these funds are used.

This unbundling requires an ability to measure the costs and revenues of each product and a focus on product performance. The unbundling will require decentralized measures of profitability and will be difficult to accomplish, given the high degree of fixed costs that must be allocated across products (for example, for computers). Pressures to measure product profitability add a new dimension to the traditional emphasis on customer profitability, whereby all products purchased by the customer are taken into account. The resulting two-dimensional product/customer matrix is further complicated by the functional dimension of resources. To measure product and customer profitability, the costs of these resources must be allocated to products and customers. The cost allocation problem has never been adequately resolved in banking, but because of competitive pressures it can no longer be ignored.

The emergence of product/customer/function matrices and decentralized measures of profit performance will result in structures and systems that generate levels of conflict never before experienced in the history of most banks. Few seem to be aware of the vast changes in their organizational processes that the strategic moves they are currently making will require. Because conflict is anathema to most bankers, many will mistakenly take its increase as a sign that they should retreat from what they are doing. Instead, they should take exactly the opposite action, and they should continue to move in the direction of the collaborative region by learning how to manage the conflict in a constructive fashion.

Many other specific problems of strategy implementation can be analyzed by managers and can also be the basis of further research by academics. An especially interesting and important problem is integrating acquisitions and mergers—something that nearly always proves to be very difficult to do and that can create so many problems that anticipated economic benefits are never obtained.[17] Are there guidelines for how much and how quickly integration should be obtained—such as according to whether the companies are of similar or different organizational types? For example, less eventual integration will be expected by two competitive organizations, but the acquisition of one cooperative organization by another may be based on the premise of an ultimate integration between the two.

Are the problems more difficult when the organizations are of dissimilar types? Is it any wonder that large cooperative organizations, such as Exxon, have had difficulty diversifying through acquiring small, entrepreneurial collective organizations?[18] How should a cooperative organization manage the acquisition of a competitive or collaborative organization, and vice versa? Do certain combinations of organizational types involved in acquisitions and mergers tend to be more successful than others? These are just a few of the practical questions, with important theoretical implications, that can be addressed by using the MAP to study the problem of acquisition and merger integration.

One other potential application of the MAP would be the problem of corporate evolution. Various stage theories have been suggested about the direction in which companies' strategies evolve and the challenges they face in moving from one stage to another.[19] In the terminology of the MAP, all organizations begin as the collective type and can vertically integrate, diversify, or some of both. Do typical paths of movements in the MAP exist, and what are the various problems companies face depending on the path they follow? Obviously, a company faces a different set of challenges when it vertically integrates without diversifying than when it diversifies without vertically integrating, although in both cases it will be faced with the challenge of implementing increasingly formal management tools. Also, in both cases, the founder and entrepreneur will be confronted with the fact that he or she can no longer maintain the same intimate degree of involvement with all aspects of the business.

Capital Budgeting

The theory contained in the MAP is entirely consistent with Bower's (1970) findings on the capital budgeting process at the company he studied and his speculations about how this process might vary in other types of organizations. National Products Corporation, the disguised name of the company in which he studied four capital budgeting decisions, is an example of a collaborative organization, as is evident from a glance at the chart of materials flow in the company (on the inside front cover of his book), which shows substantial interdependencies across many different businesses. Bower used the term "managed conglomerate" for what is called the collaborative organization here, "integrated company" for the cooperative organization, and "financial conglomerate" for the competitive organization.

Bower suggested that in cooperative organizations, capital budgeting decisions would be highly centralized in the corporate office. Speaking of the three-phase model he developed to describe the capital budgeting process, he suggested:

> In an integrated company all three phases of the task are performed in the president's office; this implies that the same individuals are responsible for *perceiving environmental trends* and defining responses in *product-market terms*, and for *measuring their own performance critically* in *financial terms*. That would seem to be a very difficult task. (p. 291, italics in original)

In contrast, since in the competitive organization, "the relationship of the parts of the corporation to the corporate whole is entirely financial . . . it is possible that portfolio theory, as developed in the field of financial economics, provides an adequate normative model for top management" (p. 293). In other words, these decisions really are made on the basis of such criteria as hurdle rates, discounted cash flow, and net present value—that is, on the basis of numbers alone.[20] When this is the case, lower-level management has much more control over the proposals for capital investment, and the role of top management is simply to say yes or no to them. Ackerman (1970), following up on the work of Bower, studied the capital budgeting process in two cooperative organizations and two competitive organizations. He found that the process was more decentralized in competitve organizations, which was consistent with Bower's hypothesis.

The capital budgeting process was much more complicated in the National Products Corporation because it required substantial top management input as a result of the strategy of vertical integration; at the same time, it required substantial input from lower-level profit center managers, who had the best knowledge of the company's many businesses arising from its diversification strategy. Bower (1970) described the differences in this process among the three types of firms:

> The point is that in the integrated company, planning and resource allocation constitute a whole task naturally accomplished by top management. In the financial conglomerate, the task is split up, but each phase is a whole and, moreover, mangement is facilitated. But, the managed conglomerate leaves no unit with a whole task. It is spread across the hierarchy of management. (p. 294)

Not only does the extent of management's involvement according to level vary according to type, but the nature of its involvement also varies.

Bower's description of how capital budgeting decisions are made in the collaborative organization is very much one of iterative processes—one of the hallmarks of this type of company. He also emphasized the necessity for top management to exercise indirect influence, the importance of middle managers being sensitive to the "inevitable imperfections" in corporate strategy, and the use of "an element of adversary process" in managing capital investment decisions in this type of organization. These, too, are distinguishing characteristics of the collaborative organization.

The fact that these general differences exist in the nature of the capital budgeting process according to organizational type is both interesting and theoretically important. The practical utility of this observation would be enhanced by translating this finding into clear prescriptions for practice. Although Bower does this to some extent for the collaborative organization, opportunities remain to establish more specific guidelines on *how to follow his advice*—just as such opportunities remain for the prescriptions about transfer pricing given in this book. Furthermore, work of the same nature needs to be done for the cooperative, competitive, and even collective organizational types.

The Distribution and Cost Allocation of Corporate Resources

I have performed some preliminary analyses of Vancil's data base regarding the extent to which corporate line and staff resources are centralized, whether or not these resources are charged or allocated to profit centers, and the allocation methods that are used when they are charged.[21] This class of problems is closely related to the transfer pricing problem, although these line and staff functions are not businesses in the way profit centers are, even though these allocations may include a profit. Since Vancil collected data only on multiple profit center firms, it is possible to address only a subset of the more general problem of if and how overhead is allocated. This problem has received a great deal of attention by accounting theorists and managers, and it has proved to be almost as difficult to resolve as the transfer pricing problem. As one manager at Paine Chemical expressed it: "There are two truisms in business. Transfer prices are wrong and charges for corporate overhead are too high."

These preliminary findings are consistent with the theory of the MAP. The principal finding is that, as expected, collaborative organizations are structurally similar to cooperative organizations in terms of the distribution of line and staff resources and similar to competitive organizations in the use of management control systems. Since collaborative and cooperative organizations are pursuing a vertical integration strategy, they tend to have higher levels of centralized line and staff resources because of economies of scale, a common underlying technology for all or most products, and the necessity to ensure coordination of the parts. Although collaborative organizations have somewhat less centralization of these resources than cooperative organizations do, because of their greater emphasis on diversification, they are more centralized than competitive organizations, which place little if any emphasis on vertical integration. In competitve organizations much more of these resources tend to be decentralized to individual profit centers.

Collaborative organizations are more similar to competitive organizations in terms of whether or not the costs of central functions are allocated to profit centers and in terms of the methods by which these costs are allocated. First, collaborative and competitive organizations are more likely to charge at least some of these costs to the profit centers. They are also more likely to use methods such as standard costs, which more clearly separate financial responsibility. In contrast, cooperative organizations are more likely to allocate these costs on an actual basis.

These allocation patterns are very complex, however, since both cooperative and collaborative organizations are more likely to charge out all costs when they do allocate them because of the "we're all in this together" consequence of vertical integration. In competitive organizations, there is a greater tendency to charge the profit centers only for what they use and to distinguish more clearly the centralized resources that support the profit centers from those that support the corporate headquarters only. Furthermore, these general patterns must also be qualified by particular aspects of the functions in question, such as its relative expense in the corporate budget and how easy it is to measure by a particular allocation method.

Next Steps

There are some obvious next steps to be taken—in terms of both the MAP generally and transfer pricing specifically—that are important to both managers and academics. Most obviously, the assertion that there are four pure organizational types that are determined by two dimensions of strategy—vertical integration and diversification—can be tested in a number of ways. The best way to do this is through in-depth field research, both within and across industries.

Closely related to this effort is the attempt to establish ways to operationalize the two dimensions and the variables in the implementation mode. This would enable managers to locate their company or subunits in the MAP in terms of past, present, and future strategies. It would also enable them to determine whether the characteristics associated with a particular location match the actual characteristics of the organization. Accomplishing this task would give practitioners a very useful management tool for implementing strategy in the same way that theories of markets have been translated into analytical techniques to be used in formulating strategy.[22]

A particular aspect of testing the theory of the MAP as it relates to the relationship between strategy and its implementation concerns transfer pricing practices. Their theory would gain support if many examples were found that conform to the assertions made here, although no number of these examples would "prove" the theory in any ultimate sense. However, the theory would be weakened if only a few counterexamples could be found that could not be readily explained by variables outside the theory.

The weight of many different forms of evidence in this book—clinical data, surveys, and research findings of others—suggests that the explanations of transfer pricing and the MAP are reasonably robust. Data are much sparser, however, on the problem of change. Substantial opportunities exist to fill in the large gaps in knowledge regarding how to change from one organizational type to another—particularly how to implement changes in transfer pricing policies.

Finally, the question remains of why organizations adopt the strategies they do. Following the work of others who have suggested that not only does strategy determine structure, but structure (and other organizational characteristics) determines strategy, the question must be asked of how strategy formulation varies according to organizational type. This question can be asked for both dimensions of strategy emphasized here. The reasons for diversification are reasonably well understood, although more work could be done in identifying the conditions in which particular reasons predominate.

Vertical integration is a much less well understood phenomenon. It has also had a somewhat ironic role in this research project, since the project began as a study of vertical integration. During the pilot phase, I decided that the problem of determining why companies vertically integrated—or why not—was too complex for me to study. Instead, I decided to focus on transfer pricing, which I had never heard of before but which was clearly an important aspect of this more general problem. I have now come full circle. Although vertical integration turned out to be central to the theory of transfer pricing presented here, I have artfully (I hope) dodged the question of why companies do or do not pursue such a strategy. Thus, the original question remains unanswered.

Appendix A: The Methodology of Practice-Based Theory

This research project did not originate as a study of transfer pricing. My initial objective was to study the general problem of vertical integration—a topic that has been and continues to be of central interest to me. This interest evolved out of my doctoral dissertation, which focused on a specific instance of vertical integration—subcontracting by general contractors in the construction industry. During the pilot phase of my study, I decided that the problem of vertical integration was too complex and narrowed my focus to a problem closely related to vertical integration—transfer pricing.

I had never heard of transfer pricing before the pilot phase of my aborted vertical integration study; in discussions with managers, however, it became apparent that it was an issue of importance to them. After reading the voluminous literature on this topic, I realized it was also a problem of some theoretical importance. Finally, I was struck by the divergence between theory and practice. My research design was simply to talk to managers in a number of companies in different industries about transfer pricing. I was neither testing a theory nor looking to develop a theory. My objective was both more modest and more ambitious—to derive some guidelines about managing transfer pricing that would be useful for practice.

Evolution of This Research Project

The seeds of this study can be traced back to my interest in the construction industry, which developed during the time I was a graduate student in sociology at Harvard University. An especially interesting problem—whether general contractors perform a trade with their own employees or use special trade subcontractors—is one of the questions concerning structure in the construction industry that I explored in my doctoral dissertation.[1]

A natural extension of my interest in subcontracting practices in the construction industry is the more general problem of vertical integration across industries. As a graduate student, I had been exposed to Williamson's (1975) "new institutional economics" approach to this issue, which, combined with the work of Stigler (1951) and Thompson (1967), had enabled me to develop a theory of subcontracting in the construction industry. Despite the utility of Williamson's work based on the concept of "transaction costs," I was not persuaded by his more general conclusions about vertical integration. Nor was I satisfied with the work of other economists, sociologists, and those who study business administration. I found most of this work either highly theoretical, with limited empirical testing and using data at very high levels of aggregation from government surveys, or individual case studies that did not posit general principles.

I decided to take the same approach I had taken in my dissertation—to go out into the field. My objective was twofold (Eccles, 1980b). First, I wanted to identify patterns of vertical integration (its existence or lack thereof across various industries) and the variables explaining these patterns. This involved both firm and individual levels of analysis to understand the process by which a firm decided whether or not to integrate vertically for a particular product. I was interested in patterns across firms and industries, but I wanted to understand variations as well. Less explicitly and consciously, I was also curious about the relationship between vertical integration and performance.

Since the fundamental question I was probing was the difference between internal and external transactions, it seemed that a particularly efficient research design would allow me to see examples of both for the same product in the same company. I called examples of this phenomenon "dual transaction goods" (Eccles, 1980a). Although I knew that instances of this phenomenon existed, I did not know how prevalent it was. As it turned out, this phenomenon of tapered integration (Porter, 1980) ended up playing only a minor role in even the pilot phase, where the focus was on vertical integration in general.

The pilot phase of my study of vertical integration was conducted in the spring and summer of 1980. I selected two industries, electronics and chemicals, since vertical integration was important in both, and I obtained access to two companies as research sites in each industry. This phase turned out to be very confusing. From interviews with a number of managers in these companies, it seemed that vertical integration had less to do with the economists' concern of cost reduction or the sociologists' concern of uncertainty reduction and more to do with a large number of factors best described as corporate strategy.

The complexity of this conclusion made it difficult to reduce to a pure cost–benefit analysis. I found examples of companies in similar circumstances making different decisions and examples of companies in different circumstances making similar decisions. Unlike my study of the construction industry, I was not able to identify patterns of vertical integration easily.

A critical turning point in this research project was a conversation I had with Professor Robert Hayes of the Harvard Business School. I had read a working paper of his on vertical integration (Hayes, 1977), and I was familiar with his work on the product/process life cycle. Because of our shared interest in vertical integration, he had played the role of informal advisor to me on the initial stages of this project. I expressed my feeling that vertical integration was too large and complex a problem for me to address at this time. He suggested that I focus on one aspect and he proposed several possibilities, including the management of internal relationships based on vertical integration and the transfer pricing problem.

I decided to focus on the transfer pricing problem within the context of managing these relationships for two reasons. During the pilot phase, I had been struck by the vehemence with which managers discussed transfer pricing. Although the subject was new to me, it came up naturally in discussions of vertical integration; from my interviews, it was clear that this was a very urgent practical problem for these managers. Thus, its practical importance was one reason I chose to focus on this problem. Walton (1983) has noted that "difficulties in practice can often be translated into theoretical puzzles" (p. 22), and this was indeed the case for transfer pricing. Claims by managers of both buying and selling divisions that they would rather engage in external transactions than internal ones seemed to strike at the very heart of the new institutional economics theory, which explained vertical integration in terms of the lower transaction costs for setting and changing the terms of a relationship and resolving disputes. If anything, the transaction costs of these internal transactions seemed to be greater than the transaction costs of external ones. Focusing on transfer pricing thus gave me a solid handle on an important part of the vertical integration problem.

The second reason for focusing on the transfer pricing problem was its theoretical importance. In the winter and spring of 1981, I read extensively in the literature on transfer pricing. Its emphasis on formal economic theory and mathematical programming made it largely irrelevant to the problems of practicing managers. There was clearly an opportunity to contribute to theory, since existing theory about transfer pricing bore no relationship to the empirical phenomenon—an important criterion for evaluating the quality of a theory.

Thus, I considered the transfer pricing problem to be important to both theory and practice. It is an example of the kind of question Walton (1983) identified as having dual relevance to both:

> An appropriate question is one that is interesting on two counts: The question is theoretically interesting, i.e., there is a gap in theory or a weak theory and a scholarly audience which will appreciate the contribution to theory. The question is practically interesting, i.e., there is an undefined area of practice or an ill-defined set of practices and a practitioner audience. (p. 21)

The absence of a theory of transfer pricing that was useful for practice, and the broader theoretical issue of vertical integration to which transfer pricing was intimately related, made the problem an excellent subject for research.

Research Design

In selecting the first four companies for the pilot phase, I sought companies that were large enough to yield interesting data but not so large as to be incomprehensible in a short period of time, and that had a reasonable degree of vertical integration, as revealed from comments and data in their annual reports and SEC Form 10–Ks. The four companies ranged in size from $700 million to over $2 billion in 1980 sales. In all cases, I obtained access by writing a letter to the company's CEO, sometimes using the name of someone on the faculty who knew this person. Figure A–1, which shows this letter, reveals my focus at that time on "dual transaction" goods. Two companies were selected in each industry, and I limited my search to companies on the East Coast, since as a new faculty member I was unsure about the level of research support I could get. Between May and August 1980, I conducted interviews with fifty-three managers in these companies.

The somewhat informal and opportunistic nature of research site selection for the pilot phase also characterized the selection of the other nine companies where I conducted interviews between May and November 1981. Once I decided to focus on transfer pricing, the only question I considered was whether or not to include another industry. I wanted to continue with the chemicals and electronics industries, because I now knew something about them and wanted to get data that would enable cross-company comparisons in addition to those I already had. Because my pilot research had revealed the importance of organizational behavior issues in transfer pricing, I thought that theory from this field could be used as a basis for creating a more rigorous research design. I had found the organic–mechanistic continuum identified by Burns and Stalker (1961), and applied to technology types by Woodward (1965), illuminating, and I used it as the basis for selecting the third industry. Since I already had continuous process (chemicals) and mass assembly (electronics) industries, I needed a job shop industry.

The search for a job shop industry proved unsuccessful. I reasoned that industries that used a great deal of custom manufacturing were likely to use job shop technologies. The candidate I selected was machine tools, but in reviewing annual reports and 10–Ks, I found that machine tool companies had few if any inter–profit center transfers. (In retrospect, this is to be expected, since an organizational design that would suit this technology would be unlikely to develop a need for transfer pricing.) Consequently, as a third industry I selected companies manufacturing heavy machinery and machinery components, in which I knew that transfer pricing existed.

I obtained access to nine other companies in a manner similar to that used in the pilot phase—a letter to the CEO that was very specific about my research interest in transfer pricing (figure A–2). The literature on transfer pricing divided methods between cost-based (including cost plus profit markup) and market-

HARVARD UNIVERSITY

GRADUATE SCHOOL OF BUSINESS ADMINISTRATION

GEORGE F. BAKER FOUNDATION

ROBERT G. ECCLES
Assistant Professor of Business Administration

SOLDIERS FIELD
BOSTON, MASSACHUSETTS 02163

April 30, 1980

(Name)
Chief Executive
Address

Dear (Name):

I am conducting a study of the management of goods and materials transfers among divisions in a firm when these goods and materials are also obtained from outside sources. Given the industry segments at (Company Name) (industry segments reported in annual report), it appears likely that such situations exist in your company.

I would like to use (Company Name) in my pilot phase. This would require interviews with key managers from your divisions with internal purchase and supply arrangements, as well as with some top corporate officers. These interviews would require one to two hours each.

Through this study I hope to improve our understanding of how managers can best decide on the relative emphasis to be placed on facilitating internal transfers versus maximizing competition between internal and external sources. My major objective is to determine the factors which must be considered by managers in order to arrive at an optimal solution.

Because the study touches on a number of issues which must be treated with the strictest confidence, all identities of individuals and companies will remain anonymous. However, I will share with all participants the important practical and theoretical findings.

My current plan is to proceed as quickly as possible with this pilot phase. Interviews will be scheduled in the months of June, July, and August. Please let me know by letter or phone (617/495-6250) if I might get together briefly with you or a representative of yours to explore the possible participation of (Company Name) in this study. If you would like to clarify any issues before I meet with you or your representative, please feel free to call me.

Sincerely,

Robert G. Eccles
RGE:ldb

Figure A–1. Letter to Obtain Research Sites for Pilot Phase Study of Vertical Integration

HARVARD UNIVERSITY

GRADUATE SCHOOL OF BUSINESS ADMINISTRATION

GEORGE F. BAKER FOUNDATION

Robert G. Eccles
Assistant Professor of Business Administration

Soldiers Field
Boston, Massachusetts 02163

April 14, 1981

Mr. (Name)
Company Name
Address

Dear Mr. (Name):

I am conducting a study of domestic transfer pricing policies and practices through case studies of six to eight companies. Although many articles have been written on this subject and a few general surveys have been conducted, few of these have proven to be very helpful for practicing managers. From pilot research I conducted in four companies last summer and from discussions with a number of managers it is clear that this can be an important general management issue. I also feel that it is difficult to find an approach to transfer pricing which satisfies all of the parties involved.

The purpose of my research is to determine how managers establish transfer prices and the conditions in which the various methods seem most appropriate. This will involve interviews with selected business unit managers (e.g., division general managers, group general managers), controllers, and top corporate executives including the CEO and COO. I will also collect basic background data on the history of the company and its current operations.

I am looking for two types of companies in which to conduct this research. The first type is composed of companies which are relatively satisfied with their transfer pricing practices and feel they are working relatively well. The second type is composed of companies which are dissatisfied with their current transfer pricing practices and are currently reviewing them. For both types the amount of internal transfers should be significant enough to make transfer pricing an important issue. In addition, I hope to split the sample into companies which emphasize cost-based methods and those which emphasize market-price based methods.

I am interested in working with (Company Name) on this project. After reviewing your annual report and 10-K, I believe your company would be an especially good research site. Any proprietary information would be disguised, of course, including the name of the company, if you so desired. Both quantitative and qualitative data could be disguised. Information which will ultimately be used in publications will be available for your review.

In return for your participation I would be happy to personally review my findings with you and discuss their implications for your company. I will call you within the next several weeks to determine if your company fits my research design criteria. If so, I hope you will be able to participate in this study. At this time I can answer any questions you might have. Thank you for your consideration.

Sincerely,

Robert G. Eccles

Figure A–2. Letter to Obtain Research Sites for Transfer Pricing Project

based, and I sought to obtain research sites that would have examples of both. I also sought a balance between companies that were generally satisfied with their management of transfer pricing and those that were not.

As it turned out, neither of these criteria affected site selection, since I accepted every offer for cooperation—but I did end up with the variety I wanted. No doubt, a certain degree of self-selection bias exists in my sample: companies that agreed to cooperate often were friends of the school, and they were especially interested in transfer pricing. Also, as a very junior faculty member, I felt fortunate to get access to them. This feeling was reinforced when rejections came in—for such reasons as IRS audits or recent reorganizations. About half of the companies solicited agreed to participate. In field-based research, formal criteria of research design may be of far less significance than enthusiastic cooperation by the companies involved. (I will always choose the extensive access that such cooperation makes available, even if the company fits the formal research design less perfectly than another company that is not enthusiastic about the project.)

Table A–1 lists the companies and number of persons interviewed, according to function. In terms of 1980 sales, the size range of the companies studied was between $475 million and over $6 billion. The number of persons interviewed varied between 2 and 21 with a mean of 11. A total of 144 managers were interviewed during 44 days in the field; I made between one and four trips to each company. The number of days at each company ranged from one to ten. The interviews lasted from a half-hour to four hours, averaging about one hour. They were largely unstructured, although there was a common pattern at each company.

My first interview at a company was always with a manager who had been designated as my company contact to help coordinate my study at the company. During this interview, I obtained background data on the company, including its history, its current strategy and organizational design, its transfer pricing policy, especially important or interesting transfer pricing situations, and current high priority management issues. Other interviews were those that I was able to arrange with managers involved in transfer pricing, within the limitations established by the company and my own time. Although I managed to interview many general managers—distinguishing this study from other field studies—I was not able to get many interviews with CEOs and COOs because of their time limitations and my low status as a researcher. As the interviews progressed within a company, less time was spent on learning about the company and its transfer pricing policies in general and more time was spent on the details of specific transfer pricing situations.

During each interview, I typically asked about the educational and career background of the person, then about his or her current job responsibilities, which became the basis for a discussion of transfer pricing. As the interview progressed and the manager became more engaged, I raised increasingly sensitive issues, such as the personality characteristics of managers involved in transfer pricing disputes and company politics. All managers were promised anonymity and were assured that what they told me would be treated as confidential in other

Table A–1
Summary of Data Collection Effort

Company Name (Disguised)	Data Collection Period	Number of Interviews: General Managers	Financial Managers	Other Managers[a]	Total	Number of Visits	Total Days On Site
Alfarabi Chemicals, Inc.	May–June 1981	5	5	4	14	2	4
Aquinas Chemicals Co., Inc.[b]	June–August 1980	3	1	5	9	2	3
Bacon & Bentham, Inc.[b]	June–August 1980	3	4	3	10	2	4
Blackstone Machinery Co., Inc.	May 1981	1	4	3	8	1	2
Cicero Systems, Inc.	June 1981	0	4	0	4	1	1
Dewey & Burke, Inc.	September 1981	3	3	1	7	1	1
Grotius Equipment Co., Inc.	July 1981	1	1	0	2	1	1
Hobbes Instrument Co., Inc.	May 1981	3	7	3	13	1	3
Hume Fabrication Co., Inc.	April–June 1981	9	8	1	18	3	5
Locke Chemical Co., Inc.	April–November 1981	5	10	2	17	3	5
Milton, Inc.[b]	May–August 1980	5	4	4	13	4	4
Paine Chemical Co., Inc.[b]	June–August 1980	14	3	4	21	4	10
Rousseau Chemical Corporation	November 1981	2	3	3	8	1	1
Total	May 1980–November 1981	54	57	33	144	26	44

[a]Primarily in manufacturing, marketing and planning.
[b]Pilot phase.

interviews, but even so, I was impressed with the openness and helpfulness of nearly everyone with whom I spoke. When documents were cited during the interviews, such as internal studies of transfer pricing or memoranda on specific transfer pricing situations, I obtained copies whenever possible. As a result, I obtained a wealth of data in each company. Although I asked many of the same questions in various interviews, I did not have a fixed set of issues to cover in each interview or each company, since I continued to identify relevant issues as the data collection progressed.

A pattern of data collection also emerged across companies. As I learned more and more about transfer pricing, I was able to probe more deeply into the phenomenon and to ask more precise questions. This enabled me to collect the same amount of information in a shorter period of time. I was also able to test tentative hypotheses suggested by interviews in previous companies. My approach was very similar to the approach used by Walton (1983):

> In the field, I try to develop rich descriptions of the situation. I search for comparative data between organizations or between different time periods in the same organization. During the early stages of making sense out of the data, I rely primarily on inductive processes. I immerse myself in the data, let it soak, and then gradually organize it, searching for themes, contrasts, and causal relationships among aspects of the situation studied. (pp. 30–31)

This approach does not lend itself to structured interviews, since it is designed to identify the relevant variables and suggest hypotheses about relationships between them, rather than to test hypotheses that have already been formulated.

The advantages of this type of data collection effort for understanding the full richness and complexity of a phenomenon are obvious, since an attentive researcher who does not collect data according to a set of preconceptions is likely to identify most of the relevant variables. The many case examples in the text illustrate how different the transfer pricing problem in practice is from that studied in most economic and accounting theoretical approaches. Another payoff from this clinical data collection effort is that it provided clarifications on two important points that have been obscured in survey research on this topic and identified another point that has been ignored.

First, this clinical research enabled me to distinguish between method and process. Most surveys confound these concepts by treating negotiation as a method, when in fact it is a process that can be applied to all methods. Second, whereas surveys treat cost plus profit markup as a cost-based method, it is more appropriately considered a market-based method, since it is used to derive a market price for differentiated or proprietary goods that are not sold in external transactions, which could help identify market price. From the beginning, my clinical data also showed the importance of the issue of whether division general managers have exchange autonomy. The few surveys conducted to date have ignored the question of whether internal transactions are mandated. When a phenomenon is not well understood, questionnaire surveys have limited analytical utility.

I decided to conclude my field research in the fall of 1981 for two reasons. First, I felt the need to begin analyzing these data, given deadlines I had set for when I would produce written reports from this project. (I did not meet these deadlines.) Second, I thought the time had come to begin the analysis because, in the last two or three companies I studied, no issues related to transfer pricing came up that I had not already identified. Instead, the situations seemed to repeat one or another situation I had already encountered. This suggested that I had a reasonably complete view of the problem, or as complete a view as I was able to see at that time, given the synthesis I had achieved during the data collection phase. I was then ready to attempt to develop an analytical framework that would account for the data I had collected.

From Practice to Theory

The primary purpose of this research project was to obtain an understanding of the transfer pricing problem that would be useful to managers. Although I did not explicitly set out to do so, I both tested existing theory and created a new one. Existing theory was tested by the fact that in the many situations I studied that were candidates for a mathematical programming approach, none of the companies used it. The theory that was developed was based on the transfer pricing practices I observed, rather than being derived from a more general theory in one discipline, such as microeconomics or organizational sociology.

Walton (1983) argued that research relevant to both theory and practice "is more likely to occur from research which is designed to *generate* concepts, hypotheses and theory than research which is designed to *test* hypotheses and theory" (p. 29). This was certainly the case with this project, which has yielded a number of very specific hypotheses (presented in chapters 3 through 9) that can be subjected to empirical test. This entire book is a theory of transfer pricing based on the concepts of strategy, fairness, and process.

A distinctive characteristic of this theory is that, since it is derived from observations about practice and focuses on a management problem rather than an intellectual discipline, it uses concepts from a number of disciplines, including business policy, control, economics, industrial marketing and purchasing, organizational behavior, and sociology. From the perspective of the researcher, Walton (1983) noted: "Working from practice issues to theory requires that one be reasonably familiar with the existing stock of theory. This can be a major difficulty because the problems in practice can be informed by many different basic and applied disciplines" (p. 23). Although this is a nontrivial difficulty, it is clear that a theory about transfer pricing that used only one or two disciplines could not comprehend the whole problem.

Since the study of administration begins with practice to develop theory, it is a methodology of practice-based theory. However, the study of administration is scientific in the sense that its theories should be consistent with existing data and should be disconfirmable by new data. Theory and practice are inseparable, as noted by Roethlisberger (1977): "Theory without practice is metaphysics; practice without theory cannot get off the ground" (p. 360). Moreover, although they are inseparable, practice comes first. As Roethlisberger (1977) noted: "Logic and theory do not come from some never-never land. They too come first from practice" (p. 354). Examples abound of how adminstrative practices first invented by managers formed the basis for more formal theories, such as the multidivisional and matrix organizational forms.

Managers need theories to make decisions, however implicit these theories may be. For the practitioner, "the distinction between theory and practice is . . . no problem" (Roethlisberger, 1977, p. 353). The role of academic researchers is to examine these implicit or explicit theories, which tend to be somewhat specific—according to company or industry, for example—and to look for patterns of similarity and variation. It is difficult for managers to know the extent to which a practice they have derived has general application or whether it is the most effective practice possible given their situation. They also cannot be expected to know which criteria are relevant for categorizing situations. The researcher's contribution is to identify relationships between situations and specific practices that contribute to effectiveness. In doing so, managers' explanations of why they adopt certain practices and what effects their actions have are valuable but not always conclusive. This is obvious, since managers' views of any situation will differ according to their role. For example, conflict between division general managers may seem dysfunctional to them, but it may be useful to a CEO, who has a different set of concerns.

This research project moved very explicitly from practice to theory. The sorting of the rich and complex clinical data into patterns went through a number of stages, involving some dead ends and much groping. However, there were also moments of a certain flash of insight. I can recall three such "flashes," each of which contributed to identifying one of the three concepts in this theory, although only after a long period of time were the three put together.

The importance of strategy was suggested early in this project by the CEO of Paine Chemical Company, who said: "Well, young man, I doubt you're going to solve this problem because there's no answer to it. But one thing I can tell you is that transfer pricing depends on strategy." The relationship between strategy and transfer pricing method was largely forgotten when I recognized the importance of administrative process. At that time, I thought any method could work in any situation if the right process was used. The third insight—about the importance of fairness—emerged when I was struggling to define what "working right" meant. At that stage, I was aware that transfer pricing was not simply an economic problem of resource allocation, and I believed that an "organizations are societies" metaphor would be a better orienting perspective on this problem. The importance of fairness became clear to me from reading political philosophy in an attempt to develop this metaphor into a more explicit theory. Although this was an example of a dead end, the importance of fairness remained.

Another contribution of this research project to theory is reported in "Transfer Pricing as a Problem of Agency," a paper presented at the Harvard Business School 75th Anniversary Colloquium, "Asymmetric Information, the Agency Problem, and Modern Business Practice" (see Eccles, forthcoming). This paper contrasts the efficiency concerns of agency theory (and economic theory in general) with the problem of fairness, which is largely ignored. The paper has implications for both agency theory and a positive theory of accounting.

From Theory to Practice

There are two ways to test the theory presented in this book. The first is to collect more data to see whether hypothesized relationships are valid. These relationships include situations in which transfer pricing is being managed effectively and situations when it is not. Similarly, data collected by someone else can be used to test this theory, as was done with Vancil's (1978) data in chapter 4 of this book. However, the assumptions that had to be made in reclassifying firms according to strategic category limited this as a test.

The second way to test the theory presented here is to determine whether managers find (1) that it is consistent with their experiences, (2) that it helps them better understand these experiences, and (3) that it suggests actions that should be taken. When actions are taken to improve the effectiveness of an inter–profit center transfer by changing either policy or process, or both, a finding of whether or not this improvement takes place (assuming that it is properly implemented) would be a very real test of this theory. Of course, the change process itself, which is utilized to change policy and/or process, becomes an important variable in determining the ultimate effectiveness of the change. Since this theory has yet to be tried in practice, the ultimate step in truly integrating theory and practice remains to be taken. This is in contrast to theories developed out of consulting projects, as described by Walton. However, whereas Walton distinguished between starting with theory and starting with an action project, a third possibility is to start with the actions of managers, even without a specific theoretical orientation.

Walton (1983) identified a continuum of research that has generating hypotheses at one end—"where the results may only increase the certainty about a phenomenon from probabilities of .2 to .6"—and testing hypotheses that are already well formulated at the other end—"where the results may increase one's certainty about the relationship among variables from probabilities of say .85 to .95" (p. 28). He argued that the former was more useful to managers:

> Managers are accustomed to making decisions under relatively high levels of uncertainty. They have little interest in that knowledge about cause and effects which merely increases the certainty of an already apparent relationship. They are decidedly more interested in either conceptual knowledge which helps them order their thinking about an action area, or plausible hypotheses that have not previously occurred to them. (p. 29)

This research project is clearly at the hypothesis-generating end of the continuum and is intended to provide a useful framework for managers who are confronted with the transfer pricing problem. The utility of this theory is as important a test for them as any test would be that used a more formal research design. Since theory and practice are inseparable, this theory should meet both tests; failure to meet either one means that changes must be made in the theory. Much formal theory in the social sciences today cannot be subjected to either test.

certainty about the relationship, and any assumptions from probabilities of say .45 to .55" (p. 28). He argued that the former was more useful to practice.

[illegible] are accustomed to reduce their complexity [illegible] with [illegible]. They have [illegible] knowledge [illegible] which [illegible] increase their [illegible] apparent relationship. They [illegible] to [illegible] knowledge which helps them [illegible] a plausible hypothesis [illegible] (p. 29).

The second product is clearly [illegible] the hypothesis is relevant and [illegible] and is intended to provide a useful framework for managers. [illegible] the smaller [illegible]. The utility of the theory is [illegible] would be that [illegible]. Since theory and practice are [illegible] this theory should [illegible] that [illegible] the theory [illegible] of the [illegible] cannot be [illegible] tests.

Appendix B: A Revision of Rumelt's Typology of Corporate Strategy

In his questionnaire survey of decentralization in 291 companies, Vancil (1978) used Rumelt's (1974) classification scheme for categorizing companies according to corporate strategy. He was unable to find any significant relationship between transfer pricing method and four major strategic types: single business, dominant business, related businesses, and unrelated businesses. The statistically strong results reported in chapter 4 were obtained by revising Rumelt's typology and reclassifying the firms in Vancil's study into a threefold scheme.[1] In this new typology, the strategic categories are single business vertical integration, distinct businesses vertical integration, and unrelated businesses.

The objective of this revision was (1) to distinguish companies to which transactions between profit centers were mandated from those in which they were not and (2) to distinguish companies in which the capacity of the selling division devoted to internal sales was treated as a manufacturing unit from those in which the entire selling division was regarded as a business in its own right. The assumption made here is that single business firms with vertical integration and distinct business firms with vertical integration require internal transactions but unrelated businesses firms do not. In single business vertical integration firms, the selling division is regarded as a manufacturing unit on internal sales; in distinct businesses vertical integration firms, the selling division is a distinct business in its own right.

The basic concept underlying Rumelt's (1974) typology is that of a discrete business: "A discrete business means one that could be managed independently of the firm's other activities" (p. 12). Thus, discrete business can be expected to be identified as a distinct profit center. Rumelt used three ratios to classify firms according to his fourfold typology. He defined the *specialization ratio* as "the proportion of a firm's revenues that can be attributed to its largest single business in a given year" (p. 14). The *related ratio* was defined as "the proportion of a firm's revenues attributable to its largest group of related businesses" (p. 16). This group of related businesses is related to the original business through (1) markets served and distribution systems, (2) similar production technologies, or (3) common science-based research. A consequence of strategic relatedness is resource sharing among discrete businesses, which creates the need for transfer pricing.

Using these two ratios, Rumelt created his four strategic categories. Single business firms are those that have a specialization ratio of 0.95 or more. Dominant business firms are those that have a specialization ratio greater than or equal to 0.7 but less than 0.45. Firms that have a specialization ratio of less than 0.7 and a related ratio of 0.7 or greater are classified as related businesses firms. Finally, firms that have specialization and related ratios of less than 0.7 are classified as unrelated businesses firms.

Rumelt also defined a *vertical ratio* as "the proportion of the firm's revenues that arise from all by-products, intermediate products, and end products of a vertically integrated sequence of processing activities" (p. 23). He noted that there are special problems in classifying vertically integrated firms that argue for treating them separately from firms that can be classified according to the other two ratios:

> Before the research began no special provisions were made for dealing with vertically integrated firms apart from the stipulation that diversification was to be considered in terms of products *sold.* It was found, however, that vertically integrated firms often did not seem to belong in any of the categories defined. Attempts to classify these firms as either Single, Dominant, or Related invariably required either too broad or too narrow a definition. Two difficult questions kept recurring. (1) Is a by-product a separate business or part of the business which produces it? and (2) Under what conditions should a firm that has integrated forward into a wide variety of manufacturing activities be considered diversified? (p. 20)

The difficulty of classifying vertically integrated firms on the basis of "discrete business" reflects the fact that in these firms, discrete businesses are not easy to identify. It is largely a matter of how management chooses to define the role of the selling division in a strategy of vertical integration. Even when a number of discrete businesses are identified at each stage of the vertical chain, "the interdependencies among the businesses of a vertically integrated firm mean that, no matter how many different forms the end products take, general management must view the firm as a whole when considering the effect of any change in operations or resource allocation" (Rumelt, 1974, p. 20). Thus, there is more diversity in vertically integrated firms than in single business firms because of separately identifiable businesses but less diversity than in the other categories because the businesses are intimately related. For simplicity, Rumelt decided to avoid creating a separate category or dimension of classification and treated vertically integrated firms as follows:

Vertical ratio greater than or equal to 0.7:

Single business if specialization ratio is 0.95 or greater.

Dominant business if specialization ratio is less than 0.95.

Vertical ratio less than 0.7:

Related businesses if related ratio is 0.7 or greater.

Unrelated businesses if related ratio is less than 0.7.

Table B–1 shows the eleven strategic types defined by Vancil, using Rumelt's classification scheme, according to each of the four basic types.

The category of unrelated businesses used in chapter 4 includes Vancil's category of the same name. The major and unrelated type was also included in the unrelated businesses category according to two assumptions. First, the single largest business unit, which represents between 70 percent and 95 percent of the company's sales, is one profit center. Thus, inter–profit center transfers between this major business and the minor unrelated businesses, or between these minor businesses, are similar to transactions between businesses in the unrelated businesses category, which is the second assumption.

Table B–1
Strategic Classification Scheme Used by Vancil

Single Business

1. *Vertically integrated*
   More than 95 percent of corporate revenues are attributable to sales of final products, by-products, and intermediate products associated with a vertically integrated raw materials processing sequence.
2. *Large single-unit*
   More than 95 percent of corporate revenues are attributable to the company's largest single business unit. A single business unit is the set of activities associated with the production and marketing of a single product/service of a line of closely related products/services. Included within a business unit are all products or product lines that require close coordination and share important resources.

Dominant Business

3. *Predominantly vertically integrated*
   Between 70 percent and 95 percent of corporate revenues are attributable to sales of final products, by-products, and intermediate products associated with a vertically integrated raw materials processing sequence.
4. *Major and common skill*
   Between 70 percent and 95 percent of corporate revenues are attributable to the company's single largest business unit. Most of the minor businesses are related to the firm's dominant business and to one another by some central skill, concept, or resource.
5. *Major and linked*
   Between 70 percent and 95 percent of corporate revenues are attributable to the company's single largest business unit. Not all of the minor businesses are closely related to the dominant business, but most have at least some relationship to other corporate activities.
6. *Major and unrelated*
   Between 70 percent and 95 percent of corporate revenues are attributable to the company's single largest business unit. Most of the minor business activities are unrelated to the company's dominant business.

Table B–1 continued

Related Businesses
7. *Related and common skill*
Less than 70 percent of corporate revenues are attributable to the company's single largest business unit, but 70 percent or more of corporate revenues are attributable to the largest group of somehow related businesses. (A business is part of a group of "somehow related businesses" so long as it is tangibly related to at least one other business in the group.) The businesses in this group are mostly related through some central skill or resource, so that each business is related to most of the others.
8. *Related and linked*
Less than 70 percent of corporate revenues are attributable to the company's single largest business unit, but 70 percent or more of corporate revenues are attributable to the largest group of somehow related businesses. The businesses in this group are not all interrelated, but each is related tangibly to at least one other business in the group.

Unrelated Businesses
9. *Unrelated merger*
Less than 70 percent of corporate revenues are attributable to the largest group of somehow related businesses. The firm merged with another firm of comparable size, producing a combined company that is active in unrelated businesses.
10. *Unrelated acquisition*
Less than 70 percent of corporate revenues are attributable to the largest group of somehow related businesses. The firm acquired a number of companies that were active in areas unrelated to the origin of the firm's businesses.
11. *Unrelated internal development*
Less than 70 percent of corporate revenues are attributable to the largest group of somehow related businesses. The firm became active in unrelated businesses through internal investment and development.

Source: Adapted from Vancil (1978) pp. 375–377.

Because of the diversity and lack of relatedness among businesses in firms in this category, each business represents a profit center, with nearly all of the necessary resources for producing and selling its products, giving division general managers substantial authority. This authority is matched with a large degree of responsibility, since the diversity of businesses makes it impossible for top management to be knowledgeable about and intimately involved in all of the businesses. The emphasis on division general manager authority includes choosing between internal and external transactions. The emphasis on division general manager responsibility for financial outcomes results in transfers that include a profit to the selling division, since it obviously is a business in its own right. In particular, since exchange autonomy exists, negotiation should be the most popular method, followed by market price and then cost plus profit markup.

For the remaining seven types, there is some basis for relationships between profit centers. The assumption is made that an explicit strategy of vertical integration, using the broad definition given in chapter 4, as opposed to its specific use in the Rumelt classification scheme, exists between these profit centers and results in mandated internal transactions. This leaves the problem of distinguish-

Table B–2
Reclassification of Vancil's Eleven Strategic Types

Vancil's Types	*Single Business Vertical Integration*	*Distinct Businesses Vertical Integration*	*Unrelated Businesses*	*Total*
Single Business				
1. Vertically integrated	7	35	0	42
2. Large single-unit	17	0	0	17
Dominant Business				
3. Predominantly vertically integrated	5	35	0	40
4. Major and common skill	19	0	0	19
5. Major and linked	14	0	0	14
6. Major and unrelated	0	0	7	7
Related Businesses				
7. Related and common skill	6	36	0	42
8. Related and linked	1	22	0	23
Unrelated Businesses				
9. Unrelated merger	0	0	7	7
10. Unrelated acquisition	0	0	63	63
11. Unrelated internal development	0	0	17	17
Total	69	128	94	291

ing between single business vertical integration and distinct businesses vertical integration, which requires the strongest assumptions in matching Vancil's eleven types to the three categories used in chapter 4. The field data collected in this study helped in reclassifying Vancil's types.

All large single-unit, major and common skill, and major linked firms were considered to be in the single business vertical integration category. The assumption was made that because of the high specialization ratio in these firms, the buying divisions, which sold product externally, represented the primary businesses, and transfers to them would be on a full cost basis. However, if the minor businesses were the buying divisions, transfers in these firms would be on a cost plus profit markup or market price basis, unless internal sales were considered to be purely incremental volume, as they were at Cicero Systems.

The remaining four types—vertically integrated, predominantly vertically integrated, related and common skill, and related and linked—were split between the single business vertical integration and distinct business vertical integration categories. It was assumed that the greater diversity in these firms would result in all profit centers being regarded as a business in their own right, which would require transfers that included a profit. However, when firms classified as one of these four types do not have inter–profit center transfers, the interdependencies are all contained within individual profit centers, each of which resembles the single business vertical integration firm. Thus, when there were no inter–profit center transfers, the firms were classified in this category. Distinct businesses vertical integration firms make much greater use of transfers that include a profit than do single business vertical integration firms. However, because exchange autonomy does not exist, negotiation is a less popular method than it is in unrelated businesses firms.

Table B–2 shows the relationship between Vancil's categories and the categories used here. The reason Vancil did not get statistically significant results on the relationship between transfer pricing method and strategic category was that his three types—single business, dominant business, and related businesses—all contained both single business vertical integration and distinct businesses vertical integration. His classification scheme, although it fairly closely reflected whether or not internal transactions were mandated, did not reflect the other essential distinction that determines transfer pricing method—whether or not the selling profit center is a business in its own right. In particular, his use of Rumelt's typology made it impossible to distinguish between vertically integrated and other dominant business firms. This suggests that the decision to force vertically integrated firms into a typology based on the specialization and related ratios is not a good one, and it may have important consequences for studies of the relationships between strategic category and other variables.

Notes

Chapter 1: The Problem with a Solution

1. The Price Waterhouse (1984) data are only for those firms using transfers that included a profit—69 percent of the total number of respondents. Data on the number of sequential transfers were provided to me in a personal communication from Daniel P. Keegan of Price Waterhouse.

2. This information was provided to me in a personal communication from Daniel P. Keegan of Price Waterhouse.

Chapter 2: Theory and Practice

1. Transfer pricing is only one example of the gap between theory and practice. Anthony (1984) cited as another example the problem of allocating indirect costs. He noted: "Fifty years ago, cost accountants were well acquainted with allocation techniques, and texts and academic literature faithfully reflected these practices. Beginning in the 1940s, however, the literature diverged from practice, and the divergence continues to this day" (p. 5). For an attempt to provide an agency theory-based theoretical justification for allocating these costs, see Zimmerman (1979).

2. Chandler (1962) restricted the use of the term *vertical integration* to refer to the incorporation within the firm of additional functions, such as distribution or manufacturing. He used the term *diversification* to refer to the development of new products. In general business parlance, vertical integration refers to internalizing a transaction formerly conducted with a supplier or customer and often results in entering a new business.

3. It is a fairly common practice for companies with a problem to set up a task force to study this problem and for this task force to talk to managers at other companies who have faced or are facing a similar problem. Several of the companies in my study did this with transfer pricing.

4. This formula shows that return on investment (ROI) is a function of both profitability and turnover:

$$\frac{\text{Profit}}{\text{Sales}} \times \frac{\text{Sales}}{\text{Investment}} = \text{ROI}$$

For a more complete discussion, see Weston and Brigham (1981, pp. 152–156).

5. The *quasi profit center* is sometimes used when an organization unit, such as the manufacturing or sales function, is turned into a profit center by being measured on the basis of both revenues and costs, even though it does not have functional responsibility for the resources that determine both revenues and costs. Thus, it is a profit center only in the most technical sense when compared to a unit such as a division, which closely approximates a stand-alone business. The definition of a profit center is discussed in more detail in chapter 4.

6. Peat, Marwick, Mitchell and Company is one of the "Big Eight" accounting firms.

7. This assumes cost plus pricing on the final good based on a fixed percentage markup.

8. See Kaplan (1982, pp. 493–497) for a discussion of shadow prices.

9. Advocates of market price have included Cook (1955), Heuser (1956), Dean (1955), Shillinglaw (1961), Dearden (1960a, 1973), Stanley (1964), Lemke (1970), Onsi (1970), Dittman (1972), Vendig (1973), Edwards and Roemmich (1976), Lucien (1979), Madison (1979), Schiff (1979), Haidinger (1970), Fremgren (1970), and Mailandt (1975). Advocates of various cost-based methods have included Stone (1956), Shillinglaw (1957), Drebin (1959), Henderson and Dearden (1966), and Goetz (1967). Those who have emphasized that the appropriate system depended upon circumstances and managements' objectives also have emphasized that all methods have problems. Advocates of the "it depends" position have included Bierman (1959), Finney (1966), Lemke (1970), Bierman and Dyckman (1976), Dascher (1972), Troxel (1973), Fantl (1974), Sharav (1974), and Schaub (1978).

10. For an example of this, see Kaplan (1982, pp. 484–488).

11. Explicit recognition of the importance of behavioral aspects was made by Anthony (1965), Arvidsson (1973), Bailey and Boe (1976), Benke and Edwards (1980), Dean (1955), Dearden (1960a), Dittman and Ferris (1978), Earnest (1979), Lambert (1979), National Association of Accountants (1956), Thomas (1980), and Watson and Baumler (1975).

12. Shillinglaw (1977) is another good example of a textbook review of the transfer pricing problem, along with Kaplan (1982) and Anthony and Dearden (1980).

13. Dean assumed this was possible after the system was put in place. He recommended that a mediator be used in the beginning.

14. One reason for this disagreement was that Dean believed that divisions should be able to buy outside, whereas Dearden did not.

15. Benke and Edwards (1980) also used Lawrence and Lorsch's framework in their model of the management control process, but they did not incorporate it into their findings in any meaningful way.

16. In general, field-based clinical studies are essential for understanding complex management phenomena such as transfer pricing. They are also extremely useful in interpreting and designing surveys.

17. Mautz (1968) found that cost-based methods were used in 40.9 percent of the cases, market-based methods in 50.3 percent, and other methods in 8.8 percent. Tang (1979) found that cost-based methods were used in 50.4 percent of the cases (as the dominant method in 56.4 percent) and market-based methods in 49.6 percent (as the dominant method in 43.6 percent).

18. Tang (1979) collected data on both dominant method and all methods. For all methods, he found that standard variable cost was used in less than 3.0 percent of the firms and actual variable cost by 0.0 percent. He also found that actual variable cost plus a lump sum subsidy was used by 0.9 percent of the firms for all methods and as a dominant method by 0.7 percent.

19. This information was made available to me in a personal communication from Daniel P. Keegan of Price Waterhouse.

20. Those that did not use markup transfer pricing also must have been fairly well satisfied, since they had given little thought to changing their transfer pricing practices. Conversely, few companies that had used a markup transfer pricing system in the past had abandoned it. These findings were also communicated to me by Mr. Keegan.

21. Tang (1979) conducted a fairly detailed analysis that focused only on international transfer pricing practices.

Chapter 3: The Case of Alfarabi Chemicals, Inc.

1. Although the term *transfer price* is typically reserved for transfers between profit centers, in some cases it is also used to refer to charges assessed to profit centers and cost centers for goods and services from cost centers. These latter charges are more commonly referred to as *overhead charges* or *cost allocations.* For discussions of this problem, see Kaplan (1982), Anthony and Dearden (1980), and Vancil (1978).

2. Transfers from the operations function in the Commodity Group to the Retail Division were, in effect, transfers from a cost center to a profit center within a larger profit center that contained the cost center that transferred to the smaller profit center.

Chapter 4: A Theory for Practice

1. All managers of profit centers are general managers, including division general managers, group general managers, chief operating officers, and chief executive officers. For simplicity, we will not distinguish between chief operating officers (COOs) and chief executive officers (CEOs) and will use the latter term to refer generally to the highest-level general managers. Some authors, such as Kotter (1982) have used the term *general manager* to refer to such positions as product/market manager or operations manager, which do not always have profit responsibility. We will use the terms *profit center manager* and *general manager* interchangeably, thereby excluding general managers who do not have profit responsibility.

2. This finding was obtained by Mautz (1968), Tang (1979), and Vancil (1978).

3. If variable cost transfer prices are used, the buying profit center is not charged for any of the fixed costs of manufacturing the product. The near absence of variable cost transfer prices in practice is especially significant because variable cost is similar though not identical to marginal cost, and thus has some of the characteristics that make marginal cost transfers so attractive to economists.

4. Andrews (1980) has established the classic definition of the most general concept of strategy—corporate strategy:

> Corporate strategy is the pattern of decisions in a company that determines and reveals its objectives, purposes, or goals, produces the principal policies and plans for achieving those goals, and defines the range of business the company is to pursue, the kind of economic and human organization it is or intends to be, and the nature of the economic and noneconomic contribution it intends to make to its shareholders, employees, customers, and communities. (p. 18)

5. A National Industrial Conference Board (1967) study of transfer pricing practices in 190 companies recognized the importance of strategy, although it did not use that term:

> The general feeling among executives faced with this problem is that each company needs to devise policies and transfer prices that are consistent with its own management philosophy and then take into account the type of business and the type of products subject to interdivisional transfers. (pp. 2–3)

Corey (1976) also recognized the central role of strategy in his discussion of transfer pricing as a special case of buyer/seller relations when both parties are within a single company:

> What is needed, then, as the basis for healthy internal relationships is a primacy of strategic objectives. Then it becomes possible to articulate each divison's objectives in terms of corporate purpose, to make trade-offs in dealing with external and internal suppliers and customers, and to measure performance accordingly. (p. 370)

6. See Schendel and Hofer (1979) and Miles and Snow (1978).

7. Jensen's (1983) use of the term *decision rights* is similar to Vancil's (1978) use of the term *authority*, which he defined as "the set of corporate resources under the custody of a manager and for which he has the power to decide how the resources are utilized" (p. 35).

8. Vancil (1978) defined *responsibility* as "the set of corporate activities with which a manager is concerned and for which he is held accountable" (p. 35).

9. Anthony and Dearden (1980) defined five different ways of measuring profitability: "(1) as the contribution margin, (2) as direct divisional profit, (3) as controllable divisional profit, (4) as income before income taxes, and (5) as net income" (p. 221).

10. An especially interesting and vexing example of this problem concerns the data processing function. To what extent should division general managers be able to choose between using a corporate data processing function and establishing its own data processing capabilities, whether within the division or through external vendors? When the division does use corporate resources, what type of chargeout system should be used? These questions apply to all other functions as well. I am exploring this issue through case studies and using Vancil's (1978) data base from his decentralization study.

11. Based on his survey data, Vancil (1978) concluded that "for managers in between the highest and lowest levels there can be an important difference between custody

and concern, between the power to control physical resources and the accountability for results that is usually measured in financial terms" (p. 35).

12. For more complete discussions on the cost advantages of backward vertical integration, see Porter (1980), Hayes (1977), Hayes and Wheelwright (1984), and Carlton (1979).

13. For a good discussion of cost (or expense) centers, revenue centers, profit centers, and investment centers, see Anthony and Dearden (1980).

14. Vancil (1978) had hoped to develop a taxonomy of profit centers, but he regarded his efforts as unsuccessful:

> At the moment, the single term "profit center" is too broad, covering wide variations in the authority and autonomy of profit center managers. Our efforts to classify profit centers based on the manager's scope (and/or type) of functional authority, or on his or her perceived autonomy for various categories of decisions, were fruitless; we could not discern any natural break-points in the data. (p. 141)

The framework presented here for describing responsibility centers may contribute to the development of such a taxonomy.

15. Davis and Lawrence (1977), Galbraith (1973), and Mintzberg (1979) are useful references on matrix organization.

16. For more complete discussions of other reasons for backward vertical integration, see Porter (1980), Hayes (1977), and Hayes and Wheelwright (1984).

17. For more complete discussions of reasons for forward vertical integration, see Porter (1980), Hayes (1977), and Hayes and Wheelwright (1984).

18. Assume, for example, that the intermediate good produced by the selling division has a cost of $50 and a market price of $100, and that the final good produced by the buying division adds additional costs of $50 and sells in the external marketplace for $200. The corporation earns a total profit of $100. Under dual pricing, profits to the selling division are $50 and profits to the buying division are $100. The total of $150 is $50 more than the $100 truly earned, since the $50 profit on the intermediate good has been counted twice, once for each division.

19. See Popper (1959) for a discussion of what constitutes the testing of a theory. He emphasized that theories can only be falsified, never verified, because data consistent with a theory simply show that it has not yet been proved false. The first piece of data inconsistent with a theory is enough to falsify it, assuming no measurement error. Since there is always measurement error, the testing of theories is not a cut-and-dried procedure.

20. Vancil (1978) had an "autonomy questionnaire" distributed by the chief financial officer (who completed the structural and demographic questionnaires) to three "typical" profit center managers. The questionnaire asked the profit center managers to indicate their degree of autonomy in making twenty decisions, including "buying from an outside vendor when the items required could be supplied by another unit in your corporation."

21. See Rumelt (1974, pp. 9–32) for a detailed discussion of his strategic typology.

22. This is partially an artifact of the way the classification scheme was developed.

23. Vancil's (1978) implicit rank order was variable standard cost, variable actual

cost, full standard cost, full actual cost, cost plus profit on sales, cost plus profit on investment, cost plus other markup, negotiation, competitor's price, market price–list, and market price–bid.

24. See Vancil (1978, pp. 148–149) for a discussion of the accuracy of the classifications based on questionnaire data.

25. This is because profit center managers were not asked about transfer pricing practices in the autonomy questionnaire.

26. Statistically significant findings were also obtained for the relationships between strategy and decisions about (1) redesigning a product, (2) expanding territories, (3) investing in plant and equipment, (4) developing a new product, (5) changing selling price, (6) changing inventory policy, (7) increasing the number of exempt personnel, and (8) increasing the number of nonexempt personnel.

27. For a discussion of these modes of conflict resolution, see Lawrence and Lorsch (1967, pp. 73–78).

Chapter 5: Exchange Autonomy: Pricing in a Market Context

1. Negotiating extremely favorable transfer prices can be a double-edged sword, however—such as when top management makes personnel changes, possibly as a way of adjusting the transfer price. An amusing story of the consequences of such changes was told by Aaron Thornton of Paine Chemical Company. A number of years ago, Randall Hill, the general manager of the selling division, had negotiated extremely favorable transfer prices with Arthur Damon, the general manager of the buying division. Then Thornton replaced Hill and Hill replaced Damon. Thornton recalled with some glee what happened:

> Randall Hill was a good friend of mine and a real wheeler-dealer. Damon was not as sharp, and Randall was hoodwinking him a bit on the transfer price. When I became general manager of the selling division and Randall was made general manager of the buying division, he came to see me. I said, "Hell, Randall, I have confidence in you on these transfer prices. If you set it up this way I know it's fair." However, pretty soon I changed the transfer price and gave him the product for three to four cents a pound less.

2. When profit center managers have exchange autonomy, the product pricing process plays a part in the marketing strategy of the seller and in the purchasing strategy of the buyer. It is a complex process that is related to a number of objectives on both sides. An understanding of behavior on both sides of the exchange is important. Webster (1979) reviewed a number of models of buying behavior and pointed out a number of environmental, organizational, interpersonal, and individual determinants. All of these factors are also relevant to marketing behavior. For a buyer-seller relationship in a single organization, the fact that it is taking place in a hierarchical setting is especially relevant.

3. See also Shapiro and Jackson (1978) and Webster (1979). These and Corey's

(1976) references are good examples of a theory of product pricing based upon companies' pricing practices.

4. For further discussion of the marketing mix in competitive bidding, see Corey (1978, pp. 54–56).

5. At least transfer pricing should be no more difficult a problem than external product pricing.

6. See Macaulay (1963) for the classic statement of this phenomenon.

7. The classic exposition of this was provided by Coase (1937). This "transaction cost" theory of vertical integration has been greatly expanded and developed by Williamson (1975).

8. Michael Jensen has suggested to me that withholding payment could be made an option on internal relationships as well.

9. For a discussion of cash cows and portfolio planning in general, see Abell and Hammond (1979).

10. I am indebted to John Pratt for this insight.

11. See Rawls (1971, p. 269) for a discussion of the prisoner's dilemma. The nature of this problem is illustrated in the following table, which shows the years in prison each prisoner will receive, depending on the outcome of separate interrogations. The essential point of this dilemma is that it is an unstable situation. What is rational for each prisoner to do—confess—can lead to a situation in which both prisoners are worse off if each follows this course of action.

	Second Prisoner	
First Prisoner	*Not Confess*	*Confess*
Not confess	1,1	10,5
Confess	0,10	5,5

12. In fact, the "hind tit" has the richest milk. The common expression is used in a way that has an opposite meaning to what is implied by the actual biology of the situation.

Chapter 6: Mandated Full Cost: Measuring the Cost of Production

1. For a discussion of fixed and variable costs, see Kaplan (1982, pp. 23–31).

2. For discussions of variance analysis, see Anthony and Dearden (1980, pp. 419–433) and Kaplan (1982, pp. 319–351).

3. Standard costs can also be used for measuring the performance of other functions.

4. For a discussion of joint and by-product costing problems, see Kaplan (1982, pp. 389–409).

5. See Kaplan (1982, pp. 226–230) for a discussion of overhead allocations in the context of full cost pricing.

Chapter 7: Mandated Market-Based: Searching for the Just Price

1. The concept of a "just price" dates at least as far back as Aristotle and was an issue of major concern in the twelfth and thirteenth centuries. For an interesting discussion of this concept in a very different context, see Baldwin (1959).
2. See Macaulay (1963) for a discussion of how firms can enforce agreements without resorting to litigation.
3. It is easy to create these incentives by establishing goals for cost reduction as well as goals for profitability.
4. Anthony and Dearden (1980, p. 236) emphasize this point.

Chapter 8: Managing Conflict for Information and Control

1. This discussion of interdependence borrows heavily from Pfeffer and Salancik (1978). See also March and Simon (1958) and Thompson (1967).
2. This is not true, of course, if the profit center is operating at such a high capacity that it is experiencing decreasing returns to scale; that is, each unit costs more to make than the preceding one.
3. See Macaulay (1963).
4. For an example of this view, see Dearden (1960a).
5. For an example of this view, see Kaplan (1982).
6. This depends on how much of the product is sold internally and on whether the selling profit center is also responsible for cost reduction objectives.

Chapter 9: Pressures for Endless Change

1. Benke and Edwards (1980) also found some unwillingness among managers in their study to change their transfer pricing policies, even when these policies were perceived to have weaknesses: "The interviewees felt that whatever the weakness of their current technique, at least those who used this technique understood it. A frequently cited reason for not wishing to change techniques was the problem of reeducating those who would be affected" (p. 10).
2. For a criticism of the product life cycle concept, see Dhalla and Yuspeh (1976).
3. An August 13, 1984, *Business Week* article stated that Rolls-Royce Motors, Ltd., makes approximately 2,000 cars per year, which sell for between $75,000 and $156,000.
4. Williamson's (1975) original formulation treated markets and hierarchies as discrete choices. Later (Williamson, 1979) he developed a statement of alternative contracting modes in terms of a continuum.
5. In general, change can be useful for its own sake.
6. An alternative approach would be for top management simply to put restrictions on budget levels and let the conflict be over service levels. This would be another way of

enforcing greater efficiency by making the cost centers responsible for greater output with the same level of resources. It is not clear why this more direct approach was not taken.

Chapter 10: The Manager's Analytical Plane

1. This follows from the fact that strategy formulation and strategy implementation are interdependent.

2. This model is very similar to those proposed by others, such as Andrews (1980) and Vancil (1978).

3. For a good discussion of the concept of process, see Weick (1979, pp. 42–47).

4. For a comprehensive discussion of vertical integration, see Porter (1980, pp. 300–323). Another excellent discussion of vertical integration from a manufacturing perspective is Hayes and Wheelwright (1984, pp. 275–307). See also Stigler (1951) and Thompson (1967).

5. Thus, this model is a type of contingency theory. The seminal work in contingency theory was developed by Stinchcombe (1959), Woodward (1965), Lawrence and Lorsch (1967), and Thompson (1967).

6. Data on each company were taken from case studies published by HBS Case Services: "IBM Corporation: Background Note" (9-180-034), "IBM Corporation: The Bubble Memory Incident" (9-180-042), "General Electric Strategic Position: 1981" (9-381-174, rev. 3/82), "Human Resources at Hewlett-Packard" (0-482-125), and "People Express" (9-483-103).

7. The collective organization is very similar to what Mintzberg (1979, pp. 305–313) described as the "simple structure."

8. The cooperative organization is very similar to what Mintzberg (1979, pp. 314–347) described as the "machine bureaucracy" and to what Miles and Snow (1978, pp. 31–48) described as the "defender."

9. The competitive organization is very similar to what Mintzberg (1979, pp. 380–430) described as the "divisionalized form" and somewhat less similar to what Miles and Snow (1978, pp. 49–67) described as the "prospector."

10. For discussions of the management practices of the competitive organization, see Berg (1965), Salter (1973), and Vancil and Lorange (1975).

11. The collaborative organization is somewhat similar to what Mintzberg (1979, pp. 431–467) described as the "adhocracy," and it also shares some similar characteristics with what Miles and Snow (1978, pp. 68–80, 140–151) described as the "analyzer" and the "Type IV" organization.

12. For further discussion of these issues, see Lorsch and Allen (1973), Salter (1973), and Davis and Lawrence (1977).

13. See Eccles (1983) for another discussion of the MAP and transfer pricing policies.

14. The creation of metrics for each dimension is an essential step in making the concept of the MAP fully operational. It is possible that this effort will involve a process designed to establish metrics specific to each company. The next step would be to establish equivalence mappings across companies.

15. This suggests the somewhat counterintuitive finding that precise measurement

can actually lead to problems, since in reality the desired degree of precision can never be obtained.

16. For further discussion on how the MAP can be used and for some hypotheses that can be derived from it, see Eccles (1984).
17. See, for example, Kitching (1967) and Meeks (1977).
18. See Kirkland (1984).
19. See, for example, Chandler (1962), Salter (1970) and Scott (1971a, 1971b).
20. See, for example, Bierman and Smidt (1980).
21. See Eccles and Carley (1984).
22. The most successful effort is that of Porter (1980 and 1985).

Appendix A: The Methodology of Practice-Based Theory

1. The other structural question concerned organization within the firm itself. For a detailed analysis of these two questions, see Eccles (1979, 1981a, and 1981b).

Appendix B: A Revision of Rumelt's Typology of Corporate Strategy

1. Kathleen Carley was a great help to me in reclassifying Vancil's data base and in conducting the statistical analysis relating transfer pricing policies to corporate strategy.

Bibliography

Abdel-khalik, A. Rashad, and Lusk, Edward J. 1974. "Transfer Pricing—A Synthesis." *Accounting Review* 49: 8–23.

Abell, Derek F. 1980. *Defining the Business: The Starting Point of Strategic Planning.* Englewood Cliffs, N.J.: Prentice-Hall.

Abell, Derek F., and Hammond, John S. 1979. *Strategic Market Planning: Problems and Analytical Approaches.* Englewood Cliffs, N.J.: Prentice-Hall.

Ackerman, Robert W. 1970. "Influence of Integration and Diversity on the Investment Process." *Administrative Science Quarterly* 15: 341–351.

Alchian, Armen A., and Demsetz, Harold. 1972. "Production, Information Costs, and Economic Organization." *American Economic Review* 62: 777–795.

Allison, Graham T. 1971. *Essence of Decision: Explaining the Cuban Missile Crisis.* Boston: Little, Brown.

Andrews, Kenneth R. 1971. *The Concept of Corporate Strategy.* Homewood, Ill.: Dow Jones-Irwin.

———.1980. *The Concept of Corporate Strategy,* rev. ed. Homewood, Ill.: Richard D. Irwin.

Anthony, Robert N. 1965. *Planning and Control Systems: A Framework for Analysis.* Boston: Division of Research, Graduate School of Business Administration, Harvard University.

———.1984. "Cost Allocation." *Journal of Cost Analysis* 1: 5–15.

Anthony, Robert N., and Dearden, John. 1980. *Management Control Systems,* 4th ed. Homewood, Ill.: Richard D. Irwin.

Arrow, Kenneth J. 1959. "Optimization, Decentralization, and Internal Pricing in Business Firms." In *Contributions to Scientific Research in Management,* Proceedings of the Scientific Program following the dedication of the Western Data Processing Center, Graduate School of Business Administration, University of California at Los Angeles, pp. 9–18.

———.1964a. "Control in Large Organizations." *Management Science* 10: 397–408.

———.1964b. "Research in Management Controls: A Critical Synthesis." In *Management Controls: New Directions in Basic Research,* edited by Charles Bonini, Robert Jaedicke, and Harvey Wagner, pp. 317–327. New York: McGraw-Hill.

Arvidsson, Göran. 1973. *Internal Transfer Negotiations: Eight Experiments.* Stockholm: Economic Research Institute.

Bailey, Andrew D., and Boe, Warren J. 1976. "Goal and Resource Transfers in the Multigoal Organization." *Accounting Review* 51: 559–573.
Baldwin, John. 1959. "The Medieval Theories of the Just Price." *Transactions of the American Philosophical Society* 49 (Part 4): 1–92.
Baumol, William, and Fabian, Tibor. 1964. "Decomposition, Pricing for Decentralization and External Economies." *Management Science* 11: 1–32.
Benke, Ralph L., Jr., and Edwards, James Don. 1980. *Transfer Pricing: Techniques and Uses.* New York: National Association of Accountants.
Berg, Norman A. 1966. "Strategic Planning in Conglomerate Companies." *Harvard Business Review* 43(3): 79–92.
Bierman, Harold, Jr. 1959. "Pricing Intracompany Transfers." *Accounting Review* 34: 429–432.
Bierman, Harold, Jr., and Dyckman, Thomas R. 1976. *Managerial Cost Accounting,* 2d ed. New York: Macmillan.
Bierman, Harold, Jr., and Smidt, Seymour. 1980. *The Capital Budgeting Decision,* 5th ed. New York: Macmillan.
Bower, Joseph L. 1970. *Managing the Resource Allocation Process: A Study of Corporate Planning and Investment.* Boston: Division of Research, Graduate School of Business Administration, Harvard University.
Bower, Joseph L., and Doz, Yves. 1979. "Strategy Formulation: A Social and Political Process." In *Strategic Management: A New View of Business Policy and Planning,* edited by Dan E. Schendel and Charles W. Hofer, pp. 152–166. Boston: Little, Brown.
Brown, F. Donaldson. 1927. "Centralized Control with Decentralized Responsibilities." *American Management Association Annual Convention Series* 57. Reprinted in *System and Profits: Early Management Accounting at Du Pont and General Motors,* edited by H. Thomas Johnson. New York: Arno Press, 1980.
Burns, Tom, and Stalker, G.M. 1961. *The Management of Innovation.* London: Tavistock.
Business Week. 1984. "Turnaround at a Humbler Rolls-Royce." August 13, p. 75.
Camman, Eric A. 1929. "Interdepartmental Profits." *Journal of Accountancy* 37: 37–44.
Carlton, Dennis W. 1979. "Vertical Integration in Competitive Markets Under Uncertainty." *Journal of Industrial Economics* 37: 189–209.
Chandler, Alfred D., Jr. 1962. *Strategy and Structure: Chapters in the History of the Industrial Enterprise.* Cambridge, Mass.: M.I.T. Press.
———.1977. *The Visible Hand: The Managerial Revolution in American Business.* Cambridge, Mass.: Harvard University Press, Belknap Press.
Christenson, Charles. 1976. "Proposals for a Program of Empirical Research into the Properties of Triangles." *Decision Sciences* 7: 631–648.
Coase, R.H. 1937. "The Nature of the Firm." *Economica* 4: 386–405.
Cohen, Michael D., and March, James G. 1974. *Leadership and Ambiguity: The American College.* New York: McGraw-Hill.
Cohen, Michael D.; March, James G.; and Olsen, Johan P. 1972. "A Garbage Can Model of Organizational Choice." *Administrative Science Quarterly* 17: 1–25.
Cook, Paul W., Jr. 1955. "Decentralization and the Transfer Pricing Problem." *Journal of Business* 28: 87–94.
Corey, E. Raymond. 1976. *Industrial Marketing: Cases and Concepts,* 2d ed. Englewood Cliffs, N.J.: Prentice-Hall.

———.1978.*Procurement Management: Strategy, Organization, and Decision-Making.* Boston: CBI.

Cyert, Richard M., and March, James G. 1963. *A Behavioral Theory of the Firm.* Englewood Cliffs, N.J.: Prentice-Hall.

Dantzig, George B., and Wolfe, Philip. 1960. "Decomposition Principle for Linear Programs." *Operations Research* 8(1): 101–111.

Dascher, Paul E. 1972. "Transfer Pricing—Some Behavioral Observations." *Managerial Planning* 21: 17–21.

Davis, Stanley M., and Lawrence, Paul R. 1977. *Matrix.* Reading, Mass.: Addison-Wesley.

Dean, Joel. 1955. "Decentralization and Intracompany Pricing." *Harvard Business Review* 33(4): 65–74.

Dearden, John. 1960a. "Interdivisional Pricing." *Harvard Business Review* 38(1): 117–125.

———.1960b. "Problems in Decentralized Profit Responsibility." *Harvard Business Review* 38(3): 79–86.

———.1969. "The Case Against ROI Control." *Harvard Business Review* 47(3):124–135.

———. 1973. *Cost Accounting and Financial Control Systems.* Reading, Mass.: Addison-Wesley.

Dhalla, Nariman K., and Yuspeh, Sonia. 1976. "Forget the Product Life Cycle Concept!" *Harvard Business Review* 54(1): 102–113.

Dittman, David A. 1972. "Transfer Pricing and Decentralization." *Management Accounting* 54(5): 47–50.

Dittman, David A., and Ferris, Kenneth R. 1978. "'Profit Centre': A Satisfaction Generating Concept." *Accounting and Business Research* 9: 242–245.

Drebin, Allan R. 1959. "A Proposal for Dual Pricing of Intra-Company Transfers." *N.A.A. Bulletin* 40(1): 51–55.

Earnest, Kenneth R. 1979. "Applying Motivational Theory in Management Accounting." *Management Accounting* 61(6): 41–44.

Eccles, Robert G. 1979. "Organization and Market Structure in the Construction Industry: A Study of Subcontracting." Ph.D. dissertation, Harvard University.

———.1980a. "Research Project on Dual Transaction Goods." Boston: Graduate School of Business Administration, Harvard University, May 2. Mimeographed.

———.1980b. "Research Proposal for a Study of the Vertical Integration Decision." Boston: Graduate School of Business Administration, Harvard University, January. Mimeographed.

———.1981a. "Bureaucratic Versus Craft Adminstration: The Relationship of Market Structure to the Construction Firm." *Administrative Science Quarterly* 26: 449–469.

———. 1981b. "The Quasifirm in the Construction Industry." *Journal of Economic Behavior and Organization* 2: 335–357.

———.1983. "Control with Fairness in Transfer Pricing." *Harvard Business Review* 61(6): 149–161.

———.1984. "Creating the Collaborative Organization." Working Paper 9-784-047. Boston: Division of Research, Graduate School of Business Administration, Harvard University, February.

———.Forthcoming. "Transfer Pricing as a Problem of Agency." In *Principals and*

Agents: The Structure of Business, edited by John W. Pratt and Richard J. Zeckhauser. Boston: Harvard Business School Press.

Eccles, Robert G., and Carley, Kathleen M. 1984. "Structure and Systems in the Multi-Profit Center Firm." Boston: Graduate School of Business Administration, Harvard University, September. Mimeographed.

Edwards, J. Don, and Roemmich, Roger A. 1976. "Transfer Pricing: The Wrong Tool for Performance Evaluation." *Cost and Management* 50(1): 35–37.

Fantl, Irving L. 1974. "Transfer Pricing—Tread Carefully." *CPA Journal* 44(12): 42–46.

Finney, Frederick D. 1966. "Pricing Interdivisional Transfers." *Management Accounting* 48(5): 10–19.

Fremgren, James M. 1970. "Transfer Pricing and Management Goals." *Management Accounting* 52(6): 25–31.

Galbraith, Jay. 1973. *Designing Complex Organizations.* Reading, Mass.: Addison-Wesley.

"General Electric Strategic Position: 1981." 1982. Boston: HBS Case Services, 9-381-174, rev. 3/82.

Godfrey, James T. 1971. "Short-Run Planning in a Decentralized Firm." *Accounting Review* 46: 286–297.

Goetz, Billy E. 1967. "Transfer Prices: An Exercise in Relevancy and Goal Congruence." *Accounting Review* 42: 435–448.

Gordon, Myron J. 1970. "A Method of Pricing for a Socialist Economy." *Accounting Review* 45: 427–443.

Gould, J.R. 1964. "Internal Pricing in Firms When There Are Costs of Using an Outside Market." *Journal of Business* 37: 61–67.

Haidinger, Timothy P. 1970. "Negotiate for Profits." *Management Accounting* 52(6) 23–24.

Hass, Jerome E. 1968. "Transfer Pricing in a Decentralized Firm." *Management Science* 14: B-310–B-331.

Hayes, Robert H. 1977. "A Note on Vertical Integration Decisions." Boston: Graduate School of Business Administration, Harvard University, April 6. Mimeographed.

Hayes, Robert H., and Wheelwright, Steven G. 1979a. "The Dynamics of Process-Product Life Cycles." *Harvard Business Review* 57(2): 127–136.

———.1979b. "Link Manufacturing Process and Product Life Cycles." *Harvard Business Review* 57(1): 133–140.

———.1984. *Restoring Our Competitive Edge.* New York: Wiley.

Henderson, Bruce D., and Dearden, John. 1966. "New System for Divisional Control." *Harvard Business Review* 44(5): 144–154.

Heuser, Forrest L. 1956. "Organizing for Effective Intracompany Pricing." *N.A.C.A. Bulletin* 37: 1100–1105.

Hirshleifer, Jack. 1956. "On the Economics of Transfer Pricing." *Journal of Business* 29: 172–184.

———.1957. "Economics of the Divisionalized Firm." *Journal of Business* 30: 96–108.

"Human Resources at Hewlett-Packard." 1982. Boston: HBS Case Services, 0-482-125.

"IBM: Background Note." 1980. Boston: HBS Case Services, 9-180-034.

"IBM: The Bubble Memory Incident." 1980. Boston: HBS Case Services, 9-180-042.

Jensen, Michael C. 1983. "Organization Theory and Methodology." *Accounting Review* 68: 319–339.

Kanodia, Chandra. 1979. "Risk Sharing and Transfer Price Systems Under Uncertainty." *Journal of Accounting Research* 17(1): 74–97.

Kaplan, Robert S. 1982. *Advanced Management Accounting*. Englewood Cliffs, N.J.: Prentice-Hall.

Kirkland, Richard I., Jr. 1984. "Exxon Rededicates Itself to Oil." *Fortune,* July 23, pp. 28–32.

Kitching, John. 1967. "Why Do Mergers Miscarry?" *Harvard Business Review* 45(6): 84–101.

Kotter, John P. 1982. *The General Managers*. New York: Free Press.

Lambert, David R. 1979. "Transfer Pricing and Interdivisional Conflict." *California Management Review* 21(4): 70–75.

Larson, Raymond L. 1974. "Decentralization in Real Life." *Management Accounting* 55(9): 28–32.

Lawrence, Paul R., and Lorsch, Jay W. 1967. *Organization and Environment: Managing Differentiation and Integration*. Homewood, Ill.: Richard D. Irwin.

Lemke, Kenneth W. 1970. "In Defence of the 'Profit Centre' Concept." *Abacus* 6(2): 182–189.

Lorsch, Jay W., and Allen, Stephen A., III. 1973. *Managing Diversity and Interdependence: An Organizational Study of Multidivisonal Firms*. Boston: Division of Research, Graduate School of Business Administration, Harvard University.

Lucien, Kent. 1979. "Transfer Pricing for the Cost of Funds in a Commercial Bank." *Management Accounting* 60(7): 23–24, 36.

Macaulay, Stewart. 1963. "Noncontractual Relations in Business: A Preliminary Study." *American Sociological Review* 28: 55–67.

Madison, Roland L. 1979. "Responsibility Accounting and Transfer Pricing: Approach with Caution." *Management Accounting* 60(7): 25–29.

Mailandt, Peter. 1975. "An Alternative to Transfer Pricing." *Business Horizons* 18(5): 81–86.

March, James G., and Simon, Herbert A. 1958. *Organizations*. New York: Wiley.

Mauriel, John J., and Anthony, Robert N. 1966. "Misevaluation of Investment Center Performance." *Harvard Business Review* 44(2): 98–105.

Mautz, R.K. 1968. *Financial Reporting by Diversified Companies*. New York: Financial Executives Research Foundation, 1968.

Meeks, George. 1977. *Disappointing Marriage: A Study of the Gains from Merger.* Cambridge: Cambridge University Press.

Miles, Raymond E., and Snow, Charles G. 1978. *Organizational Strategy, Structure, and Process*. New York: McGraw-Hill.

Mill, John Stuart. 1884. *Principles of Political Economy.* Cambridge, Mass.: Harvard University Press.

Mintzberg, Henry. 1979. *The Structuring of Organizations*. Englewood Cliffs, N.J.: Prentice-Hall.

National Association of Accountants.1956. *Accounting for Intra-Company Transfers.* Research Report No. 30. New York: National Association of Accountants.

National Association of Cost Accountants (NACA). 1925. *Proceedings of the Sixth International Cost Conference*. New York: J.J. Little and Ives.

———.1930. *Proceedings of the Eleventh International Cost Conference.* New York: Knickerbocker Press.

National Industrial Conference Board. 1967. *Interdivisional Transfer Pricing.* Studies in Business Policy, No. 22. New York: National Industrial Conference Board.
Onsi, Mohamed. 1970. "A Transfer Pricing System Based on Opportunity Cost." *Accounting Review* 45: 535–543.
Oxenfeldt, Alfred R. 1975. *Pricing Strategies.* New York: AMACOM.
"People Express." 1983. Boston: HBS Case Services, 9-483-103.
Pfeffer, Jeffrey, and Salancik, Gerald R. 1978. *The External Control of Organizations: A Resource Dependence Perspective.* New York: Harper & Row.
Pondy, Louis R. 1967. "Organizational Conflict: Concepts and Models." *Administrative Science Quarterly* 12: 296–320.
Popper, Karl. 1959. *The Logic of Scientific Discovery.* New York: Harper & Row.
Porter, Michael E. 1980. *Competitive Strategy: Techniques for Analyzing Industries and Competitors.* New York: Free Press.
———. 1985. *Competitive Advantage: Creating and Sustaining Superior Performance.* New York: Free Press.
Price Waterhouse. 1984. "Transfer Pricing Practices of American Industry." Columbus, Ohio: Price Waterhouse, March 31. Mimeographed.
Rawls, John. 1971. *A Theory of Justice.* Cambridge, Mass.: Harvard University Press, Belknap Press.
Reece, James S., and Cool, William R. 1978. "Measuring Investment Center Performance." *Harvard Business Review* 56(3): 28–40.
Roethlisberger, F.J. 1977. *The Elusive Phenomena,* edited by George F.F. Lombard. Boston: Division of Research, Graduate School of Business Administration, Harvard University.
Ronen, Joshua, and McKinney, George, III. 1970. "Transfer Pricing for Divisional Autonomy." *Journal of Accounting Research* 8(1): 99–112.
Rumelt, Richard P. 1974. *Strategy, Structure, and Economic Performance.* Boston: Division of Research, Graduate School of Business Administration, Harvard University.
Salter, Malcolm S. 1970. "Stages of Corporate Development" *Journal of Business Policy* 1(1): 23–37.
———. 1973. "Tailor Incentive Compensation to Strategy." *Harvard Business Review* 51(2): 94–102.
Salter, Malcolm S., and Weinhold, Wolf A. 1979. *Diversification Through Acquisition: Strategies for Creating Economic Value.* New York: Free Press.
Schaub, H. James. 1978. "Transfer Pricing in a Decentralized Organization." *Management Accounting* 59(10):33–42.
Schendel, Dan E., and Hofer, Charles W., eds. 1979. *Strategic Management: A New View of Business Policy and Planning.* Boston: Little, Brown.
Schiff, Michael. 1979. "A Note on Transfer Pricing and Industry Segment Reporting." *Journal of Accounting, Auditing, and Finance* 2: 224–231.
Schwab, Richard J. 1975. "A Contribution Approach to Transfer Pricing." *Management Accounting* 56(8): 46–48.
Scott, Bruce R. 1971a. "Stages of Corporate Development—Part I." Boston: HBS Case Services, 9-371-294.
———. 1971b. "Stages of Corporate Development—Part II." Boston: HBS Case Services, 4-371-295.

Shapiro, Benson P., and Jackson, Barbara B. 1978. "Industrial Pricing to Meet Consumer Needs." *Harvard Business Review* 56(6): 119–127.

Sharav, Itzak. 1974. "Transfer Pricing—Diversity of Goals and Practices." *Journal of Accountancy* 137: 56–62.

Shillinglaw, Gordon. 1957. "Guides to Internal Profit Measurement." *Harvard Business Review* 35(2): 82–94.

———. 1961. "Problems in Divisional Profit Measurement." *N.A.A. Bulletin* 42(3): 33–43.

———. 1977. *Managerial Cost Accounting,* 4th ed. Homewood, Ill.: Richard D. Irwin.

Sidgwick, Henry. 1901. *The Principles of Political Economy,* 3d ed. London: Macmillan.

Solomons, David. 1965. *Divisional Performance: Measurement and Control.* Homewood, Ill.: Richard D. Irwin.

Stanley, Curtis H. 1964. "Cost-Basis Valuations in Transactions Between Entities." *Accounting Review* 39: 639–647.

Stigler, George J. 1951. "The Division of Labor Is Limited by the Extent of the Market." *Journal of Political Economy* 3: 185–193.

Stinchcombe, Arthur L. 1959. "Bureaucratic and Craft Adminstration of Production: A Comparative Study." *Adminstrative Science Quarterly* 4: 168–187.

Stone, Willard E. 1956. "Intracompany Pricing." *Accounting Review* 31: 625–627.

Swieringa, Robert J., and Waterhouse, John H. 1982. "Organizational Views of Transfer Pricing." *Accounting, Organizations, and Society* 7(2): 149–165.

Tang, Roger Y.W. 1979. *Transfer Pricing Practices in the United States and Japan.* New York: Praeger.

Thomas, Arthur. 1980. *A Behavioural Analysis of Joint Cost Allocation and Transfer Pricing.* Champaign, Ill.: Stipes.

Thompson, James D. 1967. *Organizations in Action.* New York: McGraw-Hill.

Troxel, Richard B. 1973. "On Transfer Pricing." *CPA Journal* 43(2) 895–897.

Vancil, Richard F. 1973. "What Kind of Management Control Do You Need?" *Harvard Business Review* 51(2): 75–86.

———. 1978. *Decentralization: Managerial Ambiguity by Design.* Homewood, Ill.: Dow Jones-Irwin.

Vancil, Richard F., and Lorange, Peter. 1975. "Strategic Planning in Diversified Companies." *Harvard Business Review* 53(1): 81–90.

Vendig, Richard D. 1973. "A Three-Part Transfer Price." *Management Accounting* 55(3): 33–36.

Verlage, H.C. 1975. *Transfer Pricing for Multinational Enterprises: Some Remarks on Its Economic, Fiscal, and Organizational Aspects.* Farnborough, England: Gower.

Walton, Richard D. 1983. "Research Strategies with Dual Relevance to Theory and Practice." Paper presented at conference, "Doing Research That Is Useful for Theory and Practice," University of Southern California, November.

Walton, Richard E., and Dutton, John M. 1969. "The Management of Interdepartmental Conflict: A Model and Review." *Administrative Science Quarterly* 14: 73–84.

Walton, Richard E., and McKersie, Robert G. 1965. *A Behavioral Theory of Labor Negotiations: An Analysis of a Social Interaction System.* New York: McGraw-Hill.

Watson, David J.H., and Baumler, John V. 1975. "Transfer Pricing: A Behavioral Context." *Accounting Review* 50: 466–474.

Webster, Frederick E., Jr. 1979. *Industrial Marketing Strategy*. New York: Wiley.

Weick, Karl E. 1969. *The Social Psychology of Organizing*. Reading, Mass.: Addison-Wesley.

———. 1979. *The Social Psychology of Organizing*, 2d ed. Reading, Mass.: Addison-Wesley.

Weston, J. Fred, and Brigham, Eugene F. 1981. *Managerial Finance*, 7th ed. Hinsdale, Ill.: Dryden Press.

Williamson, Oliver E. 1975. *Markets and Hierarchies: Analysis and Antitrust Implications*. New York: Free Press.

———. 1979. "Transaction Cost Economics: The Governance of Contractual Relations." *Journal of Law and Economics* 22: 233–261.

Woodward, Joan. 1965. *Industrial Organization: Theory and Practice*. London: Oxford University Press, 1965.

Wrigley, Leonard. 1970. "Divisional Autonomy and Diversification." Doctoral dissertation, Harvard Graduate School of Business Administration.

Zimmerman, Jerold, L. 1979. "The Costs and Benefits of Cost Allocations." *Accounting Review* 54: 504–521.

Index

Abdel-khalik, A. Rashad, 24
Abell, Derek F., 273
Accounting theory, 27–35, 41, 43, 49
Ackerman, Robert W., 291
Acquisitions and mergers, integrating, 290
Actual costs, 149, 173–174; measuring, 149–151
Adams, Mike, 87, 89, 90, 170, 171
Adaptability, *vs.* stability, 37
Adjusted market price, 118–119
Administrative process, 1, 8, 10, 39, 44, 113–116
Administrative simplicity, 269; and fairness, uniformity for, 256–266
Alfarabi Chemicals, Inc., transfer pricing practices at, 49, 51, 84, 91, 107, 147; changes in transfer pricing policies of, 57–62; company background and strategy at, 51–56; conflict at, 204; discussion of, 71–75; economic decisions by, 66–68; effects of volume and business performance at, 70–71; and Manager's Analytical Plane (MAP), 281–282; performance measurement, evaluation, and reward at, 68–69; transfer pricing policies of, 56–57; transfer pricing processes of, 62–66
Allison, Graham T., 36
Ammonia Corporation, 52, 56, 61
Anthony, Robert N., 2, 31–32, 38, 130–131
Aquinas Chemicals Company, 155, 158, 169, 227, 259; conflict at, 204; and Manager's Analytical Plane (MAP), 281–282, 283; viability of actual full cost transfers at, 153–154
Arrow, Kenneth J., 21, 22, 23–24, 38
Austin, Lee, 194, 195, 219–220
Authority: and continuum of exchange relationships, 248–249; and dual pricing, 102–103; and exchange autonomy, 97–98; and mandated full cost transfers, 85–86, 151; and mandated market-based transfers, 91, 93; and strategy and transfer pricing policy, 79–80, 81

Bacon & Bentham, Inc., 99, 155–156, 157, 159; efforts to use dual pricing at, 140–141; efforts to use market mechanisms at, 138–139; internal transfers at, 100–101; and Manager's Analytical Plane (MAP), 281–282, 283, 285; mandated dual pricing at, 142–143; mismatch on marketing and purchasing at, 120–121; performance measurement, evaluation, and reward at, 100; preferences for external sources at, 131; strategy and structure at, 99–100; ultimate end of dual pricing at, 146–147; use of adjusted market price transfers at, 119; use of hierarchical encouragement at, 132–134
Banks, diversified financial services offered by, 289
Bargaining, 36
Baumler, John V., 38–39
Baumol, William, 25, 26
Behavioral model, 36, 37
Benke, Ralph L., Jr., 5, 27, 31, 32, 45, 46
Bergman, Roland, 125
Berke, Eric, 136, 187, 188–189
Berkin, Ed, 243, 244, 246
Bernard, Mitchell, 103–104, 106
Bidding, competitive, 121, 123
Birch Paper Company, 36
Blackstone Machinery Company, 266, 267, 285–286; difficulty in implementing transfer pricing at, 240–247
Bove, Ken, 88, 90
Bower, Joseph L., 36, 37, 84, 272–273, 291–292
Brady, B.A., 20
Brown, Donaldson, 17–18
Buying profit center, and product/process life cycle, 234–238
Byrne, Howard, 241, 242, 244, 245

Camman, Eric A., 19
Capital budgeting, and Manager's Analytical Plane (MAP), 291–292
Capital investment decisions, 11, 24–25, 66–68
Cartman, David, 159, 160, 209
Cedar, Bruce, 51, 68–69
Chandler, Alfred D., Jr., 16–17, 18
Change, 227–228; inherent value of, 266–267; and introduction of transfer pricing, 238–248; lack of incentives for, at Rousseau Chemical Corporation, 170–172; managing, 288; and product/process life cycle, 228–238; and reorganizing exchange relationships, 248–256; and uniformity for administrative simplicity and fairness, 256–266
Chelsea Chemicals, 52, 56
Chief executive officer (CEO): decision making by, 2; role of, in company strategy, 36
Chudnoff, Eric, 192–193
Cicero Systems, Inc., 286–287; balancing diversity and uniformity at, 259–266
Clarkson, Mike, 54
Clifford, Ed, 224
Coase, R.H., 23
Cohen, Michael D., 36
Collaborative organization, 277–279
Collective organization, 273–274
Collins, V.W., 20
Competitive bidding, 121, 123
Competitive organization, 276–277
Competitive problems, resulting from market-based transfers, 195–200
Conflict, 32, 205–206; dynamics of interdependence, 206–213; evaluating benefits of, 222–225; at Hobbes Instrument Company, 93–94, 95–96; implications for dual pricing of, 225–226; at Locke Chemical Company, 159–162; managing, 38, 39, 44–46, 116; under mandated full cost transfers, 172–174; under mandated market-based transfers, 176, 203–204; top management's use of, 213–222
Conley, Kevin, 241, 242, 243
Contracts, 121; cost-plus and fixed price, 122
Cook, Paul W., Jr., 21, 23
Cool, William R., 2
Cooperative organization, 276
Control: balance between fairness and, 270–271; use of conflict for facilitating, 213–222
Corey, E. Raymond, 119–120, 121–123
Corporate evolution, 290–291
Corporate optimization, emphasis on, at Rousseau Chemical Corporation, 90
Corporate resources, distribution and cost allocation of, 292–293
Cost allocation(s): distribution and, of corporate resources, 292–293; at Hobbes Instrument Company, 94–95; at Paine Chemical Company, 150–151
Cost-based methods, 40–41
Cost plus markup pricing, 175, 184–190
Costs and variances, managing, 172–174
Cost system, standard, at Rousseau Chemical Corporation, 88
Coulter, John, 95–97, 188, 201, 202
Customers, 16
Cyert, Richard M., 35–36

Danton, Paul, 243, 244, 246
Dantzig, George B., 25
Dean, Joel, 21, 38
Dearden, John, 31–32, 38, 130–131
Decker, Robert, 196
Decomposition algorithm, 26
Decomposition theorem, 25
Demand independence, 22
Dennis, Richard, 142, 143
Dennison Manufacturing Company, 36
Derby, Leo, 161, 165
Dergola, David, 125–126
Dewey & Burke, Inc., 286; from manufacturing unit to distinct business at, 176–178
Discounted cash flow (DCF), 89
Discounts, 121, 122–123
Disincentives: managing, 147–148; to

trade internally, 124–132. *See also* Incentives
Diversification, 16; and collaborative organization, 277–279; and collective organization, 273–274; and competitive organization, 276–277; and cooperative organization, 276; defined, 272–273; and Manager's Analytical Plane (MAP), 269, 280, 294; and model of strategy implementation, 271–273; relationship between internal transfers and, 3–4; relationship between transfer pricing policy and, 47, 107
Division, 17
Dolan, John, 181–184, 217, 218, 220, 223–225
Donnelly, Paul, 154
Doz, Yves, 36, 37, 272–273
Dual pricing, 8–9, 77, 101–103; at Hume Fabrication Company, 103–106; implications of conflict for, 225–226; incentives through, 139–143; as limited and temporary solution, 144–147; and Manager's Analytical Plane (MAP), 284–285; and mandated market-based transfers, 200–203
Du Pont, 17, 18
Dutton, John M., 214–215

Economic decisions, 8, 24, 134; affecting corporate performance, 10–11; at Alfarabi Chemicals, Inc., 66–68
Economic theory, 21–25, 35, 41, 42, 43, 49
Edwards, James Don, 5, 27, 31, 32, 45, 46
Effectiveness, of transfer pricing practices, criteria for evaluating, 10–11
Efficiency variances, 150
Exchange autonomy, 8, 77, 97–99; and adjusted market price, 118–119; at Bacon & Bentham, Inc., 99–101; disincentives to trade internally under, 124–132; dual pricing as limited and temporary solution under, 144–147; incentives through dual pricing under, 139–143; incentives through management hierarchy under, 132–137; incentives through market mechanisms under, 137–139; and Manager's Analytical Plane (MAP), 283–284; managing disincentives under, 147–148; and pure market price, 117–118; transfer pricing as external pricing under, 119–124
Exchange relationships, reorganizing, 248–256
Exxon, 290
External market-based prices, 175, 178–184
External pricing, transfer pricing as, 119–124

Fabian, Tibor, 25, 26
Fairness: balances between control and, 270–271; based on shared fate, 276; continuum of, 250; importance of, 38, 39; perceptions of, 8, 11, 25; problem of, 81–82, 134; uniformity for administrative simplicity and, 256–266
Fales, Ed, 135–136, 189–190
Falk, Don, 160, 161, 166
Fantl, Irving L., 38
Farber, Nathan, 159, 161, 208–209
Firth, Henry, 212
Fisher, Mal, 54, 63, 64–65, 68
Flaherty, Vincent, 181–184, 194, 217, 219, 220, 221
Ford Motor Company, 17
Fortune, 2, 4, 42, 46
Furman, Allen, 242–243, 244

Galani, Pat, 62
Galbraith, Jay, 38
Gaming, 23, 24, 25, 26, 163, 168
Garbage can model, 36, 37
General manager, 2
General Motors, 17, 18
Goals, vs. determinants, 37
Godfrey, James T., 26–27
Goldsmith, Mal, 259–266
Gould, J.R., 23, 24
Gould, Ken, 120–121, 143

Government regulation, of internal transfers, 124, 130–131
Gunther, Herman, 62, 64, 70–71

Hackman, Jake, 197, 198–199
Hammond, John S., 273
Hardman, Karl, 133
Hart, Leo, 241, 242, 244, 245
Harvard Business Review, 31
Hass, Jerome E., 26
Hayden, Paul, 159, 167–168, 208–209, 210
Hayes, Robert H., 83, 228, 237
Haynes, Julian, 104
Heckert, J.B., 20
Hector, Winthrop, 121, 157
Herzog, Steve, 61
Hewitt, Tom, 165–166, 209, 210
Hierarchy: disincentives to trade internally within organizational, 124, 127–129; incentives through management, 132–137
Hirshleifer, Jack, 21–23, 24, 28, 30, 38
Hobbes Instrument Company, 93, 99, 155, 156; conflict management at, 95–96; corporate transfer pricing policy at, 96–97; cost allocations at, 94–95; dual pricing for antennae at, 201–203; limitations in using markups on cost at, 187–190; and Manager's Analytical Plane (MAP), 281–282, 283–284; organization of Electronics Group at, 94; performance measurement, evaluation, and reward at, 96; prevalence of internal competition and conflict at, 93–94, 204; problems for restricting exchange autonomy at, 135–137
Hume Fabrication Company, 103–104, 132, 286, 287; Foundry Division of, 105; improved cooperation through transfer price at, 191–193; internal transactions under exchange autonomy at, 129–130; preferences for external sources of, 104; proposal for dual pricing at, 106
Hypothesis(es): 1–3, 52; 4, 54; 5–6, 57; 7–8, 61; 9, 62; 10, 63; 11–12, 64; 13–16, 66; 17, 67; 18, 68; 19–21, 69; 22, 70; 23, 71; 24–27, 147; 28–29, 172; 30–31, 173; 32, 191; 33, 214; 34, 226; 35, 237; 36, 238; 37, 255; 38, 257

Imholz, Martin, 166, 167
Impartial spectator, 277
Implementation mode, 269, 273, 274, 276, 278, 289
Incentives: through dual pricing, 139–143; through management hierarchy, 132–137; through market mechanisms, 137–139
Individual involvement, 274
Information: and mathematical programming, 27; used in setting transfer prices, 179–180; use of conflict for generating, 213–222
Interdependence(ies), 87, 108; activity, 205, 206; at Aquinas Chemicals Company, 153–154; competitive, 205; conflict dynamics of, 206–213; across and within groups, 52–53; and mandated full cost transfers, 151, 152, 169; outcome, 205, 206; between profit centers, 2, 8, 151, 205; symbiotic, 205–206; variety and, 272
Internal trading, disincentives to, 124–132
International Inks, Inc., 20

Jackson, Henry, 54, 60, 65, 67, 70
Jakowsky, Ed, 160–161
Jevon, Bill, 125
Johnson, Larry, 181, 182, 184, 195–196, 216–222 *passim*, 267

Kanodia, Chandra, 24
Kanter, Joel, 90, 170–171, 172
Kaplan, Robert S., 42, 43, 49, 85, 150; and accounting theory, 31, 32–34, 35; and mathematical programming, 27, 35

Lambert, David R., 45–46
Lampert, Steve, 170, 171
Larson, Raymond L., 5, 45, 46
Lawrence, Paul R., 38, 39, 116, 214
Linear programming approach, 25–27
Lipkin, Arthur, 159, 210–211
List price, 121, 122–123

Littel, Andrew, 51, 52, 56, 63, 66, 67
Litten, Herbert, 141, 146
Locke Chemical Company, 158–159, 164, 169, 217; ambiguity about cost and profit center roles at, 160–162; analysis of problems at, 283; calculation of transfer prices at, 164–165; conditions for erosion of competitive position of, 197–199; Consumer Division of, 211–212; disputes over variances at, 165–166; evolution of transfer pricing policy at, 251–255; examples of high and low interdependence at, 208–212; formation of Basic Chemicals Division at, 160; General Chemicals Division of, 211; improvements in transfer pricing process at, 167–168; and Manager's Analytical Plane (MAP), 282, 286; Molding Division of, 208–210; Plastics Division of, 210–211; problems in determining standard costs at, 166–167
Lorsch, Jay W., 38, 39, 116, 214
Lusk, Edward J., 24

McCarthy, Ted, 261–263, 265
McKersie, Robert G., 276, 277, 278
McKinney, George, III, 30–31
Madigan, Lee, 252
Mahan, George, 181, 217, 220–221
Malbert, Ken, 177–178
Management, top, use of conflict by, 213–222
Management Accounting, 31
Management hierarchy, incentives through, 132–137
Management theory, 35–40, 42, 49
Manager: general, 2; profit center, 2
Manager's Analytical Plane (MAP), 269, 293–294; and capital budgeting, 291–292; and distribution and cost allocation of corporate resources, 292–293; and four pure organizational types, 273–279; and strategy implementation, 269–273, 289–291; and transfer pricing, 279–288
Mandated full cost transfers, 8, 9–10, 77, 82–86; at Alfarabi Chemicals, Inc., 56–57, 61; and Manager's Analytical Plane (MAP), 281–282; managing costs and variances under, 172–174; measuring standard and actual costs under, 149–151; need for strategic clarity under, 151–162; problems in allocating variances under, 162–172; at Rousseau Chemical Corporation, 86–90
Mandated market-based transfers, 8, 77, 91–93, 175–178; at Alfarabi Chemicals, Inc., 56–57, 60–61; competitive problems resulting from, 195–200; cost plus markup pricing under, 175, 184–190; dual pricing solution to, 200–203; external market-based pricing under, 175, 178–184; at Hobbes Instrument Company, 93–97; and Manager's Analytical Plane (MAP), 282; managing ambiguity of price under, 190–195; reducing conflict in, 203–204
Manufacturing variances, 150
March, James G., 35–36, 43, 113
Marginal costs, 21–22, 24, 25, 41, 42
Market-based methods, 40–41, 43
Marketing and purchasing, mismatch on, 120–121, 124
Market mechanisms, incentives through, 137–139
Market price: adjusted, 118–119; pure, 117–118
Markets and hierarchies model, 36, 37
Martin, Fred, 65
MAT (marketing, administration, and technical) expenses, 164
Mathematical programming, 25–27, 30, 35, 41–42, 49
Mauriel, John J., 2
Mautz, R.K., 2, 3, 5, 40–43, 47
Mead, Michael, 138
Mergers and acquisitions, integrating, 290
Meston, Alfred, 89, 170, 171–172
Michels, Bernard, 156, 223, 224, 225
Milton, Inc., 159; disincentives to trade internally at, 125–127; efforts to use dual pricing at, 140–141; efforts to use market mechanisms at, 138–139; and Manager's Analytical Plane (MAP), 283, 285; ultimate end of

Milton Inc. (*continued*)
dual pricing at, 146–147; use of hierarchical encouragement at 132–134; use of pure market price transfers at, 117–118

National Association of Accountants, 5
National Association of Cost Accountants (NACA), 18, 19, 20
National Industrial Conference Board, 5
National Products Corporation, 291–292
Negotiation, 28, 33–34, 43–44, 107; role of conflict and, in transfer pricing, 213
Newman, John, 255

Ohio State University, 20
Olsen, Johan P., 36
Opportunity cost, concept of, 33
Organizational hierarchy, disincentives to trade internally within, 124, 127–129
Organizational structure, 276; at Rousseau Chemical Corporation, 87–88
Organizational types, four pure, 273; collaborative organization, 277–279; collective organization, 273–274; competitive organization, 276–277; cooperative organization, 276
Organizing model, 36, 37
Output levels, 11, 23, 24, 66
Overhold, Mark, 100–101, 141
Oxenfeldt, Alfred R., 121

Paine Chemical Company, 155, 156, 204, 267, 293; limitations in using external market prices at, 180–184; and Manager's Analytical Plane (MAP), 281–282, 283; power politics in transfer pricing at, 223–225; problem in cost allocation at, 150–151; problems of weakened competitive position of, 195–196; process resolution of plastic resins problem at, 193–195; using conflict for information and control at, 216–222
Pappas, Nicholas, 150–151, 156
Patterson, George, 189, 190, 202, 203
Peat, Marwick, Mitchell and Company, 19
Performance measurement, evaluation, and reward, 8, 11, 25, 40; at Alfarabi Chemicals, Inc., 68–69; at Bacon & Bentham, Inc., 100; effects of conflict on, 214–215; and exchange autonomy, 137; at Hobbes Instrument Company, 96; and mandated full cost transfers, 151–152, 157–158, 172–174; and mandated market-based transfers, 191; at Rousseau Chemical Corporation, 88–89
Personal code, 274
Peterson, Roger, 259, 262, 263
Pfeffer, Jeffrey, 206
Plant closings, 66–68
Pondy, Louis R., 214
Porter, Michael E., 79, 228
Practical full capacity, 149
Price Waterhouse, 4, 5, 42, 43, 44, 46–47
Pricing conventions, 121–124
Process(es): in collaborative organizations, 278; defined, 269–270; distinction between policy and, 43; elements of, 40; vs. outputs, 37; role of, 37–38; used to determine transfer price, 193–195. *See also* Product/process life cycle
Product pricing, 11, 24, 66
Product/process life cycle, 228; and buying profit center, 234–238; and selling profit center, 228–234, 235–238
Profitability, and method of successive approximations, 23
Profit center(s), and product/process life cycle: buying, 234–238; selling, 228–234, 235–238
Profit center manager, 2
Profit maximization, 15, 24, 27, 31, 39
Purchasing: and marketing, mismatch on, 120–121, 124; variances, 150
Pure market price, 117–118

Rational trust, 279
Reece, James S., 2
Reis, Keith, 99, 101

Relatedness, 272
Rennke, Helmut, 181, 183–184, 194–195, 217–221
Research design, 5–7
Responsibility: and continuum of exchange relationships, 248–250; and dual pricing, 102–103; and exchange autonomy, 97–98; and mandated full cost transfers, 85–86; and mandated market-based transfers, 92–93; and strategy and transfer pricing policy, 80–81
Return on average assets (ROAA), 242, 244, 246
Return on invested capital (ROIC), 52, 53, 68, 70, 259, 263
Return on investment (ROI), 17, 88–89, 158, 164
Return on net assets (RONA), 95, 96, 154
Return on sales (ROS), 88
Return on total operating assets (RTOA), 217
Richards, Earl, 54, 65, 67, 69, 70
Robinson, Mason, 133, 157
Roderick, Bryan, 197, 198
Rolls–Royce Motors, Ltd., 237, 238
Rome Wire Company, 20
Ronen, Joshua, 30–31
Rousseau Chemical Corporation, 86–87, 93, 99, 153, 169; compared with Locke Chemical Company, 158, 159, 160; conflict at, 204; emphasis on corporate optimization at, 90; lack of incentives for change at, 170–172, 227; and Manager's Analytical Plane (MAP), 281–282, 283; organizational structure of, 87–88; performance measurement, evaluation, and reward at, 88–89; rejection of market-based transfer prices at, 169–170; standard cost system at, 88
Rumelt, Richard P., 107, 272

Salancik, Gerald R., 206
Salter, Malcolm S., 272
Satter, Michael, 245–246
Scovell, C.H., 18
Securities and Exchange Commission (SEC), 252
Selling profit center, and product/process life cycle, 228–234, 235–238
Shadow prices, and mathematical programming, 25, 26, 27
Shared fate, 276
Shaw, Chris, 182–183, 216, 217, 221–222
Sheldon, Adam, 167
Shields, Ron, 166, 251, 253
Shillinglaw, Gordon, 38, 43
Shindell, Earl, 167–168, 211, 252, 253, 254–255
Short, Dave, 243
Sidgwick, Harry, *The Principles of Political Economy*, 15–16, 17
Simon, Herbert A., 43, 113
Simplicity: vs. complexity, 37; and fairness, uniformity for administrative, 256–266
Smith, Adam, 277
Smith, Jim, 66
Solomons, David, 5, 28–30, 31, 32, 33
Sourcing, external, 4–5, 18, 32; at Bacon & Bentham, Inc., 131; at Hume Fabrication Company, 104
Specialization, 272
Standard costs, 149, 173–174; measuring, 149–151; problems in determining, at Locke Chemical Company, 166–167
Status, determinants of, 176
Stockton, Carl, 243
Strategy: implementation of, 269–273, 289–291; need for clarity of, 151–162; transfer pricing and, 1, 8–10, 79–82, 106
Subjective judgment, 38, 153, 222
Successive approximations, method of, 23, 25
Suppliers, 16
Surveys: and empirical support for transfer pricing theory, 107–113; on extent of internal transfers, 2–4; of multiple profit center organizational form, 2; on transfer pricing practices of actual companies, 40–49
Swieringa, Robert J., 36–38

Tang, Roger Y.W., 2, 5, 40–43
Technological independence, 22

Thompson, James D., 35
Thornton, Aaron, 181, 217, 218, 219, 220
Tishman, Stuart, and transfer pricing at Alfarabi Chemicals, 51–73 *passim*
Transfer pricing: and accounting theory, 27–35; at Alfarabi Chemicals, 51–75; early theory of, 18–21; and economic theory, 21–25; inherent value of change in, 266–267; introduction of, 238–248; and management theory, 35–40; and Manager's Analytical Plane (MAP), 279–288; and mathematical programming, 25–27; nature of problem of, 1–5; origin of, 15–18; policies, changes in, 285–287; policy, empirical support for theory of, 106–113; policy, strategy determining, 8–10, 79–82, 106; practice, data from, 40–49; practices, criteria for evaluating, 10–11; and product/process life cycle, 228–238; reorganizing exchange relationships for, 248–256; research design used to develop theory of, 5–7; role of administrative process in, 8, 10, 113–116; summary of findings on, 7–11; terminology of, 287–288; uniformity in, for administrative simplicity and fairness, 256–266. *See also* Dual pricing; Exchange autonomy; Mandated full cost transfers; Mandated market-based transfers
Tretter, Charles, 203

Uncertainty, 23–24
Uniformity, for administrative simplicity and fairness, 256–266

Vallon, Victor, 161–162, 198, 211
Vancil, Richard, 5, 12, 81, 82, 85, 292; and decentralization of American manufacturing firms, 107, 271–272; and empirical support for transfer pricing theory, 107–108, 111, 112, 113; on problem of transfer prices, 1–4; on standard cost centers, 150; and transfer pricing methods in practice, 40–43, 47–49
Variances: efficiency, 150, 163; managing costs and, 172–174; manufacturing, 150; problems in allocating, 162–172; purchasing, 150, 163; volume, 149–150, 163
Variety, and interdependence, 272
Veaux, Pierre, 243, 244
Verlage, H.C., 26
Vertical integration, 16; at Alfarabi Chemicals, Inc., 51; and collaborative organization, 277–279; and collective organization, 273–274; and competitive organization, 276–277; and conflict dynamics of interdependence, 212–213; and cooperative organization, 276; defined, 79, 272; and dual pricing, 101–103; and empirical support for transfer pricing theory, 107–113; and exchange autonomy, 97; fundamental reasons for, 23; and Manager's Analytical Plane (MAP), 269, 280, 294; and mandated full cost transfers, 82–83; and mandated market-based transfers, 91; and model of strategy implementation, 271–273; and relation of strategy and transfer pricing, 8, 9
Volume variances, 149–150

Wakefield, Scott, 158–159, 252
Walker, Jason, 210, 254
Walton, Richard E., 214–215, 276, 277, 278
Waterhouse, John H., 36–38
Watson, David J.H., 38–39
Webster, Al, 93–94, 96, 156
Webster, Frederick E., Jr., 121
Weick, Karl E., 36, 37
Weinhold, Wolf A., 272
Welch, Jason, 150–151
Wheelwright, Steven G., 228, 237
Williamson, Oliver E., 23, 36, 214
Win/lose, 277, 278
Winter, David, 156
Win/win, 276, 278
Wolfe, Philip, 25
World Export Organization (WEO), 241, 242
Wrigley, Leonard, 272
Wyckoff, Dan, 54, 57, 63, 65, 67–68, 70–71

About the Author

Robert G. Eccles is an associate professor at the Graduate School of Business Administration, Harvard University. He holds degrees in mathematics and humanities and social science from the Massachusetts Institute of Technology and received the Ph.D in sociology from Harvard University. His research and teaching interests are in the areas of business policy and organizational behavior, focusing on the problems of defining the boundaries of the firm and managing relationships between business units within the firm.